The Wonder of the Cross

The Wonder of the Cross

The God Who Uses Evil and Suffering to Destroy Evil and Suffering

RICHARD A. SHENK

Foreword by Simon Oliver

☞PICKWICK *Publications* • Eugene, Oregon

THE WONDER OF THE CROSS
The God Who Uses Evil and Suffering to Destroy Evil and Suffering

Copyright © 2013 Richard A. Shenk. All rights reserved. Except for brief quotations in critical publications or reviews, no part of this book may be reproduced in any manner without prior written permission from the publisher. Write: Permissions. Wipf and Stock Publishers, 199 W. 8th Ave., Suite 3, Eugene, OR 97401.

Unless otherwise noted, the Scripture text used is the New American Standard Bible—1995 update, La Habra, CA: the Lockman Foundation, copyright © 1960, 1962, 1963, 1968, 1971, 1972, 1977, 1988, 1995.

Unless otherwise noted, all quotations from the Greek New Testament are from Novum Testamentum Graece, Nestle-Aland 27th Edition. Copyright (c) 1993 Deutsch Bibelgesellschaft, Stuttgart.

Unless otherwise noted, all quotations from the Hebrew Bible are from Biblia Hebraica Stuttgartensia (Hebrew Bible, Masoretic Text or Hebrew Old Testament), edited by K. Elliger and W. Rudolph of the Deutsche Bibelgesellschaft, Stuttgart, Fourth Corrected Edition. Copyright © 1966, 1977, 1983, 1990 by the Deutsche Bibelgesellschaft (German Bible Society), Stuttgart.

All of the above texts are cited from BibleWorks for Windows, version 6.x, 7.x, 8.x, Norfolk, VA: BibleWorks, LLC, 2007.

Pickwick Publications
An Imprint of Wipf and Stock Publishers
199 W. 8th Ave., Suite 3
Eugene, OR 97401

www.wipfandstock.com

ISBN 13: 978-1-61097-869-9

Cataloguing-in-Publication Data

Shenk, Richard A.

    The wonder of the cross : the God who uses evil and suffering to destroy evil and suffering / Richard A. Shenk ; foreword by Simon Oliver.

    xviii + 326 p. ; cm. — Includes bibliographical references and index(es).

    ISBN 13: 978-1-61097-869-9

    1. Theodicy. I. Oliver, Simon. II. Title

BT160 .S52 2013

Manufactured in the U.S.A.

to my father

Contents

Foreword by Simon Oliver | ix
Preface | xiii
Acknowledgments | xv
Definitions | xvii

Introduction | 1

PART I: The Tension of Theodicy | 13

1 The Historical Development of the Concept of Free-Will | 15

2 The Historical Development of the Concept of Evil | 58

3 Free-Will and Evil: The Historical Development of Theodicy | 101

PART II: The Testing of a Theodicy | 153

4 Hypothesis 1: Conforming-Freedom is the ultimate and singular human freedom required by God's character and goals for his people. | 157

5 Hypothesis 2: Evil & Suffering is a subordinate-metaphysical necessity, being both the intrinsic problem and the instrumental solution in God's economy. | 187

6 Hypothesis 3: Conforming-Freedom is achieved by God for his people through Evil & Suffering over four Eras of Freedom which are divided by three Creation & Crisis events. | 228

PART III: A Theodicy in the Face of Reality | 263

7 Practical Theology: Applying the Thesis | 265

8 Remaining Issues and Disconfirmatory Evidence | 283

Conclusion | 295

Bibliography | 301
Scripture Index | 315
Name and Subject Index | 321

Foreword
by Simon Oliver

THE EXPERIENCE OF EVIL and suffering is often cited as the single greatest challenge to religious faith. For any person seeking to minister in the name of Christ, human anguish and pain present the most acute pastoral and intellectual challenge. How can one proclaim the goodness and mercy of God to a family whose child is dying of cancer, or a community whose homes and livelihoods have been destroyed by the brutal forces of nature?

The more aggressive elements in the contemporary 'new atheist' movement confront Christians with the challenge of evil as if that challenge had never occurred to those of religious faith. Yet it is one of the striking elements of the New Testament that it never dodges the experience of suffering; there is no way 'around' the dereliction of the cross of Jesus Christ. As the nineteenth century Scottish author, poet and minister George MacDonald once famously wrote, 'The Son of God suffered unto the death, not that we might not suffer, but that our suffering might be like his.' Reflection on the nature of evil begins at the very inception of Christianity, finding its roots in the ancient writings of Israel and the history of God's people.

Nevertheless, the way in which Christian theology has dealt with the experience of human anguish has changed over the course of the tradition. This is why an historically sensitive approach to the questions posed by evil and suffering, such as we find in Rick Shenk's book, is so important. The patristic writers frequently begin with the conviction, derived from Genesis and brought to focus through Platonic philosophy, that God's creation is fundamentally good. Evil is an intrusion; it is alien to creation. What is ontologically fundamental is the Good, and creation is but a participation in the Good. Evil, for Augustine and other theologians of antiquity and the high middle ages, is the absence of the Good, much as darkness is the absence of light. So, unlike the various Gnostic philosophies he opposed, Augustine refused to grant evil a foothold in being. It is, in itself, nothing. This is not an empirical thesis concerning how we experience evil because, of course, we experience evil as a terrible force. However, placed within a more fundamental doctrine of creation, Augustine insists that we must see evil as the privation of the Good, as the disintegration of being and as therefore inherently unintelligible. That unintelligibility is reflected in Job's refusal to accept the justifications of his comforters. In this context, evil is not mysterious in the sense that God is mysterious. God is, in himself, most knowable and the eternal source of reason (*logos*), even though for us God is an unfathomable mystery. To enter the mystery of God requires the intensification of our finite intellect by the gift of grace. By contrast, evil is the absence of being and therefore the absence of reason. We cannot give a reason, in the sense of a justification, for cancer in a child or the loss of lives and cultures in disasters brought about by nature's apparent caprice. Such reasons would, perforce, attempt to turn evil into something 'justifiable,' and therefore something which is apparently good for us. This would be a most lamentable failure to take the destructive and nihilistic character of evil with full seriousness. This is not to say that good cannot come from evil. It is to say that Christian theology resists any sense that evil is to be justified by claiming that, despite all evidence to the contrary, in some as yet unfathomable way it is good for us in the long run. Any courage, generosity, hope, patience and spiritual growth shown by a young person dying of cancer maybe a response born of hope in God, but it is no justification (in the sense meant by, for example, 'soul-making' theodicies) of the wickedness of this disease.

The business of justifying evil does not truly gather pace until modernity. Here, in the wake of fundamental theological shifts in late medieval thought, God becomes a moral agent. In other words, God's moral credentials in the face of suffering and evil become questionable. Viewed against our criteria of what a creator God should be like, modernity finds God wanting. So although reflection on evil in the context of the doctrine of creation, as well as in Christology and soteriology, is prominent in the treatises of patristic and high medieval theologians, the so-called problem of evil becomes an apparently decisive argument against the existence of God only in modern thought.

Following this trend, the problem of evil as an intellectual conundrum requiring a solution is very prominent in the writings of twentieth century philosophy of religion, particularly in the wake of the experience of two World Wars, mechanized genocide and murderous dictatorships. More recently, theologians have responded not by pointing speculatively to possible reasons why God might or might not allow certain forms of suffering and evil, but rather by examining what Christian tradition claims God has actually done in the face of suffering and evil. In other words, what is God's response as revealed in the incarnation and testified in scripture, to which the Church seeks to witness in its life and tradition? What do Christians actually do and say when thrown into the mire of the most desperate and pointless suffering? They practice, however falteringly and with constant need of repentance and forgiveness, the virtues of faith, hope and love which are at once gifts of grace.

Rick Shenk's book belongs firmly within the field of theological responses to evil and suffering, rather than philosophical justifications of evil and suffering. Nevertheless, his work presents us with a meditation which is philosophically acute, intellectually rigorous and historically informed. It is also honest and humble, not offering a 'solution' but a series of theological proposals based on a profound reflection on scripture, a deft handling of philosophical concepts and a careful consideration of a great breadth of the Christian theological tradition. This guide through the dense thicket of human experience and anguish comes from a theologian with deep pastoral experience in ministering to God's people and preaching his Word.

Any work on evil and suffering will prove controversial and provocative, and this book is certainly no exception. Many theologians, including the writer of this foreward, will balk at the use of the term 'necessity,' whether subordinately metaphysical or otherwise, in relation to evil. At first glance, it seems to run full-square against the deeply influential tradition of privatio boni, traceable to Plato, reflected in the book of Job, and acutely expressed in Augustine and Thomas Aquinas, which focuses on the radically accidental nature of evil and its unintelligibility. Shenk knows this and believes that his work is fully consistent with this tradition. He pleads for the 'theological space' to explore the idea that a created reality will, not of logical necessity but by virtue of God's eternal character and goals, manifest evil and suffering which must be turned against itself. In essence, Shenk's proposal is that evil and suffering is destroyed by evil and suffering in such a way that, by methods of pure peaceableness, creation is brought to the fullness of being in the Good. The fulcrum upon which this meditation turns is, of course, the cross of Jesus Christ.

This is not, then, a work of abstract solutions and philosophical game-playing. It emerges from many years' pastoral experience and, in the end, a response to evil and suffering must be theologically and experientially intelligible. This is why Shenk, with characteristic and simple honesty, applies his theological response to the experience of evil and suffering in the final two chapters of this book and examines so clearly some of the most important challenges to his ideas.

This book will be all the more persuasive if God's purposes and goals have been correctly identified, and in a fashion that does not render the argument brutally circular. The claim that evil does not challenge God, but challenges his purposes, as if the two can be separated, will no doubt be scrutinized, as will the notion that anything in God—for example, his purposes and goals—can entail, however subordinately, evil and suffering. Still, theology requires many virtues, not least humility, patience and a quality of attention which one finds so abundantly in the works of Augustine and Aquinas, but finds so lacking in the loud grandstanding of much theology in our own time. Rick Shenk has allowed himself to be schooled by the best in the tradition and shows something of the qualities required of the theologian as he follows carefully where faith and reason lead. He is fully aware of the challenges I cite very briefly here and responds to them in his text. One may be very persuaded by the rigorous argument of this book, or one may conclude that its author has, like so many when tackling this most difficult topic, taken some wrong turnings. Either way, it is most definitely worth walking with Rick Shenk, listening carefully, quietly and patiently to what he has to say.

Preface

WE MAY BE ASKING the wrong question: "Why is there evil in the world if God is good and powerful?" This question seems to arise, unbidden, and intuitively. It is as if we all know that the world *should not* be "this way." But it is. For now. And so, this may be the wrong question. It may smuggle-in an unbiblical premise: God *can* and *should* use his coercive-power to relieve suffering since he is both good and able. But what if coercive-power does not work?

This book is an investigation into the possibility that it is the Cross which *must* be the center of this issue and it is the Cross which *could* reform this question. The Cross challenges us to wonder if the effectiveness of coercive-power against evil is a false assumption. Most Christians are not tempted to deny that God is good or powerful, or that evil exists. Instead many ask: Why doesn't God *use* his power to prevent suffering in the world? In response to this, I want to propose that evil, and its corresponding suffering, is destroyed *only* by enduring evil and suffering while trusting God—on the Cross and throughout our lives. At least, I propose this is the case if God's goal is to destroy evil *for* the people of God. So I want to propose that the Cross is not simply an example of "what God did in one case," but normative and necessary in all of life's experiences. For God is destroying evil, not by might, nor by power, but by a special kind of power: the power of suffering and trusting God. As we wait for his return, the Cross becomes normative for us as well.

If I am correct, this changes the question from, "Why doesn't a good and powerful God use his power to relieve suffering?" to "How is God destroying evil and suffering—and why is he taking so long?" The answer to the later and reframed question would then be, "He is using evil and suffering to destroy evil and suffering for His People; this is how long it takes."

I hasten to add that I do not believe my proposal is a "solution" to the problem of evil. But perhaps it could help us learn to delight in God in an evil world of suffering which seems at times so relentless. And even so, we cry out, "How long, O Lord!"

Acknowledgments

I AM GRATEFUL TO Simon Oliver, my primary supervisor, for his insights, challenges to my argument, and his knowledge of the field, which he shared and applied. Simon's passion for the truth of Christ comes through in all of our discussions. I am grateful to Steve Roy, who has served as a mentor and friend since this project began. He has provided critical direction and his challenges have always been on-target. I am also grateful to Mark Cartledge for taking a pastor and teaching him to write as a theologian—or at least trying tirelessly to do so.

I am deeply grateful to the staff of the Feehan Memorial Library at the University of Saint Mary of the Lake Seminary in Mundelein, Illinois: Mary, Marian, Lois, and Anna. You welcomed a stranger with help and encouragement that even included coffee, water, and homemade treats!

And what a privilege I have had to be part of a church family like Calvary who allowed me more than four weeks of dedicated study a year during four very difficult years in the life of our church. I know that God used your investment in me as a significant part of my time of healing. You are irreplaceable friends and I am still surprised that God called me away from serving with you. And I am very grateful to my new church family, Village Church, for allowing a new pastor to continue to focus on study.

I am grateful to my family. First, to my parents who provided a "room with a view" where I could study; even now I am watching squirrels fighting with doves over dropped seeds and a woodpecker alternating with a greedy starling over the suet. How I miss Dad, now. Most of all, I am grateful to my wife, Lynne, who supported me during these difficult years, including allowing me to be away and study. You all were a source of encouragement to pursue this work.

Definitions

Conforming-Freedom* or *Ultimate Freedom, is that freedom, suggested in Romans 8, which is free from Evil & Suffering (in the sense of agency and even its presence in our new world), in order that we might be as free as God in respect to evil, so that we are free to delight fully in God. This is the fourth and last era of freedom.

Compatibilistic Free-Will is that freedom which allows a person to make a choice by the free action of will, so that the decision, while it is wholly free with respect to the human will, is also fully compatible with God's sovereignty, so that having made a choice, a person could not have made a choice other than the one that was made. Bruce Ware is helpful in naming this the "freedom of inclination": we choose in response to the constellation of causes which inclines our will to a singular and explainable choice (though not necessarily explainable by us now).

Creation & Crisis is a collective-singular term for the three creation events of Scripture (creation of heaven and earth, creation of the church, re-creation of heaven and earth), and their associated crises (the Fall, the Cross, and the Judgment).

A Defection is a species of Theodicy which is an argument (biblical or philosophical) intended to modify (defect from) one of the Trilemmas of Theodicy. It is distinct from both a Theodicy and a Defense in that it is not so much a solution as a restatement of the premise(s) of the problem in order to escape the tension they create.

A Defense is a species of Theodicy which is a philosophical argument intended to show a logically sufficient solution to the Trilemma of Theodicy. A Defense is distinct from a Theodicy, which offers an argument to genuinely "untangle" the Trilemma, in that a Defense needs only to offer a sufficient solution, even if unlikely in the world as we experience it.

Evil & Suffering is a collective-singular term for evil (and on occasion, I will only use the word, evil, for simplicity), both moral and natural, and its attendant suffering. While evil and suffering are distinct, they have a common beginning and a common end, and cannot exist in isolation and do not share a common genesis with the rest of God's creation.

Forfeit-freedom (or Slavery) is that "freedom" which resulted from the rebellion of God's willful-creatures from God's laws, which led to complete loss of freedom. This is the second era of freedom.

Definitions

Hope is our confidence and joy in God which is based on our eschatological future in the person of Christ.

Libertarian Free-Will is that freedom which allows a person to make a choice by action of the will, for which the full network of all causes, including the character of the one making the choice, is insufficient to predict or determine the decision, and having decided, it is the case, that the person could (just as easily) have done otherwise. As Bruce Ware defined it, it is the freedom of indifference—the choice made cannot be explained by the summed causes so that the person acts with indifference to the summed causes.

Penultimate Freedom is that freedom which was created by Christ in his resurrection for his new-creation people, and has a Kingdom-like, "already, not yet" aroma. This is the third era of freedom.

Perfect is to be without taint of sin. This means that a person, object, or motive is "perfect" because it is untainted by sin, even if that perfection may be tainted in the future. It does not imply a unique, unchanging point of singular perfection, but freedom from all taint of evil.

Subordinate-Metaphysical Necessity is the necessity that arises subordinate to God's metaphysical necessity and therefore conditional upon God. Yet, given God's metaphysically necessary character and announced goals, "it had to happen."

A Theodicy intends to offer a solution to the Trilemma of Theodicy by offering a fourth "lemma." Distinct from a Defence, a Theodicy is not merely offering a logical reason why the Christian God cannot be dismissed in the face of evil, but attempts to offer a real-world solution to the problem of evil.

Trilemma of Theodicy is the three ancient assertions (and to some extent, the tension felt by their assertion within the theist): the omni-goodness of God, the omnipotence of God, and the presence of evil in the world that God created.

Unfettered Freedom (or Defectable or Defective Freedom) is that freedom given to God's willful-creatures at creation, a perfect freedom, but not fettered to God's perfection. In fact, it was a freedom decreed to defect from perfection in time. This is the first era of freedom.

Volitional Free-Will is the state in which the act of willing and the act resulting from that willing are in concord. It implies nothing of the influences upon the will or their effect upon willing. Volitional Free-Will endures throughout all eras of freedom.

NOTE: Because some quotes cited here already employ square bracks to indicate inserted text, I have chosen to indicate my insertions with square brackets and my initials: [RAS: . . .], except in biblical citations.

Introduction

> At the cross evil is conquered as evil.[1] —Henri Blocher

THIS IS THE WONDER of the Cross. Throughout the history of the church, Christians from all major traditions have argued that it is the shadow of the Cross, not evil, that stretches over the world. The Cross is illuminated by the light of the eschaton, shining even now into our world from God's throne. Indeed, with Henri Blocher we affirm, *at the Cross, evil is conquered as evil*. Christ has defeated evil and death, and brought life and immortality into the light for all the world to see. Still we sense evil's relentless, gnawing bite, chewing steadily through our threadbare hopes. How can this be? For the Christian, this vicious and vivified evil, which does not shrink before the Cross, is the problem of evil.

EVIL: A MYSTERY OR A PROBLEM?

> There is no harm in trying to resolve the mystery.[2] —D. A. Carson

> The refusal of God to explain His design is itself a burning hint of His design. The riddles of God are more satisfying than the solutions of man.[3]
> —G. K. Chesterton

For the Christian the "problem" of evil is more properly the "mystery" of evil; and it is an enduring mystery. It is not a "problem" to be solved, like a mathematical equation, which submits step-by-discrete-step to a singular and final solution. No elegant solution will fully exhaust the depths of this mystery. This is true in all of theology. Just as the universe is not by nature, Newtonian, nor is God by nature, Thomistic, so also no comprehensive work is the complete work and no *magnum opus* is *the telos* of theology. To say the world is not Newtonian and that theology is not Thomistic is not to undermine the work of great men, but to exalt the majesty of God and the infinite mystery of his ways. As he has designed his universe, there is always more to

---

1. Blocher, *Evil and the Cross*, 132.
2. Carson, *How Long, O Lord?*, 178.
3. Chesterton, *The Book of Job*, xxii.

Introduction

learn—even about how and why evil exists in his world. It is an enduring mystery, not a problem to "solve." But that must never be a discouragement, inhibiting us from pursuing God to new depths. In fact, we glorify God by discovering his ways, even in regard to why evil is in his world. It is written in Proverbs 25:2: "It is the glory of God to conceal a matter, but the glory of kings is to search out a matter." So "kings" like Newton, Aquinas, and many others, have done and it is properly to their glory! But, while revelation is complete in Christ, we will always have an infinite amount of work yet to do to understand. While to discover anything about him and his universe is a delight to him and to us, we will never finish the job; our God and his ways are inexhaustibly deep.[4] So, it is precisely because the problem of evil is a mystery that we are called to discover more, even if discovery cannot achieve *telos*; even if there is no hope of an ultimate, mathematics-like solution.[5] We were created by God to seek to know

---

4. That God allows evil is not simply a problem, but an engaging mystery which draws us to know him better. Marcel (*Philosophy of Existentialism*) distinguishes between "problem" and "mystery." He writes, "this world is, on the one hand, riddled with problems and, on the other, determined to allow no room for mystery" (12). By this he is indicating that a "problem" implies an issue in relation to which I can "remain outside it—before or beyond it" (16) which he rejects. Instead a "mystery" is something in which I am involved so that the subject/object distinction breaks down. So, a mystery is a "problem that encroaches on its own data" (19). In so saying, he identifies the "problem of evil" as a "clear case" of a mystery which we tend to "degrade it to the level of a problem" (19). He writes, "evil which is only stated or observed is no longer evil which is suffered; in fact, it ceases to be evil . . . being 'involved' is the fundamental fact" (19). To treat a mystery as problematical is to degrade it to the point that it is not personal or to objectify it. In this Marcel offers a welcome reminder of the nature of the world; there is a great difference between a mystery and a problem. In fact, I would suggest that it would be beneficial to communication, if, instead of using the word "problematic" to refer to a difficult situation, we used the term to mean that which is fundamentally reducible and "only a problem." Certainly, the "problem of evil" should never be considered "problematic" in that sense. So also, it might be helpful to augment Marcel by suggesting that a problem is that kind of intellectual challenge which submits to assault by rational reduction. And truly, those of us who are strongly influenced by modernism and the approach of science, tend to degrade mystery to a "problem" that is "only problematic" in this sense. Perhaps it is the case that our "problem" is not our understanding "mystery" as a "problem," but even that the concept of a "problem" is applied to just about anything. So it is the case that even "problems" of physics might be better considered as "mystery" to the extent that no one worthwhile problem will ever be so exhausted that the last chapter is written. Progress in physics and in theology may require techniques which are wholly conscious of the cross-talk between subject and object in all investigation and even the personal nature of the world in which we live—including science. So it must be emphasized that the subject *appropriately* interferes with the understanding of the object—appropriate because that is the nature of the personal relationship in which we stand with the universe and other beings. But, I have no reason to think that the distinction between object and subject is an inhibition to successful investigation. While the "mystery of the problem of evil" (my sense of the best way to state this case) can never be reduced to its *telos*, the image of God in us and the commission to rule over creation allows us (I would say commissions us!) to investigate God and his universe fruitfully and with expectation. This expectation is not of impersonal solution to a reducible problem, but a mystery in which we are deeply invested and in which God is invested with us—and in which he invests us with tools of discernment.

5. The amazing anthropomorphic reality is that we are "perfectly equipped" to study our universe. John Polkinghorne writes, "The universe is astonishingly open to us, rationally transparent to our enquiry. This is what enables scientists to make their discoveries but it is by no means a trivial fact that this is so. One would anticipate that evolutionary selection would produce hominid minds apt

him and his ways. James Moreland and David Ciocchi write, "One possible decision is to make the appeal to paradox, maintaining that although we cannot explain how for instance Jesus can be both God and man, God can."[6] We must beware of calling what is paradox, antinomy. We must beware of calling God characteristically, unknowable, instead of infinitely deep. To do so is to short-circuit the use of God-given intellectual tools. Nor should we act in a triumphalist way with hubris saying, we have made everything clear. Instead, let us assume that God has given us the ability to investigate the great depths of his glory. In this confidence, we pursue God and his ways, even to the "why" of evil.

So while evil is not a "problem-to-be-solved," and it remains a mystery, it is still appropriately called a problem, because it can weigh down our souls. It can threaten our hope and our joy. But it is even more intractable because not everyone understands this problem of evil in the same way. It is not only a mystery that resists an ultimate solution, but a mystery that resists even a common understanding of itself. Historically, it is stated this way by Epicurus (341–270 BCE):

(i) God is characteristically good; and

(ii) God is omnipotent; and

(iii) evil exists in his world[7]

This "trilemma" is clearly an expression of the anxiety that evil raises within us, but is it clear that Epicurus wrestled with this in the same way and with the same "tension in the soul" that a Christian does? That is hardly possible. His context and culture were quite different. But, it is clear that these issues were a deep challenge both for him and for Christians today. Moreover, these propositions are not even formally contradictory.[8] But the fact that these statements have mutable historical context and weight, and

---

for coping with everyday experience, but that these minds should also be able to understand the subatomic world of quantum theory and the cosmic implications of general relativity goes far beyond anything that could conceivably be of relevance to survival fitness. . . . How does it come about that our minds are so perfectly conformed to understanding the universe? It does not seem sufficient to say that this is just our luck." (*Science & Theology: An Introduction*, 72–73).

6. Ciocchi and Moreland, *Christian Perspectives on being Human*, 96.

7. This three-fold anatomy, the so-called "Trilemma," is also stated by Hume, through the mouth of Philo who echoes Epicurus: "Is he willing to prevent evil, but not able? then He is impotent. Is he able, but not willing? then He is malevolent. Is He both able and willing? whence then is evil?" (Hume, *Dialogues Concerning Natural Religion*, Part I0, 100).

8. Plantinga (*God, Freedom, and Evil*, 21) cites an even more complete set of propositions and notes that even this set is not formally contradictory. So also, Eleonore Stump, "To show such an inconsistency, one would need at least to demonstrate that this claim must be true: (5) There is no morally sufficient reason for God to allow instances of evil." ("Problem of Evil," 392). This is not an insignificant point. Not only are these standard propositions not formally contradictory, but (5) can never be proven by definition. However, if a sufficient case could be made that "a morally sufficient reason exists," disproving (5), the tension of (1)-(4) would thereby be relieved (Note: Stump divides God's omnipotence and his omniscience into separate propositions making four where Epicurus had three). Stump, at least, believes this is possible. I do, too.

Introduction

that these propositions are not formally contradictory so as to create a "real" problem, is no obstacle to their ability to articulate clearly the tension from one generation to the next of those who believe in such a God and who suffer evil. This they have done and continue to do. This trilemma remains the simplest and most common understanding of the issue—and it produces real tension.

As a result of this real tension, many have tried to frame an answer or have tried to point us in the right direction to begin to resolve the tension: Pelagius's early free-will proposal, Augustine's "trust in God in the face of all evils" response, Leibniz's "Best of All Possible Worlds" theodicy, Hick's soul-making theodicy, and many others. Each possessed a certain level of confidence in their contribution, but no proposal achieved a determinative *telos* in the church. One could argue that by the twentieth century, discouragement and perhaps even boredom had settled over the issue. It was then that John Mackie announced the wholesale *failure of theology* on this very point, *theodicy*. He claimed that any belief in God (at least the good and omnipotent God of Christianity) was wholly illogical in the light of evil. He wrote:

> I think, however, that a more telling criticism can be made by way of the traditional problem of evil. Here it can be shown, not that religious beliefs lack rational support, but that they are positively irrational, that the several parts of the essential theological doctrine are inconsistent with one another, so that the theologian can maintain his position as a whole only by a much more extreme rejection of reason than in the former case.[9]

This declaration held great currency in the philosophical world and it came to be known as the Flew-Mackie proposal because of parallel work by Antony Flew.[10] Even if his conclusion was not universally accepted, still he spoke for those who thought that theodicy was a misguided venture. However, in the face of defeat or disinterest, some, including Alvin Plantinga, took up the challenge[11] and the battle was resurrected. To some extent, Plantinga not only resurrected the whole field of philosophical theology (specifically in regard to theodicy), he even won the battle, which Mackie claimed to be previously forfeit. He did so by showing that the philosophical-theological problem was solved by any one of many possible, logically-consistent arguments. That is, as opposed to a theodicy, he mounted a defense, which does not make a claim for God's purpose in allowing evil, but instead shows that there exist internally consistent reasons, or possibilities, which could be sufficient reasons for God to allow evil. According to John Feinberg and others, Plantinga fully accomplished this.[12] So it is possible

---

9. Mackie, "Evil and Omnipotence," 200. The "former case" is the thorough criticisms of the positive traditional arguments for God that can be ignored, if the theists chooses to do so.

10. Flew, "Divine Omnipotence and Human Freedom," *New Essays in Philosophical Theology*, 144–69.

11. Alvin Plantinga's work is extensive, but his argument, that reopened the debate, is well represented in *God, Freedom, and Evil*.

12. Feinberg, *Many Faces of Evil*, 63–74. One can note what may be a resurgence of interest in

to construct a robust defense (or even many) which satisfies Epicurus's challenge and which answers Mackie.

But even a defeat of the Flew-Mackie thesis was painfully insufficient; it merely revived the issue. In the face of many overwhelming examples of evil, a system, which is merely internally consistent, but still only speculative, offers little comfort. Even if it can be shown that an all-good and all-powerful God is consistent with evil, why could God not do with a little less evil than we actually experience? The argument here is that it should be possible to evaluate the probability that God exists in the face of evidence and in light of all known defenses of God and the actual abundance of evil. Many have entered into this discussion, including Plantinga.

Still, even if a good theodicy could be developed which met the test of the evidence and probabilities, the tension would still exist. Marilyn McCord Adams and others call this the problem of "horrendous evil." It is not only the amount of evil, but the awfulness of evil, which makes us aware that evil is so vile; it is difficult to accept any logic which permits faith in God. Any solution must face the test of the Holocaust, the Stalinist purges, racial horrors of Rwanda, and each one of the singular horrors faced by every individual. What do we say of the person who dies having suffered intensely, one for whom her life was not in any conceivable way, good to her?

But even "horrendous evils" do not represent the full scope of the tension. A theodicy must address the problem of gratuitous evil, Hick's dysteleological evil. How can we address the evil for which there is no reason, no soul-making, and no God glorifying effects? This is (at least) an example of the horizon problem; our understanding has reached only so far at this point in history. And understanding, like light from a distant star, speeds through the universe, engulfing a larger horizon from which it becomes visible to more observers. So, over time, as our horizon of understanding expands so that we understand some more reasons for some evil, such understanding moves (if slowly) in the direction that reduces the sum total of those events that could be called "meaningless." Still, it must be admitted that after thousands of years, we continue to be overwhelmed by the weight of evil, which is, at least to us, meaningless. So we still must ask, how are we to understand evil that has no discernable purpose?

Finally, and most importantly, there is the problem of practical theology; the tension of the problem of evil is first, last, and at its core, personal and religious: "It hurts! Where is God!?" In common expression, before we want philosophy, we want an answer. That reflects at least one reading of Job: his friends were philosophers, but Job wanted comfort. The answer Job wanted was the (quiet) comfort of his friends, a response from God, or a quick death. A philosophical answer is essential, but any true philosophical answer must go "beyond" philosophy, and stand the test of the place of personal pain.

---

the journals at about this time. While not claiming a causal link, it is at least interesting that one significant journal of philosophical religion, *Sophia*, was birthed at just this time in the early 1960s, after Mackie's article.

Introduction

As a problem, this is in reality many problems: philosophical-religious, evidential-probabilistic, dysteleological evil, and practical-religious-personal. And, as was discussed above, this problem of evil is first a mystery. This is the warning: if by saying that the problem of evil is a mystery and without rational solution, we fail to pursue the tension further, we may fail to pursue a path that leads to knowing God more and delighting in him more deeply. We must follow this tension and see where it leads.

ON THE HUBRIS OF DOING WORK IN THEODICY

> It is dangerous to embark on the question of evil: we risk defeat, and we risk presumption as well.[13] —Charles Journet

John Hick speaks for many when he says that some consider that "the very notion of a theodicy is impious."[14] Others might understand the limited historical progress to imply that its pursuit is without merit. So, what hubris has overwhelmed me that I attempt to pursue what has eluded others? It is not hubris, but a "thorn in my mind," which God would not extract or relieve. I also fear that the lack of significant progress toward resolution of the issue of theodicy may leave too many Christians open to rational and emotional attacks upon their faith. So this thorn, this irritation, demands my attention. It is not the hubris of assumption, but the hope of a knowable God. I have no expectation of offering theological *telos*, but I do hope to offer a contribution that might in some way catalyze some progress in the conversation. In doing so, I am encouraged by a quote from Augustine's, *de Trinitate*:

> So, whoever reads this and says, "This is not well said, because I do not understand it," is criticizing my statement, not the faith; and perhaps it could have been said more clearly—though no one has ever expressed himself well enough to be understood by everybody on everything.... On the other hand, if anyone reads this work and says, "I understand what is being said, but it is not true," he is at liberty to affirm his own conviction as much as he likes and refute mine if he can. If he succeeds in doing so charitably and truthfully, ... then that will be the choicest plum that could fall to me from these labors of mine.... I do not doubt, of course, that some people who are rather slow in the uptake will think that in some passages ... I mean what I did not mean, ... Nobody, I trust, will think it fair to blame me for the mistake of such people.[15]

With this in mind, I want to pursue a measure of hope (a large, overflowing, and bountiful measure!), in a world seemingly too dominated by Evil & Suffering.[16]

---

13. Journet, *Meaning of Evil*, 18.
14. Hick, *Evil and the God of Love*, 6.
15. Augustine, *Trinity*, 68–69.
16. Evil & Suffering is considered in this project as a singular, not a plural idea. This will be explained at greater length in chapter 2.

Introduction

ON THE CHALLENGE OF PRACTICAL THEOLOGY: THE EXAMPLE OF ZOSIA

Any proposal offered to address the tension should fit real life as if it were designed by God himself to do so. There are many possible scenarios of horrendous and personal evil, historical and personal. I desire to set out as a challenge to this (or any) theodicy, a problem which is neither invented by me to be a straw-man or merely iconic.

In the late 1990s, I first became interested in studying the problem of evil as I read Gregory Boyd's *Letters from a Skeptic*. His writing here and in other places regarding Open Theism, drove me to wrestle with the issue of theodicy. It is not important to discuss Open Theism here except by way of explanation: Open Theism attempts to preserve God's goodness by elevating human-freedom to the extent that, God cannot foreknow a decision before it is made by God's willful creatures because such a decision does not yet exist. More importantly for my study is the implication: blinding God to future willful decisions *is* a theodicy.[17] If God cannot know, then he is not responsible for evil. While my goal is not to refute Open Theism, it did seem to me that a solid theodicy which meets the challenge of the Epicurean Trilemma, but also the personal-religious application, is quite important to those who want to enjoy the pursuit of God in the pursuit of truth.

If Boyd, and others, chastise orthodox theology for having failed in the area of theodicy, then I should perhaps allow Boyd to set the test. This he does in *God at War*, reproducing the eyewitness account of the story of Zosia, a Jewish girl living in the Warsaw ghetto during the Nazi occupation:

> Zosia was a little girl . . . the daughter of a physician. During an "action" one of the Germans became aware of her beautiful diamond like eyes.
>
> "I could make two rings out of them," he said, "one for myself and one for my wife."
>
> His colleague is holding the girl.
>
> "Let's see whether they are really so beautiful. And better yet, let's examine them in our hands."
>
> Among the buddies exuberant gaiety breaks out. One of the wittiest proposes to take the eyes out. A shrill screaming and the noisy laughter of the soldier pack. The screaming penetrates our brains, pierces our heart, the laughter hurts like the edge of a knife plunged into our body. The screaming and laughter are growing, mingling and soaring to heaven.

---

17. Gregory Boyd writes, "First, the most fundamental reason why I believe suffering is often gratuitous—devoid of divine reason—differs from these other approaches. Within my system the possibility of gratuitous suffering is necessarily built into the possibility of love for contingent creatures." (*Satan and the Problem of Evil*, 20). Millard Erickson agrees. In his book, *What Does God Know and When Does He Know It?*, he writes, "The open theists have wrestled at some length with the problem of evil. In fact, to some extent, this theology can be seen to exist as a response to this problem" (190).

Introduction

> O God, whom will you hear first?
>
> What happens next is that the fainting child is lying on the floor. Instead of eyes two bloody wounds are staring. The mother driven mad, is held by the women.
>
> This time they left Zosia to her mother....
>
> At one of the next "actions," little Zosia was taken away. It was of course, necessary to annihilate the blind child.[18]

Boyd explains his response to this historical evil and why it is a challenge to our understanding of God:

> Hence when I speak of "evil" throughout this work, I am not referring primarily to some abstract "absence of goodness" (Augustine) or any other merely theoretical definition of evil. I am, rather, referring to Zosia, her mother and the unheeded cries and unpunished laughter that rose up to heaven on that day. By extension (but not abstraction!), I am referring to every concrete horrifying experience that in various ways looks and feels like this one.... If God is all-loving and perfectly good, he must want to protect Zosia. And if God exercises total control over the world, he must be able to protect Zosia. Yet Zosia suffers an unspeakable ordeal, then is murdered. This makes no sense and constitutes, in its starkest form, the intellectual problem of evil.[19]

He calls this an "intellectual" problem, and to some extent it is. But the nature of it is better considered as the personal-religious problem. It is the challenge that Boyd felt sufficient to use as a test for a theodicy because it represents the very intense, real, and personal problem in its most extreme form. What could we say to Zosia's mother? What could we say to those who participated in this evil? What could we say to those who had to hear the screams? What does God say?

ASSUMPTIONS

This project began with some assumptions, which I state here for clarity and to expose my commitments. For the sake of those who would disagree, I acknowledge that these are worthy of discussion in and of themselves, even if they do not fit within the scope of this project:

Theology: YHWH is. Named within this project as God or YHWH, he (the pronoun by which YHWH identifies himself in the text) is uniquely the self-existent One and Creator of everything that is. He is Trinity, and so is both relational and personal

---

18. Boyd, *God at War*, 33–34.

19. Ibid., 34–35. This challenge of Boyd is not unlike the challenge of Ivan to Alyosha in *The Brothers Karamazov*. A young peasant boy who injured his master's dog is stripped naked and told to run. In the presence of the boy's mother, the pack of hunting dogs tear him to pieces. Ivan is eager to hear how Alyosha, his religious brother, will respond (Dostoyevsky, *Brothers Karamazov*, 288).

Introduction

by nature, having existed from eternity in perfect and loving relationship between the three Persons: Father, Son, and Spirit. He also is good and so is the Source of all goodness; he does not cooperate with goodness, but is its source and all he does is characteristically good.[20] He reveals himself to us as: omnipotent (he is able to do all that is consistent with his character and all that is his sovereign will), infinite (he is not merely greater than us in the sense of magnitude, but beyond us in domain as the infinite to the finite), omniscient (all truth is known by him and all truth flows from him), omnipresent (having created all, nothing he created is "distant" from him for he is present "everywhere"), immanent (intimately involved in our lives and his creation), and transcendent (distinct from his creation and beyond our full comprehension, but not, in that, unknowable).

Epistemology: We know God, not because of our desire to know him, but because God desires to make himself known to us. By his Word, the Son, and by his Word, the Scriptures, he makes himself personally known. Like the incarnate Word, God's written Word is both human and divine, and it fully reflects God's nature and character. As such, it is authoritative and true, and when properly interpreted, accurate in all of its claims. My means of knowing God, as for Augustine,[21] is through faith in a Triune God who makes himself known by this Word of God read through faith. This is not propositionalism,[22] but neither does it divest any authority from Scripture to any other source.[23] It is not rationalism, for my faith is not in reason. It is not fideism, for I do not

---

20. The "Source" in regard to God's goodness will be capitalized and is used as a synonym for "Fountain of Goodness" as used by Calvin and Edwards.

21. Augustine often cited Isaiah 7:9, "if you will not believe, certainly you will not stand" as "unless you believe, you shall not understand" (*Free Choice of the Will*, 1.2). This issue will be considered at some length later in this project.

22. George Lindbeck considers three uses of Scripture: cognitive-propositionalist (which uses the Bible as data and reduces it to propositions), experiential-expressive (which is existential and might be typified by the work of Schleiermacher), and his own proposition, cultural-linguistic (which makes the community the authority and the text is a linguistic rule which is true intra-textually in regard to how the community is to live) (*Nature of Doctrine*, 16–33). However, I cannot find myself in Lindbeck's system. While coming close in some respects to a propositionalist, I am not because the text is not data, nor is the Bible reducible to propositions.

23. David Kelsey argues that those who find authority in the Text have made many mistakes. He asks four great questions regarding what aspects are authoritative; what about Scripture makes it authoritative; what logical force is attributed to each specific text; and how is it used to authorize theological proposals (*Proving Doctrine*, 15). While these questions must be considered when thinking about what it means for Scripture to be an authority, his approach makes it ultimately impossible for Scripture to be authoritative. For example he writes, "'Authoritative' is part of the meaning of 'scripture'; it is not contingent judgment made about 'scripture' on other grounds" (97). Further, he claims that "authority of Scripture" as a phrase is very close to "let's play ball" (which says nothing of what ball game or what rules) and so is not a statement that conveys significant content (108–12). In part, his work is a call to carefully define terms and functionally what we intend by words like "authority." So, in choosing Scripture as authority, it is fair to require that I state in what way it is an authority. Edward Farley argues that evangelical Christians have had a distinct problem with this and he rightly attacks the "identity problem." That is, there is a tendency to flatten God's communication and what human authors say about it: "To summarize, the principle of identity involves interpreting

believe in a way that is wholly distinct from reason. Rather, like Augustine, my epistemology begins with a presupposition: faith in a personal God, which is interpreted through reason. My view of biblical authority is influenced by Kevin VanHoozer, who understands the Bible in its canonical-linguistic setting through communicative-action theory. In brief, he makes a case that all of God's multi-genre communications to us are actions and calls to action, particularly our participation in his drama.[24] This position does not exclude biblical criticism, textual criticism, or natural theology. It certainly does not exclude any of the natural sciences. It promotes scholarship and investigation, but ultimately the Bible is authoritative when properly understood. This clearly leaves much room for discussion.

Method: My approach is to begin in Part I by considering an historical overview of the development of theodicy in the Christian tradition; specifically the Western tradition. This is intended to establish the texture and contours of the concepts of freedom, evil, and theodicy in their historical setting in order to give context for my thesis in Part II.

How is theodicy to be approached methodologically? Options include philosophy, philosophical theology, biblical theology, practical theology, systematic theology, and more. Edward Farley in his book, *Good and Evil*, wrestled with just this question:

> Such a project would appear to be a systematic theology. It is not. . . . One reason this project does not fall within the genre of systematic theology is its tendency to cross the borders that demarcate the theological disciplines. According to traditional mappings of the territory of theology, systematic theology is a specific discipline set off from ethics, history, and practical theology.[25]

Can any project dealing with the problem of evil fail to touch on many eras of biblical teaching, philosophical assumptions, issues of ethics, and even details of practical theology? However the project is perceived, "borders" (if they are perceived as such) will be crossed. In that sense, I agree with Farley that his project, and similar

---

the creaturely entity as the ersatz presence of the divine, a synthesis of divine intention and human interpretation into one content, and the identity of content between what is divinely willed (revealed) and what is humanly asserted. The question is, identity in what sense?" (*Ecclesial Reflections*, 38). In brief, the one who cites Scriptures cannot, herself, assume the authority of Scripture for her argument. Well said; the line of authority stops with Scripture and judgment and humility must attach to the theologian's assertions. Interestingly, this is built on his negative assessment of the hermeneutic of salvation-history, which is itself destroyed, in his system, by the problem of evil (156–57). So, Scripture is my authority in that when rightly understood and applied, by God's Spirit and within the community of believers, it is my authority for all things. That is, faith, informed Scripture rightly understood, leads to understanding. The fact that my understanding is not whole, and not wholly correct even in what I do understand, while it is a threat to my understanding and "success," is no more a threat than are our failures to properly read the authority of nature in our physics and chemistry. Over time, and by God's Spirit, the community tests understandings and adjusts. This project attempts such an adjustment to our thinking about theodicy.

24. Kevin J. VanHoozer's ideas are clearly presented in his texts, *Is There a Meaning in This Text?*, *First Theology*, and *The Drama of Doctrine*.

25. Farley, *Good & Evil*, xvii.

projects dealing with the problem of evil, do not strictly fall within the discipline of systematic theology. Yet, I would argue that the discipline, which necessarily permits the greatest integration, is systematic theology. To accomplish its systemizing task, to move from the details to a useful construction within the broader conversation, a project must necessarily wrestle with philosophy, epistemology, historical theology, ethics, biblical studies, and more. It is, I think, better not to consider these as "borders," but perspectives, all of which are helpful and contribute to the task of construction and conversation within systematic theology.[26]

THE THESIS

So we begin. In Part I, I will investigate the historical development of the understanding of free-will (Chapter 1); evil (Chapter 2); and theodicy (Chapter 3). Against this background, in Part II, a thesis is to be tested in regard to the problem of evil—the tension between the propositions of the Epicurean Trilemma and its application to the personal experience of evil. The thesis asserts that Evil & Suffering is destroying Evil & Suffering to bring about "Conforming Freedom" for God's people in the final state. This thesis is presented in three hypotheses:

- Hypothesis 1: Conforming-Freedom is the ultimate and singular human freedom required by God's character and goals for his people (Chapter 4).

- Hypothesis 2: Evil & Suffering is a subordinate-metaphysical necessity, being both the intrinsic problem and the instrumental solution in God's economy (Chapter 5).

- Hypothesis 3: Conforming-Freedom is achieved by God for his people through Evil & Suffering over four Eras of Freedom which are divided by three Creation & Crisis events (Chapter 6).

Finally, Part III is the practical evaluation of this proposal. Chapter 7 investigates the proposal as practical-theology. Chapter 8 evaluates remaining issues, open questions, and asks the question: What if I am wrong?

Essentially, I am suggesting that we understand Henri Blocher's words, with which I began this introduction, with a change of preposition: not "at the Cross, evil is conquered *AS* evil," but "at the Cross, evil is conquered *BY* evil." Or in the specific language of this project, "at the Cross, Evil & Suffering is conquered *BY* Evil & Suffering." This is the wonder of the Cross; God uses Evil & Suffering against itself, conquering in weakness.

---

26. Even if this is granted for systematics in general, it may still be the case that the "problem of evil" is a particular "problem child," rattling doors and testing locks in every room of the house. Theodicy will stray into areas not normally on the "tour" for systematics. While this project will necessarily "rattle doors" of many disciplines, it is a theological project, first, because it hopes to consider the problem in the context of the character of God and in regard to his revealed Word. Its nature is essentially systematic in that it attempts to pull together diverse ideas and construct something useful to contribute to the ongoing conversation among all of the disciplines which touch on theodicy.

PART I

The Tension of Theodicy

WHILE THE EPICUREAN TRILEMMA is the classic statement of the problem to which theodicy addresses itself, the heart of the problem can be unfolded by a study of free-will and evil, out of which a theodicy is framed. This will involve, to some extent, a study of the ideas of God's sovereignty and goodness, but the heart of a discussion can fruitfully begin with these two issues. So this project begins by attempting to grasp the historic development of the Christian understanding of free-will and evil and the tension between them that gives rise to various theodicies.

1

The Historical Development of the Concept of Free-Will

The person who chooses has the torment of choice.[1] —German proverb

IN THIS CHAPTER, I intend to trace the development of the two established free-will perspectives: Libertarian Free-Will and Compatibilist Free-Will. I will first establish the relationship between a study of theodicy and free-will. Then, to make it possible to follow the development of the concept of free-will, I will offer working modern definitions. Though such definitions will not always be well fitted to past historical understandings, they will serve as useful benchmarks for this discussion. Finally, I will trace the historical development of the concept of free-will that has led to our modern perspectives and understandings. My intent is to suggest that the Libertarian Free-Will and Compatibilistic Free-Will perspectives are inadequate descriptors of freedom.

ON THE RELATIONSHIP OF THEODICY TO FREE-WILL

> Well, the two seem clean contrary and opposite, God's universal foreknowledge and freedom of the will. If God foresees all things and cannot be mistaken in any way, what Providence has foreseen as a future event must happen. So that if from eternity Providence foreknows not only men's actions but also their thoughts and desires, there will be no freedom of will. . . . For even if it is the case that they are foreseen because they are going to happen and not that they happen because they are foreseen, it is nonetheless necessary that either

---

1. Cited by Moltmann, *Trinity and the Kingdom*, 213.

PART I: The Tension of Theodicy

> future events be foreseen by God or that things foreseen happen as foreseen, and this alone is enough to remove freedom of the will.[2]
>
> —Boethius in dialog with Lady Philosophy

The idea of personal freedom is a deeply held belief but this belief brings us into tension with God's supremacy and sovereignty, including his foreknowledge. Jonathan Edwards said well that this great assumption of freedom comes from our experience of making choices: "A great argument for self-determining power is the supposed experience we all have of an ability to determine our wills, in cases wherein no prevailing motive is presented."[3] That is, our decisions "feel" free and uninfluenced, even when we are fully aware of significant and overwhelming influences, such as lack of sleep, drugs, or pressing circumstances. Surrounded by causes, we dream we are free. But are we free? And if we are free, in what sense are we free?

Before we begin an historical survey of the church's understanding of free-will which is intended to address these questions, it is worthwhile to state my intention in this project in regard to free-will or freedom, which I consider to be synonyms. I am proposing that Evil & Suffering is used instrumentally by God to destroy Evil & Suffering in order to produce an ultimate, conforming-freedom. This freedom is a freedom from Evil & Suffering (in the sense of agency and exclusion), in order that we might be as free as God in respect to sin (it has no intersection in us) and so are free to delight *fully* in God. I will propose that such freedom for his people is under construction within God's sovereign and sacrificial direction through four distinct Eras of Freedom:

- *Unfettered Freedom* was given to God's willful-creatures at creation, and was a perfect freedom, but wholly unfettered from God's control and character, and a freedom decreed to collapse.[4]

- *Slavery, or Forfeit-freedom*, resulted from the rebellion of God's willful-creatures from God's laws, which led to complete loss of freedom.

---

2. Boethius, *Consolation of Philosophy*, 5.3.

3. Jonathan Edwards, "The Freedom of the Will," 2.6.1 (the scheme for indication references to this work of Edwards is as follows: Part. Section. unnumbered paragraphs of this edition). Does everyone make the assumption of a certain kind of libertarian freedom from birth, collecting mounting evidence that such may not be the case—even rebelling against that evidence at times? Perhaps an Arminian position comes hard-wired into us, but an Edwardian-Reformed position must be acquired, if it is, over time, against our initial sense of the world.

4. This term is one that I take from Alvin Plantinga as the best term to describe this era of freedom. In Plantinga's case, he used it in order to "make a present" to Flew of the word "freedom," surrendering the argument about its meaning since Flew wanted freedom conditioned in a compatibilist way and Plantinga wanted a freer freedom: "unfettered" (*God and Other Minds*, 135). I also take this to mean, specifically, that the first humans were not simply "freer" in some measurable sense, but were also not tied by nature to God's goodness. God is good by character. The first humans were good by accidental necessity of creation by a good God. They were not created "God," possessing his goodness as a part of their metaphysical being. In proof of this, I simply offer that God persists in goodness because it is a part of himself. We, unfettered by that goodness, defected.

The Historical Development of the Concept of Free-Will

- *Penultimate Freedom* was created by Christ in his resurrection for his new-creation people, and has a Kingdom-like, "already, not yet" aroma.
- *Conforming-Freedom*, suggested in Romans 8, is an eschatological or ultimate freedom in which we freely conform to the image of Christ and are unmolested by evil in any way.[5]

During each of these four Eras of Freedom, Volitional Free-will (the exercise of the human will and the clear and real sense of choice and responsibility) is preserved intact (even though the will is damaged) and is sufficient for responsibility in every age of freedom. That is, in the exercise of our will, we chose and act willingly.[6]

It should be stated that this project is not about freedom or free-will as an isolated concept, but instead the freedom of God's human willful-creatures as seen or viewed from a specifically Christian perspective and in regard to theodicy. For that reason, I will primarily consider writers from the Christian era (excepting, of course, Old Testament biblical authors). While much could be learned from the study of pre-Christian authors, and from writers working outside the Christian tradition, their ideas are often cited by the writers considered here. Where they are not, work is left for another project.

FREE-WILL: DEFINITIONS AND CONTOURS

> There is no such thing as the definition of indeterminism or the definition of determinism. Instead, there are varieties of each.[7]
>
> —John S. Feinberg

A development of the precise meaning of free-will[8] has been taking shape for millennia. This in itself is instructive. Unlike the concept of "rock," which has always existed

---

5. Based on conversations during the research for this project, I also suspect that a significant question will arise in the minds of many readers as the idea of a progressive and constructed freedom is investigated: "How will our eternal, holy, and free state be preserved in heaven?" That is, if Adam fell, what is different about freedom in the final state that will ensure our eternal holiness? This question is born of the subordinate questions: Why did God not preserve Adam in holiness? Could God have preserved him? Could God have actualized a world in which Adam would have conformed freely to holiness and also met God's own goals? What kind of freedom would permit Adam to fail when first created and remain holy in the final creation? What will have changed so that God will preserve him the second time or what will have changed such that Adam will freely choose to conform in the final creation? I want to suggest that the main question forces itself on all theologies, not simply on theodicies or this theodicy. This is not a new question and there are answers in every system. One answer will be proposed here.

6. Anthony Hoekema is helpful here when he writes, "what we call 'willing' is simply another name for an activity performed by the whole person; it is the whole person in the process of making decisions" (*Created in God's Image*, 227). He says this in the context of arguing against a "faculty psychology" in which there is a separate organ of the will and in accord with John Locke.

7. Feinberg, "God Ordains All Things," 20.

8. "Free-will" will be hyphenated as a composite word in this project because it is not to be

with a certain objectiveness (though the meaning has grown richer with deeper understanding), free-will seems to be an idea that did not hold common meaning over time, nor did every era show equal interest (in fact, some were particularly disinterested, as I will note). As we begin the twenty-first century, the discussion concerning the meaning of free-will has been divided into two fundamental positions: deterministic and indeterministic free-will. Or, as they will be more commonly identified in this project, "Libertarian Free-Will" and "Compatibilistic Free-Will." While this project will not wholly subscribe to either of these positions, understanding these specific positions or viewpoints is necessary to understand the historical development and current divide. For that reason the following definitions will prove useful as benchmarks for the historical study.

Will is that "faculty of the soul," the whole person who chooses.[9]

Free-Will is the state in which the will is free to choose, while at the same time acknowledging internal and external influences upon it. It is the will that chooses.[10] So the sense of "free" here is that an action is made freely when it is in accord with the will. The word pair "free-will" is hyphenated because it is to be understood as a binary concept, which has a definition that is not simply a compound of two independent words. A few examples may serve here. If a person chooses to walk across the street, this is a freely willed choice regardless of the influences upon her. But if she is prevented from walking, against her will, by coercion (constraining causes), the act of staying, which an observer may see and which she experiences, was not by the free-choice of her will; she was coerced. So also, if a person wills to lose weight, but in the presence of food, she decides to eat, this does not mitigate against the freedom of her will. The action of eating is in accord with her will to eat. The fact that it is a choice made under the influence of external pressure (the temptation of the food) and internal influence (her undisciplined character) and though this is against another lesser-willed desire to lose weight, this does not mitigate against this being a freely willed action. This action is in accord with volition; she chose to eat. So, in this limited sense, an action is an act of the free-will when it is in accord with the will. To this extent, as will be seen, Augustine, Aquinas, Luther, Calvin (with conditions), and Edwards can agree with Irenaeus, Pelagius, Arminius, Hick, and others.

---

investigated as two conjoined and independent concepts of "free" and "will." Instead we want to understand the meaning that the two symbols "free" and "will" acquire when conjoined as "free-will." The terms, "freedom," and "human free-will" will often be used in this project as synonyms for free-will. We will also consider, separately, what it means for God to have "free-will," and what "kind" of free-will he has, in Part III.

9. In using Augustine's refrain from Free-Choice of the Will (and other writings), I am not distinguishing here, the soul from spirit, nor do I intend a separate organ of choice. By this definition, I intend to indicate the willing of the whole person in full agreement with him or herself.

10. This is true for the libertarian and compatibilist perspectives as noted by Feinberg ("God Ordains All Things," 24).

Volitional Free-will in this project is synonymous with free-will as defined above.[11] And when the word freedom is used in this project, and is not modified by other adjectives, it is to this volitional freedom that I refer. Free-will, freedom, or Volitional Free-Will is the state in which the will is free to make a choice and it is an act of free-will when the act of willing and the act coming from that willing are in concord. Nothing is implied here about how that choice is or is not conditioned. That choice may be influenced both by external influences and by the internal influences of character.

Libertarian Free-Will is that freedom which allows a person to make a choice by action of the will, for which the full network of all causes, including the character of the one making the choice, is insufficient to predict or determine the decision, and having decided it is the case that the person could (just as easily)[12] have done otherwise.[13] As Bruce Ware defined it, it is the freedom of indifference—the choice made cannot be explained by the summed causes so that the person acts with indifference to the summed causes.[14]

Compatibilistic Free-Will is that freedom which allows a person to make a choice by the free action of will, so that the decision, while it is wholly free with respect to the human will, is also fully compatible with God's sovereign control over all wills, so that having made a choice, the person could not have made a choice other than the one that was made.[15] Again, Bruce Ware is helpful in naming this the "freedom of

---

11. Volitionalism should not be confused with voluntarism (Duns Scotus and others) which shall be considered later. While it may seem somewhat redundant to position "volitional" and "free-will" together, it serves as a reminder of the meaning in certain contexts.

12. This phrase, "just as easily" is not clearly agreed upon by either libertarians or compatibilists.

13. Antony Flew writes, "to say that a person could have helped doing something is not to say that what he did was in principle unpredictable nor that there were no causes anywhere which determined that he would as a matter of fact act in this way. It is to say that if he had chosen to do otherwise he would have been able to do so" ("Divine Omnipotence & and Human Freedom," 150). In counterpoint, Plantinga puts the emphasis on freedom from antecedent conditions, which is not the same as unpredictability (Plantinga, *God, Freedom, and Evil*, 29–30). The issue still hinges on freedom to perform or not perform and having performed, the person was still free to have not performed (or vice-versa). So also this definition is supported by Plantinga: "If a person is free with respect to a given action, then he is free to perform that action and free to refrain from performing it; no antecedent conditions and/or casual laws determine that he will perform the action, or that he won't. It is within his power, at the time in question, to take or perform the action and within his power to refrain from it" (*God, Freedom, and Evil*, 29).

14. Ware, *God's Greater Glory*, 25; 85–87.

15. A negative version of this definition can be read from Freddoso's long introduction to Molina: "Bañezians are not compatibilists in any standard sense. They deny that free acts can result from deterministic natural tendencies; they even go so far as to accept the condition that an act occurring at a time *t* is free only if some contrary act is compossible with the activity of *t* of all secondary causes other than the agent of the act in question" (Molina, *On Divine Foreknowledge*, 41). It is also important to note that both Libertarian Free-Will and Compatibilistic Free-Will "permit" a person's character to strongly influence the movements of the will, though Libertarian Free-Will must stop just short of determination (Ciocchi and Moreland, *Christian Perspectives on being Human*, 91–94).

PART I: The Tension of Theodicy

inclination": we choose in response to the constellation of causes which inclines our will to a singular and explainable (though perhaps not by us, now) choice.[16]

How do these positions differ and how are they in agreement? There are many areas of agreement. For both defenders of Libertarian Free-Will and Compatibilistic Free-Will, the volition of the person is free. Both advocates of Libertarian Free-Will and Compatibilistic Free-Will, admit Volitional Free-Will because both admit the sense and the reality of actually choosing; choice is fully experienced so that the person with Libertarian Free-Will or Compatibilistic Free-Will makes real choices and both are responsible for that choice.[17] For both, issues of internal character and external cause affect the decision. For both, God is active in the world of the person making the choice. But beyond that the differences form a great gulf. While there is an important distinction in regard to cause, so that for Libertarian Free-Will the causes, including character, are not sufficient to explain the decision, the great distinction is that for Compatibilistic Free-Will, having made a choice, no other willful choice was possible.[18] It is worth pausing here to define the definition. John S. Feinberg, in "God Ordains All Things" presents an excellent discussion of the meanings of the word "could" in the phrase "could have done otherwise." He rightly notes that if the libertarian is permitted to make the definition of "can" or "could," the meaning of "can" is "contra-causal" and if so, the compatibilist could not agree. However, other meanings of "can" include conditional, ability, opportunity, rule-consistent, avoidance of ill-consequences, and reasonableness. As a result he argues that the compatibilist could accept "could" if it was defined in any way other than the first (contra-causal).[19] However, I believe it is most helpful to the discussion if we allow the libertarian's contra-causal position to stand as a point of genuine disagreement.[20]

Again, these definitions are not intended to be read back into history. My use of them in the historical survey below might seem, at first glance, to belie that statement. As much as I may observe their development in history, it is rather unfair to Job or Augustine or Ockham to say they are in this camp or they are in that camp. At best,

---

16. Ware, *God's Greater Glory*, 25; 114.

17. While this is an issue for logical discussion, it is the position of both defenders of Libertarian Free-Will and Compatibilistic Free-Will that responsibility exists fully in their system.

18. For many the difference is even greater. For example, W. S. Anglin argues that one cannot be morally good or morally evil (or even fully human) unless one has Libertarian Free-Will. He writes, "No one is morally good unless he has Libertarian Free-Will" (Anglin, *Free Will and the Christian Faith*, 108).

19. Feinberg, "God Ordains All Things," 27–28.

20. Feinberg's position is well considered and a good reminder that the best definitions themselves need defining. Yet, I do not think his contribution is ultimately helpful to the discussion. If the libertarian is permitted to define what they mean, it is helpful to allow them to do so in a way that is to their liking. If their definition reads, "could have done otherwise," where "could" is used here in a contra-causal sense, it would seem unhelpful to say, "but there are other ways we could understand the word "can," unless the word "can" is more important than the meaning they intend to communicate by it—and that is not the case.

I am observing the development of these ideas through them, seen from our vantage point in history. But it must also be said that while the modern definitions were not in their minds, the current ideas are greatly indebted to them. Also, I should say clearly that I do not intend to fully support either Libertarian Free-Will or Compatibilistic Free-Will as defined above, but hope to give evidence for various Eras of Freedom in God's design for his human willful-creatures, a conforming-freedom that liberates his creatures to fully (and freely) delight in him forever.

AN HISTORICAL SURVEY OF THE DEVELOPMENT OF THE CONCEPT OF FREE-WILL

A Drift toward a Kind of Libertarian Free-Will: The Pre-Augustinian Discussion

Clement of Alexandria (c.150–c.220) wrestled against the Gnostics, much as Augustine would later grapple with the Manicheans. In much he anticipated Augustine, including his affection for Plato, his understanding of evil as a privation, and his belief that evil did not originate with God but in the free-will of humanity. However, and more importantly for this discussion, in this he also anticipated Pelagius: he saw man's free actions as reaching fully to the bar of merit.[21] Rejecting the secret rites of the Gnostics, he insisted that the freedom of the will in obedience allowed people to aspire to perfection and achieve an understanding of all things.[22] His influence was felt most fully through his successor, Origen,[23] who assumed the role of instructor at the school in Alexandria. While his position on free-will is delineated in merely a single chapter of *De Principiis*, this issue proved to be at the heart of Origen's theology. Not only is this chapter the longest in the work, but for Origen, the fundamental teaching of the Bible in regard to providence is free-will. He writes, "Indeed, there are in the scriptures ten thousand passages which with the utmost clearness prove the existence of free will."[24]

---

21. Floyd, *Clement of Alexandria's Treatment of the Problem of Evil*, 97.

22. This is the concept of "deification," which is the conforming of people to the "image and likeness" of God by God-assisted human effort—we are saved by our own action (Floyd, *Clement of Alexandria*, 87–89). If his "Pelagianism" is not "forgivable" it is at least helpful to understand that in his time, his bent toward the possibility of human-gained perfection is influenced by his flight from (or battle against) dualism.

23. Trigg, *Origen: The Bible and Philosophy in the Third-Century Church*, 54. Origen, growing up in a non-Christian family, had only one opportunity for Christian instruction and that was his schoolteacher, Clement. While there is no direct evidence that they met, the school and Origen's succession as teacher, links them. It might also be cited that in their writing they shared a rare book title, *Stromateis*. More overtly, their theologies are intertwined: "it is almost impossible to overestimate Origen's debt to Clement and the outlook he represents" (65). He was almost lost to the Church at the age of seventeen during the persecution that killed his father, Leonides. In a well-known story, Origen intended to follow his father to prison and martyrdom. Full of physical strength and unbridled passion, his mother was unable to stop him physically, so she hid his clothes. Modesty checked what wisdom could not.

24. Origen, *On First Principles*, 3.1.6. This text has English translations of both the Greek and Latin

PART I: The Tension of Theodicy

Origen believed that only a few texts presented a problem to this position. Speaking of those who used these passages to preach a future determined by God, Origen wrote, "Now these passages are used by some of the heretics, who practically destroy free will."[25] His aversion to anything that infringed on human free-will indicates his concern for God's justice: "But since they admit that they look upon God as being just, and our view is that he is good as well as just, let us consider how one who is good and just could harden Pharaoh's heart."[26] What is Origen's solution to this seeming injustice of God? He writes, "The hardening follows as a result of the substance of evil present in the particular evil person, so that God is said to harden him who is already hardened."[27] God only confirms what is already true within the person and is already shown in their actions or "motions" of the will. It could be fairly said here that God is not the primary cause, but the secondary or indirect cause of hardening. In this he is arguing for Libertarian Free-Will, though not in its fully developed form.[28] He is arguing that man must have significant freedom that goes beyond Volitional Free-Will.

Origen confirms this in the example of Romans 9 and 2 Timothy 2 regarding "vessels of honor."

> For the Creator makes "vessels of honour and vessels of dishonour" not from the beginning by his foreknowledge, since he does not condemn or justify beforehand by that, but he makes those who purge themselves "vessels of honour" and those who allow themselves to remain unpurged, "vessels of dishonour"; so that it comes from causes older than the fashioning of vessels unto honour and unto dishonour that one was made "unto honour" and another "unto dishonour."[29]

---

texts. Unless otherwise noted, all citations are from the shorter Greek text. It should also be noted that paragraphs in this text can be different on occasion from *The Ante-Nicene Fathers* text.

25. Origen, *On First Principles*, 3.1.8.

26. Origen, *On First Principles*, 3.1.10.

27. Origen, *On First Principles*, 3.1.10.

28. Origen did accept a strong view of God's providence. He wrote, "of those events which happen to men, none occur by accident or chance, but in accordance with a plan so carefully considered, and so stupendous, that it does not overlook even the number of the hairs of the heads, not merely of the saints, but perhaps of all human beings, and the plan of which providential government extends even to caring for the sale of two sparrows for a denarius." (On First Principles, 2.11.5). This Biblical confidence in Divine providence exists side-by-side with his commitment to a kind of libertarian free will.

29. Origen, *On First Principles*, 3.1.21. Contra Origen, it should be noted that in regard to "vessel for honor" in 2 Timothy, Paul's argument concerns the responsibility of humanity but in Romans, the perspective of God's sovereignty. 2 Timothy 2:20–21 says, "Now in a large house there are not only gold and silver vessels, but also vessels of wood and of earthenware, and some to honor and some to dishonor. Therefore, if anyone cleanses himself from these things, he will be a *vessel for honor*, sanctified, useful to the Master, prepared for every good work." But in Romans 9:20–23, Paul writes, "On the contrary, who are you, O man, who answers back to God? The thing molded will not say to the molder, 'Why did you make me like this,' will it? Or, does not the potter have a right over the clay, to make from the same lump one *vessel for honorable use* and another for common use? What if God, although willing to demonstrate His wrath and to make His power known, endured with much patience vessels of wrath prepared for destruction? And He did so to make known the riches of His glory upon vessels

So, for Origen, God only confirms what is already true in the person. In fact, in a passage appearing only in the Rufinus's fourth century Latin texts of *De Principiis* (and not in the extant Greek) Origen goes even further:

> This leads us to the opinion that since, as we have frequently said, the soul is immortal and eternal, it is possible that in the many and endless periods throughout diverse and immeasurable ages it may either descend from the highest good to the lowest evil or be restored from the lowest evil to the highest good.[30]

If this passage is authentic, Origen claims here that in the immortal life of the soul, the will goes through periods of obedience and disobedience, gaining at one time perfection and at another corruption. It would seem by this that he is a universalist.[31] Jerome (c.347–420) and many others attacked him on this issue.[32] His position is not unlike that of Clement, his mentor, and Pelagius, who followed him and was directly opposed to Augustine and Jerome. For Origen, free-will is free not only as the direct cause of the "motion" of the will, but as the primary cause as well.[33] God's providence simply confirms who we already are shown to be by the action of our will.

How then does Origen relate God's foreknowledge to this proto-Libertarian Free-Will position? First, it should be observed that he does accept the reality of God's foreknowledge (as seen in the above quote) and many others like it.[34] The issue, then, is the connection between foreknowledge and free-will. As is true of most writers of his time, on both sides of what we call Libertarian Free-Will and Compatibilistic Free-Will, no link is acknowledged. He writes:

> It is, then, neither in our power to make progress apart from the knowledge of God, nor does the knowledge of God compel us to do so unless we ourselves contribute something toward the good result; nor does our power apart from the knowledge of God and the full use of the power that deservedly belongs to us cause a man to be created for honour or for dishonour; nor does the power

of mercy, which He prepared beforehand for glory."

30. Origen, *On First Principles*, G. W. Butterworth, 3.1.23. Latin text.

31. Not only in regard to humans, but for all created and rational beings (3.6.3), including demons and in his cosmology, the stars and planets as well! (Scott, *Origen and the Life of the Stars*, 163–4).

32. Origen, *On First Principles*, G. W. Butterworth, note 5, 208.

33. Interestingly, it would seem that Origen feels no tension between God's foreknowledge and causality and freedom. He writes, "In the same way God, who knows the secrets of the heart and foreknows the future" (*On First Principals*, 3.1.13). Yet, those who follow him will feel this issue acutely.

34. Origen does not debate foreknowledge, but simply acknowledges it. In *Against Celsus*, he does defend it along with its corollary; prophesy. For example, he writes, "For if He had foreknowledge of the traitor, He knew the wickedness in which the treason originated, and this wickedness was by no means taken away by the foreknowledge" (*Against Celsus*, in *The Ante-Nicene Fathers*, volume 4, 439). Note that Origen's conditional statement, in context, is fully supported.

> of God by itself fashion a man for honour or for dishonour, but God finds a ground of difference in our will, as it inclines to the better or to the worse.[35]

God's power of [fore] knowing does not link directly to our power of willing. It is the difference that is found in the will of a person that determines the action of the will, not God's knowledge. Therefore, for Origen, God knows and the will is libertarianly free.

Pelagius (354–418)[36] took an even stronger view of libertarian freedom.[37] It was perhaps his vocation as a pastor that led Robert Evans to apologize that Pelagius was more of a moralist than a theologian.[38] But who can avoid being a theologian or be excepted from responsibility for influencing others theologically? What honest pastor would want to be defended as being a pastor rather than a theologian!? When he was confronted by Augustine's *Confessions*, "Grant what you command, and command what you will,"[39] Pelagius's hand was set to theology's plow.[40] He taught that a man becomes evil by wrong exercise of the will and conversely that he can make himself good by right exercise of the will.[41] Pelagius also rejected original sin.[42] Perhaps most important, Pelagius taught that divine grace for salvation consists in (1) freedom of the will,[43] (2) the revelation of God in his Word and (3) the example of Christ.[44] In this teaching, the moralist had come up against firm theological boundaries. For Pelagius, Christ is only our example, our guide to the way of redemption, and this help

---

35. Origen, *On First Principles*, 3.1.24.

36. A layman, a monk, and a probable native of the British Isles, Pelagius was a contemporary of Patrick of Ireland. Sometime early in his career, he made his way to Rome. There, acting pastorally as a layman and as a monk, he called the people of Rome to obedience to the One God.

37. It should be noted that the extant works of Pelagius are quite limited, quoted only in the works of his adversaries, Jerome and Augustine. Jerome is most extensive (*Expositions on Paul's Epistles*, the *Epistle to Demetrias*, and *Confession of Faith*). Only fragments of others are cited by Augustine ("A Select Bibliography of the Pelagian Controversy").

38. Evans, *Pelagius*, 42, 91. The paucity of the preserved writing of Pelagius, the recent publication in English of what does exist, and a general animosity toward Augustine in some, has led to a recent "reform" of Pelagius, asking that he be excused his theological ideas as incidental and perhaps accidental affects of his greater concern for Christian morals. This is interesting, but outside of the scope of our concern about the development of the idea of freedom.

39. Augustine, *Confessions*, 10.29 (40).

40. Rees (*Pelagius: A Reluctant Heretic*, 1), quoting Augustine's own understanding of the events of 405 in *On the Gift of Perseverance* (20.53).

41. Evans, *Augustine on Evil*, 121.

42. Evans, *Pelagius*, 97. Pelagius did so, in part, because he believed that "original sin" smacked of Manicheanism in that it made sin a necessary component of human existence. It is instructive to see that Augustine's theology was not shaped by wholesale rejection of all the Manicheans taught, but by his understanding of God's Word. It is not fair to understand him as under Manichean influence or defined by rejection of all things Manichean.

43. Wiggers, *An Historical Presentation of Augustinism and Pelagianism from the Original Sources*, 193.

44. Evans, *Pelagius*, 111.

is sufficient in itself.[45] Considering the example of Christ is a sufficient "help" is a clear departure from orthodox soteriology and biblical teaching.[46] By phrases such as "natural goodness" and "man's capacity for either direction," Pelagius taught that humanity is able to be without sin.[47] This is possible for him to conceive, in part, because of his rejection of the concept of original sin. For Pelagius, Adam and post-Adamic humanity, share a common freedom (opportunity) to conquer evil, and to be good,[48] by an exercise of free-will along with the grace of God.[49] Here such Pelagian grace is not the forensic declaration of justification in Christ's blood. With a ring of eisegesis he explains this in his commentary on Romans where he ascribes the author's use of the name "Paul" (over Saul) to his growth in righteousness.[50] It is, as stated earlier, "help." This "help" (grace) is the teaching of the Word, the example of Christ, and a will kept free by God.

Pelagius might have been ignored by history, as B.R. Rees notes, had not Alaric the Visigoth's approach to Rome sent Pelagius fleeing, first to the shores of Africa and then on to Palestine in 409.[51] In Africa and Palestine, he met his two famous adversaries, Augustine and Jerome, with whom he would be thereafter locked in combat. Augustine responded in various ways, but especially with his book *On Nature and Grace* in 415. By 431, Pelagius's teaching was condemned by the Council of Ephesus.[52]

---

45. Robert F. Evans writes, "We might capture Pelagius's whole teaching on the grace of Christ as 'help' in a singular formula: Christ by the example of his life, by his commandments, and by his teaching concerning man and God has brought the final revelation of that 'way' for man which leads to life and in doing so has brought 'help' sufficient to overcome the power of sinful habit" (*Pelagius*, 111).

46. While perhaps an extension of the thinking of Clement and Origen, it is a departure from the biblical Christ who is lifted up as a propitiation for our sins (Romans 3:21–26) and resurrected as our Lord (Romans 1:1–5) and we are called not simply to follow him, but to submit to his Lordship (Romans 10:9–10; 12:1–2). The debate of course is whether Augustine was returning to orthodoxy in his understanding or creating a new orthodoxy. It is argued here that Pelagius was continuing on the divergent stream. Yet, while some may disagree with my understanding, concord is not essential in order to discern Pelagius's perspective on freedom, my primary and more achievable goal.

47. Evans, *Pelagius*, 93–95.

48. Wiggers, *An Historical Presentation of Augustinism and Pelagianism from the Original Sources*, 105. He says, "As the Pelagians admitted no original sin, but maintained that every man, as to his moral condition, is born in just the same state in which Adam was created . . . man, in his present state, has the power to do good."

49. Pelagius, *Pelagius's Commentary on St. Paul's Epistle to the Romans*, 83. Here he writes, commenting on Romans 3:28, "Some misuse this verse to do away with works of righteousness, asserting that faith by itself can suffice, although the same apostles says . . . . Clearly, [RAS: Paul means] the works of circumcision or the Sabbath and others of this sort, and not without the works of righteousness." For Pelagius, grace is first, but salvation comes by grace and works.

50. Pelagius, *Pelagius's Commentary on St. Paul's Epistle to the Romans*, 59. The passing initial reference in Acts 13:9, "Saul, who was also called, Paul" at the start of his first missionary journey leaves all to the imagination in regard to its use in regard to Paul's sanctification.

51. Rees, *Pelagius*, 1.

52. R. K. McGregor Wright, *No Place for Sovereignty*, 20. Pelagius was condemned by the church in Carthage (418), Ephesus (431), and Orange (529), but lived on in popular Catholicism and does so to this day. Some have argued for a more generous and perhaps more circumspect evaluation of Pelagius.

PART I: The Tension of Theodicy

In the fifth century, the Clement-Origen-Pelagius perspective represented a significant stream of thinking: the capacity of human willful-creatures to choose good is, if not robust, sufficient with limited help. John Calvin references Pelagian arguments as saying, necessary sin is not sin; voluntary sin is avoidable. In response he insists, "I therefore deny that sin ought less to be reckoned as sin merely because it is necessary. I deny conversely the inference they draw, that because sin is voluntary it is avoidable."[53] Without working out the specifics of Calvin's denial, it is clear that, for Pelagius, grace has something of a different nature and application than the usual understanding of Paul when he writes, "For what the Law could not do, weak as it was through the flesh, God did: sending his own Son in the likeness of sinful flesh and as an offering for sin, he condemned sin in the flesh" (Romans 8:3). Pelagius's sinful nature is quite able to turn to the good.[54] Such freedom would seem to be a libertarian freedom, liberated even from the necessity of atonement.[55]

Still, Pelagius demonstrates something true about the problem of evil by what is missing in his argument. Were I to accept his understanding of the self-redemptive operation of the will (which I do not), this would still beg the question, "Why does everyone fail this great experiment?" Pelagius would certainly reply that our will does not fully take advantage of God's grace and help. But why not? What is defective in our free-will? Without debating the mechanics of failure, the Bible and experience demand agreement that we "all have sinned" (in fact). We all begin at a deficit that shows itself in this defective action. This is the key. Free-will, as given to Adam and to Eve, was defective, not because it was not good (it was), but because it did not have the Source of what is good to sustain it step-by-step in God-like goodness that flows from God's nature alone. Therefore, freedom was bound in sin. We will return to this later.

Robert Evans wrote, "Pelagius is one of the most maligned figures in the history of Christianity. It has been the common sport of the theologian . . . to set him up as the symbolic bad man . . . which often tells us more about the theological perspective of the accuser than about Pelagius" (*Pelagius*, 66). Rees would agree that Pelagius saw himself in a better light: "Pelagius never saw himself as a heretic . . . he was a moral reformer who, as he became familiar with Christian society in Rome at the turn of the fourth century, became also more and more critical of its moral standards" (*Pelagius*, 3). He suggests that both Jerome and Augustine over-reacted. This is beyond the scope of this investigation and it will be necessary only to state his position in regard to freedom.

53. Calvin, *ICR*, 2.5.1.

54. Robert F. Evans, *Pelagius: Inquiries and Reappraisals,* 100. "The power which sin holds over men is the power of habit."

55. Or perhaps, he is anticipating the Socinian (Faustus Socinius, 1539–1604) theory of the atonement which rejects the necessary atonement for sin or that, in fact, Christ was our substitution. The scope of the project does not allow this to be pursued. Yet, while in 418 the church did overturn his views in the Council of Carthage, his ideas still persisted in the church. Called by Augustine, "the relics of Pelagius," and later named as "semi-Pelagianism" by critics of Molina, his ideas persist today.

Early "Compatibilistic" Free-will: Augustine

In the fourth century into which Augustine (354–430) was born, the drift of the theological boat was toward the shore of libertarian freedom,[56] as was shown above. It was tending even to a liberty from the need of God's redemptive grace. But it was the problem of evil which drew the theological (but not yet Christian) Augustine toward the dualism of the Manicheans.[57] For almost a decade, he accepted their worldview: a substantive and primordial Good and Evil coexist and are locked in mortal combat, and humanity stands on the level plain between them in freedom. He was taught that humanity faces this battle by overcoming Evil with knowledge.[58] Once freed from this Manichean system, Augustine along with Pelagius, combated this dualism, but it was Augustine who also opposed the prevailing current of creaturely libertarian freedom.

Augustine's journey to faith in Christ is recounted in his book, *de Libero Arbitrio*.[59] Here Augustine dialogues with Euodius much as he does with Plato (427–347 BCE).[60] His dialogue opens with Euodius asking the most critical of questions, "Tell

---

56. This pattern is observed by many, including Swinburne who writes, "all Christian theologians of the first four centuries believed in human free will in the libertarian sense, as did all subsequent Eastern Orthodox theologians, and most Western Catholic theologians from Duns Scotus (in the fourteenth century) onwards" (Swinburne, *Providence and the Problem of Evil*, 35). It could well be argued that to inflict current terminology such as "libertarian" or "compatibilist" retroactively is quite unfair to writers who did not expressly use such terms. So it is. If however our desire is to trace the roots of the development of the concepts, it is correct to perceive such ideas in the writings. That is all that is intended by their use here.

57. Augustine, *Free Choice of the Will*, 1.2.

58. Geivett, *Evil and the Evidence for God*, 11.

59. This book was written in 388–395, only two years after his conversion to Christ from the Manicheans. This journey to faith from the Manicheans was, he believed, due to his love for the truth. He understood, perhaps from Ambrose, that belief is the root of epistemology (*Confessions*, 6.5(7)). Also in *Free Choice of the Will* he cites the singular proof text Isaiah 7:9, "Unless you believe, you shall not understand" (1.2). It also appears in *The Trinity*, 7.12 (232); 15.2 (396)). While his translation was based on the LXX, that translation itself may not stand. This verse reads more accurately (both in context and by translation), "If you will not believe, certainly you will not stand." The translation is based on a word play between a verb common to both clauses, but appearing in different forms (אמן). In the conditional clause it appears in the Hiphal meaning "believe" and in the resultant clause it appears in the Niphal meaning "establish" or "stand," not "understand." The context is also damaging to Augustine's use because Isaiah is expressing the historical warning that God's people will be wiped out by the invading army, if they do not believe. Still, however mistaken Augustine may have been in regard to this text, his epistemology is still well supported biblically. For example, 2 Thessalonians 2:10–13 includes the phrase, "they did not receive the love of the truth so as to be saved" which clearly links belief in the truth and salvation in a way that supports an epistemology grounded in belief. So also, Psalm 111:10 would serve his intention well. It states, "The fear of the Lord is the beginning of wisdom; a good understanding have all those who do His commandments." A strong case could be made. So John Polkinghorne would strongly support Augustine. He writes, "there is no neutral Archimedean point of detachment from which judgment can be made; insight is gained only through participation" by which he means active belief, the judgment of which is proved by the fruitfulness of the theory which is believed (*Belief in God in an Age of Science*, 115).

60. Augustine is sometimes criticized for being a Platophile. Indeed, here and throughout this work, Augustine speaks highly of Plato, "with a glory which far excelled that of the others" (*The City*

PART I: The Tension of Theodicy

me, please, whether God is not the cause of evil." Augustine responds, "But if you know or believe that God is good, . . . God does not do evil."[61] Everything else in his book develops from the space between Euodius's question and Augustine's answer. In the conclusion to Book 1, Augustine exonerates God by making the free-will of humanity the source of evil. This conclusion is stated repeatedly throughout the books to follow.[62] In Augustine's understanding, there is nothing above the will. For example he writes, "the mind is made servant of desire by no thing but its own will."[63] By many such statements, he is arguing that the will is the unique "organ" of decision, above which there is nothing superior, inside or outside of human willful-creatures and that it acts in concert with the whole being, including memory and reason.[64] As a result, God in no way shares in the responsibility for human sin. Augustine insists that the will is good, permitting people to do right. The fact that it also permits people to do wrong is mitigated by the reality that God uses the wrong we do for his own good purposes. This does not make evil in any way desirable, yet the will is established as a "medium good."[65] This, for Augustine, exonerates God in making the will.

What then of God's foreknowledge? God's foreknowledge (which Augustine assumed) does not undermine the freedom of the will of humanity. He assures us in strong terms that they are not related.[66] Quite simply, he writes, "These two points are not contrary and logically repugnant—the fact that God knows all things future, and

---

of God, 8.4). So also in many other places, including, "It is evident that none come nearer to us than the Platonists" (*City of God* 8.5). Still he never accepts Plato uncritically. He argues against Plato often (including: 12.24–26 (creation of man), 22.11 (resurrection), 22.26 (the value of the body). In *City of God* (8.10) he expresses his wariness about all pagan philosophers: "He is on his guard, however, with respect to those who philosophize according to the elements of the world." It would seem that he is using Plato not to build a foundation for Christianity, but to contextualize the truth of the Gospel where he finds it in the best thinking of those respected by the Latins. In fact, he says this: "But we have thought it better to plead our case with Platonists, because their writings are better known. For the Greeks, whose tongue holds the highest place among the languages of the Gentiles, are loud in the praise of these writings." The comments of Chesterton in regard to Aquinas's use of Aristotle may also be appropriate here: "St. Thomas did not reconcile Christ to Aristotle; he reconciled Aristotle to Christ" (G. K. Chesterton, *Thomas Aquinas*, 28).

61. Augustine, *Free Choice of the Will*, 1.1.

62. In his conclusion to Book 1 he writes, putting his point in the mouth of Euodius: "We do wrong from free choice of the will. But I ask whether a free choice itself . . . should have been given to us by him who made us" (ibid., 1.16). He makes the same point in 3.1; 316; 3.17; 3;22, and others.

63. Ibid., 3.1.

64. Augustine's will is not a form of voluntarism as will be noted in the discussion of Duns Scotus. There is nothing above the will, but neither is it in isolation. We should also not, by his use of the word, "organ," infer that he means anything other than the willing of the whole person—as if there is a center of willing distinct from the whole person.

65. Augustine uses this term, "medium good," in ibid., 2.18–19.

66. In conversation with Euodius: "I am unsettled in a manner beyond expression—how God foresees all facts and we sin by no kind of necessity. . . . How then is the will free where there appears to be such inevitable necessity?" Augustine: "A great number of men are tormented by this question for no other reason than this, . . . they are more ready to excuse than to confess their own sins" (ibid., 3.2).

The Historical Development of the Concept of Free-Will

the fact that we sin, not by necessity, but by will."[67] His fundamental argument here is by assertion: "they do not contradict" and "if you think they do, you are raising a smoke screen for your own sin."[68] Even those who agree with him might accept that Augustine has left to others some measure of work that could be done in this regard.

In championing free-will, Augustine is not, even at this early development of his thinking, speaking of what would become known as Libertarian Free-Will. Instead, his position falls within the general scope of what we would term compatibilism.[69] He writes, "You said that you have the will [RAS: to be happy now], but as yet not the power . . . [RAS: but] our will, therefore, would not be will if it were not in our power."[70] That is, we always desire to do what we actually do and we do not act out of keeping with our will and power as if an external agent is dragging our hand into action.[71] He puts a finer point on this later in Book 3 saying (note that he has now dropped the artifice of dialogue having done so about half-way through his book):

> Is it then perhaps force that is the cause, and that one is forced against his will? . . . If the will can not resist it, the yielding to force will not be sin: . . . . Perhaps then it deceives one unaware? Let him be on guard then and not to be deceived. Perhaps fallacies are so overwhelming that they can not be avoided at all? If so then there is no sin. . . . And yet certain works done through ignorance are blamed.[72]

In other words, if the will can be forced or even deceived fully, there is no sin. But humanity is sinful and justly punished by God. This is rudimentary compatibilism; though Augustine does not address the reason deception mitigates a sinful act in light of the emphasis of sin offerings for unintentional sins in the Mosaic Law and in light of the fact that Eve was deceived and still fully guilty.

This was considered Augustine's early understanding of freedom of the will. How did it change over time? John Rist, and perhaps a majority of scholars believe

---

67. Ibid., 3.3.

68. This is not to say that Augustine does not develop his bare assertion. For example, he explains that since God, who clearly foreknows his own work, does not do his own work by necessity, he can also know our future choices without imposing necessity upon us (ibid., 3.3). Still, in the end, I do not understand his argument to add significantly to his assertion, although I do agree.

69. Hasker, *God, Time, and Knowledge*, 4. An extreme exponent of Libertarian Free-Will, he recognizes in Augustine, a "soft-determinist" or compatibilist, citing as example Augustine's insistence of "a certain order of causes" (*City of God*, 5.9) when he writes: "But it does not follow that, though there is for God a certain order of all causes, there must therefore be nothing depending on the free exercise of our own wills, for our wills themselves are included in that order of causes which is certain to God, and is embraced by his foreknowledge, for human wills are also causes of human actions." This quote is also significant in understanding the definition of Libertarian Free-Will from a libertarian's perspective.

70. Augustine, *Free Choice of the Will*, 3.3.

71. To be fully compatible with compatibilism, it would be necessary to make some claim about not being able to will and do other than we actually did will and do. This he does not do.

72. Ibid., 3.18.

that his view changed over time, affected largely by the sacking of Rome in 411 and by the spread of Pelagianism.[73] That his view matured is certainly true, but such assertions may paint with strokes too broad. Here in his early work Augustine indicates that only Adam and Eve were free to choose between good and evil.[74] Because of the work of evil, we suffer from *acrasia*, a term of Aristotle's, meaning a "weakness of the will."[75] Augustine writes in On the Spirit and the Letter, "humanity has only freedom for sin" and in The *Nature of Grace*, "The will of man is free to sin only, and not to righteousness, unless freed and aided by God."[76] This is not *libertas* in any common use of the word.

Indeed as many note, his later writing did reflect a greater dependence on grace, a comfort with God's predestination, and a clearer exposition of the effect of evil upon God's good creation, especially in his writings against Pelagius. Consider a late statement even in *Free Choice of the Will*: "Where we speak of the will free to do right, we speak of the will in which man first was made."[77] This is an important clarification. If it was only Adam's free-will that could truly do right, our will, corrupted by Adam's sin, is not free in the sense that it can freely do what is good. Showing that this is truly what he intended us to understand, he debates the obvious charge that this would be unfair to us. He charges us to cease our murmurings and fully asserts that we are still responsible. Though we can do no right, because we do not use our will to respond to him who calls us to serve, we are rightly judged. Even if we are not charged for fault we cannot avoid, still there remains the fault of not heeding him who would

---

73. John M. Rist sees this change in Augustine most clearly expressed in *City of God* written after the events of 411 (*Augustine*, 130). The significance of this date is well known. But perhaps the shock of Rome's sacking by the barbarians in 411 may be felt by us after 9/11 in New York: a shocking vulnerability after years of moral decay.

74. Did Augustine's views really change over time as some suggest? Augustine writes, "Where we speak of the will free to do right, we speak of the will in which man first was made" (*Free Choice of the Will*, 3.18). Here he has seemingly limited all his comments which sound like Libertarian Free-Will to the first Era of Freedom under Adam prior to initial corruption of creation. So, it may not be simply the maturing of his views, but his addressing the working of free-will in different Eras of Freedom that has caused some to understand his perspective to change. It is also possible that his interaction with "heretics," at different times in his life, affected the slant of his presentation and how we understand his views. That is, when he reacts against the fatalism of Manicheans, he sounds, *to us*, much more like libertarian, because he argues against fatalism. But, later, when he addresses Pelagius, he sounds, *to us* more like a compatibilist, for it is an extreme libertarian with whom he contests. Clues such as the ones cited above may be throughout his text showing us that while he has certainly matured and even changed, he is still Compatibilistic Free-Will in his approach in all of his writings. It is possible that the consistent understanding of Augustine in regard to free-will is Compatibilistic Free-Will, but interaction with different heresies make it difficult to see the consistency. The focus of this project will not allow us to investigate this fully, but it begs to be studied.

75. Rist, *Augustine*, 130. Acrasia (preferred spelling is, "akrasia") is defined as "to fail to act although one judges that one has sufficient reason to act" and first used by Aristotle in *Nicomachean Ethics, Book 7* (Mautner, *Dictionary of Philosophy*, "akrasia").

76. Cited by Wiggers, *Historical Presentation of Augustinism and Pelagianism from the Original Sources*, 114.

77. Augustine, *Free Choice of the Will*, 3.18.

heal us.[78] So, even if more fully developed later, the fundamental understanding that the fallen will is not free to conform to goodness was well established in his earliest writings. This pushes his free-will boat to the shores of the compatibilists and away from the libertarian beaches. Against a background of those who understood God's human willful-creatures as capable by their will of self-healing from the effects of evil, Augustine stood against that drift.

There is one last issue concerning freedom for Augustine. That is, the final freedom of his people will be greater even than that of the initial freedom of Adam. Rist says that for Augustine, true *libertas* is "the God given freedom to choose the good alone."[79] Clearly this state was not available to Adam. This claim is not as obvious as it might seem. In fact, it may represent just the gap that appears between Antony Flew and John Mackie in their wrestling with Alvin Plantinga in our day. This true freedom, it will be argued, which God has always possessed and which we will possess in the last Era of Freedom, is conforming-freedom—freedom that freely conforms to the good nature of God.

Hardening of the Libertarian and Compatibilist positions in Regard to Free-will: Scholastics to Present Day

Born and raised in France, Anselm of Canterbury (1033–1109) entered the Abby of Bec in 1060. In keeping with his gifts, though not his desire (for he wanted to focus solely on scholarship and pastoral care), he rose to greater and greater authority, until he became Archbishop of Canterbury in 1093.[80] Known for his work, *Cur Deus Homo*, his central concern was the issue of freedom. It was his fundamental interest in *De Libertate Arbitrii* and in *De Concordia Praescientiae et Praedestinationis et Gratiae Dei cum Libero Arbitrio* and others.[81] He was said by some to be the first one to take a fresh look at issues of freedom since Augustine[82] though Boethius might object.

Anselm's use of words and especially the words "freedom" and "will" are highly nuanced. Anselm dissected the will into three parts: (1) instrument of willing (faculty); (2) affection of the instrument (disposition); and (3) use of the instrument (act).[83] For Anselm it is the affections that move the faculty of the will, for it is unable to move of its own.[84] The will must be free in humanity in order to preserve the "ability to defect from the goals or purposes imposed on them by God."[85] In that respect, the will has

---

78. Augustine, *Free Choice of the Will*, 3.19.
79. Rist, *Augustine: Ancient Thought Baptized*, 278.
80. Hicks, *Journey So Far*, 168.
81. Kane, *Anselm's Doctrine of Freedom and the Will*, 13.
82. Evans, *Augustine on Evil*, 175.
83. Kane, *Anselm's Doctrine of Freedom and the Will*, 15.
84. Ibid., 72.
85. Ibid., 156.

a dual purpose: to move man toward God or to defect from God. Anselm argues that freedom has only one purpose, and in that sense is more limited than the will. If the will exists that we might be able to conform to God or to defect from him (it has a dual purpose), freedom is not simply the power of choice, it is only the positive "ability to fulfill one's ultimate end, i.e., to do what is right or just."[86]

Having defected, the will has no means of recovery within itself. Anselm writes, "But when free will abandons rectitude because of the difficulty of preserving it, it is afterward the slave of sin because of the impossibility of recovering it by itself."[87] Still this slavery does not remove its ability to function freely. Anselm writes, "it is without contradiction both slave and free."[88] By this, he reasserts what he explained earlier in his chapter 6 that the will is powerful even in the face of temptation and even when it fails against temptation, because it is exercised. The will was not forced against its will. He writes, "but he cannot will unwillingly, because one cannot will to will against his will. Every willing person wills his own willing."[89] This is a statement endorsing volitionalism. Volitional freedom is freedom preserved in man regardless of the corruption of his will.

Therefore, Anselm is saying, (1) the power of the will is more general than the power of freedom; (2) and the power of freedom is to conform to God. Kane summarizes by observing that for Anselm, the will is the general power of willing but freedom is one specific kind of power of willing, namely the power of willing justice.[90] It is important to note what Anselm is not saying. He is not Pelagian. The fallen will is not salvageable by moral teaching, but still a person with a fallen will does not sin by compulsion.

Returning to his idea of freedom, how does this freedom operate? Remember that for Anselm freedom is the ability to do what is upright.[91] It has a distinct vector toward the One who is Good. This raises many questions, including: what kind of freedom does God have; what kind of freedom did Adam have; and what kind of

---

86. Ibid., 156.

87. Anselm, "On Free Will," in *Anselm of Canterbury*, chapter 10 (188).

88. Anselm, "On Free Will," Davies and Evans, chapter 11 (189).

89. Anselm, "On Free Will," Davies and Evans, chapter 5 (181).

90. Kane, *Anselm's Doctrine of Freedom and the Will*, 158.

91. It is worth noting that this freedom to do what is upright (previously cited) is not undermined by Anselm's understanding of divine foreknowledge. He writes, "T: I will answer briefly now: Divine foreknowledge is not properly called foreknowledge. He who has always present all things does not have foreknowledge of the future, but knowledge of the present. Therefore since foreknowledge of a future event is going to be considered differently than knowledge of a present thing, what is called divine foreknowledge and what is properly foreknowledge do not have the same consequences" (Anselm, "De Casu Diaboli," in *Anselm of Canterbury*, chapter 21 [224]). Such foreknowledge does not, in itself, have an impact on the nature of the free-will of God's willful creatures now, or to do what is right in the Era of Conforming-Freedom; God's foreknowledge is not in the temporal-causal stream. That does not specify the causal role of God, only Anselm's understanding that his foreknowledge is not causal.

freedom will Christians have in the final state? Even, does God have less freedom than Adam since Adam was free to do all good and all evil and God is only "free" to do what is good? Conversely, will we be free in the final state, if we are unable to sin? Anselm writes:

> Teacher. I do not think free will is the power to sin or not to sin. Indeed if this were its definition, neither God nor the angels, who are unable to sin, would have free will, which it is impious to say.... Do you not see that one who is as he ought to be, and as it is expedient for him to be, such that he is unable to lose this state is freer than the one who is such that he can lose it and be led into what is indecent and inexpedient for him?[92]

This is an important point and it resonates with what is claimed about ultimate conforming-freedom in this project. True freedom for God (at all "times") and for his people in the final state is truly free in the sense that the greatest freedom is the inability to sin. The fidelity to God's goodness does not arise from external compulsion, nor from a sustaining force, but from the lack of the option for evil. Evil will have been eradicated for God's people. Anselm is correct to say that true freedom is to be as free as God is in regard to sin. The will is free when it is no longer dual (able to do good or evil), but singular (able to do only good). The will is free when it experiences, conforming-freedom. This clearly does not explain how this is accomplished, but I will consider this later.

Thomas Aquinas (1225–1274), delighted in the reliability of the senses, pursuing the clear and simple truths that reason could smelt out of the unrefined details,[93] and presented his thoughts for the "man on the street."[94] To some ways of thinking, he was an advocate for "the Philosopher," for Aristotle (384–322 BCE), over, and at times against, Augustine and his affinity for Plato. Indeed, he was born into a day that saw

---

92. Anselm, "On Free Will," Davies and Evans, chapter 1 (176).

93. Aquinas will pursue this in the context of faith, not simply reason. Rudi te Velde writes, " 'Creation' is, moreover, a word of faith, part of the Christians confession of faith. This is something Thomas is always aware of.... Thomas, however, does not stop here. That creation is something invisible, disclosed to us in the light of faith, does not mean that its truth resists rational expression and philosophical understanding" (Rudi te Velde, *Aquinas on God*, 124). That is, Aquinas is not a rationalist, but one who employs reason to investigate the truths which rest upon a foundation of faith. Moreover, he is agreeing with Aristotle on the need to distinguish between the intellect and the senses (135), allowing philosophers to proceed from the particular (the reliable sensory data) to the universal by way of reason (137).

94. This is not to say that Aquinas was a rationalist or a scholastic. He warns against the "scholasticism" of his day when he writes in the introduction to the *Summa Theologica of St. Thomas Aquinas*, "Because the doctor of Catholic truth ought not only to teach the proficient, but also to instruct beginners... [RAS: avoiding] useless questions, articles, and arguments,... we shall try, by God's help, to set forth whatever is included in this sacred doctrine as briefly and clearly as the matter itself may allow" (*ST*, preface). Aquinas's success in this may be reflected by Chesterton when he states, "Thomistic philosophy is nearer than most philosophy to the mind of the man on the street" (Chesterton, *Thomas Aquinas*, 146). If he accomplishes his assigned task and if Chesterton is correct, while he may advocate reason, the result is neither scholastic nor rationalistic.

PART I: The Tension of Theodicy

a revival of Aristotle through the work of Islamic philosophers. He could hardly have ignored this, as the revival was often perceived as a threat to Christianity. However, Aquinas did not perceive Aristotle as a threat, or as an authority, but as a pedagogic assistant.[95] That is not to say that Aquinas was a rationalist or Aristotelian, and certainly not that Augustine was an advocate for Plato or fundamentally platonic. Instead, both were able to pursue their theological and God-centered projects with the pedagogical aid of these two distinct patterns of thinking.[96]

It should not be surprising then, that Aquinas seems to believe firmly that the will of humanity is free, even free in a libertarian sense,[97] or seems to be. This sense of the free-will arising from choice is the clear impression that reason delivers to every man. That is, we seem to have free-will, so we do have free-will.

Yet, Aquinas is very satisfied that God's will is prior and eternal. That is, it is logically prior (not temporally) and it is eternal in the sense that for God all things are always present. He is outside of our time-line altogether. Seeking to explain this he writes,

> There is no succession in God's act of understanding, any more than there is in his existence. Hence it is all at once everlasting, which belongs to the essence of eternity, whereas the duration of time is drawn out by the succession of before and after. . . . Somewhat of an example of this may be seen in the circle: for a given point in the circumference, although indivisible, does not coincide in its position with any other point, since the order of position results in the continuity of the circumference; while the center which is outside the circumference is directly opposite any given point in the circumference. Accordingly

---

95. So Peter Hicks in *Journey So Far: Philosophy through the Ages,* perceives the shock of Aristotle on the Christian world and Aquinas's response. He writes, "Aquinas tried tying Aristotle in with the Augustinian tradition" (155); and "Aquinas was convinced that Ibn Rushds's teaching was a serious misinterpretation of Aristotle and set out to counteract the heresies of the Averroists and the speculations of others by expounding Aristotle's true message" (199). This does not make Aquinas an "Aristotelian" nor was he sanctifying a pagan philosopher. Chesterton writes that the growing "puppy" does not become the food he eats, but more "doggie." Again, it is worth restating, "St. Thomas did not reconcile Christ to Aristotle; he reconciled Aristotle to Christ" (*Thomas Aquinas: The Dumb Ox,* 28).

96. Mark D. Jordan, responding to Aquinas's "alleged Aristotelianism" writes that even "a term like 'Aristotelianism' does not accord with Thomas's view of philosophy in history" (*Rewritten Theology,* 60–62). However, contra Peter Hicks (and others), Jordan does not believe that the evidence indicates that Aquinas wrote to combat false readings of Aristotle from the influence of the Latin Averroists (73). Rather, Jordan argues that the very way he used Aristotle and the type of citation indicates that he used Aristotle as "a convenient but not indispensable authority" (79) or in some way other than as a foundational citation of authority. So, for Jordan, it is clear that even when Aristotle is at times cited authoritatively, "Aristotelian citations are juxtaposed with other authorities of all kinds" (83). He concludes, "For Thomas, Aristotle is not a unique or perennial authority. Aristotle is a pagan author whose texts can be brought into helpful constellation with other authorities. . . . He treats Aristotle instead as the teacher behind a set of pedagogical texts" (88).

97. Terrance Tiessen reports on Aquinas's view, "God acts concurrently with *libertarian free agents* so that the actions of moral creatures are the free choice of the creatures themselves" (*Providence & Prayer,* 178, emphasis mine).

> whatever exists in any part of time, is co-existent with the eternal as though present thereto, although in relation to another part of time it is present or future.... It remains therefore that God has knowledge of those things which are not as yet in relation to the course of time.[98]

That is, all of time is equally available to God, who is uniquely at the center, but not constrained to our limited temporal-circumference. It is as simple for God to reach any point on the circle; all points that are to us past, present and future are available to God by equal reach. His will acts, not temporally, but in a way that is prior and from an eternal present.

When God acts in such a way, God's will is always fulfilled, but yet his will is also limited.[99] Concerning fulfillment, he states, "All good things that exist, God wills to be. If therefore his will imposes necessity on things willed, it follows that all good happens of necessity, and thus there is an end of free-will, counsel, and all other such things."[100] By "an end of free-will," he does not intend that free-will has ceased, but that such an end would be obviously at odds with a strong sense of freedom. Therefore there must be a limit to God's will; "The divine will imposes necessity on some things willed, but not on all."[101] This, he says, is an effect of division of God's will into his "necessary will" and his "contingent will." The contingency of the latter will is the very house inhabited by the will of man, which though defective by reason of his finiteness and his sin, are still his house and his rightful domain. This contingent will is also the limit on God's will, contingent upon man's Libertarian Free-Will. Yet, even this contingency is the will of God: "We must understand a necessity in things willed by God that is not absolute, but conditional. For the conditional statement that if God wills a thing it must necessarily be, is necessarily true.... [RAS: However] not all things, therefore, are absolutely necessary."[102]

In regard to the will of people, this means that God does not use "necessity of coercion." In regard to necessity, Aquinas understands many ways this word can be understood: (1) "absolute necessity" which is "as when we say that it is necessary for the three angles of a triangle to equal two right angles"; (2) "necessity of utility" which is understood in the sense that "food is said to be necessary for life"; and (3) "necessity of coercion" which is "when someone is forced by some agent, so that he is not able to do the contrary."[103] The reason God does not use this latter form of necessity is, "necessity of coercion is altogether repugnant to the will." By this Aquinas means that coercion and free-will cannot cooperate, "for we call that violent which is against the inclination of a thing." Nevertheless, God is willing to employ the necessity of utility,

98. Aquinas, *Summa Contra Gentiles*, volume 1, 1.66.
99. Aquinas, *ST*, Ia,q.19,a.6.
100. Aquinas, *ST*, Ia,q.19,a.8.
101. Aquinas, *ST*, Ia,q.19,a.8.
102. Aquinas, *ST*, Ia,q.19,a.8.
103. Aquinas, *ST*, Ia,q.82,a.1.

PART I: The Tension of Theodicy

and for obvious reasons, absolute necessity. However, these preserve volition, which is understood as being "according to the inclination of the will."[104]

Humanity then has a will, but in what sense is it free? As was cited above, Aquinas states that he is committed to the Libertarian Free-Will of humanity. Indeed, it could be argued that this commitment is *a priori*. He says, "man has free-will; otherwise counsels, exhortations, commands, prohibitions, rewards, and punishments would be in vain."[105] His conclusion seems to come before the question. Still, in this Libertarian Free-Will, he continues to make room for God's sovereignty. He writes,

> Free-will is the cause of its own movement, because by his free-will man moves himself to act. But it does not of necessity belong to liberty that what is free should be the first cause of itself, as neither for one thing to be cause of another need it be the first cause. God, therefore, is the first cause, Who moves causes both natural and voluntary. And just as by moving natural causes He does not prevent their acts being natural, *so by moving voluntary causes He does not deprive their actions of being voluntary: but rather is He the cause of this very thing in them*; for He operates in each thing according to its own nature.[106] (emphasis mine).

Though he is understood as defending Libertarian Free-Will, might his position be more like what would be called compatibilism, not in full-flower, but in the seed? This is without doubt. Compatibilism accepts God's sovereignty and the priority of his will, but preserves the active, though subordinate, will of man: volition. Such is the case for Aquinas; the first cause of all things is God and the volitional cause of every human act is humanity. He further writes, "those things which are naturally inclined are not subject to free-will."[107] That is, much of our life is not free, in the libertarian sense, at all. This is not surprising, for this too, is our experience in our habits as Aquinas observed. The domain of freedom in humanity is growing smaller. Free-will is limited to this: it is the power that moves us to action when faced with a choice, and this power of free-will is "indifferent to good and evil choice."[108]

This may raise a question for the reader: what is the relationship between reason, will, and free-will? It might seem that the "will" is passive, simply desiring and that the will and reason call upon the "free-will" to make a choice. This is not Aquinas's understanding. First, the will is the same power as the free-will so that they are indistinguishable, "the free-will is nothing else than the will."[109] Secondly, reason (which is synonymous with "intellect" in Aquinas), is a separate realm from the will, for "every

---

104. Aquinas, *ST*, Ia,q.82,a.1.
105. Aquinas, *ST*, Ia,q.83 a.1.
106. Aquinas, *ST*, Ia,q.83,a.1.
107. Aquinas, *ST*, Ia,q.83 a.2.
108. Aquinas, *ST*, Ia,q.83,a.2.
109. Aquinas, *ST*, Ia,q.83,a.4.

movement of the will must be preceded by apprehension, whereas every apprehension is not preceded by an act of the will."[110] Then there are two, reason and will. Which is prior, superior, and greater? Aquinas says that reason is superior to the will, "The intellect precedes the will, as the motive power precedes the thing movable" and "absolutely, however, the intellect is nobler than the will."[111] So, in brief, the will is free and subordinate to reason.[112]

Aquinas stands as champion of a free-will, with conditions. It is free, but not free of reason nor free of God's priority. Humanity's free-will is a necessity of common experience (we are volitional) and by reason (we are responsible and that would mean nothing if we were not free). Yet, in Aquinas are seeds, not of modern Libertarian Free-Will,[113] but rather of compatibilism, because the free-will is subject to the priority of God's will. Further, an implication of the free-will being subject to reason and God's priority is that it acts as a hedge against free-will of the modern Libertarian Free-Will type, which may lean toward randomness and meaninglessness, if it cannot be externally influenced.[114] This will be investigated later.

Largely in reaction to Aquinas, John Duns Scotus (c.1266–1308)[115] investigated voluntarism, which holds the will as primary over and against reason (or intellect) and justice (or natural goodness). It is closely associated with the version of theonomy in which theology and deity's decrees are prior to logic; God (or the deity) chooses the

---

110. Aquinas, *ST*, Ia,q.82,a.4.

111. Aquinas, *ST*, Ia,q.82,a.3.

112. This is distinct from Augustine who asserts that nothing is above the will (*Free Choice of the Will*, 3.17, 18).

113. The crux of Libertarian Free-Will is not that a man makes a choice in accord with his will, but that whatever choice a man makes, the same man was free to have chosen otherwise. Even more important in the context of modern Libertarian Free-Will is that the will is not significantly influenced. Hasker writes that modern libertarian freedom is, "Augustine does not say, as a modern libertarian would say, that the free will functions as an uncaused or undetermined cause" (*God, Time and Knowledge*, 6).

114. This is indicated by the fact that Aquinas has subordinated the free-will to God's will and to the intellect or reason. As we shall see, the true libertarian philosopher cannot allow even reason and certainly not God's sovereignty to supersede the act of the will. If the will is ungoverned, is it then unpredictable? If it has no motive power behind it, is it random?

115. John Duns Scotus was most likely a Scot who was born in Duns, and so nicknamed, Duns Scotus. His birthplace is debatable, but this is the best scholarly guess according to many, including Mary Beth Ingham (*Scotus for Dunces*, 13). He was a Franciscan and is known as the "Subtle Doctor" both as a compliment for his keen mind and intense precision in argument and also perhaps because he represented the high-water mark of scholastic complexity and even tediousness. He was admired greatly by Ockham for the subtlety of his judgment (Adams, *William Ockham*, 43). Later history was not so kind. The etymology of "dunce" seems to stem from a 16th century unkind use of "Duns" (*Oxford English Dictionary*). The style of his writing made Duns Scotus inaccessible to many. His work is still without a comprehensive edition in English and there exists only fragmentary translations of his work in diverse secondary sources. Not only is this so, but his ideas on will and morality are scattered throughout his rather disconnected works. This may be due in part to his relatively early death which found him still editing *Ordinatio*, his Oxford lectures.

rules of reason that are desired as opposed to those which are in any way necessary in regard to reason.[116] In this, he was followed by his pupil William of Ockham.[117]

So subtle[118] is Duns Scotus that the precise meaning of voluntarism is not easy to state with general agreement. William Frank proposes understanding Duns Scotus as putting forward a theory of co-causality in which the contribution of people and God are both necessary but not independently sufficient so that "no increase in accidental features of either cause suffices to overcome the limitation of essence that is overcome only by the holistic integration of the two natures" which he takes from Ordinatio 2.37.2.[119] As Duns Scotus often noted, this is a partnership in causality not unlike the work of male and female in begetting offspring so that the necessary contribution of each is rooted in an essential difference. This I reject in the sense that if God *needs* a partnership with his creatures in order to accomplish his will, there is then some deficit in God. However, I will examine this concept more favorably in a specific application to evil in Part II.

Another perspective can be seen in the discussion between Thomas Williams and Allan B. Wolter. Williams argues that for Duns Scotus the will of God acts with broad independence apart from his reason and justice[120] and that Duns Scotus is an "unmitigated" voluntarist (and that this should be no embarrassment to those who endorse his views). Williams begins his case with the oft cited *Ordinatio*, 3.19 "everything

---

116. Feinberg, *Many Faces of Evil*, 23. Per Feinberg, in the case of William of Ockham (Duns Scotus's pupil, and others which I take to include Duns Scotus), there is one rule of logic that is prior to God's decisions: the law of noncontradiction (26). Still, per this system, "no action is necessarily good or evil, and God has the power to choose whatever will be good or evil" (29). It should also be understood that this sense of "theonomy," which is taken as a synonym for voluntarism, is distinct from the modern definition which declares the Old Testament law as applicable to modern society as civil law. It should be allowed that Duns Scotus does allow for necessity, in God's freedom, writing under the head, "Is there Necessity in any act of the will?," "This is obvious. God is necessarily happy; therefore, he necessarily beholds and loves the beatific object. Similarly, the Holy Spirit is God and consequently is supremely necessary in being. Therefore, since he receives being by proceeding . . . the act whereby he proceeds from them is most necessary" (John Duns Scotus, *God and Creatures*, 16.4).

117. Feinberg, *Many Faces of Evil*, 26–28. So strong was this in Ockham, that he declared that God could, if he had wanted, make it ethically required that we hate him (Ockham, *Sententiarum IV*, q. 8–9, E-F, as cited by Feinberg, 28). It is also worth noting that Duns Scotus's voluntarism, however strong or weak, did come in the context of the Condemnations of 1277 of Paris, which, among other things, implicitly strengthened the position that God's will is free of all constraints and was also an attempt to ground all things on God's love (Ingham and Dreyer, *Philosophical Vision of John Duns Scotus*, 117–8). Duns Scotus had context and fertile ground for his views.

118. It was this intellectual subtlety of Duns Scotus that established the doctrine of Mary's "Immaculate Conception." He was later called "Mary's Architect" by Allan Wolter. Duns Scotus's position on Mary is presented in *Ordinatio*, 3.3.1.

119. Frank, "Duns Scotus," 152–53. He notes that this is contrary to the work of Marilyn McCord Adams and Douglas Langston who propose a deterministic reading of Duns Scotus (158).

120. T. Williams, "Reason, Morality, and Voluntarism in Duns Scotus," 73–94. In this article, he argues not this point, primarily, but rather that this independence of God's will (our morality) from (external) reason and justice is not a problem for us to know and obey.

other than God is good because it is willed by God, and not vice versa"[121] to argue that God's willing is prior to all. While Williams maintains that "Duns Scotus's God cannot will contradictions," he can and does act from his will alone, without consulting either his divine rationality or his divine justice.[122] In regard to divine justice as a possible constraint, citing *Ordinatio*, 4.46, Williams argues that for Duns Scotus, God's one non-derivative obligation (to love and enjoy his own goodness) does not give rise to a derivative obligation to his creatures.[123] He also argues that God's rationality or intellect is divided into two senses, rational willing, and orderly willing. Citing the assertions of other scholars that Duns Scotus's God "wills everything most reasonably and in a most orderly and correct way,"[124] Williams argues that Duns Scotus's intent is nothing more than "God wills in a most orderly way, but what he wills in that orderly way is very much up to him."[125] So, distinct from the Thomistic idea of "reasonable," so intellectually ordered, he understands that Duns Scotus intends nothing more than "God acts however he wills to act."[126] This position sees Duns Scotus as a classic theonomist of the first order.

In contrast to Williams, Wolter's position ties God's will more closely to what is good and to God's reason and intellect, thus mitigating Duns Scotus's voluntarism. Referring again to *Ordinatio*, 3.19 ("everything other than God is good because it is willed by God and not vice versa"), Wolter argues "If we divorce [RAS: this affection for justice] from the divine will or ignore how it influences God's possible choices, then we get a distorted and even more shredded conception of Duns Scotus's voluntarism."[127] In other words, still understanding Duns Scotus as a voluntarist, Wolter takes the majority view that his voluntarism is mitigated by God's natural justice—that everything created has all that is proper to its nature, that is, all that is proper for God to give it because of his nature.

---

121. T. Williams, "Unmitigated Duns Scotus," 1–2. He also cites *Ordinatio*, 4.d.46.q.1,n.7, "the divine will has no rectitude inclining it determinately to anything but its own goodness" (11). So Williams concludes, "These quotations make clear the extent to which the value of creatures, as well as the rectitude of their conduct, depends on the divine will. Some of the laws of morality, Scotus says, are in force only because God wills them to be in force" (12).

122. T. Williams, "Most Methodical Lover?" 169–70. So also Ingham would agree that rationality in Duns Scotus has more to do with self-control than analysis so that "the intellect is not the rational potency" (*Philosophical Vision of John Duns Scotus*, 147) and "the will's response to whatever the intellect presents is completely free from anything outside the will's own power" (166). It should be noted that for Williams, God can will contradictions like "cold fire" in the sense that they are contradictions of extant physical laws (169), but he cannot will *a* and *not-a* simultaneously. However, nothing prohibits God from willing *a*, at time *t*, and *not-a* at time *t*."

123. T. Williams, "Most Methodical Lover?" 175.

124. Ibid., 184.

125. Ibid., 187.

126. Ibid., 189.

127. Wolter, "Unshredded Scotus," 321.

PART I: The Tension of Theodicy

This is not the venue to investigate this in any detail or to weigh in on one side or the other, but I will only display the issue as it affects the development of our understanding of human free-will. Distinct from Aquinas's emphasis on the importance of the intellect and even its superiority to the will, Duns Scotus is a voluntarist who puts greater emphasis on God's freedom. Further, his emphasis on freedom is extended also to God's willful-creatures. For example, in regard to the operation of God's foreknowledge, Duns Scotus writes, "Although the necessity of foreknowledge or of the foreknown as foreknown is one of immutability, it is not simply a necessity of inevitability or absolute determination. It is only inevitable on the assumption that God foreknows that this will take place."[128] In this, as in the primacy of the will, he agrees with Augustine. Like Augustine, Anselm and others, true freedom for God and for humanity is to be able to do the good.[129] Yet, unlike both, he perceives the human will as much freer than they do, as indicated by his statement, "the intellect is moved naturally by its object whereas the will moves itself freely."[130] In the context of his voluntarism in regard to God's extreme freedom, he seems to see the will of man as quite unencumbered as well and so he has contributed to what we understand as the Libertarian Free-Will of God's creatures.

Following Duns Scotus, a great contest over the will came in the person of Martin Luther (1483–1546). When he discovered grace in Christ and was freed of his captivity, he set about to free his fellow Christians. He desired that they be free of all hindrances to grace, including and especially those of religion that distorted knowledge of our true state before God.[131] He wrote of the will and of freedom in *Bondage of the Will* (1525), in response to Erasmus (1466–1536).[132] Early in this text, he frames the direction of his argument:

> It is, then, fundamentally necessary and wholesome for Christians to know that God foreknows nothing contingently, . . . but that He forsees, purposes,

---

128. Duns Scotus, *God and Creatures: The Quodlibetal Questions*, 16.47.

129. So also Duns Scotus writes in *God and Creatures: The Quodlibetal Questions*. In 16.30–31 he agrees with Augustine and Anselm and reasons that the will which wills the good is the freer; and "the divine will wills the divine goodness," 16.33.

130. Ibid., 16.22.

131. Within the Roman Catholic church, Luther battled against Johann Eck (Eckius) (1486–1543). At the disputation of Leipzig they battled for over two weeks in the summer of 1519. The result was the Diet of Worms in April of 1521, where Luther made his famous, "Here I stand!" proclamation. The Edict of Worms followed only a month later in which Luther, along with his views, was rejected by the Church.

132. Desiderius Erasmus was a brilliant humanist and a spiritual descendant of Pelagius. His attacks on scholasticism sometimes paralleled Luther's own, but on more fundamental issues such as the freedom of the will and on grace he shared no compatibility with Luther. In 1517 Luther clarifies his perspective on Erasmus with the words, "The human is of more value to him [Erasmus] than the Divine" (Schaff, *History of the Christian Church*, 1.2.29n). When separation from Luther became important to Erasmus, he attacked him at what he considered a most significant point when he wrote, *On Free Will* in 1524.

and does all things according to his own immutable, eternal, and infallible will. This bombshell knocks "free-will" flat. . . . God foreknows and wills all things, not contingently, but necessarily and immutably, ... When he makes promises, you ought to be out of doubt that he knows, and can and will perform, what he promises.[133]

To link God's will to His foreknowledge would seem to be counter to Augustine, who argued that to suggest that foreknowledge is a cause of anything is foolish. In fact, Luther goes even further, replacing free-will by the concept of "necessity," "From this it follows, by resistless logic, that all we do, however it may appear to us to be done mutably and contingently, is in reality done necessarily and immutably in regard to God's will."[134] But then, pulling up just short of making all human action unnecessary, he makes clear what he does not mean, "I could wish, indeed that a better term was available for our discussion than the accepted one, necessity, . . . for it suggests some sort of compulsion, and something that is against one's will, which is no part of the view under debate."[135]

What kind of necessity does Luther have in mind? To what kind of willing does he refer? It seems that he is claiming that while the will is not free, we do not act under compulsion as if our will desired one thing and we were consciously overpowered against our will. That is, we have Volitional Free-Will, as was agreed by Boethius, Anselm, Aquinas, and certainly Augustine. Clarifying further he writes, "no violence is done to his will; for it is not under unwilling constraint, but an operation of God consonant with its nature it is impelled to will naturally."[136] His words are more polemical than some might like, but his conclusion is that of the contemporary compatibilist. We have a will, which is not free to do good, but which is always in congruence with our volitional will, with which we act. As such, the will is "free."

However, unlike Augustine, he understands the sovereignty of God as above the will itself. In regard to Satan's will, Luther says by example, "Thus God, finding Satan's will evil, not creating it so (it became so by Satan's sinning and God's withdrawing), carries it along by his own operation and moves it where he wills."[137] And to Luther, this lack of a will, free to respond to God, is a comfort. He writes,

> I frankly confess that, for myself, even if it could be, I should not want "free-will" to be given me, nor anything to be left in my own hands to enable me to endeavor after salvation; not merely because in face of so many dangers, . . . I could not stand my ground and hold fast my "free-will"; but because, . . . I should still be forced to labor with no guarantee of success, and to beat my

133. Luther, "Bondage of the Will," *Martin Luther: Selections from his Writings*, 181, 184.
134. Ibid., 181.
135. Ibid., 182.
136. Ibid., 198.
137. Ibid., 193.

PART I: The Tension of Theodicy

> fists at the air. . . . my conscience would never reach comfortable certainty as to how much it must do to satisfy God.[138]

So, Luther has gone further than Augustine, and perhaps all others before him, in his understanding of the concepts of the will and of freedom. He wrote that he would eradicate the term in regard to humanity as having no meaningful content.[139]

It would seem that the content of the idea called human free-will is being stretched in both directions. Origen, Pelagius, and Erasmus are opening territory in one direction; Augustine, Aquinas, and Luther are pioneering on the opposite frontier. And it is this frontier that John Calvin (1509–1564) extends even further, in the next generation. In 1536 he published the first edition of the *Institutes* which he wrote while in exile and pastoring in Geneva. His position was that the will of man is in no way free. Still he understood that the will, as created by God, was perfectly sufficient to have permitted Adam to sustain eternal life perpetually.[140] However, Adam did fall, and in this Fall, the will itself was corrupted and freedom vanished in rebellion. So Calvin expresses his frustration with philosophers of Christianity of his day who "still seek after free choice" and who "mix up heaven and earth." That is, Calvin would agree that we have a desire for freedom, but having lost it, we cannot will it back. He writes, "Man will then be spoken of as having this sort of free decision, not because he has free choice equally of good and evil, but because he acts wickedly by will, not by compulsion. Well put, indeed, but what purpose is served by labeling with a proud name such a slight thing?"[141] Two things should be noted. First, this is as good a definition of what this project intends by the term volitional freedom as could be found: "he acts wickedly by will, not by compulsion." Second, freedom is valued, but inaccessible to humanity. Freedom, which began in heaven and on earth, now remains only with God.[142] This is synonymous with slavery, the second Era of Freedom in this project.

Why is this so? Why would God allow, even decree, that such a valuable commodity would be lost to his creation? Calvin says, "But the reason he did not sustain

---

138. Ibid., 199.

139. He writes, "So it befits theologians to refrain from using the term when they want to speak of human ability, and to leave it to be applied to God only. They would do well also to take the term out of men's mouths and speech, and to claim it for their God, as if it were his own holy and awful Name" (ibid., 188).

140. "In this integrity man by free will had the power, if he so willed, to attain eternal life. . . . Adam could have stood if he wished, seeing that he fell solely by his own will. . . . His choice of good and evil was free" (Calvin, *ICR*, 1.15.8).

141. Calvin, *ICR*, 2.2.7.

142. To the Early Church Fathers, many of whom he believed to have elevated free-will above the biblical standard, he generously said, "Yet I dare affirm this: however excessive they sometimes are in extolling free-will, they have had this end in view—to teach man utterly to forsake confidence in his own virtue and to hold that all his strength rests in God alone" (Calvin, *ICR*, 2.2.9). This generosity might be surprising to some and may indicate how thoroughly he valued God's glory above even disputes about the nature of freedom.

man by the virtue of perseverance lies hidden in his plan."[143] The only truth that we can extract from these terrible facts is this, "That from man's Fall he might gather occasion for his own glory."[144] God will be glorified and this loss of freedom is part of God's plan to glorify himself. How does this affect human responsibility? Adam, born into freedom, was and is responsible, but what of those who followed him and knew not freedom? The biblical norm requires that all after Adam are indeed responsible (including especially Romans 5 and 6). In a simple affirmation, Calvin states "Yet [RAS: a human] is not excusable."[145] What is the mechanism of responsibility for Calvin? Reason and natural law.[146] It has been argued that his system does not truly allow for responsibility, but Calvin asserts that it does and does so with wisdom. He writes, "For who is such a fool as to assert that God moves man just as we throw a stone? And nothing like this follows from our teaching. To man's natural faculties we refer the acts of approving and rejecting, willing and not willing, striving and resisting."[147] Here is a key statement, for one can assert God's active sovereignty without a mechanistic model—indeed one must! Moreover, human responsibility is not diminished in a model that attributes significant, though non-mechanistic, causation to God. This responsibility affirms the goodness of God's judgment, contrary to those who say that reward and punishment lose their meaning. So Calvin asserts, "Concerning punishments, I reply that they are justly inflicted upon us, from whom the guilt of sin takes its source."[148] In this he stands strongly, as might be anticipated, with Augustine, who also emphasized the difference between being (which stones possess), life (which animals possess), and willing (which only humans possess); we have a will and so are responsible.

How corrupted is our will and how is it affected, along with our reason? This touches on Calvin's doctrine of total depravity. In Adam's sin, all who follow him are totally without ability to help themselves or to please God by their own efforts.[149] This corruption reaches even, and especially, to the will. Yet, the will is not so corrupt that

---

143. Calvin, *ICR*, 1.15.8.

144. Calvin, *ICR*, 1.15.8.

145. Calvin, *ICR*, 1.15.8.

146. Calvin, *ICR*, 2.2.22.

147. Calvin, *ICR*, 2.5.14. It is also true that Calvin affirms God's foreknowledge. Yet unlike others who preceded him such as Augustine, he affirms its causal link between God's foreknowledge and God's decrees. That is, God's foreknowledge is related to his own free knowledge of his own actions and not of the will of humanity. Calvin makes it clear throughout (3.22.1–6).

148. Calvin, *ICR*, 2.5.2.

149. For example, 2.1.6 declares that our depravity is complete and stems from Adam, not imputation. The extent is made clear in 2.1.8, "For our nature is not only destitute and empty of good, but so fertile and fruitful of every evil that it cannot be idle. Those who have said that original sin is 'concupiscence' have used an appropriate word, if only it be added—something that most will by no means concede—that whatever is in man, from the understanding to the will, from the soul even to the flesh, has been defiled and crammed with this concupiscence. Or, to put it more briefly, the whole man is of himself nothing but concupiscence."

PART I: The Tension of Theodicy

reason is inoperable, so that it might fail to report anything truly of use to the self. He says, "When we so condemn human understanding for its perpetual blindness as to leave it no perception of any object whatever, we not only go against God's Word, but also run counter to the experience of common sense."[150] Though we are totally ruined before God, it is critical to Calvin to assert not only that the reason continues to be useful, but critically important: "Reason is proper to our nature; it distinguishes us from brute beasts."[151] In this too he agrees with Augustine[152] and with Aquinas who so strongly affirmed the senses, including the interpretation of all inputs by our reason. But it is still true that the will and its reason is incredibly damaged, even blinded, spiritually.[153]

Free-will (in the sense that it is usually used) then does not exist for Calvin among the unredeemed. Why is this important to Calvin? One could reply that it is of first importance because it is his understanding of the requirement of the Text.[154] One could also reply that such a position also has a valuable effect on fallen man, "You see that Paul has taken everything away from free will in order not to leave any place for merits."[155] This despair is a goad to salvation. This fallen will continues to be drawn to what is good, but is incapable of a free and effective response to conform to God's goodness. Also, God's foreknowledge is not an issue for Calvin in the sense that he feels no tension in God's knowing, foreknowing, and foreordaining all things. Freedom for Calvin is only volitional.[156]

---

150. Calvin, *ICR*, 2.2.12.

151. Calvin, *ICR*, 2.2.17.

152. In *Free Choice of the Will* (2.3), Augustine notes that creation enjoys three essentials from God: being, life, and understanding (reason). Inanimate objects share only in the first. Beasts share in life. Only man possesses understanding and reason and therefore, will.

153. Calvin, *ICR*, 2.2.19–20. He cites John 1:4–5, Matthew 16:17, 1 Corinthians 12:3, and John 6:44.

154. The bondage of the fallen will is an area of agreement even among many (most?) of those who still disagree with Calvin on details of freedom, such as the corruption of reason (such may be just the difference between the Reformation and Enlightenment!). For example, Alfred Freddoso writes that for Luis de Molina God is also the ultimate ("particular") cause of even those events which are perpetrated by his willful creatures. Of Molina's position he writes, God "is the first or primary cause and His causal activity is absolutely pervasive. . . . no creaturely or secondary cause is able to exercise its causal power unless God also acts contemporaneously to bring about its effect" (Molina, *On Divine Foreknowledge: Part IV of the Concordia*, 16). That is, he is not the cause of the willful creature's decision, but rather the cause of the effect of the willful creature's decision (18). Often the debate is not about the Text's position in regard to our lack of free-will, and the exact meaning of free-will (or what it is that is not free) and the implications of the lack.

155. Calvin, *ICR*, 2.5.2.

156. I do not think Calvin ever used the word "free" in regard what is called "volitional will." Yet, I think it is fair to say that he perceives it so. As an example, I cite his understanding of the will of the angels. He writes, Although the elect angels "will cannot turn away from good, yet it does not cease to be will" (2.5.1) That is, the elect angels exercise volition, a will, even though they are not free to turn from what is good. It is the sense of the exercise of the will, the sense of choice, and the responsibility for that choice, which is here intended by the phrase "free volitional will."

Trained in Calvinism, and a brilliant professor at the University of Leyden, Jacobus Arminius (Jakob Hermanzoon, 1560–1609) revolted against Calvin's God. In doing so he had to work hard to establish his orthodoxy. In an example from his work, he struggles both with himself and with those who make charges against him, stating first the accusation and then offering his response:

> Faith is not the pure gift of God, but depends partly on the grace of God, and partly on the powers of Free Will; that, if a man will, he may believe or not believe. I never said this, I never thought of saying it, and, relying on God's grace, I never will enunciate my sentiments on matters of this description in a manner thus desperate and confused. I simply affirm, that this enunciation is false, "faith is not the pure gift of God."[157]

By negating a negative, Arminius is avoiding identifying that which is active in grace beyond God's own work. While this does distance him from the Pelagians,[158] it does exclude the possibility that something else is active and it does little to clarify what, if anything, is active other than God's grace. Moreover, the context for this concern (not quoted above) is offense he takes at "irresistible grace." It is here, chiefly, that he finds the Reformed position to be an offense to truth.[159] Given this opposition, something else is active. Therefore, for Arminius, the human will is free, at least, in the sense that we must act to receive the grace God is offering to us. He is struggling to preserve a place in free-will for liberty. He expends not a few of his words refuting charges that any statements of his would undermine God's glory, sovereignty or establish some kind of partnership between God and humanity. Yet his position is hard to distinguish from what he refutes. He writes:

> But if the word "DETERMINED" be received according to the second acceptation, I confess, that I abominate and detest that axiom (as one that is FALSE, ABSURD, and preparing the way for MANY BLASPHEMIES,) which, declares that "God by his eternal decree has determined to the one part or to the other future contingent things." By this last phrase understand "those things which are performed by the free will of the creature."[160] (upper case and quotation marks original)

---

157. Arminius, *Works of James Arminius*, volume 1, section 3, article 27(vii).

158. And he very clearly does desire to avoid Pelagianism. For example, he writes, "But in his lapsed and sinful state, man is not capable, of and by himself, either to think, to will, or to do that which is really good; but it is necessary for him to be regenerated and renewed in his intellect, affections or will, and in all his powers, by God in Christ through the Holy Spirit, that he may be qualified rightly to understand, esteem, consider, will, and perform whatever is truly good" (ibid., volume 1, "A Declaration of the Sentiments of Arminius on Predestination," 5.3).

159. He also writes, "While, on the contrary, this Predestination introduces such a species of grace, as takes away free will and hinders its exercise" (ibid., 1.3).

160. Ibid., volume 1, section 3, article 7.

PART I: The Tension of Theodicy

There are two things he wants to avoid: a divine-human partnership of wills (especially in redemption), and an all-determining will of God. In so doing, Arminius clarifies several things for us. First, the human will is free of all-determining causes. This aligns with what is here called, Libertarian Free-Will.[161] Second, that God's foreknowledge, while real, is not determinative.[162]

It would seem that Arminius struck a resonant chord with his concerns. After his death, his teaching became formalized in publication as the Remonstrants.[163] Though they were rejected by the Synod of Dort (1618–1619), his ideas have greatly influenced the thinking of much of the church today. Arminius is the icon for today's Libertarian Free-Will.

If Arminius was the reaction against the "compatibilism" of the Reformation, Louis de Molina (1535–1600) wanted to chart the *via media*. A Spaniard of noble birth and a Jesuit by training, he intended to find a "concord" between irresistible grace and Libertarian Free-Will so that he could reconcile divine sovereignty and human indeterministic freedom in the *Concordia*.[164] To find such a concord between libertarian freedom[165] and grace in opposition to the Thomists of his day, Molina divided knowledge into:

- "natural knowledge" which is "God's [RAS: fore]knowledge of all the bare possibilities" prior to creation or time, "what could be,"

---

161. While "libertarian" is not a word that I could find Arminius to use, it is the sense of his meaning.

162. Arminius writes, "that things do not exist because God knows them as about to come into existence, but that He knows future things because they are future" (*Works of James Arminius*, volume 1, Disputation 4.44). He also writes, "with certainty according to the foreknowledge of God, although not necessarily and inevitably" (Disputation 10.3). That is, God's foreknowledge is real and complete, but not determinative.

163. The five "Remonstrants" or "the Remonstrance" was published in 1610 against Calvinist teaching. Barth summarizes them as follows: (i) "whoever believes is then elected also by God, and whoever does not believe is rejected" (213); (ii) "Christ died for humanity in general and for each individual, earning reconciliation and the forgiveness of sin for all, but only believers participate in it" (216); (iii) & (iv) "grace is available to every person to the extent that one needs it for one's salvation, even for the person who does not make use of it" (219); (v) "Christ stretches out his hand to them, supports and sustains them. Is there not then the possibility that they might fall again? In 1610, the Remonstrants were really raising only this question" (221). Citations from Karl Barth, *Theology of the Reformed Confessions: 1923*.

164. The full title of this work is: *The Compatibility (Concordia) of Free Choice with the Gifts of Grace, Divine Foreknowledge, Providence, Predestination and Reprobation*. It was published in 1588 after thirty years of preparation. Almost all of Part IV of the *Concordia* concerning divine foreknowledge was also published in Molina's commentary of the First Part of the *Summa Theologica*. Citations are taken here from *On Divine Foreknowledge: Part IV of The Concordia*. Luis de Molina was a colorful man. Though he was a scholar of the *Summa Theologica* and the first Jesuit to write its commentary, he found the Thomistic environment hostile to his ideas. Never one to shy from controversy, he also was a critic of the Atlantic slave trade of the Spanish and Portuguese.

165. This is not simply free-will, but strongly Libertarian Free-Will. In Molina, *On Divine Foreknowledge: Part IV of the Concordia*, 24, Freddoso writes, "Molina's conception of freedom is strongly indeterministic; in modern terms he is an unremitting libertarian."

- "free knowledge" which is "God's [RAS: fore]knowledge of all future actualities," "what will be," and between them,

- "middle knowledge," what would be under all possible circumstances especially those circumstances that are not and will not be actualized by God.[166] These are the pre-volitional (in regard to God's volition) "conditional future contingents"[167] or the "counterfactuals of freedom."[168]

Knowing what could happen and what would happen under all circumstances, God then decreed a given set of antecedents. In that decree, his free knowledge is created and the world of his choosing is obtained. In this, it would seem that Molina has logically preserved libertarian freedom and God's omnipotence and omniscience. Bruce Ware says:

> According to this theory, . . . [RAS: while] God does not and cannot control what free creatures do in any set of circumstances (they retain libertarian freedom), he is able to control certain aspects of the circumstances themselves and by this he can regulate which choices and actions actually obtain from among all those that are possible. Now (according to this theory), while God can control these sets of circumstances, he *cannot necessarily guarantee* that the choice or action he wants a free creature to perform will be done.[169] (emphasis mine)

Why then is there any doubt about God getting his wants as suggested by the words above, "he cannot necessarily guarantee"? That doubt arises from two sources, which both stem from the nature of middle knowledge. First, since middle knowledge

---

166. Molina, *On Divine Foreknowledge: Part IV of the Concordia*, disputation 52.9.

167. Ibid., 22–23. What is a *conditional future contingent*? Freddoso writes:
A state of affairs (S) is a "conditional future contingent" if and only if:

(i) S can be described as it being the case that a resultant state of affairs (R) would obtain at time t, if a trigger state of affairs (T) were to obtain at time t;
(ii) S obtains from eternity;
(iii) R, T and their interaction together at time t are metaphysically contingent (not necessary); and
(iv) it is true from eternity that if T were to obtain at time t, then R would be a contingent effect produced by secondary causes.

This *conditional future contingent*, "middle knowledge," is only distinctly Molinist when it is understood to be *prevolitional*. That is, it is known to God logically prior to his decision and decree in regard to what states will obtain and it is this that makes them distinctly middle knowledge standing between natural and free knowledge.

168. The conventional label of "counterfactuals of freedom," or the shorthand "counterfactuals," is perhaps misleading. Given many "counterfactuals" of the form: "*if A, then B*," there will be some antecedents in that set which God will actualize with the result that their corresponding consequent will obtain. This subset, the only subset with which we have direct experience: our world, are hardly *counterfactual*. The term would be more precisely used of the subset within "*if A, then B*" which do not obtain because God decides, "not A." Hasker notes that Robert Adams suggests the term "deliberative conditionals" (Hasker, *God, Time, and Knowledge*, 26). Nonetheless, the former label stands by long usage.

169. Ware, *God's Lesser Glory*, 38.

PART I: The Tension of Theodicy

is conditioned by "libertarian freedom of God's creatures," it is not an infinite set. Though God may know it perfectly, the one thing (or set of things) he desires may not be in any sub-set of what he knows in his perfect middle knowledge. If it is the case that the complete set of desired outcomes is not available to God among the set that is in his middle knowledge, while he would not be surprised at not being able to choose a particular set, he would be frustrated from all eternity.[170] The second source of doubt, though also from the nature of middle knowledge, is quite different. John S. Feinberg observes that middle knowledge is expressed in two forms: "if x were to occur, y *could* follow" or, more commonly, "if x were to occur, y *would* follow." So, for the minority, who accept that God has middle knowledge, the weak "could" stands to potentially frustrate at least some of God's expectation of the outcome of events even if they are in the set known to him by middle knowledge.[171] That is, what he knows of as "could" does not have the force of the "would" or "shall."[172] This view would seem of great value to those who value libertarian freedom. But that did not prove to be the case for most.[173]

170. Basinger, "Divine Control and Human Freedom," 55–64.

171. Feinberg, *Many Faces of Evil*, 89. Feinberg further suggests that the tension between "would" and "could" leaves Molinism unsatisfactory for both the compatibilist and the libertarian because it is both too deterministic and too libertarian. Hasker insists, correctly, I think, that "[RAS: counterfactuals of freedom] must be necessitation conditionals," excluding the idea of "could" (Hasker, *God, Time, and Knowledge*, 27). Still he says, "It is at least ironic, and perhaps significant, that the theory of middle knowledge, which was then [RAS: in Molina's day against Bañez] under suspicion because it conceded too much to free-will, should now be viewed with concern by a number of philosophers because it comes to close to determinism" (17).

172. To be fair to Molina, and in contradiction of Feinberg, Molina was quite clear that all middle knowledge is of the "would" variety. In Disputation 52, ¶ 9 he writes, "He saw in His own essence what each such faculty *would* do with its innate freedom" (Molina, *On Divine Foreknowledge: Part IV of the Concordia*, 168, emphasis mine). This would, and perhaps did, tend to make it unpalatable to those who desired a fully libertarian understanding of human free-will.

173. Without subscribing to it, John Sanders, an Openness theist sees value in this view: "A theory that shares some affinities with the view [RAS: natural knowledge, the knowledge of all possibilities] and is currently being debated by philosophers of religion is called middle knowledge, or Molinism. . . . [RAS: It is] an attempt to reconcile divine sovereignty and human indeterministic freedom. According to middle knowledge, God knows not only what could possibly happen but also what would happen if something were different in any given situation. That is God knows all the 'counterfactuals of creaturely freedom,' such as the things that would be different. . . . According to middle knowledge God does not force the will of the creatures. God simply knows how to bring it about that the creatures freely decide to do God's will" (Sanders, *God Who Risks,* 197). Further, he observes, "This does not rule out risk for God, however, since God's knowledge of the counterfactuals . . . is independent of divine will." Yet, for Sanders and others of the Openness school, difficulty remains with middle knowledge. It comes from what is for them a deeper issue: "I am not sure whether this should be classified as a member of relational theism" (notes 122 and 124, 324). In fact most theologians of libertarian freedom reject this position, though not all for reasons of "relationship," (for example, Sanders says in *God Who Risks,* 224, "What God desires is a loving relationship and libertarian freedom is simply a means to an end."), but simply because it is not possible (as they understand the world) for God to know so much and leave metaphysical room for libertarian freedom.

Bruce Ware agrees. He notes that Openness theologians (and, interestingly, Calvinists as well) should agree that Molinism does not really provide enough room for one who wants to hold

The Historical Development of the Concept of Free-Will

Molina was intent on giving a model that holds up God's foreknowledge in a way that is not causal.[174] To that end, middle knowledge initially seems to provide a concord between grace and Libertarian Free-Will. For some, he has done this.[175] For most, it is unsatisfactory, simply adding one layer to the problem of evil and solving nothing. Perhaps its claim should be weaker: it preserves "volitional freedom."[176] If so, it has moved more into the camp of the compatibilist and in so doing has simply affirmed the work of Boethius and others, but with the unnecessary step of middle knowledge.

A century later and a continent away, Jonathan Edwards (1703–1758)[177] defined the will, in the tradition of Augustine, as, "that by which the mind chooses anything.

---

to libertarian freedom: (1) God is using a subtle form of determinism, and (2) exhaustive divine foreknowledge gives God regulative power over the future (*God's Lesser Glory*, 40). He also notes that open theists will also object, contra the classic Molinist, that God cannot know the free acts of free creatures prior to their free decision.

It is problematic to determine the grounds of truth for a middle knowledge counterfactual proposition (using "counterfactual" in the most obvious sense as that which never exists in the set of free knowledge) for which the antecedent will never be actualized by God and for which the condition will never obtain as a result. In other words, what can God know of something that in no way exists either as a hard or soft fact, nor ever will?

174. As cited above, the concord of God's foreknowledge and free-will may have been more important to Molina than specifically, Libertarian Free-Will. Still, contemporary opponents of Molina coined the term "semi-Pelagianism" to refer to his doctrine of grace and he did defend Libertarian Free-Will strongly. This distinguishes him significantly from Aquinas. As he wrote, "Molina thus denies . . . that secondary causes must be *moved* by God in order to exercise their causal power. In this way he stresses their autonomy" (*On Divine Foreknowledge: Part IV of the Concordia*, 18). This is unlike Aquinas who asserted that God was the mover in all things.

175. Flint in *Divine Providence: The Molinist Account*, 176) makes a book length argument in which he deals with Thomistic attacks on middle knowledge, the grounding objection, and also William Hasker's attack. Key to his refutation of Hasker being the historic, orthodox pillar of providence which he rightly claims has no meaning in Hasker's system (137). His conclusion: "and thus we conclude that the orthodox Christian with libertarian leanings has a powerful basis for endorsing this picture of God's providential activity." Molina was also vigorously opposed in his own day, specifically by Domingo Bañez (1528–1604), a Dominican and a defender of Aquinas. Bañez insisted, against Molina, "God knows the future free acts of men, even conditional future free acts, in virtue of his predetermining decree, by which he decides to give the 'physical promotion' which is necessary for any human act" (Hasker, *God, Time, and Knowledge*, 15). The battle, reflective of the broader lines of battle between the Jesuits and the Dominicans, raged throughout Molina's life. On the day of Molina's death, 12 October 1600, the committee appointed to review his work reported adversely to Clement VIII (Joseph Pohle, "Luis de Molina," *The Catholic Encyclopedia: An International Work of Reference on the Constitution, Doctrine*, volume 10).

176. "Volitional Will" is the baseline freedom experienced by the willful-creature in making a choice. The volition is active. This is the freedom of the will (the "least common denominator" insisted upon by Augustine and Aquinas and many others): the will makes a choice for the will as it is perceived to do by the creature. As such, the will is not overwhelmed nor is it taken captive "against its will." It perceives itself to be active and feels unconstrained, though perhaps not uninfluenced. It perceives significant freedom.

177. Jonathan Edwards was born into a family of eleven children and was gifted by God with great intelligence, graduating at the top of his class from Princeton at the age of seventeen. After serving in academics for several years, this Puritan accepted the position of pastor in Northampton, MA. If he

49

PART I: The Tension of Theodicy

The faculty of the will is that power, or principle of mind, by which it is capable of choosing. An act of the will is the same as an act of choosing or choice."[178] Of the motivation of this choosing, he writes, "The determination of the will supposes an effect, which must have a cause."[179] That cause is the potential felt by the soul or will, the degree of "goodness"[180] which seems to be the most agreeable and pleasing to the mind of the one who wills.[181] In so saying, he insists that the will always seeks its own best happiness.

In saying this, Edwards is setting up his argument against those who would take the now characteristic Libertarian Free-Will position. He writes,

> And indeed, according to the hypothesis I am opposing, of the acts of the will coming to pass without a cause, it is the cause in fact, that millions of millions of events are continually coming into existence contingently, without any cause or reason why they do so, all over the world, every day and hour, through all ages. So it is in a constant succession, in every moral agent. This contingency, this efficient nothing, this effectual No-cause, is always ready at hand, to produce this sort of effects, as long as the agent exists, and as often as he has occasion.[182]

That is, he opposes the view that insists that there is no sufficient cause in the environment or in the character of the one who wills that would justify using the word "cause" in respect to the choice. What does he mean by "cause"? He writes, "any antecedent, either natural or moral, positive or negative, on which an event, either a thing, or the manner and circumstance of a thing, so depends."[183] His famous example here is that of the rays of the sun which can be a cause in presence (evaporation of moisture from the earth) or by its absence (frost or dew); he allows for positive and negative causes. In the case of our will, Edwards is insistent that there must be a cause for our willing and ultimately that that cause is God.

His argument is exposed in his Part II, sections 11–13. Starting with God's foreknowledge of all human willful decisions, he establishes his argument in the strongest

---

was a great pastor to a single church, the world profited greatly by his dismissal from his congregation. It was after his dismissal in 1750 that he was so highly productive in his writings, and so now, he pastored the world.

178. J. Edwards, "The Freedom of the Will," in *The Collected Works of Jonathan Edwards CD*, 1.1.2.

179. Ibid., 1.2.2.

180. By which he means not moral goodness, but apparent goodness, that which seems pleasing to the mind (ibid., 1.2).

181. Edwards writes, "However, I think so much is certain, that volition, in no one instance that can be mentioned, is otherwise than the greatest apparent good is, in the manner which has been explained. The choice of the mind never departs from that which, at that time, and with respect to the direct and immediate objects of that decision of the mind, appears most agreeable and pleasing, all things considered" (ibid., 1.2.23).

182. Ibid., 2.3.11.

183. Ibid., 2.3.3.

terms to show that all actions that follow from foreknowledge are (metaphysically) necessary[184] choices. He writes, "I observed before, in explaining the nature of necessity, that in things which are past, their past existence is now necessary. Having already made sure of existence, it is too late for any possibility of alteration in that respect, it is now impossible that it should be otherwise than true, that the thing has existed."[185] In so arguing, he is giving God's prior knowledge of future events the weight of that which has already occurred and so, necessary.[186] This is further than Augustine went, but at the heart of what many consider to be the logical implication of foreknowledge.[187] Foreknowledge, cause, and necessity all continue to be at the heart of the modern debate. In so stating this case, Edwards is adding an early brick, indeed many bricks, to the house of the compatibilists, the foundation that has been traced here to Augustine and others.

The debate today has been significantly impacted by Alvin Plantinga, who revived the field of Philosophy of Religion in the face of the yawning indifference of University in the twentieth century. He defined free-will in the following way:

> [RAS: free-will is] being free with respect to an action. If a person is free with respect to a given action, then he is free to perform that action and free to refrain from performing it; no antecedent conditions and/or casual laws determine that he will perform the action, or that he won't, if it is within his

---

184. Edwards writes of metaphysical necessity: "Metaphysical or philosophical necessity is nothing different from their certainty" (ibid., 1.3.12)

185. Ibid., 2.12.I.1.

186. Let me extend his argument here. He writes, "It is no less evident, that if there be a full, certain, and infallible foreknowledge of the future existence of the volitions of moral agents, then there is a certain, infallible and indissoluble connection between those events and that foreknowledge; and that therefore, by the preceding observations, those events are necessary events; . . . and so it is now necessary" (2.12.I.4) That is, he links foreknowledge tightly to the metaphysical necessity of future events. Yet, heading off the objection that knowledge alone is not necessity, he writes, "I allow what Dr. Whitby says to be true, that mere knowledge does not affect the things known, to make it more certain or more future. But yet, I say, it supposes and proves the thing to be already, both future and certain; i.e., necessarily future. Knowledge of futurity, supposes futurity; and certain knowledge of futurity, supposes certain futurity, antecedent to that certain Knowledge. . . . [RAS: this is the] necessity of the event" (2.12.III). There is no misunderstanding his position.

187. This might be called *accidental* necessity, or *contingent* necessity, as that which cannot be changed. In so saying he is arguing with Ockham who would disallow anything that is future tensed to be necessary in this sense. Edwards is intentionally blurring the distinction between past and future in light of God's foreknowledge and closing the gap between God's knowing and our willful action; a gap that Augustine even in his latest writings preserved and upon which Boethius insisted. Edwards's argument has either convinced or reflected the thinking and feeling of many; Openness Theologians (sometimes referred to as consistent Arminians) and many, if not most, compatibilists. I do not find his argument convincing, and to the extent necessary, we will return to the problem of foreknowledge when we consider theodicy itself. For purposes of this discussion, Augustine and Boethius have sufficiently preserved room for human freedom in the context of God's foreknowledge.

PART I: The Tension of Theodicy

power, at the time in question, to take or perform the action and within his power to refrain from it.[188]

This has all the elements of our working definition of Libertarian Free-Will,[189] with the exception of what is called the counterfactual: the assertion that a person having done x, could have (just as easily)[190] done y with no change to the network of causes. This difference is not unimportant to Plantinga.[191] For example, he cites the case of Curley who accepts a $35,000 bribe from the Director. In retrospect, the Director wonders if it would be the case that Curley would have accepted a lesser bribe to the same effect. Contemplating this during a sleepless night, it seemed to him that either Curley would have or would not have accepted a lesser bribe. Plantinga asks if either one of those can be said to be true.[192] In the end, he concludes, through a detailed "Plantinga proof," that indeed one or the other counterfactuals is true. However, he insists that it must then be true that Curley, himself, and not God alone (if God has created Curley free with respect to the action and all other conditions are the same up to the point of the choice), affects the truth or falsity of each proposition.[193] So, his support of Libertarian Free-Will is complete.

In demonstrating the place of counterfactuals and the necessarily broad reach of human free-will in his project, he introduces the concept of the *Leibniz's Lapse*: God cannot create "any possible" world. It is possible that God may be barred from this by *trans-world depravity*—the property of those essences that in every world depart from perfection. If, in fact, trans-world depravity holds, or is even a logical possibility, as he asserts, then God cannot (or the possibility exists that God cannot) create a world with no evil. He writes, "The essential point of the Free Will Defense is that the creation of a world containing moral good is a co-operative venture; it requires the uncoerced concurrence of significantly free creatures. . . . Thus is the power of an

---

188. Plantinga, *God, Freedom, and Evil*, 29.

189. I would observe, for clarity, that this is indeed an unusual position for a theologian who identifies himself as Reformed (who has taught at both Calvin College and Notre Dame). In reviving the Free Will Defense, it may have seemed to him necessary to accept this position, either as a defensible "possibility" for God or, more likely, his own eclectic position in tension with his Reformed stance. Perhaps we are, none of us, consistent, even the best philosophers.

190. As noted elsewhere, this phrase is a disputable one among libertarians themselves.

191. It might be worth pointing out that Plantinga, unlike others in our survey, uses the term "counterfactuals" in its truest sense. In this context, he writes not of all possibilities that fall within the scope of freedom that lie before a person for whom a choice is pending. Rather, he uses them in their truest form, to indicate those choices abandoned in the past when the moment of choice has passed; they are those acts that seem to be a choice, but are counter to the accidental necessity of the historic facts of the case.

192. Plantinga, *Nature of Necessity*, 174.

193. Ibid., 184.

omnipotent God limited by the freedom he confers upon his creatures."[194] Again, his libertarian freedom is at least as great as our working definition and may exceed it.[195]

Plantinga then uses this Libertarian Free-Will to create space into which one might permit the Christian God freedom to create and rule over his creation against the atheologian's insistence that such is a contradiction. He writes, "The heart of the Free Will Defense is the claim that it is possible that God could not have created a universe containing moral good (or as much moral good as this world contains) without creating one that also contained moral evil. And if so, then it is possible that God has a good reason for creating a world containing evil."[196] It goes beyond the scope of this chapter to deal either with evil or theodicy, but it is clear that for Plantinga, Libertarian Free-Will is critical; freeing God from "blame" for the evil that exists.

Terence Fretheim might be considered one of the fathers of Openness Theology, a movement of the later part of the twentieth century. This position attempts to find a middle road between Process Theology and evangelical theology.[197] It is considered by

---

194. Ibid., 190.

195. It would seem that very little needs to be said of foreknowledge when libertarianism is so broadly defined, but Plantinga makes an interesting point that highlights the general confusion in terms and meanings in regard to foreknowledge. He acknowledges Aquinas's argument concerning God's foreknowledge: God's foreknowledge does not precondition or limit the freedom of God's willful-creatures. This is not unlike many in his tradition including Augustine, Boethius, Ockham, and others. Specifically, for Aquinas, this is metaphorically described as the circle (of time) at which God is at the center and able to "reach" just as easily to any point on the circle of time. From a Libertarian Free-Will perspective, Molina makes an argument by way of middle knowledge that is not dissimilar in kind in that it attempts to preserve human freedom and God's foreknowledge and sovereignty. In this Plantinga notes an error: Aquinas's argument is true, *de dicto*, but false *de re*. The distinction is between the way we speak about something (*de dicto*) as opposed to the way a thing is in its being (*de re*). That is, *de re* reflects the understanding that necessity is in the thing itself while *de dicto* reflects the understanding that necessity is in the proposition. In regard to Aquinas he cites the problem in *The Nature of Necessity*, 10. I am not inclined to agree with Plantinga, but that is not significant to the overall development here. Robert Cook names this as Sleigh's Fallacy, dating from the 13th century. Cook writes, "From God's knowledge of the future it follows that what he knows will in fact happen but it does not follow that what he foresees must happen of necessity. . . . it must be insisted that libertarianism can accommodate a certain future for whether it is predestined or not, the future is surely as certain as is the past since it is as analytically true that what will be will be, as what has been has been. On either the determinist or the libertarian model it is an error to assume that the past is closed and the future is open, ... In fact they are both as open and closed as each other" (Cook, *Representative Survey and Critical Analysis of Theological and Philosophical Discussions of Divine Foreknowledge in the English Speaking World from 1970–1989*). Not only is the future open, but so also is the discussion concerning God's foreknowledge. Foreknowledge seems to be the yapping sheep dog of freedom which will not lie down quietly. This cannot be fully exposed here and need not be, but the observation may help understand some of the confusion that is extant in the discussion of foreknowledge.

196. Plantinga, *God, Freedom, and Evil*, 31. As we will see later, the essence of a "defense" (and the genius of Plantinga) is to show the power of the possible in regard to God's work in a world containing significant evil.

197. He indicates that Process Theology shows promise when he writes, "These studies promise important new developments in the understanding of the God of the OT, perhaps especially in a shift away from traditional formulations regarding the divine attributes" (Fretheim, *Suffering of God: An Old Testament Perspective*, 33).

some to be a new Reformation, saving the church from modernism, and by others to be Process Theology in post-modern clothing, changing definitions of words at will. The problem of evil is one of the key issues that motivates Fretheim's theology.[198] He observes that "we" are rediscovering metaphors for God because of, in large part, the horrors of the twentieth century. As an example of this, he cites Jürgen Moltmann's *The Crucified God*,[199] and this would seem to be reflected in the title of his own work, *The Suffering of God*. As in the case of Plantinga, his position on freedom is Libertarian Free-Will, but from the perspective of the Arminian camp.[200] He would participate fully and without reservation in the definition given above. What drives his Libertarian Free-Will is the human relationship with God. He writes, "The world is not only dependent upon God; God is also dependent upon the world. The world is not only affected by God; God is affected by the world in both positive and negative ways. God is sovereign over the world, yet not unqualifiedly so."[201] God and his creation are together part of a project, which is shaping them both. Fundamentally, God is shaped by the relationship with his creation as he observes what they do with his project, for he has limited his sovereignty, omnipotence, and omniscience by creating creatures with Libertarian Free-Will, whose decisions are wholly unknown to him in advance.[202] This voluntary limitation of God is pleasant and good to him because of what God receives in return: libertarianly free image-bearers in free relationship with himself. Specifically, this commitment to relationship means, for Fretheim,[203] God has no foreknowledge of events influenced by those image-bearers he has created. This is because God is inside time and the decisions do not exist to be known before they occur. This Libertarian Free-Will position marks a significant shift away from the historical libertarian position, which couples (by various arguments) God's

---

198. This is reflected in the writing of many who agree with Fretheim, including Greg Boyd. In one of Boyd's earliest works, in response to a question about how God can allow horrendous evil, Boyd wrote, "So God can't foreknow the good or bad decisions of the people He creates until He creates these people and they, in turn, create their decisions" (Boyd and Boyd, *Letters from a Skeptic*, 30). That is, God is not responsible because he not only did not make the decision, he could not have anticipated it. One of his more recent works, *Satan and the Problem of Evil*, clearly shows that Theodicy has impacted, perhaps molded, his thinking about Openness Theology.

199. Fretheim, *Suffering of God*, 15.

200. Not a few are surprised that Plantinga, a self-professed Calvinist, argues from a perspective of Libertarian Free-Will.

201. Fretheim, *Suffering of God*, 35.

202. In *Suffering of God*, Fretheim states this over and over and in various ways: "God is 'inside time,' not outside of it" (44); the usual understanding of God's foreknowledge is omniscience at expense of integrity (47); "God opens himself up to risk; God becomes vulnerable" (55); and "it now seems clear that the OT understands God's power as limited" (77).

203. This position is shared by many other contemporary scholars such as Clark Pinnock, John Sanders, Greg Boyd, and William Hasker. Within evangelical circles, this is a live debate and a divisive issue for The Evangelical Theological Society.

foreknowledge and human Libertarian Free-Will. Some consider Fretheim and other Openness theologians simply to be consistent Arminians.[204]

SUMMARY: BREAKING THE DEADLOCK OVER FREE-WILL

> The will, therefore, is then truly free, when it is not the slave of vices and sins.[205] —Augustine

From the time of the Early Church Fathers until Pelagius, the church drifted toward a Libertarian Free-Will understanding of freedom. In Clement, Origen, Pelagius, and others, our freedom was free enough that we could move toward God "of our own volition" and could even reach the bar of merit. This both exceeds the current definition of Libertarian Free-Will (which says nothing of achieving merit) and falls short (it says nothing of counter-factual choice or causes). Still, essentially, it appears to resonate with that intuitive sense that we are free to choose or not choose. It seems that the maturing church drifted with little intentionality into these ideas and did not face the question squarely until Augustine. Most agree that Pelagius took the project too far; the drift took him and his followers across an obvious line—justification by works.[206] But this drift caught on the rock of Augustine's writing and teaching when he asserted volitional freedom while at the same time acknowledged significant limits on how free the will is to choose among the choices that lie before it. In doing so, he defined true freedom as the freedom to choose the good, something too often missed in the earlier conversation. From his time[207] until Aquinas, the Augustinian seeds grew,

---

204. This is true of R. K. McGregor Wright who calls all Arminians (not simply Openness Theologians) who give up foreknowledge, "consistent Arminians" (*No Place for Sovereignty*, 32). I am inclined to disagree in principle. Just as in the wave-particle duality of light, we must often take positions that are unresolved. That is, we say two things that are true, but are paradoxical, though which do not really exist as an antinomy. I do not agree with Libertarian Free-Will theologians in regard to the two Eras of Freedom between the first Creation & Crisis (creation-corruption) and the final Creation & Crisis (Christ's return-new creation). Nonetheless, I cede to them the right to hold seemingly, for now, paradoxical positions because they believe both are taught in Scripture. However that does not mean I believe their position is a necessary or even preferable one, but rather an anticipatory one of the fourth Era of Freedom (discussed in chapter 6).

205. Augustine, *City of God*, 14.11.

206. To be fair to Pelagius, his writing (that preserved for us) is somewhat ambiguous on this issue. At times it seems that he is speaking more about "sanctification by works" than "justification by works." One example of this is his Commentary on Romans (5:1) where he writes, "Abraham, who was justified initially by faith alone" (Pelagius, *Pelagius's Commentary on St. Paul's Epistle to the Romans*, 89). Other statements indicate that grace is a "help" to a "good man" and not "unmerited favor" to an "evil man." But it is this very ambiguity in Pelagius which is problematic, and which will be investigated more thoroughly when we consider the issues of evil (chapter 2) and theodicy (chapter 3).

207. Time does not permit in this project, but it would be worth noting that Boethius, especially in the *Consolation of Philosophy*, advanced Augustine's thinking even closer to what would become Compatibilistic Free-Will.

PART I: The Tension of Theodicy

blossomed, and dominated the church. Aquinas's work cultivated and watered that of Augustine, becoming the official position of the church, but the innate and true sense of volitional freedom continued to give rise to an implicit sense of a deeper freedom in regard to choice. So, Pelagianism (though banned by church councils) continued to have much informal support as the "relics of Pelagius." There was little change until the advent of Calvin and Arminius when the divide became clearly visible again. Over this most recent period of history, the church rightly rejected Pelagianism (again), as well as all forms of fatalism (which itself effectively rejects even volitional freedom), as counter to the Gospel.[208] This left both Libertarian Free-Will and Compatibilistic Free-Will as "acceptable" Christian positions,[209] and now both plants grew strongly in

---

208. It is worth here saying what "fatalism" is and is not. "Fatalism" means that choices are made by absolute necessity which is rejected by compatibilists (Feinberg, "God Ordains All Things," 23, 29). Tiessen, who attempts to define a Reformed-Molinism asserts, rightly, that there is no Christian fatalistic position, despite charges of some who hold the Libertarian Free-Will position (*Providence and Prayer*, 272). Antony Flew asserts that the distinction between "predestination" (incompatible with responsibility, fatalism in my language here) and "determinism" (compatible with responsibility, providence, in my language here) is the personality of God. His language is confusing here, I think, but I agree that the distinction between fatalism and determinism does lie in the personality (or my suggestion, the Trinitarian personhood) of God. To be fair to Flew, he associates fatalism with the Westminster Confession and with this I cannot agree ("Divine Omnipotence and Human Freedom," *New Essays in Philosophical Theology*, 161). This distinction is not unwelcome—God is personal and so we live in a decidedly personal universe. If we accepted only that, Tiessen would be correct. But it is worth adding Augustine's distinction here that people exercise a will (distinct from a beast, which has life and existence but no will, and from a rock which has existence, but no life or will). It is this that I think Tiessen intended: the act of willing, of choice, however influenced, avoids the charge of fatalism. Taken together, the possession and exercise of that will, in the context of a personal universe, assures the Christian that there is no fatalistic position in regard to the creaturely will. On the other hand, fatalism could be used in a completely different context, referring to a universe, which has room for those effects, particularly evil ones, which are caused neither by human or divine willing. It is not my intent to discuss this later concept here.

209. While the focus of this project is the protestant position in regard to nature of free-will, the protestant divide is reflective of the situation in the Roman Catholic Church (RCC) between the Jesuits and the Augustinians as seen at the time of Molina, and continuing, at least informally, today. In that sense, the RCC continues to share the tension with Protestantism. The Orthodox Church, which diverged from the RCC 500 years earlier (and might therefore have made more progress or greater divergence), still shares the same tension. This is likely because all share much the same formational history and theology, including the controversies between Augustine and Pelagius. Timothy Ware (Bishop Kallistos Ware, *The Orthodox Way*) paints a picture that looks rather Pelagian. Citing Origen's threefold scheme for pursuing The Way, he writes of the first stage (purification): "by listening to his conscience and by exerting the power of his free will, [RAS: humanity] struggles with God's help to escape from enslavement to passionate impulses" (106). However, a better hearing of what the Orthodox church is intending, specifically in their doctrine of *synergeia* (which proposes "the collaboration between divine grace and the freewill of man on his way toward God"), John Meyendorff declares (what is effectively a *via media* between the heretical views of Pelagius and the views of Augustine) a union between people and God that is based on God's grace and our action (*Orthodox Church*, 175ff.). Daniel Clendenin writes, "According to the tradition of the Eastern Orthodox Church, grace and human freedom are expressed concurrently and may not be understood the one without the other. There are not two separate moments. At the same time that a person freely makes the decision from wishing for the good and for the Christian life, at the very same moment divine grace comes and strengthens him. Just as this grace is given to the individual, the individual makes a free choice. . . . Consequently,

the protestant church's garden. But is it possible that these ideas should yet continue to develop and that neither Libertarian Free-Will nor Compatibilistic Free-Will are the final word?

One final thought before I move on. Why do we eagerly desire to be free in this "libertarian" sense? It is rather intuitive that we do so. In one sense, volitional freedom, the reality of choice and responsibility, may introduce its own confusion. Its reality means that our most intuitive idea of freedom (devoid of introspective adjectives) is that we are free to exercise our will, or should be.[210] That is, intuitively, the reality of choice seems to imply significantly unencumbered choice and we identify this feeling with a libertarian like free-will, but this is volitional freedom. And the reality of volitional freedom, a real freedom that is well developed by Augustine, does not imply anything about Libertarian Free-Will or Compatibilistic Free-Will. I would suggest that our assumption of a kind of "libertarian" freedom from birth (something I suggest all parents confront from the day of a child's birth) may be an echo of the original creation and anticipation of the final creation and the ultimate freedom which God is accomplishing for his people—a Conforming-Freedom. And this kind of freedom may be that to which we feel drawn even today, so that neither Libertarian Free-Will or Compatibilistic Free-Will will be the future of freedom, but Conforming-Freedom. To this I will return in chapter 6.

---

grace is not a reward for the virtues of our human will. Nor is it, on the other hand, the cause of the so-called virtuous acts of our free will" (*Eastern Orthodox Theology*, 190–1). While it is not clear that *synergeia* wholly succeeds in rising above the Pelagian stain, that is their strong intent and it shows the continuing struggle to understand the tension. And the tension remains, though with a multiplicity of terminologies, between Libertarian Free-Will and Compatibilistic Free-Will within all branches of the Christian church.

210. This autonomous freedom has many proponents at least in the modern and post-modern West. One of such fathers is Jean-Jacques Rousseau (1712–1778) who insisted on absolute freedom with no restraints (See Ronald Grimsley, "Rousseau, Jean-Jacques," *Encyclopedia of Philosophy*, volume 7).

2

The Historical Development of the Concept of Evil

IN THIS CHAPTER, I will trace the development of the understanding of evil by God's people, particularly in regard to its nature and origin. I will first consider a taxonomy of evil's various species. I will define what I mean by "necessary" evil, even before I make any effort to support such necessity (the substance of Chapter 5). With these species in mind and a definition of "necessary" evil, I will investigate the historical development of the understanding of evil and show that there is reason to consider that something significant is still missing in that understanding.

EVIL: A TAXONOMY

> What makes something "bad," is a disruption of our proper relation to God.[1]
> —Alistair McFadyen

What is evil? Does not everyone share a common understanding of this most basic experience of life? Not at a personal and cultural level. For some, ultimate reality transcends good and evil, and to acknowledge evil is to refuse to accept the fundamental impersonality of being, or more precisely, non-being.[2] Yet, the author of Romans claims that all of humanity holds in common a knowledge and understanding of evil. Further, he claims that all people know what is good, and that we depart from God's

---

1. McFadyen, *Bound to Sin*, 201.
2. Such is Francis Schaeffer's understanding of Hinduism in *He is There and He is not Silent* (24); see also Kinsley, *Hinduism: A Cultural Perspective*. There is clearly a diversity of opinions on the reality of evil. It is beyond argument that neither a common understanding of its reality or its impact can be assumed to be shared. It would seem an epistemological basis must be declared (at least) or shared, in order for progress to be made in the discussion. However, as is noted above, the text of the Bible makes universal claims in regard to evil's common understanding or possible understanding.

goodness, following ignorance and making what is false to be our god. He writes in Romans 1:18–25:

> For the wrath of God is revealed from heaven against all ungodliness and unrighteousness of men who suppress the truth in unrighteousness, because that which is known about God is evident within them; for God made it evident to them. For since the creation of the world His invisible attributes, His eternal power and divine nature, have been clearly seen, being understood through what has been made, so that they are without excuse. For even though they knew God, they did not honor Him as God or give thanks, but they became futile in their speculations, and their foolish heart was darkened. Professing to be wise, they became fools, and exchanged the glory of the incorruptible God for an image in the form of corruptible man and of birds and four-footed animals and crawling creatures. Therefore God gave them over in the lusts of their hearts to impurity, so that their bodies would be dishonored among them. For they exchanged the truth of God for a lie, and worshiped and served the creature rather than the Creator, who is blessed forever. Amen.

That is, what we know of the good is suppressed by many people or even all people. Instead we pursue what is evil. In this text, evil is understood as that which does not participate in God's goodness. This idea informs a definition of evil which will serve as a first approximation for moral evil: *evil is that which departs from the character of God revealed in creation and by His Word.*[3]

What then is natural evil? It is all that causes grief to humans (and even to God), which is not specifically moral evil. After citing a long list of natural evils generated by John Stuart Mill, John S. Feinberg adds his own shorter list: "earthquakes, pains, droughts, floods, physical deformities such as misshapen limbs, blindness, mental retardation or deficiency, insanity, fires, and diseases."[4] Even this short list gives us enough to begin to form a picture. Plantinga puts it this way, "And finally we must distinguish between moral evil and natural evil. The former is evil that results from free human activity; natural evil is any other kind of evil."[5] Natural evil is evil that cannot be traced to the specific agency of human free-will.[6]

---

3. This statement hardly needs support, but I cite C.E.B. Cranfield who writes of this text, "Sin is always an assault upon the truth (that is, the fundamental truth of God)" (*A Critical and Exegetical Commentary on the Epistle to the Romans*, 112). Or simply, sin is to trade God for anything else: "sin does not consist first and foremost in acts that transgress God's law, . . . [RAS: but rather] a failure to give him honor and glory" (Schreiner, *Romans*, 88). It should be noted that this definition does not identify specific evils. For example, when Corrie ten Boom, a Christian in occupied Denmark, told the Nazis that no Jews were hiding in her house, she lied. Can a lie serve what is good? The above definition seems to leave room for debate. Still, as a first approximation, moral evil is defined here as departing from the character of God.

4. Feinberg, *Many Faces of Evil*, revised and expanded edition, 192.

5. Plantinga, *God, Freedom, and Evil*, 30.

6. Some would see "natural" evil as the result of angelic and demonic free-will. This would include Gregory Boyd (*Satan and the Problem of Evil*) and Plantinga as noted below.

PART I: The Tension of Theodicy

It should be noted that natural disasters (historically called, "acts of God") are not in and of themselves evil.[7] They are evil because of their impact on human life.[8] A super-nova far away from human life (the only image-bearers of which we are aware) is a thing of beauty and potentially life-giving.[9] Yet, a super-nova of a near-by star would cause our destruction. The same can be said about volcanoes. But moral evils, in contrast, are evil in and of themselves because they do not conform to God's character. This is true even if no ill effects can be traced from a specific moral evil to any person. It is not the case that a natural evil, such as a flood, is evil in and of itself.

Yet, having said this, it should be noted that the distinction between natural evil and moral evil is not so sharp and distinct for everyone.[10] In fact, the more sovereignty that is "granted" to God by a particular theodicy (theology), the less need there is to distinguish between them because all is under God's authority. Henri Blocher charges that Aquinas minimizes this to his discredit.[11] Contrary to Blocher, I think there is reason to minimize the distinction. Augustine writes in the *Enchiridion*, "We should not suppose that it is necessary to happiness to know the causes of the great physical convulsions, causes which lie hid in the most secret recesses of nature's kingdom."[12] In context, he is arguing that our perfect happiness requires that we know the causes of good and evil, but not of natural evil. So, Plantinga, writing from the perspective of Libertarian Free-Will agrees. He writes, "In fact both moral and natural evil would

---

7. One could correctly ask, to what extent any disorder relates to evil. The second law of thermodynamics calls this disorder, entropy. Complete disorder is the fate of this current universe; it will be driven to disorder without reprieve, not withstanding humanity's best sinful efforts. But it is the pleasure of God to grant a reprieve not only to his people, but also his universe (Romans 8:21, "creation itself will be liberated from its bondage to decay," and Revelation 21:1, "and I saw a new heaven and a new earth."). One could imagine that without sin, this might have been considered the "problem" to which God set humanity when he commanded his people to "rule over all the earth" in Genesis 1. According to Greg Beale ("Eden, the Temple, and the Church's Mission in the New Creation," 5–32), God called humanity to extend the small original garden into all the earth, subduing it. While it is not the intent of this thesis to fully pursue the issue of natural evil, perhaps much of what is considered natural evil is generated because we have not obeyed this first command of God. Could it be the case that without moral evil, natural evil might have been non-existent or conquered by the good stewardship of creation by humanity?

8. Or by some considerations, higher life of all forms. William Rowe, writing as an atheist, cites the problem of gratuitous animal suffering from natural evils in "The Problem of Evil and Some Varieties of Atheism," 335–41. He specifically cites the suffering death of a fawn in a lightening induced forest fire (337) as a problem for the "greater good."

9. All elements heavier than hydrogen, helium, and lithium are understood to have been made in the cores of dying stars and in the shock waves of exploding stars.

10. In fact, the Bible is not always "helpful" in this regard, seeming to mix the concepts of moral and natural evil. For example, in the King James Version, Isaiah 45:7 reads, "I form the light, and create darkness: I make peace, and create evil: I the LORD do all these things." The word for "evil" here is רע, which is a very general word for harm, disaster, or evil, or in this case, punishment. The NASB translates this "calamity" in context and the NIV, "disaster."

11. Blocher, *Evil and the Cross*, 33.

12. Augustine, *Enchiridion on Faith, Hope and Love*, ¶16–17.

then be special cases of what we might call *broadly moral evil*."[13] The subjunctive is satisfied here by understanding that Plantinga is positing that all natural evil is caused by moral free agents, nominally, demons. He suggests this in keeping with Augustine, noting that he does not have to prove that it is true, but only that it is possible. I agree with M.B. Ahern who said, "The problem of evil in its most acute form concerns human or moral evil and I shall limit my discussion to this."[14] In fact, it is possible to take this argument even further so that there is no such thing as "natural evil." Peter Hicks argues this based on the sovereignty of God saying, "all that happens in the universe is the result of action by moral beings . . . an earthquake or a storm is a moral act."[15] This has merit, as I shall argue in Part II, but it is not necessary to remove the category to make my argument.

I do not need to show that there is no natural evil, only to observe that when moral evil is no more, natural evil will be eradicated as a matter of course. The biblical reality is that when moral evil does not have any "existence" for God's people in the final Era of Freedom, there will be no more tears, pain, or hopelessness; so, natural evil will be gone. Natural and moral evils are in fact, linked. In the context of our world, they seem to come together, though they cannot always (if ever) be causally traced. In this project, the inseparable mixture of moral and natural evil will be included in the term: Evil & Suffering. I do not propose either that "Evil" means "moral evil" or that "Suffering" means "natural evil," but that the term as a whole, Evil & Suffering, encompasses all that is meant by the two terms, and the suffering that attends them, and that this reflects their inseparable nature in our world today.

ON GRATUITOUS EVIL

In the taxonomy of evil, if one suggested that natural evil and moral evil are to be considered the Kingdoms of evil, gratuitous evil is a phylum subordinate to both. Gratuitous evil is that evil for which no purpose can be discerned. It might include, in the minds of some, the evil of an infinite hell which comes in response to finite, creaturely sin, or the overwhelming destruction of an "act of God" in the natural realm which surpasses any comprehendible and ultimate good-purpose. Such evil is known by many names: "surplus evil,"[16] "inscrutable evil," "pointless evil,"[17] "meaningless evil,"[18]

---

13. Planting, *Nature of Necessity*, 193.
14. Ahern, "Approach to the Problems of Evil," 20.
15. Hicks, *Message of Evil & Suffering*, 70.
16. Howard-Snyder, "Surplus Evil," 78.
17. Also attributed to Daniel T. Howard-Snyder as noted in Michael L. Peterson's, *God and Evil*, 72.
18. Carl F. Henry writes, "But how then can sin and apparently meaningless evil be reconciled with the biblical view of the sovereign, all-knowing God who is providentially at work in the space-time creation? Nowhere does the Judeo-Christian revelation say that the living God allows gratuitous evil" (*God, Revelation and Authority: The God who Stands and Stays, part II*, volume 6, 291).

PART I: The Tension of Theodicy

"dysteleological evil,"[19] and other similar terms. But the very nature of such a phylum prevents us from being quite sure that it exits. Our statements about it reflect our ignorance, more than its "existence."[20]

As I indicated in the introduction, gratuitous evil could be compared to the horizon problem in cosmology. The horizon of the visible universe is determined by the age of the universe and the speed of light. Our knowledge of the universe is limited in part by the ever expanding light-cone, which permits us to see gradually farther into the universe as time progresses, and our horizon expands. Similarly, we can only see so much of the earth from ground level, but our horizon is expanded when we stand on a tall mountain. So also, our knowledge of the purposes for which God actually uses evil is at least limited by our finitude, and also by our understanding of divine revelation. The assumption of theology is not that we will understand God fully, for his greatness is infinite, still we also expect that we will have increasing illumination from God over time; our "light cone" expands and our mountain perch from which we view him is higher. So, time potentially expands our ability to see beyond our current horizon and understand more of God's works, including the operation of Evil & Suffering in his creation. Purposes for some evil that seems gratuitous today will be understood later; everyone has had that experience.[21] And while we may never know the purposes of each instance of evil, there is no single evil for which we can say with authority, "That has no redeeming value in God's creation!" Our horizon is not God's and we must always be aware of the limitations of our perspective.

Similarly, gratuitous evil could also be understood as an application of the "God of the Gaps" theory.[22] According to this understanding of God, God is the sum of what we cannot explain, naturally. However, as our understanding of the workings of our universe grows, God is thereby diminished. But, as inappropriate as this model for God is, it may be quite appropriate for gratuitous evil: a "Gratuitous Evil of the Gaps" theory. So, evil for which we can discern a sufficient reason (or even a possible reason) should no longer be considered, "gratuitous," shrinking the phylum. It is still evil, but it is not gratuitous evil. Such would be expected if we are finite and can broaden our knowledge horizon. It certainly is the case that a newborn cannot understand any pain, but a child understands the purpose of some pain. And that

---

19. For example, Hick, *Evil and the God of Love*, 363.

20. It is ontologically difficult to speak of evil existing in any meaningful way. This will be considered later in this chapter.

21. A child experiences this in the parental first aid treatment of a skinned knee in which the pain of washing and disinfecting seems a pointless evil in itself.

22. The "God of the Gaps" theory is often attributed to Dietrich Bonhoeffer in *Letters and Papers from Prison* (311–2) in which he argues against God as a "stop gap," who does only those things for which we have, as yet, no naturalistic explanation. He writes, "It has again brought home to me quite clearly how wrong it is to use God as a stop-gap for the incompleteness of our knowledge. Here again, God is no stop-gap; he must be recognized at the centre of life, not when we are at the end of our resources."

understanding brings a certain relief. So also it continues to be for us. If the gratuitous gaps shrink with our increasing knowledge of God's purposes (possible and actual), the mathematical limit of this function would be zero and the phylum is potentially extinguished. In this view, gratuitous evil is that evil for which we cannot *yet* "see" a purpose. Such must be the case, even if our development is slow. So, also I would agree with Douglass Geivett when he writes, "It is far easier to be sure that God exists than it is to be sure that there really are gratuitous evils in the world. . . . The argument from gratuitous evil rests upon a mistake, and that is the mistake of thinking that we know there are gratuitous evils in the world. Arguably, only an omniscient being could know such a thing."[23]

I must also argue from the character of God that nothing he does (or allows) is pointless or meaningless, a corollary of the fact that he is good. Peter Hicks, who makes this same argument, concludes: "there is no such thing as a meaningless event or meaningless suffering in the Bible."[24] That is, the category of "gratuitous evil" is fundamentally specious. Still it must be retained in this project for purposes of discussion, because it communicates an idea. However, it will not be necessary to test my thesis against it for the reasons given.[25]

ON "NECESSITY" IN REGARD TO EVIL: A DEFINITION

I will investigate more completely the issue of necessity in regard to evil in Part II. Still, a general perspective and hints at what will come may be helpful for readers following my historical survey. What kind of necessity is intended by my phrase, "necessary evil"?

Considering necessity and contingency on a continuum, *metaphysical necessity* is found at one pole. Alfred Freddoso defines a metaphysical necessity in this way: "*s* is metaphysically necessary if and only if *s* obtains at every moment in every possible world."[26] This is simple enough; "*it must exist.*"[27] From most Christian theological perspectives,[28] this would include only God. Clearly "evil" is not necessary in the same

23. Geivett, *Evil and the Evidence for God*, 180–1.

24. Hicks, *Message of Evil & Suffering*, 23.

25. It would be necessary to do so if application of my thesis could be shown to make the perimeter of the "horizon" diverge instead of converge or remain unchanged. This will not be the case.

26. Alfred J. Freddoso, editor and translator, Luis de Molina, *On Divine Foreknowledge:* Part IV of The Concordia, 11.

27. This is over and against "metaphysical contingency" and "metaphysical impossibility." Freddoso writes, 's is metaphysically impossible if and only if S does not obtain at any moment in any possible world." Also, 's is metaphysically contingent if and only if S is neither metaphysically necessary nor metaphysically impossible" (11).

28. Of course, for the theonomist, even God's character is not a metaphysical necessity, but only God's being, so that his character is "freewheeling." What is good today may be evil tomorrow. This possibility will not be evaluated here.

sense in which God is necessary, otherwise the nature of "what is" would be dualistic; "evil" would be co-existent with "good" and with God. Such dualism is not biblically acceptable.[29]

Another kind of necessity is *natural necessity*. Freddoso defines it this way, "s is naturally necessary (or obtains by necessity of nature) at t if and only if s obtains at t by virtue of the world's having at t^* (at or before t) a deterministic natural tendency toward s at t."[30] Simply said; "*it exists, intrinsic to creation.*" Under such a definition, it seems hardly possible that evil could be a natural necessity, for the universe was declared good *in every way* when it was created. If this was the case, it would also be the case that God introduced evil into creation in some immediate way, making him the efficient cause of evil. This would be in direct contradiction with God's revealed character and claims.[31]

Rejecting these two types of necessity in regard to evil, we could consider *natural contingency*. This Freddoso defines as follows: "s is naturally contingent at t if and only if s is (i) metaphysically contingent, and (ii) accidentally contingent at t, and (iii) neither naturally necessary nor naturally impossible at t."[32] Simply put, "*it did not have to be, but it is.*" This could imply that contingency is used in the sense of happening by chance. Noting this, Jonathan Edwards helpfully writes, "But the word contingent is abundantly used in a very different sense; not for that whose connection with the series of things we cannot discern, so as to foresee the event, but for something which has absolutely no previous ground or reason, with which its existence has any fixed and certain connection."[33] For Edwards, an event is contingent in just this sense, that it arose not by accident, but was foreknown by God, planned for by God, and arose out of the creation, which was wholly conditioned by God's choices, even if his choices were not to grant it any extreme kind of freedom. This last point is important. No version of what is known as the Free Will Defense precludes evil from being contingent upon God because he sovereignly granted freedom (including the freedom for evil to arise); regardless of what reasons he had for doing so. If evil arose solely due to the freedom of God's willful-creatures, and if it was their will and not God's sovereignty that was responsible, then still God's foreknowing sovereignty granted that freedom. Only those who claim that God could not reasonably anticipate the introduction of evil could maintain that God is not responsible and few, even among free-will theists,

---

29. Dualism is fundamental to "Christian" Gnosticism and other abiblical systems in which what is good is not fundamental and unique, but in competition with a rival. Such would also be the case for ancient Babylonian cults as well as Hinduism.

30. Freddoso, editor and translator, *On Divine Foreknowledge*, 15. Conversely, 's is naturally impossible... deterministic natural tendency toward [S^*] at t."

31. That evil as an intrinsic part of creation is a tenet of consequentialist ethics, which this project rejects.

32. Freddoso, editor and translator, *On Divine Foreknowledge*, 16.

33. Jonathan Edwards, "Freedom of the Will," 1.3.27 (the scheme for indicating references to this work of Edwards is as follows: Part. Section. Un-numbered paragraphs of this edition).

would take this extreme position.[34] As a result, it would seem pointless to suggest that evil, even though contingent, arose with "absolutely no ground or reason" if God decreed salvation prior to even creating the world. Still, that in no way makes evil any kind of "necessity" as we would normally understand the word.

Here the poles of necessity and contingency meet. *Natural contingency* is very like accidental necessity, a class given to us by Ockham and defined by Freddoso: "This modality has to do neither with the natures of things nor with the arrangement of causes in the universe, but rather with the passage of time. For some metaphysically contingent states of affairs become necessary simply by virtue of being fixed unalterably as part of the history of the world, regardless of their causal ancestry."[35] *More simply, "It happened."* Evil and the corruption of God's perfect creation are accidental necessities. Again, while true, this is of little help to understanding evil's relationship to God or his creation.

So, evil is neither a metaphysical necessity, nor a natural necessity, but just like everything that arose in God's world, it is in some way contingent, so that from our vantage point in history, it is at least an accidental necessity. And, unless one is willing to restrict God's foreknowledge, what is an accidental necessity for us, is wholly known to God before creation when he also planned for our salvation from evil. Since God is the creator of all, and though all was created good, it was created with knowledge that as created, it would be corrupted. In doing so, I stipulate that God was free in himself to create or not to create, contra Leibniz and other rationalistic systems, for which there is little support today (making my stipulation somewhat "safe"). However, if I grant divine foreknowledge of evil and freedom for God to create or not create as he did create, God is the ultimate cause of the appearance of evil in this world because he could have suppressed evil by not creating. This is not to make God to be the efficient cause of evil,[36] nor to say that God did evil as the proximate cause of evil, but that evil is fundamental to our world "as God planned," though not "as God created." The creation he did make, though good, was destined to corruption. In that limited sense evil was necessary.

Granted these stipulations, I propose that the necessity of evil lies somewhere between metaphysical necessity and natural (intrinsic) contingency, specifically, in *subordinate-metaphysical necessity*. If I follow Freddoso's meter, *subordinate-metaphysical necessity*, could be defined as, "s is of *subordinate-metaphysical necessity* if

---

34. One exception is John Sanders who, in *God Who Risks: A Theology of Providence*, agrees with Paul Fiddes's comment concerning God's surprise at the turn of events when Adam and Eve rebel in the Garden, "Now God has to adjust his project in response to this horrible turn of events" (48). At the other extreme, freewill theist John Hick, who represents a putative Irenaean theodicy, sees evil as an instrumental necessity which is in some way intended by God. I reject both ideas. The vast majority of freewill theists would acknowledge God's foreknowledge of the introduction of evil—and so necessarily his mediate responsibility.

35. Freddoso, editor and translator, *On Divine Foreknowledge*, 13.

36. This is addressed at length in chapter 6.

PART I: The Tension of Theodicy

and only if *s* obtains in every created world created by God, conditioned by God's metaphysically necessary character and announced goals. So, more simply, "*it had to happen.*" This definition leaves much for discussion, including God's character and his goals, but I will return to these later.[37] However, because I assert that evil falls within this definition, it serves to make it clear that I understand that evil, while not a part of the initial creation, arose within creation as the intrinsic problem, resulting from creation, but not within creation as created. The contours and sense of this term may also be reflected by John Murray when he proposes *consequent-absolute necessity*.[38] He proposes this term to explain the reality that when God decided to create, the death of Christ became necessary: a consequent-absolute necessity. Surely the death of Christ is tightly related to the existence of evil. Similarly, I am arguing that evil in God's creation is not contingent upon anything other than that which is itself metaphysically necessary, God and his character, and, contingently and subordinate to God, his decision to create (without which no worlds obtain existence, and the discussion is pointless). That is, given the metaphysical necessity of God, his character, and his goals in creating the world, evil's occurrence is in a fundamental way, necessary.[39] It

---

37. Freddoso's modality of "natural necessity" is much tighter and might commend itself, but it is tied into a determinism which I reject in regard to the introduction of evil. Also, it is worth noting that this definition ignores the element of time and assumes a time interdependence for evil arising in God's world(s). It also, like the other definitions given, struggles to show examples of "other worlds."

38. Murray, *Redemption Accomplished and Applied*, 9–18. That is, God, having made the free choice to redeem, made the death of Christ an "absolute" necessity, a "consequent-absolute necessity" (12). The full quote explaining his choice of terms is worthwhile here: "The word 'consequent' in this designation points to the fact that God's will or decree to save any is of free and sovereign grace. To save lost men was not of absolute necessity but of sovereign good pleasure of God. The terms 'absolute necessity,' however, indicate that God, having elected some to everlasting life out of his mere good pleasure, was under the necessity of accomplishing its purpose though the sacrifice of his own Son, a necessity arising from the perfections of his own nature. In a word, while it was not inherently necessary for God to save, yet, since salvation has been purposed, it was necessary to secure this salvation through a satisfaction that could be rendered only through substitutionary sacrifice and blood-bought redemption" (12). It is also worth noting what John S. Feinberg calls Consequent Necessity: "once certain choices are made (by God or whomever) certain things follow as a consequence but before these choices are made, no inherent necessities dictate what must be chosen" and "an action is free, even if it is causally determined so long as it is non-constraining" (Feinberg, "God Ordains All Things," 23–24). This is not far from what I am suggesting. However, while Feinberg is looking at the micro-level of a specific choice, and here I agree, I am considering the macro-level of the necessary direction of movement for the universe. Each of Adam's choices remained wholly free, but the entrance of evil was a subordinate-metaphysical necessity.

39. Let me make one more observation about metaphysical necessity. It is conceivable that even this lofty concept of necessity might be applicable to "evil." That is, metaphysical necessity may not be as limited a concept as was accepted above. Jonathan Edwards defines it this way: "Metaphysical or philosophical necessity is nothing different from their certainty. I speak not now of the certainty of knowledge, but the certainty that is in things themselves, which is the foundation of the certainty of the knowledge, or that wherein lies the ground of the infallibility of the proposition which affirms them" (J. Edwards, *Freedom of the Will*, 1.3.5). This is of the class of things that is *de re*. That is, those things that are necessary *de re*, are necessary in regard to their being, not simply in regard to a verbal distinction of how we understand them to be, *de dicto* (*Oxford Companion of Philosophy*, 188). But Plantinga has little confidence in *de re* modality, saying, "it is a bit thin" because it can be reduced to *de*

is however true that this subordinate-metaphysical necessity that I am proposing will reflect no necessity upon God, but rather arises necessarily in his creation. In short, God does not need evil, yet it cannot be avoided given all that he intends.

AN HISTORICAL SURVEY OF THE DEVELOPMENT OF THE CONCEPT OF EVIL

Whatever evil is, God is its Lord.[40]

—Karl Barth

As we begin considering the development of our understanding of the concept of evil, it is worth noting that the Bible is comfortable with a great deal of ambiguity in regard to the origin of evil and the nature and origin of Satan. One could (should!) even believe that God intended ambiguity. But as ambiguous as it appears to be, there are some things that can be asserted: God did not create evil; we did; we do. Another way to say this is that we are created in God's image and likeness. Because we are like God, and ontologically distinct from God, this entails a kind of freedom; freedom from being God. As humans, in his image, but not God, we failed to will to conform to his holy, perfect, and good standard, (which exists only in him who is God and not in us). I will propose, in agreement with many, that it was in this gap that evil was and is born.

In addition, two concepts deeply affect how the nature and origin of evil is understood. First, many Christian thinkers work diligently to create a system in which the goodness of God is preserved, untainted by the contingent existence of evil and, by corollary, often attack their opponent's position for failing to do that in an adequate way. Second, Christian thinkers always relate the origin of evil, and to some extent its nature, to the exercise of the will of God's willful creatures within their Libertarian Free-Will or Compatibilistic Free-Will understanding. In so saying, we remember that regardless of the systematic understanding of the nature of free-will, God's willful creatures are indeed still willful and that will make their response to God and his goodness (and God's sovereignty) distinct from that of a "rock" (that which has only being) or a "squirrel" (that which has only being and life). No distinctly Christian system is fatalistic; no Christian system is independent of God's sovereignty. The nature and origin of evil must in some way be built upon the goodness of God and in the context of the author's system of free-will.

---

dicto modality by "formula" (*Nature of Necessity*, 15–23). As true as this is on the surface, such reasoning may miss reality. That an expression can be formulaically translated to *de dicto* modality does not affect the thing itself. It is merely an observation about either our creativity or perhaps our naiveté. So, Edwards intends not that this modality is only that limited class of things which is self-existent, but also includes that which must certainly exist because of those things that are self-existent, evil might fit neatly within his definition. Yet, to avoid confusion, and to allay at least a few objections, I will use a different term as proposed: subordinate-metaphysical necessity.

40. Barth, *CD*, IV.1, §60.1 "Pride and Fall of Man," 408.

PART I: The Tension of Theodicy

Evil in the Early Fathers

To understand the Early Fathers' perspectives on evil also requires that we recall the philosophical topography of the centuries following Christ. The materialistic stoicism of the day understood evil as only apparent (not part of the only reality, matter) and that it is to be conquered by acting in accord with wisdom ("logos," also understood materially) for which an indefinite "time" (number of cycles) was given to achieve perfection.[41] Though all is infinitely divisible, all that is real (including God) is matter and is one—monism.[42] In opposition, dualism, and Gnostic dualism in particular,[43] held God (or a god) and goodness at one pole and evil, as substantive, at the opposite pole, along with all matter.[44] The Early Fathers of the church (and not a few of those who followed them) interacted with these worldviews as they wrestled with the concept of evil as well as all the rest of their theology. These two basic concepts affect our understanding of evil, for even today the discussion continues to be refracted through these philosophical glasses with their two very different lenses.

Tertullian (c.160–c.230, Quintus Septimius Florens Tertullianus) of Carthage converted late in life to Christianity, and later still to Montanism. He was the first to explicitly state the Trinitarian teaching that the Father and Son are not the same person. They are two distinct persons, three with the Holy Spirit, possessing one nature.[45] It is in this context that he argued against Marcion and in doing so wrestled with the origin and nature of evil. He observed that Marcion's God was the originator of evil, writing:

> Now . . . while morbidly brooding over the question of the origin of evil, his perception became blunted by the very irregularity of his researches; . . . that God is the author of evil, so he now applied to the Creator the figure of the corrupt tree bringing forth evil fruit, that is, moral evil, and then presumed

---

41. Mautner, *Dictionary of Philosophy*, 410. The "stiff-upper-lip" understanding of stoicism comes from the idea that suffering, of the kind which cannot be avoided, should be endured without passion as part of the valuable experience in coming into conformity with the *logos*.

42. Hicks, *Journey So Far*, 73–75.

43. The Manicheans are an example. Founded by Mani (216–c.276), a Persian who was trained in Zoroastrianism and syncretistically followed Christ.

44. Mautner, *Dictionary of Philosophy*, 169.

45. He writes, "three coherent Persons, who are yet distinct One from Another" (Tertullian, *Against Praxis*, in *Ante-Nicene Fathers*, chapter 25, volume 3). As noted by Moltmann, Tertullian is using the word, "substance" as opposed to "nature": "*una substantia—tres personae*" (Jürgen Moltmann, *Trinity and the Kingdom*, 177). It is also worth noting that as he exposited this in *Against Praxis* (see especially chapter 5), his understanding of history of the Son is distinct from the position of an eternal, personal Son. Reason, not yet properly the Word or the Son, while pre-existent was not fully distinct from the Father. While against the heresies of his day, Tertullian held Reason to be clearly distinct from the Father, he did not take position that the Son was eternally distinct in personhood. Reason was actually "in God" in the same sense that Reason is in us. He was the Word in the sense that our Reasons discourse with us. It was only "when" the Word proceeded from the Father that the Son became also the person of the Son and created the world.

that there ought to be another god, after the analogy of the good tree producing its good fruit.[46]

Tertullian rejected Marcion's dualism because it opposed the biblical (Trinitarian) requirement of only one God, possessing only one nature. He declared Marcion's position to be unstable, resulting in the generation of many "gods." One God must be good, holy, just, and merciful. The other quite different:

> Such must be the sentence to be pronounced against Marcion's god: tolerant of evil, encouraging wrong, wheedling about his grace, prevaricating in his goodness, which he did not exhibit simply on its own account, but which he must mean to exhibit purely, if he is good by nature and not by acquisition, if he is supremely good in attribute and not by discipline.[47]

A strong Trinitarian position is a "protection" against multiple gods.[48] YHWH stands alone, above his universe with no competitors. All that is true of God must be true of the One God. There is no other. Whether Tertullian proposed his own unique understanding of the nature and origin of evil is unclear, but his development of the Trinitarian theology was an early hedge against dualism and Monarchianism.

In the same battle, Clement of Alexandria (c.150–c.220) attempted to reach his Gnostic neighbors and help them to re-establish their philosophical faith as a faith based on biblical revelation and philosophy. He was seeking a way to bridge the contradiction of life: a holy God and a terrible evil. In that context he held that evil is a privation of goodness; it is not something, but something that is not. As a pothole is the absence of the road and as darkness is the absence of light, so evil is the absence of what is proper. Clement writes, "Where the face of the Lord looks, there is peace and rejoicing; but where it is averted, there is the introduction of evil."[49] In so doing he was seeking not only to answer the question, but to contextualize his Gospel to his dualistic audience.[50] His answer, a privative nature for evil, was not a toothless

---

46. Tertullian, *Against Marcion*, in *Ante-Nicene Fathers*, volume 3, 1.2.

47. Ibid,. volume 3, 1.22.

48. So also the Tertullian Trinity stands against the heresy of Praxeas who defended Monarchianism—Christ is the Father and the Father is Christ: "And so, most foolish heretic, you make Christ to be the Father" (Tertullian, *Against Praxis*, in *Ante-Nicene Fathers*, chapter 28).

49. Cited by Floyd, *Clement of Alexandria's Treatment of the Problem of Evil*, 21. Floyd explains, for Clement "evil is not some thing but a deprivation of that which is essentially good. . . . this absence of good."

50. For Clement the true Gnostic is the true Christian. He wrote to this effect repeatedly. One example is in Book 2 of his *Miscellanies*, "Well, then, if the Lord is the truth, and wisdom, and power of God, as in truth He is, it is shown that the real Gnostic is he that knows Him, and His Father by Him" (Chapter 11). However, the true Gnostic was not a theistic dualist, but knew One God: "For in everything love attends the Gnostic, who knows one God. 'And, behold, all things which He created were very good.' "(Chapter 12). So also here we are reminded that all that is, is created good by the One God. Evil then is something else—or rather is not a substance of creation (quotes from *Ante-Nicene Fathers*, volume 2) It would appear that he wanted to make them "redeemed Gnostics."

compromise. Correct or not, it was a hearty answer, which although it established a difficult contradiction, real suffering and only a *privative* evil, "his" privative evil was so violent that he understood the first evil, the Fall, to be the interruption in man's progress from the "likeness" of God to the "image" of God.⁵¹

It is this primitive, privative understanding of the nature of evil that was developed by Origen (185–254). Like Clement, he understood freedom from a libertarian perspective, so it is not surprising that he also understood all people to be born with an equal and God-given ability (for only God is good, essentially) to freely do what is either good or evil. He wrote, "we have often shown that souls are by their nature capable of good and evil."⁵² He shows this by example in his exposition of Romans 9:13–14 in which Paul addresses the distinction between Jacob and Esau. In this, Origen turns Paul's argument on its head,⁵³ when he claims this passage shows that it was wholly up to Jacob and Esau to respond to the equal potential for good and evil to which they were born. He writes,

> A different position of service is prepared by the Creator for each one in proportion to the degree of his merit, which depends on the fact that each, in being created by God as a mind or rational spirit, has personally gained for himself, in accordance with the movements of his mind and the disposition of his heart, a greater or less share of merit, and has rendered himself either lovable or it may be hateful to God.⁵⁴

This example of Jacob and Esau is representative for Origen, not exceptional; he applies it to all people. He writes, "I think it right that the same sentiment should be employed in considering the case of all creatures, since, as we said above, the righteousness of the Creator ought be apparent in all."⁵⁵ So, for Origen, evil is something that we "do"; it is the doing of evil that determines that we are hated by God. Conversely, it is

---

51. Floyd, in *Clement of Alexandria's Treatment of the Problem of Evil*, writes, "Now it was Clement's opinion that the Fall interrupted man's progress in this creative process of arranging himself after the 'divine likeness'" (92). This idea becomes important for Irenaeus and later John Hick in the development of their theodicies.

52. Origen, *On First Principles*, 2.6.5. In this particular quote, Origen is concerned with explaining the impeccability of Christ. His emphatic summary statement of his position on good and evil in all men is particularly helpful. This point is emphasized repeatedly. For example: "Our contention is, however, that among all relational creatures there is none which is not capable of both good and evil. But it does not necessarily follow that, because we say there is no nature which cannot admit evil, we therefore affirm that every nature has admitted evil, that is, has become evil. Just as we may say that every human nature posses the capacity to become a sailor, and yet this will not result in every man becoming a sailor;" (1.8.3, Latin only). Another example: "He created all his creatures equal and alike, for the simple reason that there was in him no cause that could give rise to variety and diversity" (2.9.6, Latin only).

53. John Piper has an excellent extended exegesis of this text which he develops in a single chapter of his published dissertation: *Justification of God: An Exegetical and Theological Study of Romans 9:1–23*, 151–81.

54. Origen, *On First Principles*, 2.9.7 (Latin only).

55. Ibid., 2.9.7 (Latin only).

resisting evil, or the positive doing of what is good, that gains for us "merit" with the result that we are loved by God.

But what is evil for Origen? He speaks often of evil as the "opposite" of good. For example, arguing with opponents in regard to a point in regard to the nature of justice, he writes,

> Let us add also the following remarks, which are necessitated by their subtle arguments. If the just is different from the good, then since evil is the opposite of good and unjust of just, undoubtedly the unjust will be different from the evil; and as the just man according to you is not good, so neither will the unjust man be evil; and again, as the good man is not just, so also the evil man will not be unjust.[56]

The content of evil is that which is not good. So it would seem that he is asserting that evil is a privation. This becomes clearer from his many positive arguments that evil is born when we do not do what is good, while not arguing for good to be similarly born. So he writes:

> Now to withdraw from the good is nothing else than to be immersed in evil; for it is certain that to be evil means to be lacking in good. Hence it is that in whatever degree one declines from the good, one descends into an equal degree of wickedness. And so each mind, neglecting the good either more or less in proportion to its own movements, was drawn to the opposite of good, which undoubtedly is evil.[57]

"Evil" is "withdrawing" from God's goodness; it is a privation.[58] Still, it is worth noting that Origen also saw evil, at times, as rather "substantive," especially in regard to the devil, who has himself become "evil." Yet, though this appears somewhat inconsistent, it is not necessarily an idea in conflict with itself. It must be recalled that he is both avoiding the Gnostic notion of evil as a substance in opposition to God, and the Stoic concept of evil as insubstantial, even imaginary. So, he affirms: that which is evil exists as a deprivation of goodness and it is still very real.

This, along with the foregoing discussion, also raises another interesting point. Evil for Origen is understood not only as the sinful act, but as a potential. That is, at birth no one has sinned, but we have a potential for evil. Would Origen then distinguish between "evil" and "sin"? He may be saying, "Evil is the potential for sin." If that is the case, evil is the potential and sin is the outworking of the potential, but that would not fit neatly with all that he claimed about evil. Nevertheless, we are left with

---

56. Origen, *On First Principles*, 2.5.3 (Latin only).

57. Ibid., 2.9.2 (Latin only).

58. We might also add such evidence as J. C. Smith, in *Ancient Wisdom of Origen*, who cites his translation of Origen's Commentary on John (2.13), "all evil is nothing, since it is also non-being," as well as other quotes from this section of the commentary (74).

PART I: The Tension of Theodicy

a question: Are "evil" and "sin" to be distinguished?[59] But what is clear from this brief survey of representatives of this era is that the lines between dualism and privation are not as sharp and distinct as one might desire. However, these two positions seem to represent the fundamental positions then available to the philosopher-theologian in regard to the nature of evil.

Evil As a Habit: Pelagius

Here perhaps, in Pelagius (354–418), something other than dualism or privation can be found as the nature of evil. As we saw when we examined his position in regard to freedom, Pelagius understands that evil arises as a corruption of free-will and is recovered by free-will's right exercise. That is, for Pelagius, all possess a "natural innocence"[60] which permits the will the capacity to do either good or evil. Augustine wrote, citing Pelagius, "he asserts that, whether we will or not, we have the capacity of not sinning—a capacity which he declares to be inherent in our nature."[61] And this capacity is there whether or not we use it, just as a man may or may not walk, but still he has the capacity to do so. This perspective would make evil merely a habit, and one which we can break by right application of our effort and God's help. So, Robert

---

59. It is worth considering the contribution of Plotinus (205–270) and his disciple, Porphyry (c.232–c.304). They were dualists who understood evil to be embodied by matter itself, though such matter is quite different than our modern scientific conception, though created, and it borders on non-being (Hick, *Evil and the God of Love*, 47). Hick also notes that it is difficult to discern Plotinus's position on evil. Plotinus might be saying it is a deprivation. The point is disputed. The origin of this evil substance is the defection of the particular created-soul from the World-Soul, though this understanding is debated. Michael Lloyd makes this argument in "The Cosmic Fall and the Free Will Defence," 110–11. Interestingly, Lloyd notes that N.P. Williams, who follows Plotinus, moves the Fall from individual souls to the World-Soul, nearly bumping the Fall into the Godhead, though he does insist that the World-Soul to which he subscribes is created and personal. Nonetheless, in his system, all emanates from The One, through Reason, through Soul and finally to matter and created-souls which are evil. Evil, then, is substantive. But Hick notes that such a conclusion may not be so clear. Citing several characteristic passages, he supports the majority view cited above. More subtly, he notes that evil in Plotinus is, "the absence of order, which when isolated by abstract thought becomes the foe of order" (Hick, *Evil and the God of Love*, 49). The quote cited is from Dean Inge in his Gifford Lectures. He makes it clear that this is not simply a random reflection of Plotinus that is off-center for his normal thinking, but rather a deeply seated idea. Hick writes, "And this too is a response to a real feature of the Plotinian system, perhaps even representing its dominant emphasis and tendency." That is, evil is not a positive power of resistance to goodness, but a lack of good order, which is evil. This understanding, he would claim, is more of a privation. The solution to this difficulty may not be as important as the fact that it highlights the difficulty understanding not only evil, but what it means to say that evil is a privation. If Hick is correct, even a strong dualist slips not only into privationist language, but seems to require privative ideas to support his dualism.

60. R. F. Evans, *Pelagius: Inquiries and Reappraisals*, 93. This is also cited by B. B. Warfield in his introduction to volume 5 of *A Select Library of Nicene and Post-Nicene Fathers of the Christian Church* (book 1, chapter 57) when he quotes Julian of Eclanium, "God creates men obnoxious to no (sic) sin, but full of natural innocence, and with capacity for voluntary virtues."

61. Augustine, "On Nature and Grace," chapter 57 ("It Does Not Detract from God's Almighty Power, that He is Incapable of Either Sinning, or Dying, or Destroying Himself").

F. Evans wrote of Pelagius's understanding of evil, "the power which sin holds over men is the power of habit."[62] Evil is an unfortunate turning from the path which can be corrected, per Pelagius, by the "help" of Christ—turning us again to the right path. At root, the only real power of sin over people is that of a well-worn path from which everyone (not just anyone) can depart at any time for the right path.

Pelagius is distancing himself from Manichean dualism:[63] nothing of significance opposes God or even the people he created—they are free, under grace, to sin or not sin.[64] So, B.B. Warfield cites Pelagius, "Nothing that is good and evil, on account of which we are either praiseworthy or blameworthy, is born with us—it is rather done by us; for we are born with capacity for either, but provided with neither."[65] But his was a reaction against not only the Manicheans's dualism, but also against what seemed to him to be Augustine's "baptizing" of some of their teaching. This included Augustine's strong stance against (what we would call) Libertarian Free-Will. This, Pelagius feared, made God directly responsible for evil. That is, a just God would not require us to live up to a command or standard of holiness, unless we were able to do so. So, Augustine quotes Pelagius as writing, "that God is as good as just, and made man such that he was quite able to live without the evil of sin, if only he had been willing."[66]

But if evil is not a great power set against God, and if we are actually free to obey with God's "help," then what is the nature of evil for Pelagius? It is not a privation, but a defect of will. For Pelagius, evil seems to be the substance of the action of the will which fails to serve well under the "help" given to us by God. Such a substantive position is not to say that sin is tangible and certainly not part of God's good creation. But it also is not the absence of something. It is rather the positive failure of the creaturely free-will.

Though Pelagianism was condemned by the church in various counsels, first in Carthage (418) and then in Ephesus (431),[67] still semi-Pelagianism (though itself condemned at the Council of Orange in 529) continues to have a great influence in

---

62. Evans, *Pelagius: Inquiries and Reappraisals*, 100.

63. Pelagius seemed to think that Augustine was something of a repackaged Manichean. For example in regard to the original sin (Evans, *Pelagius: Inquiries and Reappraisals*, 97). So also Augustine saw in Pelagius a tendency to steer so sharply away from the obvious ditch on one side of the road that he falls into a nearby ditch which is even murkier. He writes, "He shows too great a fire against this evil." This evil being false claims against which Pelagius and Augustine would concur (Augustine, "On Nature and Grace," chapter 1 ("The Occasion of Publishing This Work; What God's Righteousness is")).

64. Augustine quotes the Pelagian bishops' letter when he writes, "That God is the Maker of all those that are born, and that the sons of men are God's work; and that all sin descends not from nature, but from the will" ("Against the Two Letters of the Pelagians," 4.2). That is, we have no bent to sin and are free to obey from our will aided by grace.

65. From "Introduction to the Pelagian Controversy," in *A Select Library of Nicene and Post-Nicene Fathers*, series 1, volume 5.

66. Augustine, "On Nature and Grace," chapter 50 ("God Commands No Impossibilities").

67. R. K. McGregor Wright, *No Place for Sovereignty*, 20.

PART I: The Tension of Theodicy

the church.[68] Such semi-Pelagianism may also include a sense that evil is not privative, but substantial, the sin itself, and arises from those times when our free-will does not do its duty.

Evil as a Privation of God's Goodness: Augustine

When Augustine (354–430) considered the nature and origin of evil, he agonized. He wrote in *Confessions*, "Who made me? Is not my God not only good, but the supreme good? Why then have I the power to will evil and to reject good?"[69] He also wrote quite dramatically, "I searched for the origin of evil, but I searched in a flawed way and did not see the flaw in my very search. . . . But being God, God created good creatures. . . . Then where and whence is evil? How did it creep in?"[70] Similarly in *The Free Choice of the Will* he asked, "Whence do we evil?" and explained, this "drove me, tired out, to associate with heretics [RAS: Manicheans]."[71] His question about the nature and origin of evil was the most enduring and challenging question throughout his lifetime.[72] Indeed, given that God is good, it seems most strange, and not only to Augustine, that evil could exist at all. But, as early as these first two major works,[73] having been freed from the hold of the Manicheans, Augustine began to define and defend a view of evil that held its origin is in the will of God's willful creatures who depart from God's goodness, and its nature is privative.

His argument in *Confessions* might be outlined in this way. (1) Evil is not a substance because substances were created good.[74] (2) No substance exists that was not

---

68. Just as we are born self-centered as babies, we are all born "Pelagian," thinking that there is something we can contribute to our own salvation. So the official denunciation of this position has only limited effect. Evans defined semi-Pelagianism as that position which arises from a discomfort with Augustine's election while hoping to find a way which is not Pelagian (Gillian Rosemary Evans, *Augustine on Evil*, 171). This is not easily accomplished. The position of Council of Orange, still official position of the Roman Church and the Reformers, is that "the grace of God is something which needs to be accepted by the men to whom it is offered, but this acceptance is itself an action which can only be performed with the assistance of God's grace" (C. J. F. Williams, "Where the Semipelagians went Wrong," 21). Taking this as an adequate summary of Orange, the semi-Pelagian is the person who insists that acceptance of a gift requires no grace, for the gift itself is grace enough to preserve God's sovereignty. Per Williams this argument is subject to the accusation of infinite regression since each grace needs another grace to accept as well as offer. So the semi-Pelagian says, "When we allow God to give us something we do not thereby give him something" (24) and this Williams claims to be fairly in accord with Paul in 1 Corinthians 4:7, "What do you have that you did not receive?" He argues that this simple, not regressive definition should be allowed.

69. Augustine, *Confessions*, 7.3(5).
70. Augustine, *Confessions*, 7.5(7).
71. Augustine, *Free Choice of the Will*, 1.2.
72. Rist, *Augustine: Ancient Thought Baptized*, 261.
73. Augustine, *Free Choice of the Will* written, 388–95, and *Confessions* between 397–400.
74. He wrote, evil "is not a substance, for if it were a substance, it would be good" (*Confessions*, 7.12(18)).

The Historical Development of the Concept of Evil

created.[75] (3) So, as a substance, evil does not have existence.[76] (4) But evil, though not a substance, exists because the human will does not align with God's goodness.[77]

What does he mean by this? We begin at the end with the assertion that God is good in some fundamental way: God is good by nature; He is the source of goodness. So Augustine intends when he writes, "Is not my God not only good but the supreme good?" By this he does not mean, "God is good all the time." To say this would be to imply that there is some mechanism by which God conforms to "goodness." But there is no external standard of goodness. Nor is he saying, "God is intrinsically valuable." That would reduce God to a useful commodity which is wholly inconsistent with Augustine. Instead, Augustine is saying that God's very character is goodness itself. Of God's goodness in *City of God*, he writes, God "is the fountain of our happiness. He is the end of all our desires."[78] What good flows into God's creation, to be observed by his creatures, and all that he does which is observed by none but himself, is all flowing from the fountain of goodness that is characteristically God. This is a given for Augustine's argument.

Now, going back to the beginning, he asserts that evil is not a substance. He says, "Evil has no existence except as a privation of the good."[79] And, "Accordingly, whatever things exist are good, and the evil into whose origins I was inquiring is not a substance, for if it were a substance, it would be good."[80] To exist is to be God or to be created by God; to be a substance is to be created by God. As is established above, God is good and as Augustine and the Bible testify, all that God made, all substances (including persons), are created good. There is no substance that does not conform to God's goodness in its creation. Evil therefore does not exist as a substance. Yet, evil appears in God's good creation. It happens in this way: people, created in God's image, have no source and no fountain of goodness within. A person could not be such a

---

75. This is implied in his writings for he assumes this fact from John 1:1–3.

76. He wrote, "For you evil does not exist at all, and not only for you but for your created universe" (*Confessions*, 7.13(19)). And he wrote, "Evil has no existence except as a privation of the good" (*Confessions*, 3.7(12)).

77. He wrote, "free choice of the will is the reason why we do wrong" (*Confessions*, 7.3(5)). And he wrote, Evil is "a perversity of will twisted away from the highest substance, you O God" (*Confessions*, 7.16(22)). Edward B. Pusey has a different translation of this, "And I enquired what iniquity was, and found it to be substance, but the perversion of the will, turned aside from Thee." I am inclined to think this a typographical error in his text because of the contrasting conjunction, "but" in regard to "substance." That is, Augustine is saying, "and found it to be no substance, but the perversion of the will" (*The Confessions of Saint Augustine*, 7.16, Kindle Edition, originally published Springfield, OH: Collier Books, 1961).

78. Augustine, *City of God*, 10.3. It should be recalled that *City of God* is written in response to the sack of Rome by Alaric in August 410. He is not writing of God's easy bounty. Indeed the opening chapters of this work are dedicated to how the Christian virgin is to respond to the horrendous personal evil of rape.

79. Augustine, *Confessions*, 3.7(12).

80. Ibid., 7.12(18).

PART I: The Tension of Theodicy

fountain of goodness, for God is the unique source of goodness.[81] So a person can only cooperate with God's goodness. Unless God sovereignly chose to sustain his willful creatures in obedience, and Augustine affirmed that he did not do so, humanity falls. So, Augustine says, it is by free-will that we deviated from God's goodness, saying, "free choice of the will is the reason why we do wrong."[82] This deviation of the will from God's goodness gave birth to evil and has continued to do so. He writes, "For evil has no positive nature; but the loss of good has received the name evil."[83] That is, evil is born from a lack of goodness in the choice of the will, a privation.[84] Evil is born when the soul becomes its own satisfaction—a place too small for God's goodness to dwell.[85] This leads to a question. What is the cause of the will's defection? Augustine writes:

> If the further question be asked, What was the efficient cause of their evil will? there is none. For what is it which makes the will bad, when it is the will itself which makes the action bad? And consequently the bad will is the cause of the bad action, but nothing is the efficient cause of the bad will. For if anything is the cause, this thing either has or has not a will. . . . and that we may not go on for ever, I ask at once, what made the *first* evil will bad? . . . I ask if it has been existing in some nature.[86]

We can answer his latter question quite clearly from what he has previously told us: he intends to assert that evil did not exist in the nature of the will as created. And in regard to the efficient cause of the first evil will, it was a result of failure of the will to conform to God's goodness.

Now, considering this answer, and before wrestling with the implications of a privative nature of evil for Augustine, we should consider the origin. The origin of evil is in God's willful-creatures.[87] Yet, when Augustine writes that its origin is in "the free choice of the will" his words sounds much like those of Pelagius. As we have seen

---

81. In fact, Augustine says just the opposite. We are actually "fountains of evil which spring out of defeat rather than superfluity" (*Enchiridion on Faith, Hope and Love*, ¶ 24, 31).

82. Augustine, *Confessions*, 7.3(5).

83. Augustine, *City of God*, 11.9.

84. It should be understood here that there is a distinction between the will, which is good and a "substance" in the sense that it was created by God, and the creaturely exercise of the will. Geivett writes, "Augustine's account depends upon a subtle distinction between the having of human free will and the exercise of human free will. The former obtains through divine agency, the latter through human agency" (Geivett, *Evil and the Evidence for God*, 15).

85. Augustine, *City of God*, 14.12–13.

86. Ibid., 12.6.

87. This position is a rejection of dualism. It is also worth noting that dualism is rightly precluded on grounds of symmetry. He writes, "Accordingly, there is nothing of what we call evil, if there be nothing good. But a good which is wholly without evil is a perfect good. A good, on the other hand, which contains evil is a faulty or imperfect good; and there can be no evil where there is no good." And, "good, however, can exist without evil" (Augustine, *Enchiridion on Faith, Hope and Love*, ¶ 13, (13) and ¶ 14 (15)). Such an asymmetrical relationship and parasitic dependence of evil upon good, precludes dualism. And this gets us close to the very challenge that God presents himself in creation.

The Historical Development of the Concept of Evil

above, the function of the free-will is understood to be of one of two mechanisms; we cooperate with God's goodness either by a Compatibilistic Free-Will or a Libertarian Free-Will understanding of the nature of the will. Augustine's position could be described in my terminology as Compatibilistic Free-Will, though again, such terminology is used here for convenience in tracing ideas and is not wholly accurate if forced upon Augustine.[88] But for Augustine, true liberty (a liberty that God uniquely enjoys) is not understood either by compatibilistic freedom nor by libertarian freedom, for neither is tied to God's goodness. There is a greater liberty, a liberty to choose God's goodness alone and God's goodness always, a liberty even Adam did not posses.[89] This, without dispute, radically distinguishes him from Pelagius.[90] But it is even more important to note, as did Augustine, that Pelagian free-will requires that God's human willful-creatures are themselves a source of God's goodness.[91] So, the origin of evil is found in the free-will of Adam[92] and continues in the denatured free-will of all willful creatures who followed.[93]

If the privative nature of evil is easily stated, its exact implications are not as clear. For context, it should be understood that this position did not originate with

---

88. Though some would argue his Compatibilistic Free-Will-like position matured over time from a Libertarian Free-Will-like position, I have shown in Chapter 1 reasons to consider that the change was one of semantics, not of position. In any case, there is general agreement that Augustine's final position is Compatibilistic Free-Will-like.

89. Rist writes of Augustine, "Libertas . . . is the God given freedom to choose the good alone" (*Augustine: Ancient Thought Baptized*, 278). Augustine, speaking of the ultimate freedom that we will enjoy in eternity, says we will always choose the good, "and yet this will constitute no restriction on the freedom of his will. On the contrary, his will shall be much freer when it shall be wholly impossible for him to be the slave of sin" (Augustine, *Enchiridion on Faith, Hope and Love*, ¶ 105, 123).

90. It may also be significant that Augustine clearly separates the act of the body from the motion of the will. He writes, "The wicked deed, then — that is to say, the transgression of eating the forbidden fruit — was committed by persons who were already wicked. That 'evil fruit' could be brought forth only by 'a corrupt tree.' But that the tree was evil was not the result of nature; for certainly it could become so only by the vice of the will, and vice is contrary to nature" (Augustine, *City of God*, 14.13). Pelagius may emphasize too much the actual commission of evil acts as opposed to the person (in this case Adam) becoming evil before acting evil.

91. Evans wrote, "Pelagius's hypothesis was that if a man can make himself evil by a wrong exercise of his will, he can make himself good by a right exercise of his will. Augustine found two serious faults in this view: it implies that a man can himself be the source of good, and that is a creative act Augustine held to lie with God alone; and it takes no account of the effect Adam's sin had upon all his descendants" (Evans, *Augustine on Evil*, 121). Ignoring the second here, the first fault is well noted!

92. In Augustine, Adam's free-will was of a somewhat different character than that of all who followed. He wrote, as a caveat to *Free Choice of the Will*, "When we speak then, of the will free to do right, we speak of the will in which man first was made" (Augustine, *Free Choice of the Will*, 3.18). Note also that the loss of God's goodness and the origin of evil lies with the fallen angels (Augustine, *City of God*, 11.11) and with Satan (11.17) as well.

93. In *Free Choice of the Will*, Augustine writes, "Either therefore the will itself is the first cause of sin, or else there is no first cause of sin" (3.17). This is expanded and explained in 3.22, but it will serve no purpose here to further explicate; the point is clear.

PART I: The Tension of Theodicy

Augustine, but he was simply the first to give it significant development.[94] But to say evil is of no substance and results from a privation of God's goodness leaves much open to interpretation and misinterpretation. Two current examples will suffice to show the scope of the misunderstanding.

For example, J.S. Whale, a predecessor of John Hick, wrote that privation is "a philosophical theory which explains that experience away by denying that evil is real. Evil exists only as a semblance; it is the negation or privation of good."[95] With this statement he hopes to dismiss privation as foolishness by choosing to understand Augustine as denying evil's reality. Hick, a philosophical adversary of Augustine, still rejects this shallow understanding. He writes, "The privative doctrine is not offered by Augustine, Aquinas, Leibniz or others in the same tradition, as a solution to the problem of evil. All that it does is to rule out a dualist solution and thereby to advance the definition of the problem a stage by posing the question, How does privation of good come about in a universe that is created and ruled by a good God?"[96] Hick is quite right. As he puts it, Augustine has rightly placed a "No Thoroughfare" sign over the dualistic option.[97]

Another, David Ray Griffin, argues that, ultimately, the Augustinian solution is to reject the reality of evil. He argues that in *City of God*, Augustine states that there is no "natural evil" and takes this to mean that "there is nothing whose 'nature' is evil, nothing that is 'naturally' bad . . . there is no genuine evil in the universe below the level of creatures with freedom."[98] That is, there is no "natural evil" and for Augustine, this leaves only "sin, or evil willing." Thus far, Griffin gives us a correct understanding of Augustine. Yet he is reductionistic and not fair to Augustine when he disposes of this as genuine evil in Augustine's system saying, "suffering, is never genuinely evil, for it is always a just punishment for sin . . . accordingly there is no genuine evil in reality."[99] However, in context, this citation from *City of God* (11.22) means that "there is nothing whose nature is created evil." This is in keeping with his understanding that a good God created a good world. Augustine's point is not that evil is nothing, and certainly not that evil is neutral, redeemable, or merely apparent. Quite the opposite. Instead, he is asserting that he trusts a good God in the face of terrible and privative evil. Yet, it is not so simple to defend Augustine. Charles T. Mathewes notes that some charge that "Augustine's ontological account of evil as privation elides the reality of

---

94. M. B. Ahern notes, "Catholic philosophers usually solve this difficulty through the privation theory of the nature of evil which was proposed in elementary form by Aristotle and developed by Christian thinkers like Augustine and Aquinas" (Ahern, "Note on the Nature of Evil," 17).

95. Whale, *Christian Answer to the Problem of Evil*, 58.

96. Hick, *Evil and the God of Love*, 187.

97. Still, Hick may not give Augustine's privative argument sufficient weight. Geivett notes that that Hick criticizes Augustinian privation as not adequately accounting for the "positive and powerful" reality of evil (Geivett, *Evil and the Evidence for God*, 42).

98. Griffin, "Augustinian Theodicy," 212.

99. Ibid.

The Historical Development of the Concept of Evil

evil in a glibly triumphalist (and escapist) manner."[100] To such as these, someone could cite Augustine's writing about evil in *Confessions*,

> Then where and whence is evil? How did it creep in? What is its root and what is its seed? *Or does it not have any being? Why should we fear and avoid what has no being?* If our fear is vain, it is certain that fear itself is evil, and that the heart is groundlessly disturbed and tortured. And this evil is the worse for the fact that it has no being to be afraid of. Yet we still fear. (emphasis mine).[101]

If Augustine meant that we need not fear evil *because* it is toothless, it would be against our common experience and biblical teaching. Psalm 23 tells us that the only reason David could find for not fearing evil was the presence of God. So also, "He will not fear evil tidings; His heart is steadfast, trusting in the LORD."[102] Much of the message of the Bible and of our own experience is that evil is capable of great damage to our bodies and souls. But perhaps, and in context, Augustine was only musing. In this particular chapter of his *Confessions* we find wonderings and heart rending cries to God for clarity, all introduced by "I searched in a flawed way and did not see the flaw in my very search." It seems very unlikely that this is an expression of his position and nowhere else does he speak of evil as powerless *because* it is privative in nature.

Therefore I claim that it is a misunderstanding of Augustine, even a gross distortion, to assume or assert that a privative nature of evil is a denial of evil's reality or evil's power. That is not the position of Augustine or Aquinas (or even Origen or Leibniz) and is in fact much closer to the non-privative position of Pelagius. It is more likely that the position of Pseudo-Dionysius (late fifth century CE) is reflected back on Augustine. He sounds very much like Augustine in that he asserts that evil's nature is privative. However, unlike Augustine, his understanding of evil was so "privative," that it is almost something that can be dismissed.[103] His shadow should not fall over Augustine. Geivett maintains, "By calling evil a privation Aquinas [RAS: or Augustine] is not denying the reality of evil."[104] Augustine has established a robust but privative evil, over and against a substantive and dualistic evil.

---

100. Mathewes, *Evil and the Augustinian Tradition*, 65.
101. Augustine, *Confessions*, 7.5(7).
102. Psalm 112:7.
103. For example, he writes, "But neither is it this which we affirm—the 'privation fights against the Good by its own power'; for the complete privation is altogether powerless, and the partial has the power, not in respect of privation, but in so far as it is not a complete privation. For, whilst privation of good is partial, it is not, as yet, an evil, and when it has become an accomplished fact, the nature of the evil has departed also" (Dionysius, "On Divine Names," 4.29.
104. Geivett, *Evil and the Evidence for God*, 20.

PART I: The Tension of Theodicy

Scholastic Evil

Evil got a bad name during the middle ages; scholasticism dominated the discussion. Boethius (c.477–524) was perhaps the last Roman scholar or the first scholastic. He certainly understood evil as a privation. He wrote, "You [RAS: Lady Philosophy] argued that God rules the universe by the helm of goodness, that all things obey willingly, and that evil is nothing."[105] But his argument leading up to this conclusion sounds quite "scholastic." He writes:

> LP: No one could doubt that God is omnipotent.
>
> B: No one, at any rate, who is in his right mind would have any doubt about it.
>
> LP: But there is nothing that an omnipotent power could not do.
>
> B: No.
>
> LP: So then evil is nothing, since that is what He cannot do who can do anything.

While this reads like boiler-plate "scholasticism," that does not mean the conclusion should be dismissed as irrelevant. It should be noted that Boethius's preserved reflections come in the context of his own raw pain. His story is like that of Job: wealthy and an advisor to Kings, yet he lost all through no evil of his own and wrote while awaiting death in a Roman jail. If he is a scholastic, it is not because he has time for philosophical word games. In fact, he even responds in this same discussion to Lady Philosophy, "You are playing with me, aren't you, by weaving a labyrinth of arguments from which I can't find my way out." Evil, and the suffering he faces, is no word game for this condemned man. The culture may affect his argument, but he is seeking his soul's *consolation* in God's goodness in the face of raw evil. In so doing, he perceives it to have a privative nature.

Later, Anselm of Canterbury (1033–1109) struggled with the concept of privation as he inherited it from Augustine. In fact, his exhaustive detail can be confusing, instead of enlightening. It could even seem that he degraded Augustine's ideas so that his own description of the will sounds vaguely Pelagian, but this is not the case, at least because he understood the fallen will to be in need of much more than "help." In the end, fighting through the cloud of detail created by the three-fold nature of Anselm's will,[106] Anselm seems to be saying little more than Augustine has already said, and it

---

105. Boethius, *Consolation of Philosophy*, 3.12. All three quotes in the above section are from this same section.

106. Anselm's complex understanding of the will (in three parts: (1) faculty or instrument; (2) disposition or inclination; (3) use or act) results in a more nuanced understanding of evil's nature and its origin which is found in the will, or not found, to be exact. Anselm strongly agrees that the nature of evil is privative. He writes, "And when [RAS: the will] abandoned [RAS: God's goodness], it lost something great, and acquired in exchange only the privation of justice we call injustice and that has no positive being" (Anselm, "De Casu Diaboli," in *Anselm of Canterbury: The Major Works*, chapter 9 (206)). It should be noted that by "justice" Anselm is using a synonym for God's goodness.

is not clear that his nuanced description advances our understanding of the nature or

He writes, "moral good, which is called justice" ("De Casu Diaboli," Davies and Evans, chapter 12, (213)). Also, Davies notes that in Latin, "righteousness" is lexically indistinguishable from "justice" (315). So also in Greek; 1 John 1:9 is a robust example. But he seems to struggle against the seeming unreality of something simply privative. He asserts that the privative nature of evil is not ontologically different from the nature of what is good: "S. When you say that evil is the privation of the good, I agree, but none the less I see that good is a privation of evil" (Anselm, "De Casu Diaboli," chapter 10 (206)). Because this statement is put forward by Anselm's "student" (S), we would be right to wonder if Anselm himself, as the "teacher" (T), agrees. In fact, he does. Anselm writes, "T: Hence evil in truth is nothing and nothing is not real, and yet in a way evil and nothing are something because we speak of them as if they were real, . . . in the same way we say 'I did something and I did a good thing.'" So we deny that what someone says is in any way something: 'what you say is nothing.' For 'what' or 'this's which are properly said only of realities, here are not said of realities but of quasi-realities" (Anselm, "De Casu Diaboli," Davies and Evans, chapter 11 (210)). If such is his meaning, however, it misses the fundamental grounding of goodness positively within God, himself. Privation is ontologically a "one-way street." That is, good is not a privation of evil, because of God, himself. Good is not a lack, but a fullness, because God exists. Good, so grounded in God, cannot be privative. I suggest he is getting lost in his own scholastic complexity here; he has managed to distinguish himself from Augustine, but perhaps to no useful advancement in thought. Essentially what he is asserting is a "privative reality" and Augustine, as was shown earlier, has already done this more simply and straightforwardly. In "Prologion," Anselm uses the illustration of light in order to understand God. We do not see light, but the things that it illuminates. As a result we see "everything," but not God, just as we do not see "light," but what it illuminates. It is by this light we see the Good and so "do not see" evil (Anselm, "Prologion," in *Anselm of Canterbury: The Major Works*, chapter 16 (96)).

However, in regard to the origin of evil he seems to distinguish himself from Augustine, but then again, maybe not. Anselm asserts that evil's origin is not to be found in the will itself, "Therefore a bad will is not itself the evil which makes men evil, just as a good will is not itself the good which makes men good. What I have said of will can also be said of the inclination of the will" ("De Casu Diaboli," Davies and Evans, chapter 8 (206)). It would seem that for Anselm evil is the specific privation of justice in the act, itself—in the specific action of the will in a specific act. But the problem for us as readers is that Anselm's will is subdivided. In the statement above, he is talking about the will that acts. But in regard to the instrumental will he writes, "T. Understand that the will that I am calling the instrument of willing has an inalienable strength that cannot be overcome by any other force, but which it uses sometimes more and sometimes less when it wills. . . . [RAS: A man] turns himself to that which he more strongly wills" (Anselm, "On Free Will," in *Anselm of Canterbury: The Major Works*, chapter 7 (186)). This sounds much like Augustine's, "there is nothing above the will." Then again, in another context, he speaks of evil as originating not from the will, but a failure to receive perseverance in righteousness, writing: "T. So I say that the devil did not will what he should have willed when he should have willed it, not because he lacked the will (and lacked it because God did not give it to him), but because, willing what he ought not to have willed, he drove out the good will when the bad will supervened. Therefore God did not give him the good will to persevere, and he did not receive it, not because God did not give it, but on the contrary, God did not give it because he gave up willing what he should have willed, by abandoning and not retaining it" (Anselm, "De Casu Diaboli," Davies and Evans, chapter 3, (p 201)). Readers who wonder if something said of the Devil should apply to human will, can at least note that for Anselm they are held in equivalence. Anselm's contribution to the nature and origin of evil is slight. If I might note here (with insufficient support), that this is very like a similar concept in quantum dynamics in which a particle will not radiate, unless it lies in a cavity which is of a size to "allow" such a packet to exist. If it is the case that it does not lie so, then it will not radiate the quantum packet it would otherwise have radiated. So the conclusion of the Student here, "I grasp what you say" is understandable if he is prescient with quantum principles . . . . In other words, I find the Student's easy, "okay," a bit of a surprise, yet, today physics does give us an analogy that might just sustain Anselm in his assertion.

PART I: The Tension of Theodicy

origin of evil. Such was even the case for Aquinas who came after him.[107]

In regard to the nature of evil, William of Ockham (c.1285–1347) separates himself from many of the major thinkers before him, but draws close to Peter Lombard (c.1100–c.1160) and others as he asserts that God is wholly free in regard to his divine action—free even from any standards of what is good.[108] For Augustine, Anselm, and Aquinas, the actions of God's willful creatures are good or evil because they do or do not conform to a standard. And though that standard is not external to God—for it is God himself; the Source and Fountain of goodness—a standard still exists. As such, Ockham's ethics lean more towards theonomy. Gordon Leff writes, "A meritorious act [RAS: for Ockham] then is whatever God accepts as such; . . . nothing of itself is intrinsically meritorious, only God's acceptance makes it so."[109] That is, it is not God's character, but his free choice, that defines a free act to be virtuous. So also, Marilyn McCord Adams writes,

> So far as conceptual theologism is concerned, Ockham declines to analyze the logical possibility in terms of divine power . . . Ockham does use theological theses that cannot be proved by natural reason alone, as premises from which to draw philosophical conclusions, . . . [RAS: but he also] uses philosophical premises about what is logically possible to draw conclusions about what God can do. In short, the textual picture is chaotic.[110]

In other words, Ockham does whatever is necessary to maintain his chief concern in regard to God; God must be wholly free; even free of any constraint of character. If what is good (or meritorious or virtuous) is related to God's free-will, which is not identical to God's character, the nature of goodness is quite different from the understanding of Augustine and his peers. So, Ockham insists, that God is not obliged to perform any act and therefore, by the fact that God wills something, it is justly done. Adams explains, "Thus even if God treated like causes differently—as Ockham suggests He does with Jacob and Esau—He would not act unjustly, because He would

---

107. Aquinas supported the privative nature of evil. He wrote in *Summa*, "Hence it cannot be that evil signifies being, or any form or nature. Therefore it must be that by the name of evil is signified the absence of good. And this is what is meant by saying that 'evil is neither a being nor a good.' For since being, as such, is good, the absence of one implies the absence of the other" (Ia,q.48,a.1). Also he wrote, "Evil imports the absence of good. But not every absence of good is evil. For absence of good can be taken in a privative and in a negative sense. Absence of good, taken negatively, is not evil . . . . But the absence of good, taken in a privative sense, is an evil" (Ia,q.48, a.3). This is simply Augustine. And like Augustine, Aquinas's privative evil is terrible indeed. So also in regard to the cause of evil, he writes, citing Augustine, "Augustine says (Contra Julian. i, 9): 'There is no possible source of evil except good.' "(Ia,q.49, a.1). In so saying, he agrees that it is the errant or evil human will which is the "accidental cause."

108. Leff, *William of Ockham*, 1257.

109. Ibid., 476. In support he cites *Ordinatio*, d17, q.1, Q; q.2, c.

110. M. M. Adams, *William Ockham*, 1255.

The Historical Development of the Concept of Evil

not thereby fail to live up to any of His obligations."[111] Ockham's conclusion in this is, "Whatever He does for us, He does by grace alone."[112] This is his freedom.

So, for Ockham, God is free of all constraint. As Adams explains, "since for Ockham, what counts as acceptable or sinful, does so by God's free and contingent choice alone."[113] The result is that Ockham does not have a privative understanding of evil. This is so, not because he refutes privation (he does), but because privation has no meaning in a world where no act is itself "good" (or "meritorious"). He writes, "Nor is sin the privation of any good that actually inheres or inhered in the past, but the privation of a future good that should have inhered if he had not sinned."[114] So, sin is not a privation in the sense of Augustine, but neither is it "something" or anything other than the contingent, free declaration of God in regard to a specific, free and purposeful choice of one of God's willful creatures. Augustine, the privationist, would identify evil with defection from God's character. Ockham, the theonomist, would identify evil as defection from God's will.

Based on this understanding of the nature of evil, the origin follows directly. The origin of evil is in the freedom of God's willful creatures. But the origin is not precisely in the act itself (or the lack of an act), for no action is intrinsically good or evil. Rather the origin of evil is in the purposeful action of a willful creature, to which God in his freedom attributes evil.

This is an important defection from dualism or privation. Clearly Ockham is not a dualist—the chief philosophical antipode of Augustine and others. Clearly Ockham's focus results in the surrender of God's character to near insignificance. Yet, like Augustine and even Edwards, he has a great desire to preserve God's freedom and glory and freedom in grace. No privationist, he is still helpful to us in understanding that evil is not substance and is that which God opposes with all his being.

Evil in the Reformation

The Reformation was an Augustinian creation. In the *Bondage of the Will*, Martin Luther (1483–1546) writes, "He impels us to act by His own acting upon us according to

---

111. Ibid., 1264. Here she cites *Ordinatio* 7 and 8.

112. Ibid., 1274. This position sounds not like Pelagius, but rather like Luther or Augustine.

113. Ibid., 1277. This is the sticking point for some who charge him with Pelagianism. Ockham himself refutes this charge. "Ockham insists that nothing could be further from the case. First, while it sounds Pelagian to say that a human being can be saved without grace, he thinks that this misimpression will be dispelled when it is realized that 'grace' is taken two different ways. One way it stands for the infused quality of grace or charity, and that is the way Ockham understands it when he denies that grace is either logically necessary or logically sufficient for salvation. Another way, it stands for God's generous act of willing . . . eternal life for someone, and that grace is both logically necessary and logically sufficient for divine acceptance and eternal life" (1279). In other words, he is preserving God's freedom, against religious rite, which many have believed to be infused with grace. This he rightly denies.

114. Ibid., 1276. This quoted from *Ordinatio* 7, 223–4.

PART I: The Tension of Theodicy

the nature of His omnipotence, good though He is in Himself, He cannot but do evil by our evil instrumentality; although, according to His wisdom, He makes good use of this evil for His own glory and for our salvation."[115] This is representative of Luther's thought and while some might argue that this is beyond Augustine, it is still Augustinian in kind. In regard to evil's origin, we are the proximate cause of evil, which is done by our will, not by God's will. But it should be noted that Luther demands much of the willful creaturely will. He writes, "Thus God, *finding Satan's will evil*, not creating it so (it became so by Satan's sinning and God's withdrawing), carries it along by His own operation and moves it where He wills."[116] So, for Luther, Satan's will became evil at some point after being created perfect—or at least unblemished (as perfect in the sense that God is perfect would also entail its being incorruptible—that it was not). So also this text reminds us that Luther understands evil's nature as a privation of goodness, God's withdrawing. It is that absence that denatured that will. In Luther, we have the two basic tenets of Augustine: origin (the creaturely will), and nature (privation). And it is in this context that Luther, sensing the frustration of some at such an explication of the nature of evil and God's interaction with creaturely wills, says, "grumbling will not change God!"[117]

In the same era, John Calvin (1509–1564) was more concerned with the effects of evil than with its nature or origin. He begins with God as the source and fountain of goodness. He writes, "Again, you cannot behold him clearly unless you acknowledge him to be the fountainhead and source of every good. From this too would arise the desire to cleave to him and trust in him, but for the fact that man's depravity seduces his mind from rightly seeking him."[118] However, there is no similar source of evil in the reality that gave birth to evil. He makes it quite clear that it is not possible to attribute the source of evil to the devil—or by extension, to any evil power:

> To God he [RAS: Mani] attributed the origin of good things, but evil natures he referred to the devil as their author. If this madness held our minds ensnared, God's glory in the creation of the universe would not abide with him. For since nothing is more characteristic of God than eternity and self-existence—that is existence of himself, so to speak—do not those who attribute this to the devil in a sense adorn him with the title of divinity? Now where is God's omnipotence, if such sovereignty is conceded to the devil that he carries out whatever he wishes, against God's will and resistance?[119]

In so saying, he excludes any shades of dualism. The origin of human evil is in Adam; when he diverged from this fountain of goodness, he was corrupted: "Yet it is at the

---

115. Luther, "Bondage of the Will," *Martin Luther: Selections from his Writings*, 193.
116. Ibid. (emphasis mine).
117. Ibid., 195.
118. Calvin, *ICR*, 1.2.2.
119. Calvin, *ICR*, 1.14.3.

same time to be noted that the first man revolted from God's authority, not only because he was seized by Satan's blandishments, but also because, contemptuous of the truth, he turned aside to falsehood.... Unfaithfulness, then, was the root of the Fall. But thereafter ambition and pride, together with ungratefulness arose."[120] As with Augustine and others, Calvin must make it clear that this failure did not come from an imperfection in Adam's character as created by God. It was a "natural wickedness" in Adam, but not one created there by God; it is a "corruption of his work."[121] As was shown above, Calvin understood that humanity had the capacity to continue in perfection, but we did not. So the origin of evil is in God's perfect creatures. The origin is not in their created nature, but arose, naturally, even in perfection, because they were separated from the fountain of goodness, ontologically.

But Calvin says very little about the nature of evil. Such terms as "privation" or "nothingness" or even philosophical explanations do not arise from Calvin in regard to evil. In regard to those who have followed Adam, he does say,

> For our nature is not only destitute and empty of good, but so fertile and fruitful of every evil that it cannot be idle. Those who have said that original sin is "concupiscence" have used an appropriate word, if only it be added—something that most will by no means concede—that whatever is in man, from the understanding to the will, from the soul even to the flesh, has been defiled and crammed with this concupiscence. Or, to put it more briefly, the whole man is of himself nothing but concupiscence.[122]

The kind of "privation" which is common to Calvin is a privation of goodness in the soul and nature of Adam's successors and followers. But this is in regard to our nature, not the nature of evil itself. Still, in his emphasis on God as the fountain of goodness, it would seem that he has no need to enter into the specifics of the nature of evil, for it is that which does not participate in goodness and it is clear that he is no kind of dualist.

Louis de Molina's (1535–1600) contribution is essentially this: his unblinking willingness to assert that God is the pervasive and primary cause of all that occurs in this world. Even the actions of willful creatures are decoupled from the actual working out of the effects, for God himself brings about every effect of such secondary wills, directly. Still, Molina protects God from any conclusion that he is responsible for evil. He denies that God in any way motivates the choice of his willful creatures; he perceives God as neutral. Still, this would seem to make God quite active in regard to the origin of evil, both indirectly (his creation of a universe that permitted evil) and, significantly for Molina, directly (his implementation of freely willed evil choices). But, deflecting a charge that this takes evil into God, Molina insists that secondary causes are quite robust, even under the conditions described:

120. Calvin, *ICR*, 2.1.4.
121. Calvin, *ICR*, 2.1.11.
122. Calvin, *ICR*, 2.1.8.

PART I: The Tension of Theodicy

> For, indeed, Sacred Scripture attributes operations of this sort to secondary causes in such a way as to signify that these operations are truly effected by their causes. Mark 4:28, "For of itself the earth bears the crop, first the blade, then the ear, etc." Luke 21:29-30, "Behold the fig tree and all the trees; when they now produce of themselves their buds . . . ." Thus in *De Civitate Dei*, 7, chapter 30, Augustine says, "God administers all things which He has created in such a way that He also allows them to exercise and perform their proper acts."[123]

So, the responsibility and origin of sin still belongs entirely to God's willful creatures, but God is the cause. Given his position on freedom, the origin of sin (and evil) is clearly in the freedom of God's willful creatures, but of the nature of freedom, he is not significantly interested.

Representatives who bridged the Reformation and the modern era include Descartes (1596-1650), Gottfried Leibniz (1646-1716), and Jonathan Edwards (1703-1758). All were rigorous philosophers, as well as theologians. On one pole, Descartes, an early rationalist, asserted that the will is free—clearly and distinctly free, unfallen, and godlike in its freedom from error.[124] So the origin of evil lies not in the will, but in lack of knowledge upon which the will operates.[125] And the nature of the evil is privative, but in quite a different sense than Augustine or the Reformers. He writes, "For

---

123. Molina, Disputation 25.5: "On God's concurrence with secondary causes with respect to each of their actions and effects," edited and translated by Alfred J. Freddoso, published only on his website. It could be added here that he dedicates a whole disputation to this very point: Disputation 32: "The reason is explained why it is not God but created free choice alone which is the cause of sin." Moreover, as noted by Freddoso, the scope of Molinistic freedom exercised by God's willful creatures is quitnarrow, "As Molina sees it, God is the paradigmatic indeterministic cause, an all-powerful being capable of freely impeding any and every deterministic natural tendency in the created world. He is the first or primary cause and His causal activity is absolutely pervasive. . . . no creaturely or secondary cause is able to exercise its causal power unless God also acts contemporaneously to bring about its effect" (Freddoso, *On Divine Foreknowledge*, "Introduction," 16-17). Responding to Domingo Bañez and Duns Scotus, Molina writes, "Again, what grievance will God have on Judgment Day against the wicked, since they were unable not to sin as long as God did not efficaciously incline and determine them to the good, rather solely by His own free will decided from eternity not so to determine them? Most assuredly, if this position is accepted, then our freedom of choice is altogether destroyed, and God's justice with respect to the wicked vanishes" (Molina, *On Divine Foreknowledge*, Disputation 50.14, 139).

124. Descartes writes, "It is only the will, or freedom of choice, which I experience as so great that I can't make sense of the idea of its being even greater . . . when the will is considered not relationally, but strictly *in itself*, God's will does not seem any greater than mine" (Descartes, *Meditations*, Meditation 4, paragraph 8 (4.8).

125. In *Meditations*, 4.9 he writes, "So the power of willing that God has given me, being extremely broad in its scope and also perfect of its kind, is not the cause of my mistakes. Nor is my power of understanding to blame:
God gave it to me, so there can be no error in its activities; when I understand something I undoubtedly understand it correctly. Well, then, where do my mistakes come from? Their source is the fact that my will has a wider scope than my intellect has, so that I am free to form beliefs on topics that I don't understand."

error isn't a mere negation . . . rather it is a privation, that is, a lack of some knowledge that I should have."[126] Leibniz, also a rationalist, understood evil as privative and, rather than a lack of knowledge, it stood in opposition to God. More important, he argued that a privative evil can be substantive in its effect.[127] While important to the discussion and development of theodicy, neither was exceptional in helping us to understand evil. This was left to Edwards.

To understand Jonathan Edwards's perspective on evil it is important to begin with his teaching on the decrees. For Edwards, everything that God has done was decreed before time in exact and specific detail. In regard to their operation with respect to evil, he writes:

> Therefore, I shall take these two things for positions granted and supposed in this controversy, viz., that as to God's own actions and forbearings to act, he decrees and purposes them beforehand; and that whatsoever God designs or purposes, he purposes from all eternity, and thus decrees from all eternity all

---

126. Descartes, *Meditations*, 4.5.

127. Leibniz believed that there is far more good than evil in the world; this will be important to his Best of All Possible Worlds theodicy which we will explore later. He wrote, "there is incomparably more good than evil in the life of men, as there are incomparably more houses than prisons" (Leibniz, *Theodicy*, 3.148). It is in this context, he wrote of evil's origin, saying, "It is an imperfection in our freedom that makes us capable of choosing evil instead of good" (Leibniz, *Theodicy*, 3.319). In so saying, he sounds much like Augustine in regard to evil's origin. He also writes, "man is himself the source of his evils: just as he is, he was in the divine idea. God, prompted by essential reasons of wisdom, decreed that he should pass into existence just as he is" (Leibniz, *Theodicy*, 3.151). That is, man, with his God given freedom, is the source and origin of evil.

Of its nature, he wrote, "The explanation of the cause of evil by a particular principle, per principium maleficum, is of the same nature. Evil needs no such explanation, any more than do cold and darkness: there is neither primum frigidum nor principle of darkness. Evil itself comes only from privation; the positive enters therein only by concomitance, as the active enters by concomitance into cold. We see that water in freezing is capable of breaking a gun-barrel wherein it is confined; and yet cold is a certain privation of force, it only comes from the diminution of a movement which separates the particles of fluids. When this separating motion becomes weakened in the water by the cold, the particles of compressed air concealed in the water collect; and, becoming larger, they become more capable of acting outwards through their buoyancy. The resistance which the surfaces of the proportions of air meet in the water, and which opposes the force exerted by these portions towards dilation, is far less, and consequently the effect of the air greater, in large air-bubbles than in small, even though these small bubbles combined should form as great a mass as the large. For the resistances, that is, the surfaces, increase by the square, and the forces, that is, the contents or the volumes of the spheres of compressed air, increase by the cube, of their diameters. Thus it is by accident that privation involves action and force. I have already shown how privation is enough to cause error and malice, and how God is prompted to permit them, despite that there be no malignity in him. Evil comes from privation; the positive and action spring from it by accident, as force springs from cold" (Leibniz, *Theodicy*, 3.153). It should be noted that he is quite clearly supporting a privative position, here and elsewhere as well (Leibniz, *Theodicy*, 1.20 (deficient cause), 1.30 ("the formal element [RAS: cause], which lies in privation") and elsewhere). But more than simply asserting that evil has a privative nature, he explains that something privative can by its very nature have a powerful effect. One could argue with his examples here, yet the examples are provided not as proof, but by way of experiential analogy. So they stand as a symbol of his understanding, while not necessarily of scientific accuracy. Evil can be privative in nature and exercise a terrible force and reality.

PART I: The Tension of Theodicy

his own actions and forbearings to act. Corollary. Hence God decrees from all eternity, to permit all the evil that ever he does permit, because God's permitting is God's forbearing to act or to prevent.[128]

So, in regard to evil, God is responsible, because evil, like creation and salvation, flows from the priority of the decrees. God is the necessary cause, though not the immediate creator, or author, of evil.[129] He works carefully to ensure that God is not the efficient cause of evil, but rather that it arises from the acts of God's willful creatures.[130] He has permitted all evil and every specific evil, and without his permission, it would not have occurred. Whatever is true of its specific origin and nature, Edwards does not try to absolve God of ultimate responsibility for evil.

In regard to its nature, Edwards writes, "Divines are generally agreed, that sin radically and fundamentally consists in what is negative, or privative, having its root and foundation in a privation or want of holiness."[131] With these divines, he funda-

---

128. J. Edwards, "Miscellanies," *Collected Works of Jonathan Edwards CD*, 763.2.

129. Unusual for Edwards, he seems to get a bit tangled while arguing against the idea that God is the "author" of evil, while allowing that he is (in my words here) the necessary cause. He writes, "In this sense, I utterly deny God to be the Author of Sin; rejecting such an imputation on the Most High, as what is infinitely to be abhorred; and deny any such thing to be the consequence of what I have laid down. But if, by the Author of Sin, is meant the perimeter, or not a hinderer of Sin; and, at the same time, a disposer of the state of events, in such a manner, for wise, holy, and most excellent ends and purposes, that Sin, if it be permitted or not hindered, will most certainly and infallibly follow: I say, if this be all that is meant, by being the Author of Sin, I do not deny that God is the Author of Sin (though I dislike and reject the phrase, as that which by use and custom is apt to carry another sense), it is no reproach for the Most High to be thus the Author of Sin" ("Freedom of the Will," *Collected Works of Jonathan Edwards CD*, 4.9.II). My understanding is supported by Dr. Williams, the editor of the 1806 edition of Edwards's works. He wrote (as a footnote to "Freedom of the Will," 2.12), "21. In reality, DIVINE DECREES (as before hinted) are nothing else than a wonderful chain or series of positions, which are so many antecedents, counteracting defects arising from the hypothetical nature of things. Whence it necessarily follows, that if there were no PASSIVE POWER there could be no DIVINE DECREES. For if good, and only good, arose from the nature of things; the decree, which has good only for its object, would be superfluous, and therefore unworthy of divine volition" (CAPS original in all Edwards's quotes). In other words, evil arises specifically and only from the "passive power" and the "hypothetical nature of things" but these are the objects of God's creation and God is the antecedent of antecedents.

130. Arguing that God is not the efficient cause of evil, having not created his willful creatures with sin already in their hearts, he writes, "I answer, 1. It was meet, if sin did come into existence, and appear in the world, it should arise from the imperfection which properly belongs to a creature, as such, and should appear so to do, that it might appear not to be from God as the efficient [RAS: cause] or fountain" ("Freedom of the Will," *Collected Works of Jonathan Edwards CD*, 4.10.3). But he does not waiver in regard to the decrees which are prior to all creative action. In this sense, God is the necessary cause, though he is as bashful of any use of "cause" as he is of any use of "author" in regard to sin.

131. J. Edwards, "Treatise Concerning Religious Affections," *Collected Works of Jonathan Edwards CD*, 1.10.4. He also writes, in regard to a positive cause for evil, that it does not exist. This also aligns him with the general privative (and non-dualist either by ontology or creation) position. He writes, "there is not the least need of supposing any evil quality, infused, implanted, or wrought into the nature of man, by any positive cause, or influence whatsoever, either from God, or the creature; or of supposing, that man is conceived and born with a fountain of evil in his heart, such as is anything properly positive" ("Doctrine of Original Sin Defended," 4.2.2).

mentally agrees, but privation does not really get to the heart of what he considers as sin's nature. Fundamentally, sin (let "sin" stand for "evil" here) is a self-love without God. This is his perspective here (through some difficult syntax) when he writes, "All sin has its source form [RAS: *sic*] selfishness, or from self-love, not subordinate to a regard to being in general and natural conscience chiefly consists in a sense of desert, or the natural agreement of sin and misery."[132] He is arguing that it is a breaking of the first, second, and third commandments, positive idolatry, that results in sin. All sin is first, idolatry.

> [RAS: Original sin] is self-love, in conjunction with the absence of the image and love of God . . . . There is nothing in the actions we call sin, but only the same self-love that necessarily belongs to that nature, working and influencing without regulation from that superior principle that particularly belongs to our nature and that is necessary in order to the harmonious exercise of it.[133]

So, while he understands evil to be in some measure a privation of the good, he understands it positively as the work of self-love in the absence of a God-ward focus and the love of God that is the result of only a God-ward focus.

The origin of evil for Edwards is in Adam's choice to rebel in the garden. For him the account is historical and the first three chapters definitive.[134] Evil was born in the first people God created, all the future generations were tainted with original sin, and each one of us has acted out our evil part afresh.[135] Evil has its origin specifically in Adam and the drama is replayed in us because of God's judgment upon Adam. So Edwards accepts privation, but his focus is on the idolatrous self-love as the nature, which is in effect, the origin of sin.

The State of Evil in Modern Scholarship

Before we consider the developments within the Protestant tradition, it is worth noting that the position of the Roman Catholic Church continues, unperturbed, to accept the privative nature of evil outlined by Augustine and confirmed by Aquinas. At the end of the twentieth century, Pope John Paul II (Karol Jozef Wojtyla, 1920–2005) wrote for the Roman Catholic Church in *Salvifici Doloris*, "We could say that man

---

132. J. Edwards, "Two Dissertations: The Nature of True Virtue," chapter 7, paragraph 10.

133. J. Edwards, "Miscellanies," *Collected Works of Jonathan Edwards CD*, Sin, 301.

134. He writes in "Doctrine of Original Sin Defended," "And doubtless it was expected, by the great author of the Bible, that the account in the three first chapters of Genesis should be taken as a plain account of the introduction of both natural and moral evil into the world. [RAS: This is] the history of Adam's sin" (*Collected Works of Jonathan Edwards CD*, 2.2.18).

135. This is due, not just to the course of things, but to God's specific judgment on Adam and his progeny, withdrawing his grace. He writes, "But here I desire it may be noted, that I do not suppose the natural depravity of the posterity of Adam is owing to the course of nature only; it is also owing to the just judgment of God" ("Doctrine of Original Sin Defended," *Collected Works of Jonathan Edwards CD*, 4.2.9).

suffers because of a good in which he does not share, from which in a certain sense he is cut off, or of which he has deprived himself."[136] This is a privative position and one that understands privation to be the lack of participation in the goodness of God, the only One from whom flows all good. So also the Orthodox Church, sharing much of the critical historical development, has not diverged from this historic position.[137]

In contrast, the Protestant church continues to be in flux. One of the critical thinkers in regard to the question of the nature of evil is Karl Barth (1886–1968). Whole studies are deservedly done in regard to his concept of *das Nichtige*; an extreme and possibly the ultimate extreme of the tradition of privation; a brief overview will suffice here. In its origin, creation is "on the frontier of nothingness and oriented toward it."[138] This nothingness is related to Augustine's concept of privation (*malum est privation boni*). He writes,

> Augustine used the term quite correctly to define the purely negative character of evil, i.e., the nullity of sin, evil and death, its nature and opposition both intrinsically and in relation to God and his creature. For Augustine, privation is *corruptio* or *conversio boni*. It is not only the absence of what really is, but the assault upon it. Evil is related to good in such a way that it attacks and harms it.[139]

In the same paragraph, he complains that when Leibniz used privation, he made it a mere negation: "the creature is a creature and not God, and does not therefore possess the divine attributes." But for Barth, evil is not mere negation, but the yawning maw of the deadly abyss. Evil is "given" its non-being by the fact of God's refusal to preserve or rule it.[140] So, the nature of evil is privative to an (almost) overwhelming extreme—to a point where as non-being, it becomes an "alien factor" that gives God and his creatures "opposition and resistance." In that sense it does smell distinctly of dualism, though Barth would clearly reject this rightly citing that evil has its origin from within (or rather in the context of) creation, and therefore metaphysically subordinate to God.

Barth's view is important in that it is an extreme which is worth exploring. It searches for the fullest possible meaning of the Augustinian tradition, rejecting all who lightly partake.[141] But he is not well received in this. John Hick refutes him on

136. Wojtyła, "Salvifici Doloris," §7.

137. Timothy Ware writes, "evil as such is not a 'thing,' not an existent being or substance" and cites Augustine, Gregory of Nyssa, and others, also noting that being nothing does not diminish its "forcefulness and dynamism" (Ware, *Orthodox Way*, revised edition, 47). So also, Thomas Hopko writes, evil "has no being of its own . . . a negative presence and a destructive power" ("On God and Evil," 181). So also, Michael Pomazansky, "evil is not some kind of essence which has any actual independent existence" (*Orthodox Dogmatic Theology*, 151).

138. Barth, *CD*, III.3, (§50.2) "God and Nothingness," 296.

139. Barth, *CD*, III.3, (§50.3) "God and Nothingness," 318.

140. Barth, *CD*, III.3, (§50.1) "God and Nothingness," 289.

141. Leibniz, for example (Barth, *Church Dogmatics*, III.3, [§ 50.3] 316–19).

the basis of both language and of the character of God. In the case of language, he rejects Barth's concept because Barth errs in that he proposes reality for a simple verbal abstract. Hick writes, "The term 'being' generates the cognate term 'non-being' but it does not follow that there in any sense is or exists anything of which this is the name."[142] In regard to God's character, Barth's position is defective because God's choice of being (good) over non-being (evil) in creating, seems to presuppose that such realities existed outside of God's character for him to choose. This is the road to the dualism of the Manicheans rejected by Augustine.[143] I agree. Greg Boyd argues more simply that "the trouble for Barth is that there is nothing 'false' or 'menacing,' let alone potentially 'evil' about bypassed possibilities. . . . Possibilities can become false, menacing and evil, however, if and when they are chosen over and against actual reality by a free, morally responsible agent."[144] While not linking arms with either of these theologians' other conclusions, they make good judgments in regard to Barth's concept of evil.

But John Hick goes too far. In what could seem like a return to Descartes, rather than Irenaeus, he suggests that evil is immaturity—perhaps he could be understood to mean, a lack of knowledge. Hick is a towering figure in modern British scholarship, and world-wide, in regard to the problem of evil.[145] He is also a self-avowed critic of evangelical theology[146] and a Modernist Christian who is a universalist.[147] Not having displayed Hick's thought in the previous chapter in regard to free-will, it should be said here that he argues as libertarian.[148] By way of illustration, I quote from his argument: "However, this is not taking place—it is important to add—by a natural and inevitable evolution, but through a hazardous adventure in individual freedom."[149] So, as a libertarian, he understands evil as the product of the actions of creaturely freedom. But Hick's starting-point to understand evil is that of an Irenaean theology over and against the more traditional Augustinian positions.[150] He argues that evil, in

---

142. Hick, *Evil and the God of Love*, 192.

143. Ibid., 193.

144. Boyd, *Satan and the Problem of Evil*, 289.

145. As a young man he converted to evangelical Christianity after an air raid (Hick, *John Hick: An Autobiography*). He notes that he accepted Christ in March of 1941 while in college, after a terrible air raid: "I experienced a powerful evangelical conversion to fundamentalist Christianity" (27). Also, he writes, "I accepted as a whole and without question the entire fundamentalist theological package—verbal inspiration of the Bible, creation and fall, Jesus as God the Son incarnate" (34).

146. Hick, *John Hick*, 35.

147. This is a corollary of his views on "many lives; many worlds."

148. However, he does not support a free-will defense of any kind.

149. Hick, *Evil and the God of Love*, 292.

150. Hick writes, "Fortunately, there is another and better way. As well as the 'majority report' of the Augustinian tradition, which has dominated Western Christendom, both Catholic and Protestant, since the time of Augustine himself, there is the 'minority report' of the Irenaean tradition" (ibid., 289).

PART I: The Tension of Theodicy

the case of the Augustinian position, must arise out of necessity and perhaps also from some necessary defect in the created:

> To say they do is to postulate the self-creation of evil *ex nihilo*! There must have been [RAS: by Augustinian reasoning] some moral flaw in the creature or in his situation to set up the tension of temptation; for creaturely freedom in itself and in the absence of any temptation cannot lead to sin.[151]

So what then is the nature and origin of evil for Hick? As noted above, its origin is not in some historical event on earth. Instead, people were created in an immature state—there is no historic "Fall." We are created at an epistemic distance from God. Explaining this he writes,

> [RAS: God] must be knowable, but only by a mode of knowledge that involves a free personal response on man's part, this response consisting in an uncompelled interpretive activity whereby we experience the world as mediating the divine presence. Such a need for a human faith-response will secure for man the only kind of freedom that is possible for him in relation to God, namely cognitive freedom.[152]

This is a description of the "epistemic distance": a knowable God, the knowledge of whom is mediated by the distance creation puts between us and the knowledge of God.[153] For Hick, the fall is a state of spiritual existence at this epistemic distance, created so by God to give freedom. This is what it means to be fallen—there was no temporal fall from some prior state of grace. As such, evil is under the "sole ultimate sovereignty and responsibility of God" even though it is the "enemy of God and man."[154] As an enemy it will be defeated when we achieve complete freedom, but as a tool of God to create mature human beings, it is part of God's good purpose.[155] So

---

151. Ibid., 286.

152. Ibid., 317.

153. There is no need to debate Hick on the issue of the need of epistemic distance in order to evaluate his case or to set forth mine in Part II of this project. Still, I am eager to at least observe some possible difficulties for Hick in this regard. What is the meaning of those who met with God face-to-face and still sinned such as Adam and Cain? If it is claimed they are not historical characters and their stories only have the value of myth, why then do the stories intentionally close the epistemological gap before they tell the story of sin? What of Moses who lived with God face-to-face, but could not win the argument face-to-face with his wife to circumcise their sons? For that sin he almost died. And it was not to allow epistemic distance to work out their freedom, but to save their lives, that God proposed removing himself from their camp after the events surrounding the Golden Calf in Exodus 32. What of Eli who came and went into the presence of God and knew his voice, but could not bear to discipline his sons? What of all those who lived with Jesus and either fled from him, or betrayed him, or crucified him? Perhaps his fleshly cloak provided the epistemic distance, but many of his sayings would seem to make this assertion doubtful. It is possible that the Bible asserts that our inclination to sin overwhelms even the holy and close presence of God. If so, epistemic distance fails as a device for maturing purposes.

154. Ibid., 393.

155. I will avoid explicating his theodicy of soul-making until chapter 3.

for Hick, evil has its origin primarily in God himself: he created man (immature), at a "sinful" distance from himself. The nature of evil is to continue to live at this epistemic distance from God and so fail to become what God created us to be. This is sin: "Sin, then is a disorientation at the very centre of man's being where he stands in relationship with the Source and Lord of his life and the Determiner of his destiny."[156]

So, though I have presented Hick's thoughts here as the testimony of a "hostile witness" into the courtroom of the problem of evil, his work is distinct and significant and will be even more so when we consider theodicy. We will see that there is something significantly true about epistemic distance that is not in itself a theodicy (as Hick might claim), but still a truth. Moreover, we can agree that God does have ultimate responsibility for sin (evil) in that he has created the conditions that necessarily lead to sin, whether one comes from an Augustinian or Irenaean position.

John S. Feinberg's position on the nature and origin of evil is not remarkable for one in the Calvinist tradition; as such, it is typical and so helpful to see here. In regard to evil's nature, he is a privationist. He writes, "Moral evil is not a substance that God created when He created other things. It is not a substance at all."[157] Since all things (substances) created by God were good, God did not create evil and it is not a God-created substance. What then is its origin? Its origin is in the desires of God's willful creatures. He writes, God "neither created our actions themselves nor does he perform them. Hence, we cannot say that God must have intended for there to be moral evil because we have it in our world. God intended to create and did create agents who can act; He did not create their acts (good or evil)."[158] In order to avoid contradiction in his compatibilistic system, he goes "behind" the will to desires: "in accord with James 1:13–15, I hold that morally evil actions ultimately stem from human desires. . . . Morally evil acts, then, ultimately begin with our desires. Desires in themselves are not evil."[159] So, we have a position that is classically Augustinian, nuanced from "free-will" to "desire."

Beyond his agreement with Augustine, there is something else worth noting in Feinberg's understanding of evil. He asserts that since God did not immediately create evil, so also God did not intend evil in his creation. This is an important point for Feinberg. What Feinberg means by "intend" is not immediately clear. What he seems to be claiming is that while God did not intend evil in and of itself, he did intend certain other things which were to him a higher value than preventing evil. Specifically, that higher value is a certain kind of human. He writes, "He intended to create a being with the capacity to reason . . . , a being with emotions, a being with a will that is free (compatibilistically free, though freedom is not the emphasis of my defense), a being with desires, a being with intentions (formed on the basis of one's desires), and

156. Ibid., 300.
157. Feinberg, *Many Faces of Evil*, 127.
158. Ibid.
159. Ibid., 128.

a being with the capacity for bodily movement."[160] As a result, while not intending evil (primarily), God has created the kind of world he intended, including evil, which he did not intend (primarily). Moreover, "God can remove evil if that is all He wants to do in our world. However, I will argue that God cannot remove evil without . . . contradicting other valuable things he desired to do."[161] So, we have here by Feinberg a tentative, and even perhaps unintended, defense of some kind of necessity in evil.

It was in 1955 that J.L. Mackie pronounced the death of, not God (others had done that!), but theism.[162] To this M.B. Ahern has replied at length as a modern privationist in books and a series of articles in *Sophia* spanning four years. In those articles, he declares himself to be committed to Libertarian Free-Will and also to a privationist view of evil and thus intends to avoid the challenge of Mackie and others. He finds that he must carefully define what privation is and is not: "Evil can only be something negative but not wholly negative. . . . it is not wholly negative in as much as what is missing ought to be there."[163] To be privative is not to be merely a negation: "Privation will cause harm in proportion to the value of the good which is lacking."[164] Evil is a "real" privation. Still, Ahern acknowledges that this is not a sufficient answer to the problem posed by Mackie (and argued also by McCloskey and Bradley). Yet, privation is the precursor to a theodicy. While I am getting ahead of myself, it may be useful to explain, citing Ahern. First, given privation, and the implication that God did not create evil, Ahern can then assert from a certain practical point of view, that Christians are uniquely united in their opposition to evil:

> Dr. McCloskey continues his very remarkable answer: "Unlike the theist . . . the atheist will act to prevent and to reduce the suffering." This does not seem to square at all well with the fact that, not uncommonly, it is the theists who band together to run hospitals, homes for the handicapped and the aged, and so on, though no doubt, they should do even more.[165]

Secondly, from a logical perspective, if God did not create evil, then we are free to question why it can be asserted that he must eliminate it (on our time schedule):

> It is at this point that Bradley's argument breaks down completely. He does not show that God is obliged to prevent X or that there can be no justifying

---

160. Ibid., 126.

161. Ibid. In the original context of this quote he allows two other reasons: "(2) casting doubts on or directly contradicting the claims that He has all the attributes predicated of Him in Scripture, and/ or (3) performing actions that we would neither desire nor require Him to do, because they would produce a greater evil than we already have in our world." In Feinberg's ultimate argument, these are disallowed, in favor of (1) above.

162. He wrote, "Here it can be shown, not that religious beliefs lack rational support, but that they are positively irrational" (Mackie, "Evil and Omnipotence," 200).

163. Ahern, "Note on the Nature of Evil," 17.

164. Ibid., 23.

165. Ahern, "Nature of Evil," 43.

reasons for His not preventing X. As this is not shown, the final conclusion that He is not perfectly good, is not established.[166]

This is a significant advantage, if Ahern is correct, and a blow to Mackie's position.

Alvin Plantinga walks the interesting line of being a reformed theologian who defends Libertarian Free-Will. Like M.B. Ahern, he too is writing in response to Mackie, citing him as the one who highlights the "embarrassment" of evil for theists.[167] The origin of evil for Plantinga lies in the nature of the world which God created (and even in the nature of all possible worlds): "The sad truth . . . that it was not within God's power to actualize a world in which Curley produces moral good but no moral evil. Every world God could have actualized is such that if Curley is significantly free in it, he takes at least one wrong action."[168] In this he introduces his idea of *trans-world depravity*. This is based on his presumption (his "defense") of Libertarian Free-Will as a value of God for his willful creatures. That he laments (in ironic tone) this condition can be heard in the words, "the sad truth." But perhaps he also rejoices in this fact, because it provides for him an understanding of evil's origin.

Plantinga has been credited with single-handedly destroying the force of Mackie's argument as well as with the revival of philosophical-theology in the last century. I will not investigate his contribution to theodicy until the next chapter, but if *trans-world depravity* bears weight, it may act to reinforce the thread of the argument for the necessity of evil and the ultimate responsibility of God for it. That is, the nature of evil is privative; the cause and origin is in God's willful creatures; but evil may have been unavoidable to them, given God's announced goals and character and the fact that he did create a world which must result in some evil.

But this must be observed: though the Roman Catholic Church, the Orthodox Church, and a significant portion of the Protestant church follow Augustine, overall, no common understanding of evil or its origins has emerged out of thousands of years of debate. And, informally, much of the church continues to be dualistic or monistic, and among great minds, the debate of the nature and origin of evil continues, unresolved.

ON THE DIFFERENCE BETWEEN EVIL AND SIN

This is sin: an endless vertigo[169]

—Charles Mathewes

Henri Blocher wrote, "In the biblical perspective it is sin that is the great evil. It is the foremost evil and the very essence of evil: it is the worst evil."[170] Augustine saw evil

---

166. Ahern, "Good & Evil—a Note," 25.
167. Plantinga, *Nature of Necessity*, 164.
168. Ibid., 185.
169. Mathewes, *Evil and the Augustinian Tradition*, 245.
170. Blocher, *Evil and the Cross*, 58.

PART I: The Tension of Theodicy

as a privation of the good and sin as a perversion of the will. So, is there a difference between evil and sin, and if so, what is that difference? I raise this question for clarity of terms. Specifically, is there such thing as evil, which could be considered logically prior and separate from an evil act, a sin?[171] If the difference in the terms is merely semantic, such difference, while interesting, would not be fruitful for this project. But if the difference is more than semantic and reflects the deep structure of our universe, then there exists an ontological distinction worth considering here.

In Origen's Libertarian Free-Will-like system, people are born with a potential for evil or good. In that sense evil is both the potential and the act. Is it the case that evil can be considered merely a force that pulls us one way, while good pulls us another? That is, is evil the force and sin the act? A strict privationist should reject this, for evil is "nothing." This "nothing" may be devastating, horrible, and in its experience, damning. But only in a dualistic system could evil exert a force, for before the act (or evil non-action), there is truly nothing—which is the whole point of the privationist project. There exists no evil "pole" opposite God.

I must be careful here. I am not being quite fair to Origen. He does not speak in "potentials," but in "acts." He is concerned with the "doing." So, I am not saying, as I noted above, that Origen raised this question or that it was in his mind. I do not assert that his system must answer this question. But the question seems to emerge from his system. And it is, I think, obvious that no such question arises for a dualistic system, for a dualistic system would be "at peace" with an evil potential or force; it even demands one. So also, it does not arise for a Compatibilistic Free-Will-like system, which understands God as the only "force" and grants him the right to determine conformity to his character or divergence (evil) based only on his sovereign choice. So, it would seem that it is only for Libertarian Free-Will-like systems, such as Origen's (which assume generalized neutrality on the part of willful creatures at birth), which face this issue: is there an evil potential that draws the newborn from neutrality?

Perhaps not. John S. Feinberg rightly notes that James 1:13–14 may incline us to say that such a force exists. The text reads, "Let no one say when he is tempted, 'I am being tempted by God'; for God cannot be tempted by evil, and He Himself does not tempt anyone. But each one is tempted when he is carried away and enticed by his own lust. Then when lust has conceived, it gives birth to sin; and when sin is accomplished, it brings forth death." The lust (desire)[172] in a person for evil provides the potential or force and the outcome (if the desire is given its head) is "sin." But where does a "potential" (force) come from in a privationist, non-dualistic system? This is an important text for John S. Feinberg's understanding of the origin of evil, as noted

---

171. Here such internal "actions" as lust and covetousness are included as sins as well as non-action where right action would be the good action.

172. The text of James reads, ἐπιθυμία, which may be best translated by the neutral word "desire" as suggested by Feinberg and as translated in the NIV. See also Feinberg, *Many Faces of Evil*, 128 and *Deceived by God*, 109.

The Historical Development of the Concept of Evil

above his system is privationist and Compatibilistic Free-Will. So, it would seem this issue could also be raised in any privationist (non-dualistic) system. Is there an evil "force" or potential? If so, from where does it arise?

One response would be to say that the "force" or "potential for evil" is simply an expression—again, semantics, not ontology. Such a response would suggest that "desire" expresses not a force, but a *lack* of resolution. Indeed, we have desires, God-given desires, and what we should do with them has not been resolved. The as-yet-unmade decision of the willful creature is not an as-yet-unseen accidental necessity, and so fatalism. Note that I state this including Compatibilistic Free-Will and Libertarian Free-Will in the same container—and this is fair because both contend for a will that is volitional and unresolved in the will prior to the event; neither Libertarian Free-Will nor Compatibilistic Free-Will contend for accidental necessity of willful decisions. It remains a future event, humanly unresolved, no matter how conditioned or unconditioned by character, environment or by God.

So, ontological dualism is excluded, but evil is real, even if privative. Such a non-ontological-dualism cannot (must not) collapse into monism. What is it that keeps them apart, if not ontology? First, God is eternal and evil is not; there was no evil prior to creation or in creation. Second, and perhaps more importantly for this project, eschatologically there will be no evil (at least for God's people who are with him eternally). The final Era of Freedom, Conforming-Freedom, is distinct from the first Era at least in this respect; evil is gone for God's people; it has no intersection with them and it is existentially divided from the place of God's dwelling with his people. So, in this project, there is also no eschatological dualism. Evil, at least for God's people who will enjoy him forever, is temporary, not just limited and finite. God's goodness does not entail evil.

Based on this discussion, I suggest that it can be stipulated that if a Christian system is non-dualistic, then there can be no absolute force for evil, even though evil exerts a significant and terrible influence. At the level of human action, Satan could be acknowledged, for by orthodox understanding of God's economy, Satan exerts a force for evil. But clearly, he is not an ontologically necessary force for evil, or he could not have been corrupted himself. He was good as created; now, he is evil. Yet, if he was corruptible without dualism, Satan adds only a petty-dualism to the universe, however destructive or real his influence. Evil is not ontologically real. It has no force of its own. It is contingent.

So, I cannot agree that evil is a force and sin is the evil action. Rather evil is a description of all that is not in conformity with God; so is sin. And both can be used to describe accidentally necessary actions which lack conformity with God's character. What then is the reason for corruption, if no necessary force for evil exists? That has not been answered yet and it will be taken up again in Part II of this project.

PART I: The Tension of Theodicy

SUMMARY: THE SUBORDINATE-METAPHYSICAL NECESSITY OF EVIL

The above historical discussion of evil has tipped my hand; I understand the privative understanding of the nature of evil to have the fewest problems. I also understand privative evil to be fully real, terrible, horrifying, and destructive. As Charles Journet wrote, "The paradox of evil is the terrible reality of its privative existence."[173] In fact, consistent with an orthodox reading of the Bible, I understand it to be overwhelming to man and creation, stopped only by the death and resurrection of Christ. Though this is not at issue here, it is worth stating that a privative evil can be so horrible that it results in the death of the Son of God. Henri Blocher got it right when he wrote "Privation is not just any kind of absence. . . . The paradox of evil is the terrible reality of its privative existence."[174]

I also understand evil to originate with God's willful creatures. Willful creatures are the proximate, volitional, and efficient cause of evil. They are also "necessary" in the sense that God could not cause evil directly, nor could he be the cause of evil in any way, if he had not created volitional beings. The immediate cause of evil or sin, is the will of God's willful creatures.

Considering the nature and origin of evil, it may appear that there is little progress beyond our early understanding at the start of the Christian era. Christians agree in their rejection of dualism. We agree that the origin of sin lies generally in the will of man. But we do not enjoy thorough agreement about "privation"—or at least we do not agree to its meaning or its implications. One implication may be that evil is in some way, necessary. Few are willing to stray close to the idea that God is responsible for evil or that evil is necessary—and for good reason. Evil is the antithesis of God's goodness and if God is a source and fountain of what is good, how could evil be necessary in his universe, for if it is, he must be the cause! So, while I have shown that the privationist views of Feinberg, Plantinga, Ahern, and others, representing various positions on the nature of free-will, imply that evil is in some sense necessary,[175] most theologians would insist that evil is not necessary. For example, Calvin told us that God's willful creatures, at least the race called "Man," *could* have continued in perfection. Necessity in regard to evil is foreign to our way of thinking, even if it is implied by our systems.

---

173. Journet, *Meaning of Evil*, 47.

174. Blocher, *Evil and the Cross*, 27.

175. Ahern attributes God's omniscience and his decision to create as sufficient to make *only* the possibility of sin necessary in creation (Ahern, "An Approach to the Problems of Evil," 20). It is worth noting that it is the Catholic teaching of the sinlessness of Mary which establishes this for him, for if one can be sinless, any could be sinless. In regard to Feinberg, as noted above, this is the implication of the fact that he created the world he intended (Feinberg, *The Many Faces of Evil*, 126–8). In case of Plantinga, the idea of necessity arises out of his concept of "trans-world depravity" as shown above.

To take this a bit further, let me change the question: Is evil avoidable? If evil is not avoidable, then evil is necessary in some sense. But if evil is avoidable and if there is, in fact, evil in this world, then the question naturally progress to this: If evil is avoidable, why not start over? That is, why did God not destroy what he made, condemn the willful creatures who sinned, and start again to achieve a world without evil? There is a biblical assertion that he did something like this in the days of Noah. And the biblical record attests that he was not effective, if avoiding a sinful world in the future was his goal. Of course, this anecdotal evidence clearly does not require that we assert that evil is therefore not avoidable. Perhaps evil is avoidable and more divine "redo's" are required; we simply have not discovered, or cannot discover, the "why not" of God's refusal to perform many successive divine "redo's." That is, perhaps evil is avoidable, and successive acts of destruction and creation would accomplish a good world, but God does not choose to do so. But this is, in itself, the very theodicy question that we are pursuing! How could an omni-good and omni-powerful God fail to prevent evil? And this will be considered. But here, in regard to this question, "Is evil avoidable?" we have only the claim, on the part of some that it is avoidable. But all evidence points in the other direction. I suggest that there is no philosophical or existential evidence that evil is avoidable, only logical cases which are against experience. Instead, all evidence which we have uncovered indicates that willful creatures do depart from God's goodness—consistently! Perhaps evil is even necessary as is implied (even if unwillingly) by various systems. And if evil is necessary in some sense, perhaps in the sense noted previously as a *subordinate-metaphysical necessity*, it would change the theodicy equation and allow us more latitude in framing an understanding of the whole project of theodicy. To this we are about to turn.

Still, something more must be said about evil before I go on to consider theodicy, specifically. If we rightly understand evil to be privative in nature and originating from the wills of God's willful creatures—even if we understand evil as necessary, we must never accept it. The Cross insists that we cannot accept evil and that we must fight against it. It is fundamentally evil and "irredeemable" no matter how necessary or what good end may be brought about through it. I agree with Bruce Ware who wrote, "So let's be clear: evil is evil, suffering is suffering, and death is death. No amount of good that may be brought about through them can change what they are in their essence."[176] So, we must never concede to its residence in our world as part of the necessary balance of a willful ecology. "Evil is not there to be understood, but to be fought."[177] Indeed, nothing we might understand about its nature, origin, or necessity would minimize the truth that it is to be resisted as we were shown by the example of Christ on the Cross. If we are called to glorify God by seeking to understand his universe, even the evil that is in it, still we also hear the call to fight the battles God calls his people to fight. Evil & Suffering is the enemy. How shall we combat it? We

---

176. Ware, *God's Greater Glory*, 166.
177. Blocher, *Evil and the Cross*, 103.

PART I: The Tension of Theodicy

will do so with the singular tool used by God on the Cross: the evil of the Cross and the suffering of the Christ. We too will fight Evil & Suffering with Evil & Suffering in our own bodies. This is the wonder of the Cross; mere understanding is never enough.

3

Free-Will and Evil: The Historical Development of Theodicy

> Buddha concluded that the existence of suffering made the existence of any supreme God impossible. More recently Western thought has tended to see the fact of suffering as a powerful argument against the existence of the Christian God. The New Testament writers turned that argument on its head. Instead of suffering settling the issue of whether or not God was real, the reality of what God was and what he had done settled for them the issue of suffering.[1]
>
> —Peter Hicks

I HAVE CONSIDERED THE historical development of ideas regarding human free-will and evil's nature and origin in our world in an attempt to understand the relationship of human free-will to evil. Now I will further seek to understand this relationship by probing the theological mystery and experiential problem of theodicy. I intend to begin by making the tension within theodicy explicit and then I will consider the ethics of the theological systems that have contributed to the conversation about theodicy. Before considering the historical development of theodicy, I will first consider the taxonomy of theodicies to give a framework by which theodicies can be understood. Finally, and to no one's surprise, I will claim that there is more work to be done.

THEODICY: THE THEOLOGICAL TENSION

> If the universe were just electrons and selfish genes, meaningless tragedies like the crashing of a bus are exactly what we should expect, along with the equally meaningless good fortune. Such a universe would be neither evil nor good in intention. It would manifest no intentions of any kind. In a universe

---

1. Hicks, *Journey So Far*, 112.

PART I: The Tension of Theodicy

> of blind physical forces and genetic replication, some people are going to get hurt, other people are going to get lucky, and you won't find any rhyme or reason in it, nor any justice.[2]
>
> —Richard Dawkins

A tension, as we have seen, arises out of friction between free-will and evil in this sense. Evil seems too terrible a price to pay for free-will. How is it that God did not make another way, less evil, or less free-will, if free-will must be this "expensive"? Our desire for free-will is in tension with our anger, shock, and horror at the evil that results. We cry out to the sovereign God that it is too much. With Job, we ask for an explanation or an end to our pain—or both.

But this tension between freedom and evil exists only for the theist. While the atheist experiences the offense of pain and suffering, the lack of a good God in her system results in no tension. So, at least on this point, I agree with Dawkins as quoted above: either God's personal, creative sovereignty provides meaning to the universe or there is no meaning to be discovered. Either the universe is observed by One who creates and sustains it, or all the experiences of humanity are without significance. Life would then be a play without an audience, without a playwright, and without a director. But Christians claim there is such a One: YHWH, who is immanent and transcendent, sovereign and intimate. It is his personal presence that permits us to recognize evil and even causes us to be shocked by it. There is no "natural tension" between evil and free-will. The atheist, who has no personal Creator, requires no theodicy. She is likely to be shocked and distressed by evil, but there is nothing to be understood by it in relationship to God.[3] So, Laplace (perhaps anticipating Carl Sagan) said as much to Napoleon about God and the world as he found it: "Sire, I have no need of that hypothesis." So, Jürgen Moltmann wrote, "If there were no God, the world as it is would be all right. It is only the desire, the passion, the thirst for God which turns suffering into conscious pain and turns the consciousness of pain into a protest against suffering."[4] The economy of the atheist can afford to ignore the issue: "the problem of evil is obviously very acute [RAS: only] for theism."[5] So, this project seeks not to defend God to the atheist, who has no reason to have tension in this regard (even if she finds evil shocking and horrendous), but rather seeks to offer hope to the theist. It

---

2. Dawkins, *River out of Eden*, 132–3.

3. Many theists have become atheists in the face of great evil. Such are the well known experiences of Voltaire and of Elie Wiesel. Atheism relieves not the terror of evil, but the metaphysical pain of evil. No theodicy is needed. We will return to this in our discussion.

4. Moltmann, *Trinity and the Kingdom*, 48.

5. Whale, *Christian Answer to the Problem of Evil*, 28. Also, John Hick, "If there is no God—except as a thought in men's minds, a concept operating within our theistic language—then the destructive power of suffering is just a dreadful fact, and that's that" (Hick, "Remarks," 123). Note, while it is true that some, like Hans Küng, have said something like, "the problem of evil is the rock of atheism" (as cited by Peterson, *God and Evil*, 10), that is meant as an anti-apologetic and makes this same point: evil is a problem for those who believe in God and not for those who do not.

attempts to wrestle with the shock of evil, within the experience of human free-will, and address the question that arises: How can this world be a world overseen by God!? Where is the God who says to his people, "For the eyes of the LORD move to and fro throughout the earth that He may strongly support those whose heart is completely His" (2 Chronicles 16:9)?

As we consider a history of the conversation concerning possible solutions to this tension, it is helpful to keep in mind the core ideas from the study of free-will and of evil. First, human free-will stands. There are no orthodox Christian positions on the nature of free-will that completely remove human free-will; there is no Christian fatalism. Many have traded on the basic idea of Augustine that people are not rocks (which only have existence) and they are not animals (which have only existence and life). People, created in the image of God, have a will, as well as existence and life. Even considering the fallen nature of humanity, there remains a God-given will, which we exercise with what we call freedom, however conditioned or attenuated. Likewise, evil also exists. However fuzzy its origin or complicated its nature, it remains a reality of our world, even a *privative* reality. And no study of evil's nature and origin can render it acceptable to us.

Every conversation needs a benchmark. For theodicy, the oft cited benchmark is the words of Epicurus: "Is he willing to prevent evil, but not able? Then is he impotent. Is he able, but not willing? Then is he malevolent. Is he both able and willing? Whence then is evil?" This challenge is still potent.[6] Yet, this is not the only perspective. Some would agree with Madeleine L'Engle who writes, "Terrible things happen, and God does not prevent them. But the purpose of a universe created by a loving Maker is to be trusted."[7] In the face of unrelenting evil, Epicurus and L'Engle seem to show us opposing poles of agnostic anxiety and faithful trust. Both represent a "faith" of a sort. And both are in need of further examination in light of the reality of evil and the experience of our will. This is the tension between evil and free-will: given that evil and free-will exist, we hunger to understand God's place in relation to both.

---

6. Hume, *Dialogues Concerning Natural Religion*, part 10, 100. Hume (1711–1776) puts this quote on the lips of Philo, the careless skeptic, citing Epicurus as he debates Cleanthes, the theist. Perhaps the oldest attribution to Epicurus is Lactantius (260–330) in "A Treatise on the Anger of God" (*The Ante-Nicene Fathers,* chapter 13). He writes, "God, he says, either wishes to take away evils, and is unable; or He is able, and is unwilling; or He is neither willing nor able, or He is both willing and able. If He is willing and is unable, He is feeble, which is not in accordance with the character of God; if He is able and unwilling, He is envious, which is equally at variance with God; if He is neither willing nor able, He is both envious and feeble, and therefore not God; if He is both willing and able, which alone is suitable to God, from what source then are evils?" But this is still separated from Epicurus by half a millennium. Augustine is also credited with a very similar version of this: "Either God cannot abolish evil or he will not: if he cannot then he is not all-powerful; if he will not then he is not all-good" (Flew, "Divine Omnipotence and Human Freedom," *New Essays in Philosophical Theology,* 144). Though many reference some version of this in Augustine, I could not find this quote in Augustine's works.

7. L'Engle, *Two-Part Invention,* 149.

But not all are eager to examine the issue. A reviewer of Marilyn McCord Adams wrote, "The current debate resembles a series of disparate conversations among fewer and fewer people."[8] Centuries, even millennia of searching for a satisfying solution to the problem of evil have discouraged many from hoping for more light on this issue. It seems to respond like a black hole, absorbing all attempts to illuminate it. There is some reason to think even pursuing the issue is foolish, even presumptuous.

Yet, most who subscribe (or desire to subscribe) to Epicurus's assertions about God and evil, do seek a solution to the problem of evil, whether or not creating a "theodicy" is something we explicitly intend. Our minds, unbeckoned, cast about for ways in which the pieces might fit together. This is the issue theodicy forces upon us when we accept the reality of evil and willful-human beings before God. In this context, C.S. Lewis states it well when he writes, Christianity "creates, rather than solves, the problem of pain, for pain would be no problem unless, side by side with our daily experience of this painful world, we had received what we think a good assurance that ultimately reality is righteous and loving."[9] While one cannot easily let go of any of Epicurus's three assertions, the pieces do not settle into a comfortable patterns on their own. This tension is not simply removed by logic; it is particularly sticky in our souls.

ON THE ETHICS OF A THEODICY

Consequentialism and non-consequentialism define the two possibilities which describe how we could understand the "functioning" of evil within any theodicy. John S. Feinberg writes, "Consequentialism (known as teleological ethics) claims that what makes an action good or bad, right or wrong are the consequences that result from it. Non-consequentialism (often referred to as deontological ethics) says that whatever makes an action right or wrong . . . is something other than consequences."[10] For Feinberg, a non-consequentialist, this definition could seem to turn evil into "evil light," for by tautology, it has no evil "consequences." However, in the text on the same page, Feinberg writes: "the existence of evil is justified [RAS: for consequentialists] because God will use it ultimately to maximize good."[11] This is, I think, more exact. Consequentialism is more exactly a species of theodicy that not only uses evil instrumentally, but also justifies evil as instrumentally necessary to God. The difference is significant.

8. Zupko, "Review: Marilyn McCord Adams," 137.

9. Lewis, *Problem of Pain*, 14.

10. Feinberg, *Many Faces of Evil*, 55 n. 1. It is worth noting that consequentialism is not the only kind of teleological ethics, as the wording of this quote might indicate. In Kantian terms, this is parallel to "hypothetical imperative" as opposed to "categorical imperatives." Teleological ethics are those ethical choices we make to improve our ends and this includes consequentialism.

11. Feinberg, *Many Faces of Evil*, 55.

Free-Will and Evil: The Historical Development of Theodicy

Examples of both systems will be displayed in the historical survey that follows. Consequential systems include that of Hick, building upon Irenaeus. In such systems, it is generally proposed that: evil is a part of the system that God created; people are created immature; and evil essentially operates upon them to form them from the image and into the likeness of God. So, evil is the instrument by which God's willful-creatures are matured. Non-consequentialist systems propose: that God created the world good; that evil is an enemy to be destroyed; and that evil is of no essential value to the system, even if God uses it for his own purposes. This is the perspective of Gregory Boyd, a theologian who distances himself from Augustine and positions himself as an Openness-of-God theologian. In *Satan and the Problem of Evil*, he understands the creation of God to be going through a cosmic battle between Good and Evil, in which God is at war with an evil enemy. But, quite distinctly, it is also the ethical system of most who follow Augustine.[12] So, Feinberg identifies his own system, and Reformed systems in general, as non-consequentialist.

It is worth noting some flexibility in how ethical systems are understood and implemented. It is not as clearly defined as one might expect from the definition. As is seen above, Openness-of-God theologians and Augustinian theologians generally have the same system of ethics. But just as Augustine did not think in these terms, so we may be too eagerly categorical. By way of illustration, it would be possible to propose that the Reformed position of Calvin and Edwards is consequentialist in most respects—an ethical position which few, if any Christian theologians would espouse:

(i) God decreed evil and salvation prior to creation

(ii) God created the world good; no evil existed in the world God created

(iii) Evil entered as the mediate result of God's choice to create as he did create; but as an immediate result of the volitional action of God's willful-creatures

(iv) God was right in creating such a world, which would fall into evil and suffering, because he would be glorified supremely in its final redemption[13]

Let me first deal with an obvious objection. I have stated above, following Feinberg, that consequentialist systems usually understand the world to be created so that it is composed of both good and evil, however, it is not the case that the consequentialist systems require that creation include evil. Rather, it is more exact to state that non-consequentialist systems require that creation be created wholly good, while this is not a condition upon the consequentialist.[14] In the case of the Edwardian-Calvinistic

---

12. Though these are not terms in which Augustine would have mapped his ideas, and so it is not "his system," these concepts are concepts that developed (as was shown previously) from his ideas.

13. Private exchanges with John S. Feinberg in 2005 resulted in his agreeing with this as a valid way to frame the Calvinist/Edwardian perspective.

14. Rather it is the non-consequentialist who can only have a world created good. The consequentialist can be consequentialist with a creation permitting evil or not. The issue is how necessary evil is to the good goals.

system, God, having decreed evil from eternity, has distinct mediate responsibility for evil. And evil is justified in Edwards's system by the ends to which God uses it—a distinct feature of a consequentialist system. In his case the end is this: God is glorified supremely and more fully in that and is able to display character qualities that would not otherwise be displayed, such as justice and mercy.[15] While I am not asserting that the Edwardian system is consequentialist, this does have the ring of consequentialism by Feinberg's definition.

If this observation is of value, it is because it highlights the difficulty in determining what is meant by saying that a system is consequentialist. Is that identical with understanding evil as instrumental? It is not impossible to assess, but it is, perhaps, elusive. In my proposal, it will be important to establish in what way Evil & Suffering is used, instrumentally, to destroy Evil & Suffering and to ask if this implies a consequentialist or non-consequentialist ethic. It will also raise the question of whether this proposal minimizes the evil of Evil & Suffering. While I will address this more thoroughly in Part II, I will state here that this proposal employs a non-consequentialist ethic and, while Reformed, it is free of the possibility of reframing it in consequentialist terms. In so doing, I am asserting that Evil & Suffering is irredeemable and of no intrinsic value to God. It was neither created nor permitted in order to gain some greater good. It was a necessary enemy, as a result of God's character and his goals in creation.

THEODICY: A TAXONOMY

As background for my proposal, I want to first consider what varieties and kinds of theodicies arise within theistic systems. I propose Defections; which, rather than offering solutions, propose to change the nature of the problem; Defenses, which propose a philosophically (internally) consistent solution; and Theodicies, which propose a resolution that is offered as theologically sufficient and philosophically consistent.[16]

---

15. Swinburne's position is not unlike this as he understands that God is able to bring about certain "higher-order goods" by permitting evil—something that would not be possible without it, though in his understanding the suffering for "higher-order goods" must be for limited duration for each individual (Swinburne, *Providence and the Problem of Evil*, 248–9; *Existence of God*, chapter 11, particularly 216–28).

16. What of necessity? Would it not be of value to propose a resolution which is sufficient and necessary? In regard to any model in either theology or the physical sciences, the standard of necessity for a proposed model is unattainable. Time and testing of human models never prove necessity, but only degrees of fitness. How much more when modeling infinity in finite expression! Theology, including theodicy, is a human model of a divine reality. It seeks, rightly, to explore reality about God. We will approximate and fit various pieces, seeking understanding. We can know, but we cannot know all or know fully. No model, and certainly not the proposal of this project, will reach or claim to reach, the pinnacle of necessity. Yet, modeling is appropriate to man and honoring to God. He calls us to know him.

Defections

> Holding on to both ends of the chain, affirming both the reality of God and the reality of evil, stops the human mind gravitating into absurdity either by denying God or denying evil, and saves it from suicide.[17]
>
> —Charles Journet

In attempting to sort out the taxonomies of theodicy, it will serve to identify the first order classification which could be called Defections. Such theodicies achieve that status by doing what Epicurus would exclude: by changing the character of God or by making evil something less than terrible or even less than real. The reason seems to be that for some, when a few pieces fall together, one piece falls on the floor. For that reason, Defections are not true theodicies, offering a solution, but rather seek to change the nature of the problem. In fact, they seek to change the reality that posed the problem in the first place. Such defections are logically permissible, but they do not "solve" the problem of evil or even lead us toward a solution to the problem, to which all of these three truths must be held: God is omni-Good; God is omnipotent; evil exists. I will consider each of the three possible conclusions under this head.

Faulty Goodness: First, we consider that God is not good. If God is not good and yet he is all-powerful, what would that world look like? This includes the world of the Greco-Roman gods. While these gods would at times act benevolently towards humans, they most often acted whimsically and out of selfishness and self-pleasure. These gods were described in the tales as overgrown children, who got drunk, hacked each other to bits, swallowed each other, delighted in lewd behavior, acted with wanton cruelty, and helped humans—if it pleased them to do so. Their solution to suffering could be represented by the god Bacchus, who gave men wine which "when they drink their fill, banishes the sufferings of wretched mortals and brings forgetfulness of each day's troubles in sleep. There is no other cure for sorrow."[18] Such a system might be perceived as a significant part of the problem of evil rather than a solution.[19] There is a similar diminution of God's goodness in earthy paganism. While there are many examples, consider what the Israelites discovered when they crossed into Canaan. They encountered gods like Baal, the god of the earth, and his consort (and mother!) Asherah, the goddess of fertility. Together they governed fertility and crops.

---

17. Journet, *Meaning of Evil*, 59.
18. March, *Cassell Dictionary of Classical Mythology*, 136.
19. It is worth noting in this context that it is against the background of such "passions"—those of the unrestrained and self-indulgent Greco-Roman gods—that the very idea of impassivity was given form. Plato and Aristotle's rejection of the poetic conceptions of gods of passionate vagaries became the apathetic God. This serves as a reminder that it is critical to understand the characterization of God in the context of the argument. So, while God is not apathetic—he is the God of the Cross—he is also not like the gods of wanton passions.

PART I: The Tension of Theodicy

The worship rites for such gods included prostitution and other lascivious behavior,[20] and even the burning of their sons on Baal's altars.[21] Like the gods of the Greeks and Romans, these gods did not claim to be good or claim to pursue the best interests of humans. If God was like these gods, we are relieved of the tension of the problem of evil, because he could make no claim to goodness. If gods are cruel, it is frustrating to humans, but no more, for it would be a reality which we have no power to change.

Attenuated Power: Second, we consider that God's power is somehow attenuated. Few are comfortable asserting that God is not good; however, more are willing to diminish his power. In short, this view says, "God would like to help us, but He is unable to do so." One such attenuation of God's power is offered by Process Theism—an almost omni-immanent view of God.[22] In his Gifford Lectures, preserved in *Process and Reality*, Alfred North Whitehead exposes such an understanding of God. For Whitehead, this flows out of the life of Christ, as opposed to world systems.[23] His understanding is that both God and the creation are in process together, without attribution of sovereignty to one or the other. They are engaged in process and God cannot supersede that process by using power, anymore than the creation can do so.[24] We work through the process and as such, there is no problem of evil to solve, because neither God nor the world has the power to destroy evil. Rabbi Harold Kushner offers a popular version of attenuated power in his book, *When Bad Things Happen to Good People*.[25] While not an academic work, it is a work that resonates with the basic

20. 1 Kings 14:22–24.

21. Jeremiah 19:5.

22. Alfred North Whitehead writes, "The notion of God as the 'unmoved mover' is derived from Aristotle, at least so far as Western thought is concerned. The notion of God as 'eminently real' is a favourite doctrine of Christian theology. The combination of the two into the doctrine of an aboriginal, eminently real, transcendent creator, at whose fiat the world came into being, and whose imposed will it obeys, is the fallacy which has infused tragedy into the histories of Christianity and of Mohometanism" (*Process and Reality*, 342).

23. Whitehead writes, "There is however, in Galilean origin of Christianity yet another suggestion which does not fit very well with any of the three main strands of thought. It does not emphasize the ruling Caesar, or the ruthless moralist, or the unmoved mover. It dwells upon the tender elements in the world, which slowly and in quietness operate by love; . . . Love neither rules, nor is it unmoved; also it is a little oblivious as to morals. It does not look to the future; for it finds its own reward in the immediate present" (*Process and Reality*, 343).

24. Whitehead writes, "It is as true to say that God is permanent and the World fluent, as that the World is permanent and God is fluent. It is as true to say that God is one and the World many, as that the World is one and God many. It is as true to say that, in comparison with the World, God is actual eminently, as that, in comparison with God, the World is actual eminently. It is as true to say that the World is immanent in God, as that God is immanent in the World. It is as true to say that God transcends the World, as that the World transcends God. It is as true to say that God creates the World, as that the World creates God" (*Process and Reality*, 348).

25. Kushner's first words betray a certain bias, "There is only one question which really matters: why do bad things happen to good people" (Kushner, *When Bad Things Happen to Good People*, 6). It is worthwhile to say here that, while the problem may be an issue only for a certain kind of theist, it is not the most important matter for Christians. In fact, the problem cannot be solved and does not matter unless there exist matters that are far more important. So it is claimed in Romans 8:18: "For

Free-Will and Evil: The Historical Development of Theodicy

"feelings" of many. His thesis is this, "we will simply have to learn to live with [RAS: suffering], sustained and comforted by the knowledge that [RAS: it is] not the will of God, but represents that aspect of reality which stands independent of His will, and which angers and saddens God even as it angers and saddens us."[26] That is, God is not all-powerful. He concludes by asking us to love and forgive a God who is doing the best he can.[27] This has a certain attraction for some: God's compassion and mercy are softly lit against the backdrop of his willing inability: "God would like to help us, but he can't. Please don't hold it against him." But like the offering of the Greeks, it has in fact modified the problem rather than offering a solution. Also the recent approach of Openness of God theists uses a variant of this thinking. These theologians do not directly limit God's power, but propose that God himself preemptorily limits his knowledge and so limits the exercise of his power. In correspondence with his skeptical father, Gregory Boyd responds to his father's concern: How could a good and powerful God allow all the evil in the world? Boyd responds this way, "God can't foreknow the good or bad decisions of the people He creates until He creates these people and they, in turn, create their decisions."[28] In this way God is understood to be protected from responsibility for the moral failure of his free agents because, not only did he make them free, but he went so far as to blind himself to their future decisions (or rather their freedom blinds him). This option offers us something that is satisfying, because God is, in a significant sense, going through evil with us, like a suffering partner. Yet, this does seem to collapse the distance that separates God's *potentia absoluta* (his unmediated use of his power), and his *potentia ordinata* (his mediated use of his power), so that all the space between the natural and supernatural is removed.[29]

I consider that the sufferings of this present time are not worthy to be compared with the glory that is to be revealed to us." The same assumption seems to be behind 2 Corinthians 4:17, "For momentary, light affliction is producing for us an eternal weight of glory far beyond all comparison." Pain is significant, but understanding it may be less important than knowing what greater things are true. God's higher purposes are one example of "more important matters." What is the purpose of man? The answer of the Westminster Confession is, "to glorify God and enjoy Him forever." Our suffering is not trivial, but if it becomes central, we are indeed only left with despair. This issue is dealt with much more fully in Chapter 4 of Part II.

26. Kushner, *When Bad Things Happen*, 55.

27. "Are you capable of forgiving and loving God even when you have found out that He is not perfect, even when He has let you down and disappointed you by permitting bad luck and sickness and cruelty in His world, and permitting some of those things to happen to you? Can you learn to love and forgive Him despite His limitations, as Job does, and as you once learned to forgive and love your parents even though they were not as wise, or as strong, or as perfect as you needed them to be?" (Kushner, *When Bad Things Happen*, 148)

28. Boyd and Boyd, *Letters from a Skeptic*, 30. This statement is made in response to the problem of evil, raised by his father. It is intended to relieve the pressure of evil on God's character. But Boyd himself in a later development tells us that it fails to explain why evil exists at all: "the problem of evil remains, even within a warfare worldview. But unlike the futile quest for the elusive good divine motive for any particular evil within the world, this metaphysical question is answerable . . . [RAS: it is] a spiritual opponent to be overcome" (Boyd, *God at War*, 21). I would say that Boyd's analysis is correct.

29. While Boyd and others do not intend to take the modern route of philosophical theology that

PART I: The Tension of Theodicy

Like other Defections, the Openness of God proposal changes the problem: God's sovereignty is diminished and so the tension is relieved.[30] But the problem is not solved.

Ephemeral Evil: Third, under the head of Defections, we consider that Evil is ephemeral. As in other defections, the problem is changed: if evil does not exist, there is no problem to solve. So, if we experience pain, it is not really as we perceive it. This is reflected in Hinduism, Buddhism, and the New Age religion of western Buddhism.[31] The basic principle is *karma*, which impersonally brings into each life what is deserved. Since nothing is intrinsically evil, for there is no such thing, we need not resist, but accept. The final state, after sufficient tutoring by *karma*, is neither evil nor good, but is instead one of freedom from the material, physical, and even the personal.

A world without evil, in which all there is (including "evil") is in God; is a monistic world. Benedict Spinoza (1632–1677), a contemporary of Leibniz, was an early advocate for monism, rejecting any objective meaning to the concept of evil.[32] In our day, Christian Science is a popular philosophy, which also maintains that evil does not exist. Mary Baker Eddy, in her book *Science and Health with Key to the Scriptures*, maintains that matter does not exist and the only reality is God and his mind. Matter, evil, and even suffering are all illusions. Evil and goodness are merely perceived constructs, useful to us but created in our own minds. All impressions of good (or evil) are inventions of our mind. They are a construct through which we process the world. The right way to process experiences is the one that results in the most effective survival strategy.[33] Again, the problem has been changed, not solved.

---

brings God into the "natural," destroying the supernatural, such a move may in effect do the same thing. To be fair, Boyd would not agree, and he would assert that God is so superior to us, he is able to work through the natural without overwhelming the freedom of his creatures.

30. While Boyd's proposal in *Letters* seems to be offered only in passing, the theology of Openness Theism is thoroughly developed in his many other books including, *God of the Possible,* and also by many others, including William Hasker (*God, Time, and Knowledge*), Clark Pinnock (*Most Moved Mover*), and John Sanders (*God Who Risks*).

31. Of course, in Buddhism (and its derivatives), everything, including evil, is ephemeral, so it is perhaps hardly significant to suggest a unique distinction in regard to evil. A "Christian" version which considers evil to be ephemeral is expressed by G. W. Allen who proposes that evil is an illusion to drive us to the good and to God (Allen, *Mission Of Evil*).

32. Spinoza wrote, "After experience had taught me that all the usual surroundings of social life are vain and futile; seeing that none of the objects of my fears contained in themselves anything either good or bad, except in so far as the mind is affected by them, I finally resolved to inquire whether there might be some real good having power to communicate itself" (Spinoza, *On the Improvement of the Understanding*, 1.1). With this beginning, he seeks for objective good and fails to find it. He writes, "we must bear in mind that the terms good and evil are only applied relatively, so that the same thing may be called both good and bad according to the relations in view, in the same way as it may be called perfect or imperfect" (12.1).

33. It is worth interjecting, because it may not be obvious, that to deny evil is to mount an attack on God's character. As was discussed in chapter 2, evil is the failure of the willful creature to conform to God's holiness—so the reality of evil is tied up with God's objective goodness. God requires people to be active students of the difference between good and evil: "But . . . the mature, who by constant use have trained themselves to distinguish good and evil" (Hebrews 5:14, NIV). Isaiah writes, "Woe to those who call evil good, and good evil; Who substitute darkness for light and light for darkness"

Fading Evil: Another logical Defection is Fading Evil. Perhaps evil is not permanent, but transitory within time. That is, human advance and specific progress in the arts and sciences could, over time, diminish and eventually eradicate evil. Evil is real today, but it will one day disappear by human perseverance and progress. For some this would have the effect of exonerating God; for others, of elevating people. But the start of the World War in 1914 and its extension into the death camps of Auschwitz, the mass graves of Stalin, and the xenophobic and misogynistic atrocities throughout the century, were a jarring obstacle to such a position.[34] Evil did not disappear with the great advances in math, science, political science, or psychology humankind had achieved; far from it—it increased. Martin Buber (1878–1965), influenced by Søren Kierkegaard and conscious of the atrocities of the early twentieth century, proposed something similar. He wrote, "Man's task, therefore, is not to extirpate the evil urge, but to reunite it with the good."[35] Evil fades, not by the scientific advance of the "I-it" encounter, but by the spiritual advance of the "I-thou" encounter and is absorbed into the good. In the case of evil, its nature is transitory and metaphysically weak. While this view suffers from optimism or from a failure to confront the terrible reality of evil, it attempts to change the problem as opposed to solving it.

Making Peace with Evil: Lastly, under Defections, we consider making peace with evil. When the Allies attempted to end the World War with an armistice, establishing the League of Nations to keep evil empires at bay, it failed. It might even be construed that World War I resumed as World War II and the Cold War.[36] The world sickened even more. So, also, it must be said from thousands of years of experience with evil, no solution to the problem of evil can afford to make an armistice with evil. One only has to look once at the Cross to be overwhelmed by God's unwillingness not to "excuse" evil or to make "peace" with evil. He has made war against evil and has destroyed death (2 Timothy 1:10). If armistice is precluded, perhaps the solution to the problem of evil requires that we make real peace with evil, not just bring an end to

---

(Isaiah 5:20). Like the other options, denying the reality of evil is logically possible, and in many ways sensible, but the denial of evil is as much an attack on God's character as it is an attempt to reduce his goodness or power.

34. In the introduction to *The Justification of God: Lectures for War-time on a Christian Theodicy*, P. T. Forsyth rejects a belief in "progress." He writes that "The War" ("the magnitude of our present calamity") has forced people to consider the problem of Theodicy—the reality of evil—even when they would rather not do so (v.) More specifically, the hope for the world is "not that of civilized progress" (197). "Progress" is also rightly rejected by many others, including N.T. Wright (*Evil and the Justice of God*, 23).

35. Buber, *Good and Evil*, 95. As to the origin of evil, Buber understands it to be a corruption of "imagery" that God created "very good." Buber understands the Hebrew noun formed from יֵצֶר (which is a common verb for "form" or "make" and is used for creation) in Genesis 6:5 and 8:21 as "imagery" or "possibilities" (90), which is something like a human attempt at Middle Knowledge which is evil: "this imagery of the possible, and in this its nature, is called evil" (91). And it is now called evil, because we "made it so" (95).

36. This is the extended thesis of Niall Ferguson in *The War of the World: Twentieth Century Conflict and the Descent of the West*.

hostilities. Francis Schaeffer observed this impossibility, citing Camus as an example: Camus "argued that if there is a God, then we cannot fight social evil, for if we do, we are fighting God who made the world as it is."[37] Could it be that Christians would offer a solution to the problem of evil that requires us to in some way make peace with evil? May God, who died on the Cross combating evil, forbid it! Schaeffer argues that the Christian who believes God created man good (through whom evil was brought into the world, thus we are not abnormal), is able to fight evil: "On this basis, we can have a real ground for fighting evil, including social evil, and social injustice."[38] The basis is the work of Christ on the Cross, which for the Christian of any stripe, is a forceful declaration of war against evil. In the end, we are able to test a good theodicy because it will have this characteristic: we are able to hate evil, love the good, and fight along with God, even as his champions, against evil. No explanation may permit us to make an armistice—or even peace, with evil.

Ultimately, all Defections are unsatisfactory. I agree with J.S. Whale who declares, "Given these three presuppositions, Christian thought dare not slur over any one of them in the interests of neat and easy logic. . . . The Christian answer to the problem of evil begins, therefore, by rejecting all those tempting solutions which would simplify the issue by getting rid of the triangle."[39] If an argument, which is put forward to address the problem of evil, can be shown to be a Defection (though such categorizations are not indubitable, as in the case, for example, of Openness Theism), such an argument can be set aside by the Christian theist.

Defenses

> [a] proposition might be both necessary and such that on a given occasion the rational thing to do is to give up or deny it.[40]
>
> —Alvin Plantinga

Distinct from Defections, which merely decline to solve the problem of evil rather than offer a solution, a Defense is a sufficient and logical solution that seeks to assert all of the tenets of Epicurus's trilemma. And while Defenses are not only "not necessary," but often seem to depart even from objectivity, they can still achieve status as a solution. However, a Defense does not seek to assert a specific solution, but instead attempts to show "it is conceptually possible" in regard to the problem of evil.

Alvin Plantinga is the modern revivalist of a particular version of this solution, the Free-Will Defense. Compared to a theodicy, a defense is weaker in its claim, which

---

37. Schaeffer, *He Is There and He Is not Silent*, 28.
38. Ibid., 31.
39. Whale, *Christian Answer to the Problem of Evil*, 16–17.
40. Plantinga, *Nature of Necessity*, 4.

paradoxically, may be stronger in its effect. Plantinga writes, "So there is a significant difference between a Free Will Theodicy and a Free Will Defense. The latter is sufficient (if successful) to show that set A is consistent; in a way a Free Will Theodicy goes beyond what is required."[41] That is, if a successful case can be made that nothing bars a particular proposal, other than the fact that we are not sure that proposal is necessarily true, then the Christian God has a legitimate Defense. Plantinga is credited with accomplishing just this against the seemingly fatal objections of J. L. Mackie who wrote, referring to the Epicurean trilemma: "Here it can be shown, not that religious beliefs lack rational support, but that they are positively irrational, that several parts of theological doctrine are inconsistent with one another."[42] For Mackie (and others like Antony Flew), this is not the problem of evil—a problem with which to wrestle, but The Invincible Problem *from* Evil. A Defense, in this case a Free-Will Defense in contrast to a Theodicy, must only show that it is possible that Mackie is not correct. R. Douglass Geivett puts the difference this way:

> A defense is supposed to show that no contradiction can be made out between the existence of God and the existence of evil. But this does not show that God actually has a justifying reason for permitting evil. A theodicy, it is often thought, is supposed to show what justifying reasons God actually has for permitting evil. But theodicies are not generally convincing to non-theists impressed by the reality of evil.[43]

This observation is a good one. The Defense, limited as it is and not dependent upon truth claims, certainly not upon a correspondence theory of biblical truth, is an effective tool for an external discussion with non-theists. It is the Defense that Plantinga used so well against Mackie and Flew's strong, seemingly damning, case against

---

41. Plantinga, *God, Freedom, and Evil*, 28.

42. Mackie, "Evil and Omnipotence," 200. In fact, it is worth noting with David Bentley Hart that the atheist who argues against God is much influenced by God. So I would agree when he writes, "The atheist who argues from worldly suffering, even crudely, against belief in a God both benevolent and omnipotent is still someone whose moral expectations of God—and moral disappointments—have been shaped at the deepest level by language of Christian faith" (Hart, *Doors of the Sea*, 23–24).

43. Geivett, *Evil and the Evidence for God*, 60. We could also note Terrence Tilley's definitional assessment in regard to the difference between a Theodicy and a Defense. He wrote, "The purpose of a theodicy is not to show that the atheologian's attempted rebuttal is unsuccessful. Rather, the believer seeks to show that the warrants for her or his own conclusion are reliable. Here the believer must make the argument" ("The Use and Abuse of Theodicy," 308. In other words, the Defender can attack the Warrant of the atheologian's claim against God based on evil, but the Theodicist must produce a positive warrant for God in the face of evil.

PART I: The Tension of Theodicy

Christian theism.[44] But as Jerry Walls observed, "Plantinga must move out of the relatively modest realm of defense into the bolder arena of theodicy."[45]

Theodicies

> I may assert Eternal Providence, And justify the ways of God to men.[46]
>
> —John Milton

The word most commonly associated with the problem of evil, theodicy, was likely coined by Leibniz who wrote *Theodicy: Essays on the Goodness of God, the Freedom of Man, and the Origin of Evil* in 1710. But the idea of justifying God's ways is older still, dating from long before Milton's famous lines of 1667. The book of Job, placed in a patriarchal setting, appears to propose an ancient "market" for theodicy.[47] Many people have a deep desire first to understand but also to show God to be just and justified in the face of terrible evil. We desire to silence our anxiety as we stand in the gulf between the sovereign goodness of God and the raw evil of our experience.

---

44. Plantinga was successful in making his case, refuting Antony Flew and J. L. Mackie. In fact, Flew became a theist (Deist) in 2005 at the age of 81, open to the possibility of special revelation (Flew and Habermas, "My Pilgrimage from Atheism to Theism"). It is worth noting here that a Defense may be more likely an argument within the discipline philosophical theology than systematic theology. It is suited to rules of logic rather than hermeneutics because it does not deal with truth (necessarily) but with consistency. A Theodicy may be seated in philosophical halls and it may attempt to show its necessity on philosophical grounds, but it may legitimately choose to dwell with theologians, meeting exegetical tests. It cannot escape logic, but its benchmark intends to be God's revealed truth. So not only does a Theodicy set itself a double-edged task of being both sufficient and necessary, but it assumes the presumption of the test of Truth.

45. Walls, "Why Plantinga Must Move from Defense to Theodicy," 333.

46. Milton, *Paradise Lost*, 1.25.

47. Robert Gordis, in *Book of God and Man*, acknowledges that there can never be agreement on even the "basic meaning" of the book of Job (v.), but his perspective is that in the story Job deals with the "the most agonizing issue confronting men—the mystery of evil" (7). Elsewhere he calls it "the mystery of suffering" (135) in which suffering is the concrete (to the abstract of "evil") in opposition to the Greeks penchant for the abstract (135–6). He also writes, "the Book of Job belongs to the category of higher Wisdom . . . concerned with ultimate issues. High if not highest on the list was the problem of man's suffering in a world created and governed by a good God" (53–54). He also writes, "the major issue in biblical religion was the problem of evil. From the need to resolve the tension between faith in God's retribution and the spectacle of injustice triumphant in the world came most of the deepest insights of biblical faith" (146). That includes this book: Job. His argument is based on the clear statement of the book taken as a whole. Thousands of years later, people constantly turn to Job when they feel the existential pain of suffering in the presence of a God they believe to be both good and all powerful. And whether its subject is understood or misunderstood, Job continues to have a vast and dedicated "audience." While Gordis believes the date of book to be post-exilic (500–300 BCE, 216) and I lean to an earlier date (for reasons I will give later), the book has always been one that has grabbed the attention of its readers, insuring its duplication and ultimate position in the Canon. If Gordis is right in saying that it is about the "mystery of evil," as I also believe, then these two facts together (its immediate acceptance as a masterpiece and its subject) imply a ready audience for a book about the mystery of evil in God's good world.

Whether by argument or by epic poem, a Theodicy hopes to exceed a Defense in the way it touches reality and serves as a testable model. Michael Peterson separates a Defense from a Theodicy in this way:

> Defense: The aim of defense is to show that anti-theistic arguments from evil—either logical or evidential—are not successful on their own terms.
>
> Theodicy: The general aim of theodicy, by contrast, is to give positive, plausible reasons for the existence of evil in a theistic universe.[48]

So, a theodicy is not merely offering a logical reason why the Christian God cannot be dismissed in the face of evil, but attempts to offer a real-world solution to the problem of evil. However, if a theodicy desires to really justify God, it is quite a hopeful argument as well. Again, one could say that such a claim is a presumption: a band-aid over a fatal wound in God; an argument foolishly exalting itself over centuries of confusion. Such a disparaging view of theodicy is not limited to atheologians such as Mackie. Such a position is the hallmark of Paul Ricoeur, who wrote: "Must not the eternal theodicy and its mad project of justifying God, although it is God who justifies us, be denounced? Is it not the absurd rationalizing of the advocates of God which now inhabits the great Saint Augustine?"[49] John S. Feinberg wrote in regard to the logical problem of evil, "A theodicy purports to offer the actual reason God has for allowing evil in our world. A defense is much less pretentious, for it claims to offer only a possible reason God might have for not removing evil. . . . A defense is defense enough; a theodicy [RAS: God's actual reason] is not required."[50] In fact, Feinberg concludes his study of the logical problem of evil by writing, "Why not simply forego this current world and create that other world from the beginning?" He answers: "I respond that the most any of us can say (free-will defender, soul-building theodicist, and I) is that it pleased God to create our world prior to and perhaps even preparatory to that next world. Beyond that, God simply has not told us why."[51] After so many pages of investigation, his answer calls us to no further inquiry into God's purposes. Feinberg seems to indicate that an honest theodicy cannot be drafted: we are not to know God's purposes. Similarly, Peterson says, "theodicists embracing classical theism have to justify each actual evil or kind of evil by linking it to some actual good or class of goods—an effort that is extremely difficult and probably doomed."[52] Blocher

---

48. Peterson, *God and Evil*, 32.

49. Ricoeur, *Conflict of Interpretations*, 281. See also pages 345 ("'presumption' of theodicies"), 351 ("I renounce my viewpoint; I love the whole as it *is*"), and 370 ("the problem of the failure of theodicy"). This is not a minor point for Ricoeur. Robert Williams writes, "Paul Ricoeur gives powerful expression to the tragic sense of history in his condemnation of the entire enterprise of theodicy. . . . It fails because it is a theodicy—a view of the world as ethically ordered and governed" ("Theodicy, Tragedy and Soteriology," 396).

50. Feinberg, *Many Faces of Evil*, 1994, 19.

51. Ibid., 141–42.

52. Peterson, *God and Evil*, 104.

PART I: The Tension of Theodicy

also despairs even of the value of pursuing the subject. He says, "the problem of evil remains without any rational solution."[53] With an echo of Macbeth, some might assert that the problem of evil will remain a mystery to *the last syllable of recorded time.*

Such views are daunting and might discourage a project that hopes to pose as a Theodicy, as does this one. But as was observed in the introduction, a theodicy project does not have to be the last word to be "successful." Its role is to offer a fruitful direction for the discussion to be continued. Such is my desire with this project.

But even theodicies come in two varieties. Let me label the first, as described above, a Miltonian theodicy, which intends to justify God to man. It is inherently anthropocentric. There is a place for such theology, just as there is a place for apologetics. Yet, the theodicy that I intend to put forward in this project will involve making a move to grasp "reality," and I will label it a theocentric theodicy. This is not to make an inflated claim for such a model, and certainly not for this project, but rather it is a perspective. If there is something to say about theodicy, I seek to know something about the "reality" that is in God. Such a model does not claim to encompass all of reality, but rather intends to seek truth about God, his character, and his goals, that will allow us to understand him. He is not to be defended, but held up to view. In this model, Job could represent the first theodicy, not because God's ways are justified, but because in the context of pain, God is revealed and known to be sufficient. Hope in a world seemingly full (far too full!) of Evil & Suffering is found in knowing more of God. God does not need to be justified, but to be revealed.

We see this in Job. While some would strongly argue that Job is not a theodicy, I want to consider it so under the rubric defined above: the true answer to the problem of suffering is for God to be revealed. So, it would be distracting to start writing of the history of thinking about theodicy if we did not allow the first speaker to speak: Job. Out of civility to the text, I will grant the author his staging.[54] According to the epic poem, the drama, Job lived in cosmopolitan Mesopotamia. The text appears to make Job a wealthy contemporary of Abraham, two men who inhabit our historical horizon at the edge of recorded human history.[55] Having left the mists of creation, flood, and Babel behind, we have moved into the times of the first libraries—or so the play is staged. In that sense, this first drama is about the problem of evil in the "real" world. Did it arise for the author and his readers because they are now comfortable

---

53. Blocher, *Evil and the Cross*, 128.

54. While substantial critical issues exist in regard to the text of Job, the resolution of authorship, dating, and more will not change the claims of the text—an epic drama of suffering that the author wants the reader to hear. It is that issue, the epic drama, that is important to this project and not the details of dating and authorship. No one would argue against Job as a story of suffering, a proposed solution, and that the story is placed by the author in a setting that is contemporary with Abraham.

55. Again, the facts may be otherwise. The author and date of Job are debated and most would date the book very late. These details will be taken up later in Chapter 6. For our discussion here, this is the author's "drama" and we want to understand it as he "staged" it, as well as the facts in regard to its date of writing.

and wealthy, putting them in a position to be shocked by evil? The play makes some implicit assumptions that it would serve to make explicit: 1/ God is sovereign and all happens by his authority. This is seen as *God alone* licenses the Adversary to attack Job (Job 1&2). It is observed when *God alone* brings the time of suffering to a close (Job 37). It is implicit when *God alone* restores Job (Job 42). No one within the drama doubts God's sovereignty in all things; 2/ God has an Adversary. This Adversary comes to us in the first two chapters without introduction as if we would recognize him. His calling card: malice; and 3/ We are normally unaware of (or at least do not pay attention to) the contest between God and the Adversary (though the author is letting us peek "behind the curtain" in chapters 1 and 2). However, people do suffer the effects of this battle. So, like us in our own lives, Job is ignorant of most of what happened in the first two chapters between God and the Adversary. Indeed, from the perspective of the audience, that ignorance is the source of much of Job's ongoing pain. We, who know, have hope while Job, who does not know, despairs of hope. Was this a pedagogical device of the author to move us to God's perspective in regard to the problem of evil? While I will attempt to unpack Job more fully in Part II, let me expose here what is lying on the surface of Job to be gleaned by all readers—the Book of Job presents a God-centered theodicy. This can be seen in the introduction in which God is not only the sovereign over the Adversary, but also the instigator of the Adversary's actions. It is seen in the conclusion in which God never invites Job to share his pain, but rather calls Job to look upon YHWH in his majesty (chapters 38–41). This dovetails with many of the statements in the New Testament including Romans 9:20: "Who are you, O man, who answers back to God?" This is a God-centered, almost anti-anthropological, theodicy. God says, "Forget your tormenters; look at me!" It calls for us to understand that to behold God's glory is the antidote for Evil & Suffering. I will also argue that it is an eschatological theodicy and has in common something with both Irenaeus-Hick and Augustine—an unlikely pairing! But that must wait.

As we begin to consider theodicy, there is something that must be restated: theodicy is not the most important of theological issues. The core issue in all of life is personal; it is about the Person; God, who is three persons: Father, Son, and Spirit. Yet if theodicy is important at all, and it is, it is helpful to understand why we are driven to try to understand it and how its study reveals the beauty of God and ultimately draws us to him.

PART I: The Tension of Theodicy

AN HISTORICAL SURVEY OF THE DEVELOPMENT OF THE CONCEPT OF THEODICY

> The authors of past ages are thus assumed to provide a rich stock of atemporal resources for the present-day theodicist who is prepared to do some preliminary "demythologizing"; they become timeless grist for her ahistorical mill.[56]
> —Kenneth Surin

By looking at the church's response to the problem of evil, I want to display Theodicies and Defenses as they emerge historically, so that the development of the various lines of thought, their interweaving and even their knotting, can provide context. At the same time, Surin's rhetorical caution is important. Texts must be exegeted in their context, not smeared onto our theodicies or questions like icing on a cake. I trust this survey demonstrates attention to this caution. Accepting this caution, one of the delights of studying history is to see the confluence of influences and attempt to discover why certain ideas develop at the times they do. So, at the outset, Alan Jacobs's observation about why and how thoughts about theodicy may have developed is worth considering:

> It is my view . . . that the rise of the "problem of evil" is the result of alterations in the typical European forms of life. It is a function of, among other things, urbanization. The people who first raise the problem of evil—or, at least, who first make it central to European intellectual life—are people of the cities: Paris above all, but also London, Berlin, Edinburgh. They tend to be—in that curious and resonant term borrowed from the French—deracinated, uprooted from their native soil. They have disconnected themselves from the life-forms of their ancestors, and no longer do the work those ancestors did or worship in the parish churches those ancestors occupied. And as the eighteenth century yields to the nineteenth and then to the twentieth, they live in increasing health: with better nutrition, fewer diseases. In the latter third of the nineteenth century, the great cities begin to clean themselves up, to dispose more healthily of their wastes, to develop cleaner fuels and thereby improve their air. The patterns of life and death, of expecting suffering and unexpected health, that were all Europeans had known receded further and further into the fog of history. In 1702, . . . Matthew Henry wrote: "Since I set out in the world, I was never so long without the death of children or others near and dear to me." How long a period was he referring to? Three years. Yet the "problem of evil" was not an issue for Matthew Henry. It is, strangely and yet (when you think about it) understandably enough, only when European and American life gets noticeably cleaner and safer and healthier that certain

---

56. Surin, *Theology and the Problem of Evil*, 3.

> intellectuals begin to think that the greatest difficulty for Christianity to deal with is the fact that anything bad happens at all.[57]

Is Jacobs right?[58] His perspective is certainly worth considering as a backdrop to the historical canvas of Christian theodicy. If such thinking is catalyzed by the conflict of comfort with pain, then we owe a debt to both pain and comfort as goads to developing our understanding of God.

No project could even hope to canvass all that has been said, but the selections made are intended to show how such lines developed organically. In order to do so, some Defections will be noted, but they are generally outside of my concern for the reasons noted above. The goal will be to lay the groundwork for my Theodicy project that I will present in Part II.

A Theodicy of Moral Freedom and Human Maturity: Irenaeus to Pelagius

Wrestling with dualism was critical to the development of early Christianity. It was a maturing influence, forcing the early Christian Fathers to sharply define their own understanding of God. As the Gnostic view of God was torn down, the biblical view of God became more vivid, the implicit became explicit.[59] And to the extent that they were successful, not in destroying Gnosticism among the Gnostics but in supporting the faithful,[60] the need to think deeply about the problem of evil also became explicit, for Gnosticism is fundamentally a theodicy. The Gnostic theodicy pulls God apart from God, inserting mediate aeons and separating what is good (spirit) from what is evil (matter). In so doing, God is rescued from any immediate participation in evil. So as early Christianity exposed the flaws of this Gnostic teaching, the need to replace its explanatory power became more obvious. Evil could be not attributed to some other force or being who would share some kind of ontological parity with him. So, it becomes the responsibility of the challenger of dualism to initiate a proposal.

---

57. Jacobs, *Shaming the Devil*, 78.

58. Surin would extend this to say that "a benevolent divine omnipotence and the existence of evil were not seen by the Christian thinkers of the Middle Ages as an obstacle to belief" (*Theology and the Problem of Evil*, 9).

59. This is hardly a point in dispute, however, it might be worth citing Theodore de Bruyn, who in his introduction to Pelagius's commentary of Romans noted a similar point, "The conflict with the Manichaeans may, in fact, have contributed to the 'renaissance' of Pauline studies in the latter half of the fourth century" (Pelagius, *Pelagius's Commentary on St. Paul's Epistle to the Romans*, 15).

60. To whom were the Early Church Fathers preaching: the "sheep" or the "wolves"? Irenaeus, at least, was preaching to the wolves, not only in address, but also in hope of changing their minds, as he declares in the preface to Book 4. Yet, in my opinion, it seems likely that it was the sheep who benefited most. It was the sheep, and those who gained intellectual divorce from the Gnostics, who needed a theodicy.

PART I: The Tension of Theodicy

That responsibility seems to have fallen first upon Irenaeus (c.130–202).[61] Raised in Asia Minor under the influence of Polycarp,[62] he was in effect, a direct spiritual descendent of the Apostle John. Later, as Bishop of Lyons in Gaul (France), he defended Christianity against the Gnostic teachings which aggressively contended for hearts and minds in the second century of the church. In writing *Against Heresies*[63] he outlined much of the Gnostic teaching in as complete a form as it is anywhere preserved. This fact alone would attest to an effective contribution.[64]

The singular difficulty the Early Fathers faced in dealing with the Gnostics was that instead of repudiating Scripture (relatively easy to contend against), Gnostics appropriated Scripture for their own purposes. Irenaeus writes, "They . . . dismember and destroy the truth. By transferring passages . . . and making one thing out of another, they succeed in deluding many . . . adapting the oracles of the Lord to their opinions."[65] That is, instead of loving truth so as to gain salvation, they love what advances their system. Something that sounds like the ringing bell of John's Gospel and especially his Epistles against error.[66] In this, Irenaeus was John's heir. And it is

---

61. William E. G. Floyd claims, "Clement of Alexandria is one of the first Christian theologians to feel the contradiction of evil in God's world" (*Clement of Alexandria's Treatment of the Problem of Evil*, 99). Clement, along with Origen, responded to this contradiction by highlighting the created will of humans and invoking a weak sovereignty of God which anticipated the simplest version of the Free Will Defense, one that is still valued and perhaps the most commonly held. But Clement, and his successor Origen, were second to Irenaeus.

62. Irenaeus, *Against Heresies*, in *The Ante-Nicene Fathers*, volumes. 1, 3.3.4.

63. *Against Heresies* is the common name for this work, the original being: *Detection and Overthrow of the False Knowledge*. The only other works surviving are *Proof of the Apostolic Preaching*, which is a doctrinal overview, and scattered fragments which indicate an extensive body of lost works.

64. Carl Mosser ("Evil, Mormonism and the Impossibility of Perfection *Ab Initio*: An Irenaean Defense") makes a helpful clarification about the context and meaning of Irenaeus's argument. Mosser explains that Irenaeus's "developmentalism" is an argument against dualism, which is itself a theodicy that he is rejecting. Dualism insists that if God created *ex nihilo*, he has every choice. It is in this context that Irenaeus offers his proposal of developmentalism—to defend God. That is, the dualist would say that God has all choices: anything created by God *ex nihilo* can be whatever God wants *ab initio*. Per Irenaeus, God cannot create anything that requires process in order for it to be a specific kind of thing and so, God cannot create human beings who are mature. Contingent creatures need experience: 1/ to sustain obedience to God's command until one develops an immutable moral stature and 2/ for redemption and to be transformed into moral likeness and incorruptibility. God created morally innocent beings, but not an already developed moral fortitude which could only be gained by experience. This is the inverse of what happens to people who give themselves over to certain vices. Or it could be given by the means of redemption which gives something to a creature's character which could not be gained by fortitude of obedience. If Irenaeus is correct, not even God can create an uncreated being. So, God created a world he knew would fall and let them fall to create persons who more fully reflect his image and likeness. To create a race of people who hate evil like he does means they must have experienced and learned to hate it, but are also redeemed. So, according to Mosser: 1/ Irenaeus's distinction was not that God created immature beings by necessity of his character and declared goals; and 2/ that Irenaeus's argument was an attack upon dualistic theodicy which permitted God to create mature humans.

65. Irenaeus, *Against Heresies*, 1.8.1.

66. Almost half of the New Testament occurrences of αληθεια are in John's writings. But not only

Free-Will and Evil: The Historical Development of Theodicy

in this spirit of defending the flock and proclaiming truth that Irenaeus attacks the Gnostic myth.

Having destroyed what amounts to the popular theodicy of the day, he is now called to construct one. But it is not until he reaches the very last four chapters of Book 4 that he begins to address the problem of evil. When he does so, it seems an aside in both its brevity and depth. Even more, I would argue that nothing in the first four books anticipates this discussion, except that he has destroyed the Gnostic (Valentinian) doctrines in detail—obscure point by obscure point.[67] What he produces is a version of what will come to be called a Free-Will Theodicy: a justification of God in light of the good and godly free-will God gave to humanity. At the same time, Irenaeus is not providing a modern free-will theodicy, but one that is somewhat in harmony with Augustine (a shock to some who misappropriate him). His pre-modern theodicy is one that calls us to love God truly in Christ, as Surin noted.[68] It is worth reconstructing his argument. He first establishes man's free-will in the "ancient law of human liberty, because God made man a free [agent] from the beginning, possessing his own power, even as he does his own soul, to obey the behests of God voluntarily, and not by compulsion of God. For there is no coercion with God."[69] Building upon free-will, he asserts that people are not created so that some are good and some are evil, but rather that all are alike and neutral in regard to good and evil.[70] This had to be the case, he argues, otherwise responsibility would be lost. That is, if people acted from a

---

the word, but some of the most passionate and poetic calls to truth centered on him who is the Word of God: John 8:32 "and you will know the truth, and the truth will make you free"; John 17:17 "Sanctify them by the truth; your word is truth"; 2 John 1:4 "I was very glad to find some of your children walking in truth." This is not to say that Irenaeus's work is to be taken as truth, only that his passion for truth is a rich inheritance. For example, he claims that Christ was crucified at age 50 (based on John 8:56–57) and lived on with his disciples (after the resurrection, it is assumed) into the era of Trajan, making him approximately 98 when he left to take his place in heaven (*Against Heresies*, 2.22.5).

67. In the preface to Book 4, (*Against Heresies*, 4.pref.2), he writes, "The man, however, who would undertake their conversion, must possess an accurate knowledge of their systems or schemes of doctrine. For it is impossible for any one to heal the sick, if he has no knowledge of the disease of the patients. This was the reason that my predecessors-much superior men to myself, too-were unable, notwithstanding, to refute the Valentinians satisfactorily, because they were ignorant of these men's system;" He intends to be thorough and decisive.

68. Surin, *Theology and the Problem of Evil*, 19.

69. Irenaeus, *Against Heresies*, 4.37.1. Anticipating a counter argument, perhaps even from within, he writes, "Those, again, who maintain the opposite to these [conclusions], do themselves present the Lord as destitute of power, as if, forsooth, He were unable to accomplish what he willed; or, on the other hand, as being ignorant that they were by nature 'material,' as these men express it, and such as cannot receive immortality" (ibid., 4.37.6). This is a fair point. It is not to "save God" that we should assert God's sovereignty and control. And we should not imply more than the Bible does—we still have something called "will" and "choice." If there is more to say on this, it must wait until Part II of this project.

70. It might be worth observing that this could be considered a circular argument from the conclusion to the premise, but that is not important here because we are only seeking to demonstrate his place in the historical debate and are not contesting his ideas in this project.

PART I: The Tension of Theodicy

bias created by God, it would be acting "by nature rather than by will."[71] This would undermine personal responsibility. Thus God is implicitly freed of responsibility for evil, and evil is explained as a product of something of high value: human free-will. And evil is then used to mature his people. Now, in the following paragraph Irenaeus shows his skill, offering a theodicy, however undeveloped, in a single paragraph (I should be so economical!). It is built upon this patience of God—the lack of coercion, and the goals of God: to mature humans. For its compactness and insight, it is worth reproducing in full:

> God has displayed long-suffering in the case of man's apostasy; while man has been instructed by means of it, as also the prophet says, "Thine own apostasy shall heal thee;" [Jeremiah 2:19] God thus determining all things beforehand for the bringing of man to perfection, for his edification, and for the revelation of His dispensations, that goodness may both be made apparent, and righteousness perfected, and that the church may be fashioned after the image of His Son, and that man may finally be brought to maturity at some future time, becoming ripe through such privileges to see and comprehend God.[72]

This is the critical paragraph that establishes his offering as something more than a simple Free-Will Theodicy; it is a theodicy of necessity. For Irenaeus, it was necessary that God permit sin in order to "perfect righteousness" and to fashion us "after the image of His Son." Evil's necessity as a tool to mature his people, and so God's consequentialist permitting of evil, is the core of what is now known as the Irenaean Theodicy. He then anticipates the obvious question which his offering raises: Was evil *really* necessary? Again, his words are densely packed and significant and should be fully noted here:

> If, however, any one say, "What then? Could not God have exhibited man as perfect from the beginning?" let him know that, inasmuch as God is indeed always the same and unbegotten as respects Himself, all things are possible to Him. But created things must be inferior to Him who created them, from the very fact of their later origin; . . . . But inasmuch as they are not uncreated, for this very reason do they come short of the perfect.[73]

His argument is that God cannot do what cannot logically be done; the uncreated (perfect) cannot make something uncreated. While God had the power to give all to us, we could not receive it due to our lack of maturity. This could only be accomplished over time: "but man making progress day by day, and ascending towards the perfect, that is, approximating to the uncreated One"[74] We must wade through this process of

---

71. Ibid., 4.37.6.
72. Ibid., 4.37.7.
73. Ibid., 4.38.1.
74. Ibid., 4.38.3.

Free-Will and Evil: The Historical Development of Theodicy

our evil immaturity until we are finally "made after the image and likeness of God."[75] That is, we were made in the "image" of God, but now must be completed by the Spirit into the "likeness" of God as new creations.[76] Whether his argument is correct or not is less important here than the fact that he anticipated major issues of the debate: a significant definition of a free-will theology and the question of the logical possibility in creating perfected human beings.

In these four short chapters (a tiny fraction of *Against Heresies*) Irenaeus has presented his "sin as [RAS: a] maturing instrument of God in redeeming the world" theodicy. He has shown that God did not create evil, but that it arose from the free-will of the people he created. It should, however, be noted what he did not do or anticipate. It does not seem that Irenaeus is driven by the question, "Why is there so much evil in the world?" This could be interpreted as being in agreement with Alan Jacobs's claim that this question will wait for the social infrastructure developments of a wealthier time. It is also in accord with Surin's concern that Irenaeus was intending to demonstrate the continuity of the two Testaments against the Gnostic antinomy.[77] Nor does Irenaeus seem bothered by the question, "Why does God not intervene?" The key to Irenaeus's motivation is his patience with his understanding of God's instrumental use of man's sin as shown when he directs us to Jeremiah 2:19. If this is a correct reading, the problem of evil for Irenaeus is, "What is the relationship of God to evil and how is he using evil in redemption?" In that, he calls us to respond to evil by loving God rightly, as will Augustine, and in this they will have significant agreement.

Origen (185–254) seems to build and even amplify the thinking of Irenaeus in this regard. He teases apart the ideas of "image" and "likeness" much more clearly, though not at great length. While most of his citations of "image and likeness" are presented as a collective noun and not distinguished,[78] there is a key passage:

> Not the fact that he said, "He made him in the image of God," and was silent about the likeness, points to nothing else but this, that man received the honour of God's image in his first creation, whereas the perfection of God's likeness was reserved for him at the consummation. The purpose of this was that man should acquire it for himself by his own earnest efforts to imitate God, so that while the possibility of attaining perfection was given to him in the beginning through the honour of the "image," he should in the end through the accomplishment of these works obtain for himself the perfect "likeness."[79]

---

75. Ibid., 4.38.4.

76. Ibid., 4.38.3–4; 5.6.1; 5.8.1; 5.10.1; 5.12.4.

77. Surin, *Theology and the Problem of Evil*, 15–16.

78. For example, in *On First Principles* 2.10.7 and 2.11.3, he cites the "image and likeness" as the ultimate end for all, expressing what seems to be a form of universalism and "image and likeness" are not distinguished from each other.

79. Origen, *On First Principles*, 3.6.1 (Latin only). He also makes a similar claim for a division based on this text of Genesis in *Against Celsus* (in *The Ante-Nicene Fathers: Translations of the Writings of the Fathers Down to AD325*, volume 4) where he writes, "If however, he had known the difference

PART I: The Tension of Theodicy

Here we have a clear and unambiguous statement of the kind we might have expected to read from the pen of Irenaeus, given that this idea is attributed to him. Here we have all of the elements: (1) an exegetical reason for separating "image" from "likeness"; (2) a clear statement that people received only the image and not the likeness; (3) a purpose in God for doing so, which is in effect a theodicy; and (4) an eschatological vision in which all is accomplished. To this we could add that Origen also tells us specifically where the image is located. In another work, *Against Celsus*, he writes: "for it is the soul, and not the body, which bears the likeness of the Creator."[80] However brief, this is much more developed than Irenaeus.

It is worth noting what this means in regard to soteriology—a close cousin of theodicy. Romans 8:13 reads, "for if you are living according to the flesh, you must die; but if by the Spirit you are putting to death the deeds of the body, you will live." To this Origen comments, "But when they reach maturity to the point that there is no longer any trace in themselves of any sinful thought, word or deed, then they may be reckoned to have completely mortified the deeds of the flesh and passed from death to life."[81] Without disputing or supporting Origen's exegesis, many of the elements of his theodicy are present here in dynamic inter-relationship: "maturity," perfection, and salvation. This serves as a good illustration of his focus.

For Origen, like Irenaeus, evil is the result of human choices: God has influenced the will of people toward the good, but people still choose evil. And because evil is used to mature individuals into God's "likeness," it serves a positive function. So God is twice relieved of responsibility; he did not cause the evil and he will instrumentally use the evil to bring about good. Origen is therefore an ethical consequentialist and so needs no further development of his theodicy; the tension is relieved.

Pelagius's (354–418) influence upon the concept of free-will and evil has been already examined in previous chapters. Indications of a significant dependence upon Origen and Irenaeus have been already shown. And while there is continuity of thinking,[82] I might imagine that both Irenaeus and Origen would have taken exception to the development of their ideas into "Pelagian Doctrine"! But how strong was that influence? If it was strong, one might anticipate a further development of the

---

between man being created 'in the image of God' and 'after His likeness,' and that God is recorded to have said, 'Let Us make man after Our image and likeness,' but that He made man 'after the image' of God, but not then also 'after His likeness,' he would not have represented us as saying that 'we are altogether like Him'"(4.30).

80. Origen, *Against Celsus*, 8.49.

81. Origen, "Put to Death the Deeds of the Body," 215.

82. Of course, these ideas were not unique to Irenaeus, Origen, or Pelagius, though they provided the backbone for transmission and amplification. For example, Gregory of Nyssa (c.335–395) citing the perfected life of Moses, wrote that the purpose of our existence is to see restored the image of God in us (*Gregory of Nyssa: The Life of Moses*, 136–7, §317–21.) And as cited by (then) Cardinal Joseph Ratzinger (Pope Benedict XVI), "According to Tertullian, God created man in his image and gave him the breath of life as his likeness. While the image can never be destroyed, the likeness can be lost by sin (*Bapt.* 5, 6.7)" (*Communion and Stewardship*).

division "image" and "likeness" in some extant Pelagian mention of Genesis 1:26–27, but it is not there. A philological comparison between Pelagius and the writings of these other two men has not been systematically investigated, though comparisons exist.[83] Still, he had access to their writings and his writing clearly reflects their influence.[84] And though we cannot find Irenaeus explicitly in Pelagius, we can discover Pelagian seeds in Irenaeus.[85] For example, in supporting his proto-Libertarian Free-Will framework, Irenaeus writes, "Wherefore he has also had a two-fold experience, possessing knowledge of both kinds, that with discipline he may make the choice of better things."[86] Words like "knowledge" and "discipline" jump out of this sentence as the helps to "better things"—key ideas of Pelagius. In the next paragraph, he continues, "But by preserving the framework thou shalt ascend to that which is perfect."[87] Again, the stress is on our ability to move from free-choice between good and evil to ascend, by helps of knowledge (as opposed to grace of forensic declaration of forgiveness) and discipline to perfection. This is clearly not everything that Irenaeus teaches about soteriology,[88] but it is distinctly his and it does foreshadow Pelagius. Could it be this line of thinking that prompted Pelagius and so aroused the anger of Augustine and Jerome? That cannot be known, but it can be stated that Pelagius is congruent with a line drawn through the work of Irenaeus and Origen that extrapolates their initial thoughts to, by some ways of thinking, their logical conclusion—even if that conclusion was not one that Irenaeus reached or would have supported.

But it is just this thinking that composes a kind of a theodicy. While it does not seem that questions of theodicy drove Pelagius, it is the case that such an extreme

---

83. For example, Robert Evans in the *Four Letters of Pelagius*, writes of the juxtaposition of drunkenness with anger that is infrequent in Latin, but appears more than once in both Origen and Pelagius (127, n. 27).

84. Robert Evans asserts that in order to write his commentary on Romans, it would have been necessary to have Origen-Rufinus at hand (*Four Letters of Pelagius*, 20). So also in his commentary on Romans, Pelagius records many insights that seem to allude to Rufinus (per the translator's footnotes, comparisons can be found on almost every page). So also Theodore de Bruyn, who writes in his introduction to Pelagius's commentary on Romans, "Pelagius was among those who benefited from the translators: he read Origen's commentary on Romans in the abridged translation by Rufinus of Aquileia. The extent of Pelagius's debt to Rufinus's translation of Origen has been well documented." He also writes, "Apparently, Pelagius was comfortable with denouncing the errors of Origen without proscribing his works altogether. For Pelagius, as for Rufinus of Aquileia, Origen's works were still helpful in answering troublesome questions about divine providence and human freedom" (Pelagius, *Pelagius's Commentary on St. Paul's Epistle to the Romans*, 5 and 18).

85. It is important to say again that Irenaeus's focus was combating Gnosticism. He may have been more focused on saying exactly what is false, than building a systematic case for what is true, especially in *Against Heresies*. While he does seem to say at times that works have a value in God's redemptive economy (as noted above), he more often emphasizes the work of Christ and the Spirit. If he may not be "forgiven," he may be "understood."

86. Irenaeus, *Against Heresies*, 4.39.1.

87. Ibid., 4.39.2.

88. As he stated the Rule of Faith, while there is a stress on the role of works, the focus of his soteriology is the saving work of Christ and the grace of God (ibid., 1.10.1).

PART I: The Tension of Theodicy

free-will position leaves God independent of all acts of evil. It is an exaggerated Libertarian Free-Will theodicy (one could even suggest the phrase, autonomous free-will) that minimizes God's role at the moment of self-chosen human conversion and leaves man alone on the road to sanctification.[89] God is then free of responsibility for our sin and choices. The three-way tension is broken: God is understood to value human freedom above all, even above acting with sovereign goodness to relieve humans of their false steps. This line of reasoning seems to build powerfully for three hundred years, and there is little on the theological horizon to anticipate the great shift which is about to take place. Out of the conflict with the Gnostics, this would seem the settled direction of theology.

A Theodicy of God's Sovereignty: Augustine

However a change was just below the horizon. Two hundred years after Irenaeus, the Christian world was still wrestling with dualism; the Valentinian threat had been superseded by that of the Manicheans.[90] Now Augustine (354–430), having successfully escaped from the Manicheans, was combating their ideas; however, this battle would be contested in a way that was contrary to the strong stream of inherited Christian reasoning.[91] As a result, his enemies were not only the Gnostics, but also some of his Christian peers. He would prevail against both groups. As Elaine Pagels, no lover of Augustine, notes, "the majority of Christians in the fifth century [RAS: were] persuaded to give up this primary theme [RAS: (free-will)] of Christian doctrine."[92] But as he fought these two battles, it was not exactly a theodicy that he formed, at least not in the traditional sense. We have already shown the development of Augustine's thought in regard to evil (its privative nature) and free-will (its corrupted freedom). And it is out of these understandings that a traditional theodicy might have been formed,

89. For example, commenting on Romans 4:5, he writes, "One's initial faith is credited as righteousness to the end that one may be absolved of the past, justified for the present, and readied for future works of faith." And on Romans 5:1, "Abraham, who was justified initially by faith alone" (Pelagius, *Romans*, 85, and 89).

90. The connections between the various Gnostic sects is not wholly clear, but these and others had an affinity for the name Thomas (perhaps to distinguish them from the church of Peter). The famous quote of Cyril of Jerusalem shows the common wisdom of the day: "This man has had three disciples, Thomas, and Baddas, and Hermas. Let none read the Gospel according to Thomas: for it is the work not of one of the twelve Apostles, but of one of the three wicked disciples of Manes" (Cyril of Jerusalem, "The Catechetical Lectures," lecture 6.31). So also, Herbert Merillat notes, "Valentinians and Manicheans share an interest in Thomas and are most likely possessed by the *Acts of Judas Thomas* and the *Gospel of Thomas*" (chapter 30). If Irenaeus was successful in his day, recent interest in the Gospel of Thomas and other influences have resulted not only in a current thread of Gnosticism, but one that specifically calls itself Valentinian.

91. Elaine Pagels writes, "Representatives of Christian orthodoxy, from Justin through Irenaeus, Tertullian, Clement, and Origen, had denounced Gnostic interpretations of Genesis in the name of moral freedom" (Pagels, *Adam, Eve and the Serpent*, 152). To this we should certainly add Pelagius.

92. Ibid., 152.

Free-Will and Evil: The Historical Development of Theodicy

but Augustine stops short. He is not overly concerned with the problem of suffering, but rather with the problem of why we receive mercy from God at all. His position does depend, as we have seen, on an understanding that there is nothing above the human will. While it is corrupted and captive, the human will is still functional and its existence lies at the heart of what it means to be human: we are distinguished from all creation in that we have existence, life, *and* a will and understanding.[93] But it is important to understand that Augustine does not value human will supremely. This is not a point in passing; the will is not a high order good or of highest value. He writes of the human will that it is a "medium good" and does so at some length, listing many greater and lesser goods.[94] He elevates the will to a point that it alone acts in human decision, but it is God who is of supreme value and God's will that is supreme in the affairs of his universe. His theodicy is therefore not a free-will theodicy, but rather a "this-is-a-God-centered-world" theodicy.

To begin to understand Augustine's approach, it will be helpful to consider the opening four books of *The City of God*. It is here that Augustine asks and begins to answer the problem of suffering by looking at the most shocking and destructive event of his day, the sacking of Rome. His argument may be disturbing to some modern, Western-Christian perspectives. In the face of destruction, looting, torture, rape, captivity, and death, he responds:

1. Rome received more mercy than has ever been experienced in other historical conquests, including her own. Alaric was uniquely merciful to all who trusted God and fled to churches.[95]

2. Further, suffering is not a fundamental problem for Christians because:

    a. in it God is bringing pagan neighbors to "lay hold of life eternal";[96]

    b. death is common to all sooner or later;[97]

    c. Christians do not value material goods;[98]

    d. lack of burial is not a problem for Christians; and [99]

---

93. Augustine, *Free Choice of the Will*, 2.3.
94. Ibid., 2.19.
95. Augustine, *City of God*, 1.7.
96. Ibid., 1.9. He writes, "They are punished together, not because they have spent an equally corrupt life, but because the good as well as the wicked, though not equally with them, love this present life; while they ought to hold it cheap, that the wicked, being admonished and reformed by their example, might lay hold of life eternal. And if they will not be the companions of the good in seeking life everlasting, they should be loved as enemies, and be dealt with patiently. For so long as they live, it remains uncertain whether they may not come to a better mind."
97. Ibid., 1.10–11.
98. In ibid., 1.10 Augustine writes, "They lost all they had. Their faith? Their godliness? The possessions of the hidden man of the heart, which in the sight of God are of great price? Did they lose these?"
99. Ibid., 1.12

PART I: The Tension of Theodicy

e. God is with the captives wherever they are taken.[100]

Then he spends the largest single section of this first book (1.16–28) dealing with the sexual violation of virgins and continent Christians. He deals with their conscience and their response, specifically excluding suicide. But it is his conclusion that is the high point of this section:

> We must further notice that some of those sufferers may have conceived that continence is a bodily good, and abides so long as the body is inviolate, and did not understand that the purity both of the body and the soul rests on the steadfastness of the will strengthened by God's grace, and cannot be forcibly taken from an unwilling person. From this error they are probably now delivered. For when they reflect how conscientiously they served God, and when they settle again to the firm persuasion that He can in nowise desert those who so serve Him, and so invoke His aid and when they consider, what they cannot doubt, how pleasing to Him is chastity, they are shut up to the conclusion that He could never have permitted these disasters to befall His saints, if by them that saintliness could be destroyed which He Himself had bestowed upon them, and delights to see in them.[101]

Not only is the will the ultimate actor in human decision making, but it is also the will that determines reality over and against and greater than that which is forced upon a person in her experience. His pastoral response gets right to the heart of the sufferer's concern: guilt. Augustine's assurance is that no man can take what God has given, if we do not surrender it by our will (recall that for Augustine there is nothing above our will!). Those who are violated by man are still the delight of God.

It is wonderful to see what is *missing* here in this extended section on suffering: any philosophy of religion or exposition of the logical problem of evil. He does not shy from this as if he is unwilling or unable. Instead, he deals with suffering by looking to the realities beyond the suffering. He does not minimize their suffering, but acknowledges the reality of the evil they suffer, referring to it as a "horror," "slaughter," "hideous," "pitiable" and other realistic and compassionate terms. Still his antidote is not an explanation, but Christian duty and Christian hope, centered on an eschatological vision of God.

His "theodicy" continues by placing responsibility for Rome's sacking squarely on God's shoulders. He insists that the destruction of the Empire is not the responsibility of pagan gods, "but on the will of the true God."[102] It was God who visited destruction

---

100. Augustine, *City of God*, 1.14.
101. Ibid., 1.28.
102. Ibid., 2.23.

on Rome.[103] And, in balance, because he does see the will as critical, he acknowledges that the sins of Rome are very great and deserving of destruction.[104]

What then is Augustine's theodicy, if any? It is worth observing that there is nothing of Irenaeus's free-will consequentialism here, and indeed, the Irenaean tradition will lie dormant for hundreds of years until Schleiermacher and Hick. Like Irenaeus, however, he does not seem as disturbed by the problem of evil as we might desire; it matters, but other things matter more, including a God-ward focus in response to evil. Perhaps Alan Jacobs is correct: the social development (or perhaps decline) of civilization is not yet ripe for a fully developed theodicy in the modern sense. Perhaps this must wait for post-Enlightenment Europe. Kenneth Surin would agree that social movement greatly affects what we mean by theodicy, and what kind of theodicy seems adequate *to us*. Specifically, he would agree here that Augustine is on track by biblically responding to the concerns of his day. He writes, "If Irenaeus and Augustine are right, and holiness and conversion are the only authentically Christian responses to 'the problem of evil,' then the only remotely adequate way of resolving this 'problem' will be one which begins by moving the theodicy-question into another, and quite different, theological context . . . redemption."[105] So, even as Augustine considers the greatest single "evil" of his day, he puts God, not people and not human will, at the center of his concerns. He calls us to accept the Evil & Suffering that we receive as less than what we deserve and to accept it as something which can be used in God's providence to serve his ends, our good, and the salvation of our pagan neighbors. So the focus is on God and the light by which we understand Evil & Suffering is eschatological—our final state in God, and the final destination of our persecutor. This is not a "theodicy" in the sense of our post-Enlightenment expectations, but it is a theodicy in that it is an attempt to expose the character of God in the light of evil events and help us understand how to live in that reality. In fact, I will claim in Part II that this is a proper theodicy and will make an attempt to extend it.

A Theodicy Pending: Augustine to the Reformation

Theodicy did not see much development over the next one thousand years. There were great thinkers and great thoughts and the world saw enough turmoil to warrant the possibility of further development of theodicy. Wars, famine, and plagues touched every civilization and all of the centers of Christianity. But theodicy neither advanced beyond nor turned from the benchmarks of Augustine. The ideas of Irenaeus, Origen, and Pelagius in contrast seemed to wither. Likewise, Boethius (c.477–524) formed

---

103. Though in so saying, he also noted at length that God was more wonderfully merciful in building and then sustaining Rome than should have been expected given Rome's sin.

104. In book 2 of *City of God,* Augustine spends much space condemning the morals and entertainment of Rome.

105. Surin, *Theology and the Problem of Evil,* 23.

PART I: The Tension of Theodicy

no theodicy beyond the already examined ideas of freedom and evil that we have examined previously. And in these respects, he faced his death in agreement with Augustine. Lady Philosophy sounds like the "ghost of Augustine" admonishing him in his prison cell. His very personal and immediate theodicy is the statement of a compatibilist (type) free-will, a privative evil, a sovereign God, and happiness which is found in knowing YHWH. If he followed his own teachings, he faced his own death unwillingly, but deeply content in the love of his sovereign God. Anselm of Canterbury (1033–1109) prepared us for Aquinas in the sense that he also agreed with Augustine in the essentials and emphasized the meaning of freedom in respect to the will. That is, not that the will is libertarianly free, but rather that a person who acts not under compulsion, acts with a free-will. This is not a theodicy, but like Augustine, it represents all of the building blocks of one. As has been previously shown, Thomas Aquinas (1225–1274), for all his massive work, agreed with Augustine in regard to the problem of evil. There are differences, however. If both men proclaim the same truth, Aquinas does so from the details and with a certain academic detachment. In contrast, Augustine proclaims one idea in many different and passionate ways which sheds light on the details. If Aquinas exceeds Augustine, it is in his relentless development of the logic of goodness, his agreement about the privative nature of evil, and his affirmation of our ability to rightly perceive the world that we see. As such, the world we see is the best possible given the things which do exist;[106] the perfection of the world requires that we have the corruptible, resulting in evil;[107] and goodness and perfection need the notion of plenitude, and the completeness of all that God planned in creation.[108] He has taken the ideas logically further than Augustine, but he has done no more than to set the stage for Leibniz. But why would a great thinker, or such great thinkers, not pursue the development of these ideas? Perhaps we should not expect him to do so. No theologian addresses every possible issue or even every important issue—even one who writes the Summa. Rather, he is most likely to wrestle with those that are stirred up in her culture by the present theological climate. Nothing had changed, significantly, in the climate since Augustine theologically and logically carried the day with Pelagius in regard to the will and evil. The fact that Pelagius carried (and perhaps continues to carry) a large and informal following does not mean

---

106. For example in *The Summa Theologica of St. Thomas Aquinas*, 1a,q.25,a.6, Thomas Aquinas writes, "God cannot make a thing better than it is itself; although He can make another thing better than it."

107. For example in *ST*, 1a,q.48,a.2, Aquinas writes, "so the perfection of the universe requires that there should be some which can fail in goodness."

108. For example in *ST*, 1a,q.25,a.6, Aquinas writes, "The universe, the present creation being supposed, cannot be better, on account of the most beautiful order given to things by God; in which the good of the universe consists. For if any one thing were bettered, the proportion of order would be destroyed; as if one string were stretched more than it ought to be, the melody of the harp would be destroyed. Yet God could make other things, or add something to the present creation; and then there would be another and a better universe." It is worth noting that plenitude is an issue that Aquinas did not hold unwaveringly, but that is not an issue that needs to be resolved here.

Free-Will and Evil: The Historical Development of Theodicy

that there was obvious work to do. The theological and especially the logical problem (of most interest to Aquinas) had been laid to rest. If many followed Pelagius, no one was defending him publicly and no events were challenging Augustine's thinking. The Book of Job provided the practical theology. The package was tight. To that, we might add that suffering was the rule and not the exception in the culture of the Middle Ages for the vast majority of the people (as it is still for much of the world, today). So, even if evil was terrible, it was not shocking or unexpected.

Yet even as history moved toward the Reformation, Martin Luther (1483–1546), too (for reasons considered above), was not particularly interested in the problem of evil. His problem was waking up from slavery to the law and freeing those who labored under chains of sin without grace. His desire was to shake up a church that was more concerned about money and politics than the souls of Europe. As such, he became a megaphone for Augustine, declaring "righteousness by faith." But in regard to the problem of evil, he goes as far as Augustine and no further. So also, Calvin, a reformer with a different agenda, did not find this "problem" on his agenda. Thus, Theodicy lay dormant for more than a millennium.

The Best of all Possible Worlds: Gottfried Wilhelm von Leibniz

Alan Jacobs's words stay with me as I pursue this project; there is a reason that discussion specific to theodicy heated up at a certain point in history after lying dormant for more than 1000 years. The Gnostic and Christological controversies of the early church gave birth to new insights into what was already true, but yet unexamined. Per Jacobs, perhaps the growing wealth and comfort of Europe served as a goad to cause Christians to examine the problem of evil more deeply.

As Leibniz (1646–1716) approached the problem of evil, he came to it as a rationalist:[109] all is subject to human reason, and by reason, all rational things become necessary. Two examples from his preface on reason will serve us here. First, he placed reason on equal standing with faith:

> But since reason is a gift of God, even as faith is, contention between them would cause God to contend against God; and if the objections of reason against any article of faith are insoluble, then it must be said that this alleged

---

109. The distinction here is between theonomists, rationalists, and modified rationalists. Theonomy understands God to be prior to all logic and reason; nothing is metaphysically necessary except for God. This includes, for example, numbers and assumptions of logic, such as the law of non-contradiction. A theonomist understands that reason and morals function as they do because God determines it so, but could change them at will. Under this view, good or evil have the value God places on them and that value also may change. A rationalist believes that reason and morals are necessary and either prior to God or flow from his unchangeable character. A modified-rationalist values reason, but does not believe that all things are subject to reason, nor that reason compels God, for example, to make any world, let alone the "best possible." Good and evil are static and based on God's unchangeable character (Feinberg, *Many Faces of Evil*, 23–25, 54–55).

PART I: The Tension of Theodicy

> article will be false and not revealed: this will be a chimera of the human mind, and the triumph of this faith will be capable of comparison with bonfires lighted after a defeat.[110]

In other words, Reason is a gift of God that has no superior. Second, he gives us his famous illustration of the tower seen in a distance. A square tower, seen in the distance will appear to be round; our senses lie to us. Admitting this, he is delighted to point out that this simply makes his point! Our senses may fail us, but Reason is sounder in its duty.[111] Reason can always be trusted because it is simply a chain of truths well perceived. In this, he has every confidence.

Also, key to his understanding of the world and the problem of evil is his use of the word, "good," for it is more distinctive than his understanding of evil for purposes of this project. At bottom, "good" means metaphysical fullness or plenitude, as examined in the first chapter of this project.[112] This contrasts with his extreme privative understanding of evil as "lack of being," something which is almost Barthian in its description. Consistent with Leibniz's understanding, God is responsible to create the metaphysically best (fullest) world possible—he has no choice with respect to creating or about what he creates. He writes that God who is "supreme wisdom, united to a goodness that is no less infinite, cannot but have chosen the best."[113] Again, his confidence in reason seems "over-the-top" because, as a result of this confidence, God seems to be constrained not by Reason, but by our understanding of him. This reasoning makes Leibniz's answer to the problem of evil almost programmatic; his answer is almost extruded from his assumptions. Thus, we have the Best of all Possible Worlds theodicy. Since God is good, and despite the fact that we see so much evil around us, this created world is, by reason and by necessity, the best of all possible worlds. How

---

110. Leibniz, *Theodicy*, "Preliminary Dissertation," §39.

111. Ibid., §64. Here he writes, "Therefore my answer to this objection is that the representation of the senses, even when they do all that in them lies, is often contrary to the truth; but it is not the same with the faculty of reasoning, when it does its duty, since a strictly reasoned argument is nothing but a linking together of truths. And as for the sense of sight in particular, it is well to consider that there are yet other false appearances which come not from the 'feebleness of our eyes' nor from the loss of visibility brought about by distance, but from the very nature of vision, however perfect it be. It is thus, for instance, that the circle seen sideways is changed into that kind of oval which among geometricians is known as an ellipse, and sometimes even into a parabola or a hyperbola, or actually into a straight line, witness the ring of Saturn." This is, of course, borrowed from Descartes, *Meditations*, 6.7 and Leibniz makes the same point—the supremacy of reason (will). It is also interesting to note that "ring of Saturn" must now be "rings of Saturn," for the very reason he indicated.

112. We could argue the correctness or even the value of plenitude here. John Hick does, writing that the theory of plenitude has no philosophical value to the Christian (*Evil and the God of Love*, 76–81 and 195). I might agree with Hick, but an evaluation of plenitude is not as important as understanding his position on reason. If plenitude were weak to us, even if we are wrong in our reason, it would tend to undermine his sense that sound reason is always successful. This is more to the point of revealing a problem with the Best-of-All-Possible-Worlds theodicy.

113. Leibniz, *Theodicy*, 1.8.

could God do this? He is able (being the greatest intellect) to know all possible worlds and from them to actualize the world that is best. And he has done so.

Strictly speaking, the Best-of-All-Possible-Worlds theodicy has no need of free-will at all—even in God. It requires only a God who acts always for the greatest good in what he actualizes. It is only in the details of experienced reality that free-will would arise—or not, but interestingly, Leibniz's Best-of-All-Possible-Worlds theodicy is laced with a strong kernel of a Free-will Theodicy.[114] Consistent with his position, Leibniz is almost a determinist in his reasoning. For example, he writes, "this determination comes from the nature of truth and cannot injure freedom."[115] And again he writes, "the foreknowledge of God renders all the future certain and determined."[116] These are representative of many statements. But he pulls up short in many other assertions: "And if I am for the Molinists in the first point, I am for the predeterminists in the second, provided always that predetermination be taken as not necessitating." He is almost everything a determinist can be while still affirming a kind of free-will. That along with his Best-of-All-Possible-Worlds theodicy would preclude any need to consider a Free-Will Theodicy. Yet he writes, "whatsoever dependence be conceived in voluntary actions, and even though there were an absolute and mathematical necessity (which there is not) it would not follow that there would not be a sufficient degree of freedom to render rewards and punishments just and reasonable."[117] This seems to be a walk in the path of a Free-Will Theodicy and Compatibilistic Free-Will at the same time. Similarly he writes, "finally I hold that God cannot act as if at random by an absolutely absolute decree, or by a will independent of reasonable motives. And I am persuaded that he is always actuated, in the dispensation of his grace, by reasons wherein the nature of the objects participates. Otherwise he would not act in accordance with wisdom."[118] This sounds a similar note and he seems to be arguing for responsibility, as would a defender of a Free-Will Theodicy or even a Free-Will Defense. No, he does not discuss the relative value of free-will and its relationship to evil, but it is possible that at heart the Best-of-All-Possible-Worlds is a variety of Free-Will Theodicy and may suffer from similar flaws, if flaws are shown in such positions later.

But how did Leibniz evaluate and summarize himself—what was he trying to say? He wrote: "I think I have sufficiently proved that neither the foreknowledge nor the providence of God can impair either his justice or his goodness, or our freedom."[119]

---

114. We shall examine this in a later section, but a Free-Will Theodicy asserts that, on balance, human free-will is a greater value for God's purposes, than human evil is a loss. Free-will is therefore worth the exchange for any necessary evil.

115. Ibid., 1.37.

116. Ibid., 1.2.

117. Ibid., 1.67.

118. Ibid., 3.283.

119. Ibid., 3.377.

PART I: The Tension of Theodicy

It was his belief that our freedom (our free-will) and God's sovereignty (including his foreknowledge) are compatible. We must allow him to assert what he has said.

Historically, his theodicy failed.[120] This is due in part to the popular writing of Voltaire, who was famously troubled by the Lisbon earthquake of 1755 and the Seven Years War, which began the following year. He wrote *Candide* in 1759, specifically as a spoof upon Leibniz's *Theodicy* of 1710. At one point in his story, Candide cries out to Pangloss (Leibniz's inadequate defender with such an obvious and satirical name), " 'such horrid doings never entered your imagination. Here is an end of the matter; I find myself after all, obliged to renounce your optimism.' 'Optimism,' said Cacambo, 'what is that?' 'Alas!' replied Candide, 'it is the obstinacy of maintaining that everything is best when it is worst.' "[121] *Candide* was devastating and the Best-of-All-Possible-Worlds theodicy has never recovered. But it may be that the deepest flaw in his theodicy—the first whole-cloth theodicy ever presented to the Christian world—was a dependence upon philosophical reasoning to answer the cries of the heart.

What should be salvaged from his theodicy? I think we must salvage the eschatological assumptions buried within it. The Best-of-All-Possible-Worlds theodicy is only what it claims to be when all is said and done. Douglass Geivett cites Martin Gardener, "Leibniz's world is the best possible only in its incomprehensible totality, and in the long run, which of course includes an afterlife" and adds his affirmation, "Leibniz stands firmly within the tradition of Augustine and Aquinas by incorporating this eschatological assumption into his solution to the problem of evil."[122] Geivett is correct about Leibniz and Leibniz is correct in regard to the eschatological nature of any satisfactory answer to the problem of evil.

John Hick: Irenaeus Remixed or a Soul-making Theodicy

As John Hick presents his theodicy, it is worth noting his perspective. His aim is not apologetic, that is to assert that "Christianity is true," but rather to insist that "Evil does not make it false."[123] In that sense, this sounds like the more modest goals of a Defense, instead of a Theodicy. But, Hick retains the word theodicy, asking us to

---

120. Perhaps more tellingly, many would say Leibniz failed logically—or rationally. Robert Merrihew Adams supports the alternative position: "even if there is a best among possible worlds, God could create another instead of it, and still be perfectly good." He raises the possibility that there is no ultimate best (like there is no largest number), but even if there is a best, God did not have to create it. Adams's argument for this lies in God's grace which is "an important part of perfect goodness" (Robert Merrihew Adams, "Must God Create the Best?," 24–36). Feinberg addresses this similarly in *The Many Faces of Evil* as the modified-rationalist position which asserts that there is no best possible world and God is free to create any of the good possible worlds or to create nothing (54–55).

121. Voltaire, *Candide, or Optimism*, 77. It is well to note with Hart that Voltaire, "was not an atheist," but a deist and therefore a theist. He was renouncing only Leibniz's philosophical optimism. He still affirmed his deistic God (Hart, *Doors of the Sea*, 17).

122. Geivett, *Evil and the Evidence for God*, 27.

123. Hick, *Evil and the God of Love*, x.

understand it, not in the sense of justifying God to man, but rather in the sense of seeking to understand God: a pursuit of why he may have done things as he has done them.[124] And in presenting a theodicy, he claims to be reviving and building upon the thinking of Irenaeus in opposition to that of Augustine:

> There is thus to be found in Irenaeus the outline of an approach to the problem of evil which stands in important respects in contrast to the Augustinian type of theodicy. Instead of the doctrine that man was created finitely perfect and then incomprehensibly destroyed in his own perfection and plunged into sin and misery, Irenaeus suggests that man was created as an imperfect, immature creature who was to undergo moral development and growth and finally be brought to the perfection intended for him by his Maker.[125]

Hick is grieved to note that the Augustinian approach was so successful that "the Irenaean or eschatological approach to the problem of evil lay virtually dormant within Christianity from the time of Augustine until . . . Schleiermacher (1768–1834)."[126] In regard to the problem of evil, Schleiermacher, like Hick, understands people to have been created in an immature and free-willed state, with sin arising from that unstable combination. Our suffering (in general) arises from our sin (in general) and not from God's specific response to our sin in judgment. Hick writes approvingly of Schleiermacher's position that this "does not mean that God specifically sends suffering upon us, but that God's good world becomes evil to us as the result of our own sinful way of living in it."[127] And it is this sin and even the suffering that follows it, which Schleiermacher understands as the preparation for grace—a reversal of the Augustinian tradition upon which Hick builds.

Hick's reversal of the Augustinian tradition, or the revival of the work of Irenaeus, is built upon several components: human free-will, the nature of evil, epistemic distance, and soul-making. Hick links three of these ideas together very tightly: "Moral evil is a virtually inevitable result of the epistemic 'distance' from God that is entailed by man's creation as a morally independent being inhabiting his own world."[128] This is a helpful integrating statement and one in which I find intriguing possibilities; possibilities that I will consider in Part II of this project.

---

124. Ibid., 5, 6. At the time he writes, he is still a Presbyterian and is a self-identified Christian. He seems to be wrestling with God and eagerly desires to show him to be just. As he progresses here and in later works, he seems willing to change the Christian church's perception of God and the canonical testimony. In his autobiography he wrote, "I came fairly soon to see that for Christianity the problem of religious plurality hinged on the central doctrine of the incarnation. If Jesus was God incarnate, Christianity alone among the world religions was founded by God in person and must therefore be superior to all others" (Hick, *John Hick*, 227). Indirectly, this gets right to the issue of the goodness of God and theodicy. Directly, it justifies God by modifying God's own canonical claims.

125. Ibid., 220.
126. Ibid., 225.
127. Ibid., 233.
128. Ibid., 389.

PART I: The Tension of Theodicy

For Hick, it is this arrangement of the constellation of ideas that leads him to his key idea, "soul-making":

> But if moral evil is thus a "virtually inevitable" outcome of God's own creative work, how can it truly be hateful to Him, truly at enmity with Him, truly at variance with His purposes and inimical to all good? Again, I have suggested that pain and suffering are necessary features of a world that is to be the scene of a process of soul-making; and that even the haphazard and unjust distribution and often destructive and dysteleological effects of suffering have a positive significance in that they call forth human sympathy and self-sacrifice, and create a human situation within which the right must be done for its own sake rather than for a reward.[129]

Here he makes the extrapolation from his seed ideas to that of "soul-making" which reflects his sympathies with Irenaeus.[130] To his credit, he does so, unblinkingly, even in the face of meaningless or "dysteleological"[131] evil. For Hick the terrible reality of evil is necessary for our immature souls to grow and mature into that which God intended. He writes, "Instead of regarding man as having been created by God in a finished state, as a finitely perfect being fulfilling the divine intention for our human level of existence, and then falling disastrously away from this, the minority report sees man as still in process of creation. . . . [RAS: People as created are] only the raw material for a further and more difficult stage of God's creative work."[132] That is, God is drawing us from immaturity to maturity; our souls are being formed into his likeness by the interaction with Evil & Suffering. But this stage is more difficult for God: "it cannot be performed by omnipotent power as such. For personal life is essentially free and self-directing. It cannot be perfected by divine fiat, but only through the uncompelled responses and willing co-operation of human individuals."[133] This is then a distinctly eschatological theodicy because the answer to the problem of evil lies in the idea that evil could not be avoided. Instead, evil is necessary and useful for the work God desires to do in us. Evil is an instrumental good for Hick. As such, the environment God created will work upon our will—"through a hazardous adventure in individual freedom."[134] Such a theodicy is eschatological because it does not look

---

129. Hick, *Evil and the God of Love*, 389.

130. Here he reflects not only Irenaeus, but also on John Keats, who drew the distinction between "vale of tears" and "vale of soul-making" when he wrote, "Call the world if you please 'The vale of soul-making.'" (from his letter to George and Georgiana Keats on 21 April 1819 (a collection of letters written from 14 Feb to 3 May) in *Letters of John Keats*, edited by H. E. Rollins, volume 2, Cambridge, MA, 1958, 101–2.

131. This is his unique and very useful term for meaningless evil. That is, it is evil which seems to serve no eschatologically useful purpose. See *Evil and the God of Love*, 371ff.

132. Ibid., 289–90.

133. Ibid., 291.

134. Ibid., 292.

to the past for an answer to the problem of evil, but to the ultimate future of God's willful creatures.

At this point, it is helpful to understand how Hick himself interprets the distinctions between the Irenaean-type and the Augustinian-type theodicies. I abstract this into a chart:[135]

Augustinian-Type	Irenaean-Type
Created beings responsible for evil while God is only indirectly responsible for evil	God has ultimate omni-responsibility for evil as creator of universe in which evil is inevitable, even inherent
Philosophical	Theological
Evil as non-being	Evil as fundamental and substantive
God: predominantly impersonal	God: personal
Catastrophic: looks to past	Eschatological: looks to the future
Fall plays a central role	Fall is less significant or non-existent
Heaven and Hell as final states	Universalist—no damnation

While it is not essential to debate Hick in regard to his characterization of the Augustinian-type at length, it must at least be stated that material already presented in this project could be considered a refutation of some of the characterizations for his Augustinian-type. First, I have already shown that Augustine's concept of evil was robust and substantive and those who evacuate Augustine's privative evil of terror and reality, misunderstand him. Second, as I stated earlier, I find the observation of an impersonal God can arise only from reading into Augustine.[136] Hick, of course, is quite right to note that the Augustinian-type theodicy does have a central place for the Fall. And if for the Irenaean-type it is "not necessarily denied," Hick does deny it in fact—which places Hick as a centrist in current biblical scholarship. The burden is upon the Augustinian-type theodicy to show that the Fall is historic or even theologically sound. I hope to show that the Fall is not an impediment to developing a theodicy which has some characteristics in common with those of Irenaeus and perhaps even Hick. But this chart is also useful to remind us that much is valuable in Hick's work. In regard to his forward looking, eschatological theodicy, he is right to warn the Augustinian tradition (more than Augustine, himself) against looking overmuch on the catastrophe of the Fall. He rightly calls us to anchor theodicy in our future, our *telos*. This is what I also hope to do. Hick is also correct to note that those

---

135. This chart is an abstraction of Hick's material in ibid., 262–66.

136. Augustine's doctrine of the Trinity advanced the work of Tertullian in strongly personal ways, even to a definition of personhood from an understanding of the Trinity. This would seem ample refutation. If however the Augustinian "type" is read through those who followed him, Aquinas might be excused as a child of his age. And if Aquinas did see God through the impersonal eyes of logic, certainly later followers of Augustine had a very personal God; Luther's God is intensely personal and so is John S. Feinberg's.

of the Augustinian tradition are shy about allowing God to be ultimately responsible for evil. I hope to make the case that, while God did not sin, he is, to use Hick's phrase, "omni-responsible" for his own creation and the sin which did arise because of the conditions he set, regardless of how free people were created. The common ground of the philosophical debate offers some enticements that, while valid and even necessary, are not the primary ground for theologians. Yet, Hick's work reveals a neglect of exegesis and a paucity of biblical citations. In fact, he does not equate "theological" with "biblical." Instead, he writes, "By Christian theology I mean the attempts by Christian thinkers to speak systematically about God on the basis of the data provided by Christian experience."[137] Such statements call into question the significance of his biblical citations. Still there is something here—a call to know God, not to reason about God. This is a caution I want to respond to, even if it seems to me that it is one that Hick did not sufficiently heed himself.

Finally, it is possible that Hick attributes too much to Irenaeus. Might it be the case that Irenaeus would not be at all be pleased to have his name attached to Hick's development of ideas, which are not very recognizable as his own?[138] Perhaps. Yet,

---

137. Ibid., 282.

138. Though Hick credits Schleiermacher, and rightly so, he identifies his theodicy as of the "Irenaean-type." Mutely, the scholarly world seems to have accepted this nomenclature and heritage. For example, the Reformed scholar, R. Douglas Geivett, who writes to refute Hick, allows Hick's credit to Irenaeus stand unchallenged (*Evil and the Evidence for God*, 151). It should at least be stated that the ideas that Hick revives must be understood as a revival of the Irenaean thread only after it has passed through Origen, Pelagius, and others, where it was braided and twisted together with their own ideas into a much stouter cord. In fact, it is only recognizable to Hick *after* passing through Schleiermacher. Ken Surin notes this as well, "There is a 'problem of evil' for Irenaeus, but it has absolutely nothing to do with this kind of 'soul-making' . . . the attempt to align this second-century appreciation of the 'problem of evil' with the post-seventeenth century theodicy involves a conflation of two radically different, even incommensurable, intellectual contexts. It is mistaken to assume that Irenaeus and the modern theodicist, . . . are in fact addressing themselves to the same questions" (Surin, *Theodicy and the Problem of Evil*, 19). To be fair, Hick admits this in part when he writes, "it is permissible and convenient to name this approach after Irenaeus's (*Evil and the God of Love*, 225). So also of Schleiermacher's work Hick writes, "unfolding the implications of Irenaeus's starting-point much further than he himself had done" (*Evil and the God of Love*, 240). So he also has done! But would Irenaeus be pleased, even with Hick's caveats? If we are contrasting an Irenaean-type and an Augustinian-type, it should be remembered that historically, it was Pelagius, and not Irenaeus, with whom Augustine contested. Still, Hick makes a significant case that his theodicy is distinctly Irenaean (*Evil and the God of Love*, 217–21) citing several texts in *Against Heresies* and *Proof of Apostolic Preaching*, showing that Irenaeus believed that Adam possessed the image of God, but had to mature into the likeness of God through the path of sin. This has significant merit. But as was noticed previously, these texts in Irenaeus are few and not fully developed. In all of Irenaeus's work, the distinct concept of "image" and "likeness," in this respect, are found only in *Against Heresies*, 5.6.1; 5.8.1; 5.10.1; 5.12.4; 5.16.1–2 and even some of these passages do not make a clear distinction. Moreover, there is no exegetical warrant given by Irenaeus to tease-out this distinction from Genesis 1:26, 27 into a theology of "image" and "likeness," however, Origen did do this later (see for example, *On First Principles*, 1.2.6; 3.6.1). Further, in several instances, Irenaeus seems to say that prior to the Fall, Adam and Eve were created with both the "image and likeness." He writes, "if He did not really become man, restoring to His own handiwork what was said [of it] in the beginning, that man was made after the image and likeness of God" (*AH*, 5.2.1). And he also writes, "And again, those persons who are not bringing forth the fruits

Hick revived and extended a perspective that challenges the dominant one in some helpful ways: God is doing something with Evil & Suffering and this doing is at least part of the solution to the problem of evil.

An Atheodicy: J. L. Mackie and the Response of Alvin Plantinga

J. L. Mackie said very clearly what many were thinking in his now classic essay entitled, "Evil and Omnipotence." In it, he cites the classic trilemma problem and responds, "There seems to be a contradiction between these three propositions, so that if any two of them were true the third would be false." In other words, it just doesn't work! On the basis of this, he writes in the opening page of his essay:

> I think, however, that a more telling criticism can be made by way of the traditional problem of evil. Here it can be shown, not that religious beliefs lack rational support, but that they are positively irrational, that the several parts of the essential theological doctrine are inconsistent with one another, so that the

---

of righteousness, and are, as it were, covered over and lost among brambles, if they use diligence, and receive the word of God as a graft, arrive at the pristine nature of man-that which was created after the image and likeness of God" (*AH*, 5.10.1). In these texts he seems to indicate that both the image and likeness were present in the couple prior to their rebellion against God. That is, in their "pristine nature," and that it is this state that we will return to teleologically. Even more explicitly he writes, "For the Word was as yet invisible, after whose image man was created. Wherefore also he did easily lose the similitude. When, however, the Word of God became flesh, He confirmed both these: for He both showed forth the image truly, since He became Himself what was His image; and He re-established the similitude after a sure manner, by assimilating man to the invisible Father through means of the visible Word" (*AH*, 5.16.2). Here the word translated "similitude" is used as a synonym for "likeness" (as can be seen in the parallelism here and in 5.6.1) and it is claimed that man lost the similitude (likeness) in the rebellion. Irenaeus also seems to reverse his use of "image" and "likeness" at times. For example, he writes "For the knowledge of God renews man. And when he says, 'after the image of the Creator' he sets forth the recapitulation of the same man, who was at the beginning made after the likeness of God" (*AH*, 5.12.4). Here, writing of how the corrupted flesh is made immortal in Christ, he indicates that at the beginning we were made of the likeness. Even more striking is this passage: "But because man is possessed of free will from the beginning, and God is possessed of free will, in whose likeness man was created, advice is always given to him to keep fast the good, which thing is done by means of obedience to God" (*AH*, 4.37.4). Again, he seems to reverse "likeness" with his usual use of image. Even in regard to the idea of "maturity," Irenaeus is not developed. There are only three significant references to "mature" or "immature" in *Against Heresies*: 4.5.1, 4.37.7, 5.12.4. He writes in 5.12.4, "Now the final result of the work of the Spirit is the salvation of the flesh. For what other visible fruit is there of the invisible Spirit, than the rendering of the flesh mature and capable of incorruption?" This possible inconsistency of Irenaeus projects no blame upon him, but it may indicate that Hick attributes more credit to Irenaeus that he might desire. It is not that what Hick observes in Irenaeus is not there, but rather that his observations are taken from sparse and immature ideas, cross-bred with new species and bearing fruit very different than Irenaeus himself would have eaten. It is not only the matter of nearly two millennium, which separate the philosophical and theological contexts between Hick and Irenaeus and their different problems of evil, but when under Irenaeus's name, Hick rejects the Fall, neglects soteriology, and promotes universalism, Irenaeus might desire an opportunity to write a new edition of *Against Heresies*.

PART I: The Tension of Theodicy

> theologian can maintain his position as a whole only by a much more extreme rejection of reason than in the former case.[139]

He has laid down the gauntlet. He is saying that all adequate solutions must reject one of the three lemmas. Almost simultaneously, Antony Flew made a parallel proposal.[140] He writes, "If there is no contradiction here then Omnipotence might have made a world inhabited by wholly virtuous people; the Free-will Defense is broken-backed; and we are back again with the original intractable antinomy."[141] In the article he proceeds to show how it can be observed that this is the case. This "Flew-Mackie Principle" is stated by Geivett this way: "If it is logically possible for free creatures to always choose to act rightly, then it is logically possible that God could so constitute them at creation that they would always choose to act rightly; and, if God is good, then he should have so constituted human individuals, rather than allowing the possibility for evil to accrue."[142] This is an atheistic, atheodicy. Without a viable Free-Will Defense, no theodicy can be put forward that rescues him in his classical (biblical) formulation; logically, God cannot exist.

This position was a significant challenge for theologians. Ninian Smart proposed that if Flew and Mackie are correct, their arguments could be summarized in two theses: 1/ the Compatibility Thesis which states that causal determinism is compatible with free-will; and 2/ the Utopian Thesis, which follows directly from the Compatibility Thesis, that God could have created man wholly good.[143] However, Smart does not agree that the latter follows necessarily from the former. From his perspective, Utopia is ill-defined and not shown to be superior to the world God did create. So also, M.B. Ahern attacks this proposal by asking if it is true that evil is rationally disallowed by omni-benevolent omnipotence. Ahern writes:

> Now, I believe that this principle, in every sense that it can bear, is far from self-evident and so it will be necessary to delineate clearly in what senses this statement is certainly true; [1] . . . evil cannot exist within the constitution of God; [2] . . . evil cannot exist in God's choices; [and 3] . . . to approve evil must be excluded from such a being. . . . What is in question must be solely the permission of evil. . . . God cannot give permission for evil in this [RAS:

---

139. Mackie, "Evil and Omnipotence," 200.

140. Flew writes, "Professor J. L. Mackie . . . has since published in *Mind* a paper which runs parallel to this one in many parts, I wish to point out that our papers were entirely independent, and his was in fact completed before mine" ("Divine Omnipotence & and Human Freedom," 144, note 1).

141. Flew, "Divine Omnipotence & and Human Freedom," 149.

142. Geivett, *Evil and the Evidence for God*, 195.

143. John S. Feinberg, following the discussion between Smart and Mackie, indicates that Mackie signed-on to Smart's assessment, though not his conclusion, that the Utopian Thesis does not necessarily follow from the Compatibility Thesis (*Many Faces of Evil*, 62–63).

positive] sense. . . . Negative permission . . . is the only kind of permission which can be predicated of God.[144]

It was however left to Alvin Plantinga to decisively deal with this logical problem of evil. Feinberg asserts that "he not only answers Flew and Mackie, but also gives the free will defense its most complicated and sophisticated expression, an expression that has convinced many."[145] Key to Plantinga's approach is what he calls the "Leibniz Lapse"—an errant assumption that God had more freedom that he actually had. He writes, "The atheologian is right in holding that there are many possible worlds containing moral good, but no moral evil; his mistake lies in endorsing the Leibniz Lapse so that one of his central contentions—that God, if omnipotent, could have actualized just any world he pleased—is false."[146] As was investigated in the previous two chapters, this limitation in God rests on the proposed concept of "trans-world depravity."[147] If someone objects: "But how do you know!?," Plantinga would simply respond that he does not know. He merely shows the logical possibility and if such a logical possibility cannot be shown to be in error, then the Free-Will Defense stands as a defense: this could be the way the world is, logically. God has a possible (that is not to say probable or even plausible) reason for creating a world containing evil.

But Plantinga admits that trans-world-depravity does not settle this issue, completely. Could God not plug this gap with his omnipotence? In his chapter, appropriately titled, "Free-Will Defense Triumphant," he closes the logical gap by showing that the assertion of free-will implies a voluntary dependence of God upon his willful creatures.[148] Concisely stated, he writes, "what is really characteristic and central to Free Will Defense is the claim that God, though omnipotent, could not have actualized just any possible world He pleased."[149] Essentially, he is substituting Libertarian Free-Will for Flew and Mackie's Compatibilistic Free-Will.[150] While only the conclusions of his argument are presented here, it serves to demonstrate that the Free-Will Defense, specifically, the Libertarian Free-Will defense, is sufficient to show that the three ancient lemmas are not a formally contradictory set.[151]

144. Ahern, "Approach to the Problems of Evil," 21. Here and in a series of four articles in *Sophia* he continues to wrestle with Mackie and others who join the discussion. His conclusion in the last article is finally that it is not shown that God is responsible, because he is good, to prevent all evil (Ahern, "Good & Evil—a note," *Sophia* 6/3: 1967, 23–26).

145. Feinberg, *Many Faces of Evil*, 63.

146. Plantinga, *Nature of Necessity*, 184.

147. Ibid., 186.

148. He writes, "If he aims to produce moral good, then he must create significantly free creatures upon whose cooperation he must depend. Thus the power of an omnipotent God is limited by the freedom he confers upon his creatures" (Ibid., 190).

149. Plantinga, *God, Freedom, and Evil*, 34.

150. Plantinga, "Free Will Defense," 109, cited in Feinberg, *Many Faces of Evil*, 65. As Feinberg notes, this leaves work to do for the Compatibilistic Free-Will defender for whom Flew's argument in particular would still stand.

151. Osmond Ramberan makes an even stronger claim. Not only does the existence of evil not

PART I: The Tension of Theodicy

Again, this settles only the logical problem of evil.[152] And it is fair to say that this significantly changed the discussion so that the focus was no longer a sharp focus on the logical issue, but it extended the conversation into issues that are more existential.

Marilyn McCord Adams: All Is Answered at the Cross

In her article, "Redemptive Suffering: A Christian Solution to the Problem of Evil," Marilyn McCord Adams begins, "Christians believe that God is effectively dealing with the problem of evil through the Cross—primarily the cross of Christ and secondarily their own . . . yet these points are rarely mentioned in discussions of the problem of evil among analytic philosophers."[153] She has here put her finger on what is, I think, the critical issue of theodicy, but I judge her to be in error in one important respect. Christians, by definition, do believe that God in Christ has uniquely dealt with the problem of evil on the Cross; the solution to the problem of evil is soteriological. And, I would agree that analytic philosophers do overlook this, perhaps just as modern cosmologists overlook God's creative work, concerned that to accept God as creator would be to deny a real place to the scientific endeavor.[154] However, I do not agree that Christians are generally and specifically really aware of this concept. Christians do not generally reason from the Cross to our own lives, but rather consider the Cross as a unique, even exceptional, way in which God dealt with the problem of evil. But she is correct that it is Christian teaching.[155] Citing Luke 9:22–25, Adams asserts that God's dealing with evil in Christ has continuity with how God deals with evil through us.

---

result in a formal contradiction, given the standard formulation of the trilemma, but it results in *reductio ad absurdum*. So he writes, " 'the problem of evil' is shown to be logically absurd in that it denies the law of non-contradiction. And if this is so, it cannot be a threat to the theist in the sense of implying the non-existence of God" ("Evil and Theism," 36). Richard Swinburne offers an instructively useful set of propositions as a replacement for the usual trilemma that is formally contradictory, or as he frames it, would lead necessarily to Mackie's conclusion:

1/ if there is a God, he is omnipotent and perfectly good;
2/ a perfectly good being will never allow any morally bad state to occur if he can prevent it;
3/ an omnipotent being can prevent the occurrence of all morally bad states; and
4/ there is at least one morally bad state;

The result must be that there is no God or one of the propositions must be falsified, which Swinburne rightly indicates is (2) (*Providence and the Problem of Evil*, 7,10).

152. It is worth noting that many years later, Antony Flew, at the age of 81, renounced his atheism in favor of unfocused theism after a twenty-year friendship with Gary Habermas. This is discussed in a conversation between these two men in the Winter 2004 issue of *Philosophia Christi*.

153. M. M. Adams, "Redemptive Suffering," 169.

154. John Polkinghorne addresses this better than I could but this is not the place to enter into this discussion. I raise it only by analogy.

155. Paul Fiddes says something very similar and with which I agree, though he bases our shyness in a philosophical commitment to God's impassibility. He writes, "While Christian theology has, until quite recently, been hesitant to speak of the presence of God in the suffering of all mankind, it has always wanted to affirm the presence of God in the suffering and death of Jesus. Here at least we might

Though thirty years had passed, Marilyn McCord Adams still wrestled with the Flew-Mackie argument; she was not satisfied with Plantinga's "victory." Like Plantinga, Adams rejects Compatibilistic Free-Will and argues from a Libertarian Free-Will or incompatibilist position.[156] But, her approach, while analytic, is not focused on the logical problem of evil,[157] but the existential problem of evil—suffering is awful, but God is trustworthy. In her judgment, each life (antemortem and postmortem, combined) must be worth living to the person herself. She rejects the approach of Plantinga as not satisfying to Christians. It is insufficient, she asserts, to suggest possible answers to the logical problem that do not correspond to the factual reality and the truth of the Bible. Such possibilities do not increase our trust in God in the face of terrible suffering and overwhelming evil.[158] For this reason it is important to understand that she is rejecting not only Mackie, who argues that in regard to preventing evil, God is "damned if he didn't," but she is also rejecting the normal Free-Will Defense which argues that God is "damned if he did."[159]

Instead, her Libertarian Free-Will approach is rooted deeply in an interpersonal understanding of God's relationship to the Saints. This can be seen as she sets out God's goals:

> (T6) God's primary interest in creation is the rational creatures, particularly the human beings, whom he has made.
>
> (T7) God made human beings to enter into non-manipulative relationships of self-surrendering love with himself and relationships of self-giving love with others.[160]

---

expect to find theological talk about the suffering of God. As a matter of fact, however, traditional theology has wanted to escape this conclusion, usually by the route of asserting the 'two-natures' doctrine of Christology; that is, it has affirmed that the divine Son suffered in the flesh, but only in the strict sense that the human nature of Jesus suffered, the divine nature remaining impassible" (*Creative Suffering of God*, 26).

156. She makes it clear that her perspective excludes both manipulation and chance—the logical extremes often attributed as necessary consequences of Compatibilistic Free-Will and Libertarian Free-Will respectively. Yet in even attempting to walk this line, she refers to the willful sinning of humans as something (given God's character and goals) God is "powerless to exclude." There is something interesting here. While her argument proceeds from this basic belief and value (T7), it will be shown that this is not a necessary starting point to arrive at some of the same conclusions.

157. In fact, she does address this and it is important to her: "I believe that Christianity does provide a distinctive resolution of the 'logical' problem of evil for believers and an answer to the 'factual' problem as well." To her credit, she is reaching for much more. She is rejecting Plantinga's possible solution and his "defense," and looking for factual, biblical authority for stating what God is actually doing and how we can engage with him in his work (Adams, "Redemptive Suffering," 171).

158. M. M. Adams, *Horrendous Evils and the Goodness of God*, 54.

159. Ibid., 59.

160. M. M. Adams, "Redemptive Suffering," 173.

PART I: The Tension of Theodicy

Given these goals of God in regard to people and in light of the reality of evil in the world, she intends to take this beyond the logical to the biblically factual. She prompts us with painful and challenging questions:

> Q1/ How can I trust (or continue to trust) God in a world like this (in distressing circumstances such as these)?
>
> Q2/ Why does God not do more than he does to prevent or eliminate evils?
>
> Q3/ Why did God make a world in which there are evils of the amounts and kinds found in this world, instead of one with fewer or less severe kinds?
>
> Q4/ Why did God make a world such as this instead of one entirely free from evils?
>
> Q5/ How does God fit evils, of the amounts and kinds we find in this world, into his redemptive purposes?[161]

Her fundamental answer is that for Christians, Q1 and Q5 are answered in the Cross and in God's suffering. This is seen in the Bible and can also be exegeted from the history of the church. In short, she seems to be claiming that Evil & Suffering is used by God to destroy Evil & Suffering. The key, which goes beyond all the reasoning, is that "intimacy with God is the incommensurate good."[162] This good is the eschatological good of living in the presence of God (and to some extent even in the contemporary context of our lives) which overwhelms temporal pain. She notes that this is the argument of Romans 8:18, which tells God's people that their light and momentary suffering does not compare to the joys to be revealed in and to his people at the appearing of Christ. This echoes the ancient argument of Augustine, highlighted by Edwards and others: people were made to be happy and specifically, to be happy in God.

Going further, Adams believes that when all is understood, each person's life is an intrinsic good to them. That is, she insists that a functional theodicy must comprehensively address the intrinsic good in every life—with no exceptions. It is not enough for a theodicy to demonstrate that there is good for a majority or even that the system as a whole is the best possible. She rejects "higher harmonies" along with Ivan Karamazov;[163] each and every life must be an intrinsically good to the individual. It is worth noting that regardless of the merits of this approach, her argument is not based on biblical facts, but on an extrapolation of her understanding of God's goodness. As with all extrapolations, she may be correct, but she offers no biblical, exegetical support of her specifically Christian position. Moreover, that assertion is at odds with the long-standing and traditional understanding of other issues, for which there exists

---

161. M M. Adams, "Redemptive Suffering," 171–73.
162. Ibid., 182.
163. M. M. Adams, *Horrendous Evils*, 149.

significant agreement among Christian theologians (at least until recently): eternal judgment. She adopts universalism and rejects hell and eternal punishment.[164]

Adams identifies her model as limited and raises the objection, that if to enjoy God is the greatest good to which God calls the saints, is not "this vale of tears a waste (foolish mismanagement) for him as well as 'a pain' for them," unless evil is in some way logically necessary?[165] And if evil is not necessary, then God should have done more to prevent or eliminate evils. She notes that Christians do not support the idea of necessary evil, so the answer must lie in God. The answer she proposes is "thus enduring temporal suffering, God's people share in the divine commitment to the temporal order."[166] But this answer seems to lean toward being circular: we suffer with God because God suffers with us. But this is not an answer and she seems to understand that. The result is that all suffering does not give conclusive evidence of redemptive value and so Q2–Q4 are not answered; they "remain a mystery." She writes that "the evils of sin, sickness, and death were not part of God's original intentions but a by-product of his creation of free persons and/or a plurality of mutually interfering natures . . . and the Christian does not know . . . why he permits so many of them."[167] No one can fault Adams for a model that answers some, but not all questions, but it is possible that she has not pursued her own argument as far as it might carry her. Referring to an "incompleteness gap" she is willing to concede that Christianity does not have the resources for these questions. Yet, I believe that her core paradigm is part of a larger biblical idea that will at least close the gap, even if it fails to answer all the questions.

164. Ivan declares, "When the mother embraces the fiend who threw her child to the dogs, and all three cry aloud with tears, 'Thou art just, O Lord!' then, of course, the crown of knowledge will be reached and all will be made clear. But what pulls me up here is that I can't accept that harmony" (Dostoyevsky, *Brothers Karamazov*, 290).

And in regard to universalism, Adams writes in *Horrendous Evils*, "Nor would it follow from the fact that some humans die unconverted, without recognizing Divine presence, that the Divine Mother lets any out of Her nurturing arms. . . . eventually, . . . everyone will recognize the omnipresent tender loving care of God!" (105). In regard to hell, rejecting it as apocalyptic soteriology, a Grade B Western, she writes that in this model, "evil is not defeated . . . [RAS: it is] torment in hell . . . the wicked are not redeemed, nor does suffering come to an end" (138). She rejects the "grim hell" of "retributive justice" and proposes the "mild hell" of self-chosen consequences (argued over 43–48). Also she writes, "let creatures 'do their damnedest' and still [RAS: God will] win them over to heavenly bliss" ("Problem of Hell," 304).

She is not alone in challenging this long held biblical doctrine. For example, Rowan Williams writes, "Being Christian, if it means acting for these goals and for these reasons, is believing the doctrine of the Trinity to be true, and true in a way that converts and heals the human world. It is not to claim a totality of truth about God or about the human world, or even a monopoly of the means of bringing divine absolution or grace to men and women" (*On Christian Theology*, 179, emphasis mine). Here Williams's Christianity seems to have joined a universalist consortium. And in *Truce of God*, he rejects hell, writing, "If salvation is for any, it is for all. And Christianity in its way goes even further than Buddhism by coming near to suggesting that if it is not for all, it is not really for any" (*Truce of God*, 30). Neither Adams nor Williams are alone in this.

165. M. M. Adams, "Redemptive Suffering," 183.

166. Ibid., 184.

167. Ibid.

PART I: The Tension of Theodicy

While disagreeing with her universalist extrapolations, I find that her core idea brings significant insight to the discussion. Her point is this: the Cross is the paradigm. Redemptive suffering is the paradigm and not an exceptional action of God. As such, suffering is the godly means of destroying Evil & Suffering for his people, but we also join him in the fellowship of suffering with Christ. If it is also true that Evil & Suffering is in some way necessary to God's goals (T6 and T7), as I hope to explore, then it would it be true that suffering is our co-laboring with God in the work of destroying Evil & Suffering. And not only that, but there would be no possible accusation of foolish management on God's part because the battle would be real and not construed. Sharing in the divine commitment to the temporal order would be an all-out war against a real enemy.

Jürgen Moltmann: A Fully Trinitarian Theodicy

The trauma and raw suffering of World-War II strongly influenced Moltmann: as a teenager, he was imprisoned as a British P.O.W. During this time he was confronted with the horrors of the German extermination of Jews, and as a young theologian at Göttingen, he was lectured by the survivors. So he writes, "A theology which did not speak of God in the sight of the one who was abandoned and crucified would have nothing to say to us."[168] This is not only the key to his theology, but also to his thinking about theodicy. Like the horror of the atrocities of the War, the Cross is also a horror: "Christians who do not have the feeling that they must flee the crucified Christ, have probably not yet understood Him in a sufficiently radical way."[169] It is offensive on many levels, but perhaps the most significant is this—it is the last thing that anyone expects—or even wants—of a god or of God.[170] It is the issue of theodicy that drives Moltmann's theology: "But if there were no theodicy question, where would the risk of faith be?"[171]

His theodicy is not so much an answer to the "why" of suffering—the classic demand made of any theodicy—but rather the "meaning" of suffering. He concludes *The Crucified God* with these words, "Brotherhood with Christ means the suffering and active participation in the history of this God. Its criterion is the history of the crucified and risen Christ. Its power is the sighing and liberating spirit of God. Its consummation lies in the kingdom of the triune God which sets all things free and

---

168. Moltmann, *Crucified God*, 1. Later in the book, this is even more clearly stated, "The death of Jesus on the Cross is the centre of all Christian theology. It is not the only theme of theology, but it is in effect entry to its problems and answers on earth" (203). So also, it is the entry into the problem of theodicy.

169. Ibid., 38.

170. Ibid., 47. This is the unanticipated uniqueness of Christianity and part of the scandal of the Cross: that our sin is so horrific that God would pay so terrible a price—God abandoned God.

171. Quoted in Blocher, "Evil and the Cross," 9.

Free-Will and Evil: The Historical Development of Theodicy

fills them with meaning."[172] The meaning of suffering is to know God by participating with him in his sufferings. Indeed, it is the nature of the world God made, and of God himself, to suffer: "the history of the world is the history of God's suffering."[173] This hints at some disagreements that I would have with his soteriology, and as it is connected to his panentheism, it is problematic to my understanding, but neither of these are my concerns here. It is important to see that the meaning of suffering is found in the Cross and fellowship with the One who suffered upon it. Beyond seeing meaning in suffering in the Cross, he understands that the history of the created world (which includes the emergence of evil and its solution) is a history in the Trinity and not external to it.[174] Citing Berdyaev, he lofts his words as insight into the passion of God. He writes, "His theology of the Cross is the answer to the theodicy problem, which arises from the theology of history and freedom: "Evil and suffering exist because freedom exists; but freedom has no origin; it is an ultimate frontier."[175]

Henri Blocher rejects Moltmann as ultimately Hegelian: in fusing metaphysics and history, he is distorting soteriology,[176] and as universalist in his panentheism.[177] I agree. Yet, for both, the central event in theodicy is the Cross:

> At the Cross, who would dare entertain the blasphemy of imagining that God would, even to the slightest degree, comply with evil? . . . At the Cross, God turned evil against evil and brought about the practical solution to the problem. He has made atonement for sins, he has conquered death, he has triumphed over the devil. He has laid the foundation for hope.[178]

Here, preserving the atonement as atonement, he still shows the centrality of the Cross for our understanding evil. And more than understanding, the Cross is the means by which God wages war against evil and by which he calls us to war as well. It is this war against evil and the centrality of the Cross which is critical for both. Blocher writes, "With admirable insight Moltmann warns us against every theory that would seek to explain the problem of evil and also against every attempt to attenuate it."[179] So,

---

172. Moltmann, *Crucified God*, 338.

173. Moltmann, *Trinity and the Kingdom: The Doctrine of God*, 4.

174. One could cite numerous passages of Moltmann here, but let it suffice to note his section on "The Tragedy in God" in *Trinity and the Kingdom of God* (42–47).

175. Ibid., 47.

176. Blocher's argument is worth reading as he defends divine judgment—something fewer and fewer are interested in doing. Blocher shows that Moltmann's elevation of divine philanthropy and rejection of punishment is foreign to the Bible and constitutes a rejection of the very work of Christ and a distortion of evil into something good—which cannot be (*Evil and the Cross*, 87–90).

177. Ibid., 75–76.

178. Ibid., 104.

179. Ibid., 82. He also goes on to note that Moltmann did not take his own advice! God cannot incorporate evil into the life of God.

PART I: The Tension of Theodicy

theodicy is found in the Cross and our response to evil is found in the Cross: "Evil is not there to be understood, but to be fought."[180]

But there is a tension here. If God has fought evil "to the death" and won, why is evil still present in this age of "Kingdom Come"? Blocher writes, "The kingdom of God is not established in the form that the majority of people were expecting; it does not put an end to evil at a single blow, but its liberating march of conquest extends over a period of time. For that period of time, evil continues to thrive."[181] Concerning the Roman occupation, we marvel at the slowness of the disciples to comprehend the purposes of God in not removing the Romans—but in regard to evil, we also continue to be confused. Ultimately, evil is not explainable for Blocher: it is not an ingredient of existence or creation and it was not raised up by God instrumentally for other greater purposes. It is that which is contrary to the will of God.[182] But the lack of understanding the full nature of evil does not prevent a Cross-centered theodicy. God is at war with evil: "at the Cross evil is conquered as evil."[183] It is in this truth that we are consoled.

Greater Good Defense: Keith Yandell and Charles Journet

The Greater Good Defense is a species of the Free-Will Defense. In Keith Yandell's formulation of this system, evil is that which frustrates a man's attainment of his greater good.[184] In this case, the nature of evil is hardly privative or substantive, but it is instrumental. Evil is predicate; it has effect, rather than being. And freedom, incompatibilist, libertarian freedom, is essential to this system, for he writes, "This view of moral agency, of course, assumes . . . that moral agents are necessarily free agents, and that free agents are necessarily not determined."[185] This positions this system as consequentialist and evil as an essential component of the work of producing the good. So he writes, "Every evil is logically necessary to some good, some evil is overbalanced by some good to which it is logically necessary, and no evil overbalances the good to which it is logically necessary."[186] Evil is necessary and instrumentally used to accomplish the Greater Good and it is outweighed by the good, which is a greater part of the system.

---

180. Ibid., 103.
181. Ibid., 122.
182. Ibid., 128–29.
183. Ibid., 132.
184. Yandell writes, "It seems, then, a relevant (if perhaps partial) theistic characterization of evil to say that anything which frustrates (either prevents or diminishes) a man's attainment of his greatest good is evil. To the degree a man's own free actions and choices frustrate his self-attainment, he is evil. If God brings about, or allows, something to occur which frustrates such development . . . He is not all-good" ("Greater Good Defense," 2).
185. Ibid., 11.
186. Ibid., 4.

Like the work of Adams and Plantinga, the context for this proposal is the Flew-Mackie challenge and like Adams, Yandell is not satisfied with mere logical possibility as a defense. It might be more appropriate, given the above definitions, to call his work a Theodicy, one painted with wide brush strokes. In his 1974 article, he proposes that the Greater Good Defense is the theodicy into which all orthodox solutions to the problem of evil must fall.[187] This is a large claim given that the Greater Good Defense is exclusively limited to Libertarian Free-Will type arguments. However there is not much interest in this proposal. Feinberg dismisses it on a number of grounds, but perhaps the most significant is that he asserts that there is no logical tie between moral evil and free will.[188] It is also worth noting that this defense is not a current debate in the literature, nor did Yandell, himself, pursue the idea at any great length. However, more usefully, Charles Journet's formulation of the Greater Good Defense, as a Roman Catholic, is closer to Augustine and Aquinas and is not a response to the Flew-Mackie challenge, but rather a response to Dostoyevsky's, Ivan. As a result, he emphasized the terrible reality of privative evil, which is permitted by God in order to achieve the great good of the final state of his people.[189]

To some extent, the Greater Good Defense could be ignored by this project, but there is something worth noting in Yandell's argument in particular. First, the idea of evil as predicate is helpful when trying to grasp the nature of a terrible nothingness, though as I will explain in the conclusion to this project, I believe we can still assert that evil is the "nothing that is." More significantly, he asserts that theists must agree that God had a morally sufficient reason for creating or allowing evil[190] and he proposes one of the few substantially orthodox consequentialist ethics within a defense or a theodicy. While it seems that his sufficient reason is too much like that of Hick ("evil's instrumentality" exceeds even Hick),[191] nevertheless, he challenges us to consider something usually rejected by Christian thinkers: our formulation of the problem of evil may overlook the importance of deeply investigating God's purpose in allowing evil.

---

187. He writes, "the orthodox theist is committed to the truth of some version of the greater good defense" (ibid., 1).

188. Feinberg, *Many Faces of Evil*, 108.

189. Journet writes in agreement with St. Francis de Sales, "Our loss was a gain for us, since human nature has in effect received more graces by the redemption of its Saviour than it would have received by the innocence of Adam. . . . he was making ready to compensate for it abundantly by an even more incredible miracle" (Journet, *Meaning of Evil*, 258–9).

190. Yandell, "Greater Good Defense," 3.

191. Feinberg would agree, "Yandell reduced the Greater Good Defense to the soul-building theodicy" (*Many Faces of Evil*, 111). Feinberg, whose concern in evaluating various systems is to assess internal consistency, notes that Yandell has distorted the free-will defense which rests upon non-consequentialism, distinct from his consequentialism; an inconsistency.

PART I: The Tension of Theodicy

SUMMARY: MORE WORK IS LEFT TO DO

> It is the glory of God to conceal a matter,
> but the glory of kings is to search out a matter.
>
> —Proverbs 25:2

The depths of this mystery have not been sounded. The depths have eluded our best and most probing efforts—and will continue to do so. Though progress is slow, like physics, an arguably infinite project, the joy of attempting to unfold the mysteries of God keeps us from turning away.

My contribution will not be a defense of God, so that a possible reason for his action is put forward. And it is not an apologetic, so that the person of God will be made acceptable to the atheist—or even to the theist! Instead, the direction of my investigation is to follow the character of God, and the purposes he has revealed for his universe, to a better understanding of what he has declared and what he is doing. In so doing, I anticipate that God will be better known to those who seek him, and the hope of those who seek him would be increased. Yet, to be clear, no theodicy can relieve pain or take away the reality of evil. Rather, a good advance in our understanding of theodicy would inject hope into pain to the extent that it exposes reality, like Augustine did. If I am proposing to follow the tension between "necessary evil" and "conforming freedom" to hope, it is worth defining hope here as I close this section. Hope is our confidence and joy in God which is based on our eschatological future in the person of Christ. It is towards this truth that a theodicy must point us.

With that as a goal, and noting the key themes which I have just outlined, an advance in our understanding of theodicy should be like that of Augustine, who proposed a God-centered theodicy as we saw in *City of God*, initiating a stream of thought that then flowed also through Aquinas, Calvin, Edwards, and others, even if not wholly, or fully. One possible reading of these is that evil might be something needed in order to show off God's goodness and glory. As much as that is true, they all diverge from Augustine. God might be glorified in all things, including evil, but evil is in no way necessary to him.

Also, an advance should be eschatological. Both Hick and Augustine approached the problem eschatologically. For Hick that meant that a theodicy must necessarily be eschatological, looking for an answer in the future, not in a past catastrophe. But, *pace* Hick, Augustine's theodicy is also eschatological. While Hick has no room for Augustine's prior catastrophe, the Fall, it is not to this past event that Augustine looks for his Theodicy. It is rather to the character of God, the death of Christ, and to the future hope for his people (even those persecutors that have not yet surrendered to God, but will) to which we look. So, my theodicy will stand in light of the eschatological freedom which was promised by God implicitly in the creation story and explicitly in the Revelation of John. In other words, hope arises not merely because God is observing us now, but because we live in the light of his eternal gaze through Christ who is now seated in heaven with him.

Also, an advance should acknowledge the instrumental value of Evil & Suffering, as does Hick and others. While the problem of evil is not a problem which has a "rational solution" or *telos*, Evil & Suffering is a threat in God's creation that will be overcome. The Christian asserts with the author of Revelation that "every tear will be wiped away!" On the Cross, evil is destroyed as evil; at the Throne, evil has been extinguished. How has that been accomplished? In God's economy, Evil & Suffering is an essential part of God's response to the problem of evil. While for Hick evil is essential, for my project it is, instead, unavoidable. That difference, which is at least the difference between a consequentialist and a non-consequentialist ethic, will be explored.

Finally, I suggest that an advance should be cross-centered and acknowledge that what happened on the cross was normative and not exceptional. That is, just as Evil & Suffering destroyed Evil & Suffering on the Cross, so also this is the normal means of God to destroy Evil & Suffering. This does not make evil essential to God's world, but rather it arises from God's good creation and is used by God as an essential part of the solution in the Cross. God suffers evil; evil is destroyed. So, agreeing with Adams, Moltmann, and Blocher, and others, the Cross is and must be the focus of any Theodicy. The greatest evil in the world is death and the greatest victory is the death of death. A Cross-centered theodicy is the crucial step to a God-centered theodicy, though Adams has shown that it is possible to do otherwise! What does a God-centered, Cross-rooted, eschatological, instrumental, non-consequentialist theodicy look like? It is one that understands that God uses Evil & Suffering instrumentally to destroy Evil & Suffering. It is one in which the shadow of the Cross stretches over all of history, lit by the light of the freedom to come in the third creation, the eschaton. This is our hope. To make clear the details in this picture, we must turn to Part II.

PART II

The Testing of a Theodicy

> The person who is torn by suffering stands alone. There is no explanation of suffering which is capable of obliterating his pain, and no consolation of higher wisdom which could assuage it.[1]
>
> —Jürgen Moltmann

IN THIS NEXT SECTION I intend to unfold my offering to the conversation. I will do this in three hypotheses. First, I will make a case for "Conforming Freedom" which is the singular eschatological intent of God for his people in regard to freedom. Second, I will make the case that evil is an intrinsic problem necessarily appearing within God's project (though not in God, himself) and that it is used instrumentally as God's solution to the problem of evil, itself. Finally, I will argue that this final and eschatological freedom is created by God over four Eras of Freedom which are bounded by three acts of creation and associated crises. And it is this that leads us to hope.

I make no pretense of "solving" the problem of evil here. This is not modesty, though such modesty is well advised, but a confidence that this is a problem without an exhaustive solution. Possible solutions, that are biblical and philosophically sound (of which there are not a few), do not remove the radical disorientation of suffering from the sufferer or the observer—or even the tormenter (so said Moltmann). If a "solution" could be offered that "dries every tear," we need go no further than the Cross to change our minds. There the Son, the God-man, who knew all that a man could know of God, uttered a deep cry of dereliction, a cry of infinite pathos. And the

---

1. Moltmann, *Trinity and the Kingdom*, 47.

torturer and the watchers hid their faces. And so did the Father. The hope of the Cross did not overwhelm the infinite loss, even in light of eternal gain.

It might be the case that the Cross could be a warning to theodicists: "No Trespassing—Holy Ground! Violators will be Persecuted!" But, in fact, such a sign does not exist. Rather, the Cross is a call to come close (even if, as Moltmann argues, we are inclined to run away) and understand suffering. And when we come close, we see something more offensive to our thinking and expectations than any horror. The author of Hebrews instructs us, "let us run with endurance the race that is set before us, fixing our eyes on Jesus, the author and perfecter of faith, who for the joy set before Him endured the Cross, despising the shame, and has sat down at the right hand of the throne of God" (Hebrews 12:1b-2). Here is something intriguing, even offensive: joy. The author of Hebrews has intent neither to diminish the anguished prayer in the Garden, nor to minimize the horror of the execution. But he will not let us look away from hope. Instead of a warning, we have warrant for pursing a theodicy. A desire to understand Jesus should overcome our hesitancy. In pain, God offers us joy and hope.

But something else must be said here. God does not take away pain and replace it with joy. Joy is the *paraklesis* that came "along side," not the anesthesia that blocked the pain. So much is clearly evident from this text and every other text about suffering. While God may relieve suffering at times, we are still called to suffer. But he does offer us joy and hope in the middle of the pain. As much as any theodicy is true, as much as what I am saying is true, it will direct us to a *paraklesis* in our pain. This is a test of a theodicy.

There is another kind of test, three challenges given to us by David and Randall Basinger that seem worth listing in detail:

> *Challenge #1*: It is quite likely that God could have done more to eliminate evil without negatively affecting the relevant divine goals. In fact, it is so unlikely that all of the evil we experience is necessarily connected to divine goals that the theodicy (and thus theism) in question must be considered implausible.
>
> *Challenge #2*: Even if all of the evil we experience is necessarily connected to divine goals, it is unlikely that all of the relevant divine goals are, or could be, morally acceptable. In fact, in relation to some evils, it is so unlikely that any morally acceptable goal necessitating such evil could exist that the theodicy (and thus theism) in question must be rejected as implausible.
>
> *Challenge #3*: Even if all the evil we experience is necessarily connected to morally acceptable goals and the inherently negative value of evil is appropriately acknowledged, it is doubtful that the God postulated by the theodicy in question remains worthy of worship. In fact, since the relevant being so clearly fails to possess the minimum attributes required of a deity, any theodicy (and

thus theism) that postulates a being with such attributes must be viewed as an implausible response to the evil we experience.[2]

These could be dismissed as a rather wordy reincarnation of the Epicurean Trilemma (with appropriate logical extensions to cover the amount and intensity of evil). However, they seem to have a certain "street sense" that commends them to any project like sheep dogs, helpfully nipping at the heels of the theodicist. So, we will return to both the hope of joy and the Basingers's challenges in the conclusion.

---

2. Basinger and Basinger, "Logic of Theodicy," paragraphs 37, 42, and 49. These are presented in the context of comparative theodicy between determinism, freewill theism, and process theology. The challenges do not represent their conclusions, but challenges they offer to each system in order to assess their "non person relative" plausibility. Their conclusion: "our claim is only that we are aware of no objective basis for claiming justifiably that any one of our three theodicies (and thus theisms) is in fact more plausible than the others" (paragraph 64).

4

Hypothesis 1

Conforming-Freedom is the ultimate and singular human freedom required by God's character and goals for his people.

As God is free, so likewise man is free.[3]

—Bishop Kallistos Ware

IN THIS CHAPTER, I intend to offer a proposal for the particular kind of eschatological freedom which God's people will enjoy in God's presence: Conforming-Freedom. Groundwork will be laid for this by examining God's character and ultimate purpose, his purpose in creation, and his promise regarding this particular kind of freedom for his human willful-creatures, which arises out of his character and goals.[4] In so doing I will define Conforming-Freedom.

This ultimate, eschatological freedom must be of a different character than that which we have witnessed so far in history. Having investigated freedom in Chapter 1, and taking the position that God's first human willful-creatures were created perfect and "free to choose" between obedience and disobedience, I ask how is it that God's

---

3. Timothy Ware, *Orthodox Way*, revised edition, 51.

4. The very title of this chapter declares a strong underlying assumption—we can rightly attempt to speak with some confidence concerning the purposes of God. Is that a presumption? As I indicated in my introduction, I do not intend to address the issue of the possibility of epistemology other than to state that I am committed to a correspondence theory of truth, which applies to our theology just as much as to our physics. That does not mean that I believe that I, or anyone, knows all or even most of what can be known about any subject, especially of God. But it does mean that we can know truly. In fact, so core is this belief to the Christian, that even our salvation is wrapped up in the possibility of intimate knowing: "This is eternal life, that they may know You, the only true God, and Jesus Christ whom You have sent" (John 17:3). We not only can know God, but there is a correspondence between knowing God and eternal life, our salvation. Part of that truth is an understanding of God's purpose or purposes in creation.

people will persevere in goodness in heaven, if human willful-creatures did not do so in the perfect garden? Of course, such an eschatological "perseverance of the saints" should not be confused with the safe keeping of the souls of his people in Christ between the second and third creations. I am considering here why the situation after the creation of the new heavens and new earth will be different from Adam, who though perfect in creation, did not remain so. If indeed Adam failed after the first creation and even God's people continued to sin after they were created new in Christ, how is it that they will persevere eternally throughout the new creation?

The two basic perspectives on freedom, Libertarian Free-Will and Compatibilist Free-Will, give rise to different classes of answers. All Libertarian Free-Will positions hold in common that God values the free-will of his willful-creatures above sustained perfection. Yet, while this is the most intuitive answer and while it has been reasoned in detail, no Free-Will Defense is adequate to the task of being the foundation for a Theodicy.[5] Moreover, by only solving a rather esoteric philosophical question in regard to free-will as a response to the problem of evil, the theodicy question is merely shifted to other questions, such as the amount of evil and the net balance-of-trade for each individual between good and evil experienced. So called, Irenaean free-will defenses, with their emphasis on maturing humans by the evil that results from free-will and God's epistemic distance, do imply an answer: God's people will be matured into the likeness of God, and so persevere. But the theodicy itself does not adequately establish the reality of epistemic distance, and further it has not been shown that even if epistemic distance were the case, that it would have the desired effect of drawing people toward maturity and a rejection of evil. Worse, a single lifetime of evil is inadequate to the most prosaic advocate of this system; Hick requires the repeated opportunity of "many lives; many worlds" and an open cycle of evil tutelage to hope to accomplish the desired end.

Another major class of free-will responses understands the future actions of God's free-creatures to be unknowable to God in fundamental ways. Terence Fretheim, John Sanders, Gregory Boyd, and others (previously considered) assert that God's plan or purpose is a risky one whose end is less than established. This seems to avoid the issue of perseverance after the third creation altogether because defenders of this position

---

5. Kenneth Surin says well of Plantinga, and the Free-Will Defense in general, that it is not an acceptable vindication of God's moral blamelessness or even of his moral perfection (*Theology and the Problem of Evil*, 76). Robert C. Mesle notes, approving of Hick, that the Free-Will Defense cannot distance God sufficiently from responsibility for evil in his project ("The Problem of Genuine Evil," 412–30, especially 414). Beyond this, the Free-Will Defense (and free-will theodicy) are by-and-large strangers to the Bible, something that Bart Ehrman notes in his thorough assessment of the biblical material: "this standard explanation that God had to give human beings free will and that suffering is the result of people badly exercising it plays only a very minor role in the biblical tradition" (*God's Problem*, 12). While Ehrman's thesis is the stark failure of biblical Christianity to address the issue of theodicy, I agree with him in this: the Bible does not fundamentally use "free will" to explain evil. As I have shown above, human free-will is not even a critical concern of the biblical authors or God and it will not be shown to be a solution to the issue of theodicy.

expect God to be able to so "control the game" that the third creation will occur and heaven will be populated. But how will perfection be eternally ensured? This position does not generally consider that question. Free-will defenders are not always clear about the means of perseverance and one defender of this position at least hints that God may shift the nature of freedom to something like compatibilist free-will after the third creation.[6] I doubt that this view will be widely subscribed to among other free-will defenders, but even if it is, I will consider that below in the second division.

The second perspective, which holds to Compatibilistic Free-Will, understands that, in some way, God wills it so. That is, by compatibilist free-will, God willed the Fall (at least willed not to prevent the Fall), willed redemption and then, in heaven, wills perseverance. That is logically possible and within the omnipotence of God. But for what purpose does God require such terrible Evil & Suffering? The answer of the Reformers and those following them is that the Fall permitted God's display of his glory by revealing his justice and mercy that would otherwise have had no venue.[7] While this is clearly true in fundamental respects, it is missing something that, if it is claimed to be the complete answer, seems (to many) to make God to be other than God-like in respect to his mercy and love. Are there any clues that point us to what else might be the reason?

I am proposing that what is desired by those who assert that God values human free-will (and coordinate with that, true and loving relationships with him) is not wrong. However, it seems that to pursue human free-will as an explanation for the problem of evil leads only to more problems.[8] But that does not mean the position is not pursuing something good and true about God and his intent for his willful-creatures. I am also proposing that those who understand God's will as determinate in all things are correct. But compatibilists who attempt to explain the working of God in an evil world do face a difficulty not unlike the Mackie-Flew challenge. And clearly, Plantinga's response, even if it was considered successful beyond creating unlikely

---

6. John S. Feinberg notes this ambiguity in the position in general (*Many Faces of Evil*, first edition, 141) and in *Satan and the Problem of Evil*, Gregory Boyd hints that he considers that Libertarian Free-Will may give way to Compatibilistic Free-Will in our final state. Citing the angels as an example, he writes: "Contingent creatures spend their potential one way or the other, and once spent we become what we choose. Libertarian freedom gives way to compatibilist freedom conditioned by the character an agent acquired by the use of their libertarian freedom" (171).

7. This was observed above in theologians as diverse as Edwards and Swinburne.

8. Many observations along these lines have been cited previously. Here let me only cite G. Stanley Kane who said (in "Theism and Evil"), "what sort of theistic account would provide an adequate explanation of evil that actually exists in our world? . . . Such an account would have to explain the beginnings of evil in such a way that neither God's goodness nor his power is compromised. The only major solution apart from dualistic ones which seeks to explain the existence of evil in terms of its beginnings is the free-will solution. A serious difficulty with the free-will solution is that while it has an initial plausibility as an explanation for moral evil it seems to offer no plausible account of natural evil" (20). And also, "The natural evil that is employed as a necessary means to the good must not occur in quantities greater than that required for bringing about the good" (21). This has been addressed, but not satisfactorily.

PART II: The Testing of a Theodicy

possibilities, is not an option for the compatibilist. And while the compatibilist has an answer that is true, I have given reasons to consider that it may be incomplete. So, I am proposing that something is missing in the standard trilemma, which, when perceived, changes the problem sufficiently so that neither the standard Libertarian Free-Will position nor the standard Compatibilistic Free-Will positions are adequate to encompass it completely. The pursuit of that missing piece may lead us to a deeper understanding of God and his purposes.

The modification of the Trilemma that I am proposing is to add the statement: Evil & Suffering destroys the Evil & Suffering which arose as an intrinsic problem from creation, but not in the creation as God created it. If Evil & Suffering is destroyed (at least for his people), and not just suppressed, a particular kind of freedom would result, one that I believe God has desired for his people all along. If this is correct, it may be sufficient to answer the question: how is it that anyone will persevere after the third creation? That is, if this time of Evil & Suffering really does destroy Evil & Suffering for his people in some fundamental way, God's redeemed willful-creatures would be made as free as God in regard to evil. Just as evil does not exist in competition with God, nor does God interact with evil such that he is tempted, so also if evil is gone for his people, it holds no power over his people. If this is the case, then God's people will have no intersection with evil in the final state, so that they might achieve the vision of Bishop Ware, "as God is free, so likewise man is free."

Yet, to start there, would be to start in the middle—even to be anthropocentric. It would be a misstep for a theological project, especially theodicy, to begin anywhere other than with YHWH and his purposes, or at least as much as he may have revealed them to us. So, in this chapter, I want to begin with God's purpose and character, consider his purpose in regard to creation and finally attempt to establish his goal for ultimate human freedom which arises from his character and goals: Conforming Freedom.

GOD'S ULTIMATE AND CHIEF END: HIS OWN GLORY

> The true vision of evil demands an exalted view of God.[9]
>
> —Charles Journet

In displaying the case for God's glory as his first and highest value, there is no better tutor than Jonathan Edwards. In using him, I want to be careful in two ways. First, I am not pursuing a specifically Edwardian argument for my hypothesis in this chapter, but rather I am displaying his argument for the centrality of God's glory as the ground for my hypothesis. And second, I want to affirm that as far as I will pursue Edwards in this context, the centrality of the Glory of God, it does find common ground among

---

9. Journet, *Meaning of Evil*, 23.

many Christian theologians regardless of their view of free-will, though not always explicitly so.[10] Moreover, I would argue that this must be common ground for any theodicy. As noted above, Charles Journet, a free-will defender, writes, "The true vision of evil demands an exalted idea of God, and by similar inversion an exalted idea of God offers a deeper understanding of evil."[11] So it does. And so I desire to go no further with Edwards in this project than common ground will take us. Of course, terminology does vary between theological systems, but even here I hope to be careful, simply defining what Edwards means, rather than adopting his language as essential to my argument.

In Edwards's scheme, there are two classes of ends: ultimate and subordinate.[12] It is worth noting that he is not using "ultimate" in its usual sense of being the last in a sequence of lesser to greater, so that it is the greatest. Instead, ultimate ends for Edwards are those ends that are valued in, of and for themselves, alone. And, as will be shown below, even ultimate ends can then be comparatively ranked. Subordinate ends are those ends which are valued only because they lead to ultimate ends. But ends are not absolute, in that they are either ultimate or subordinate only in respect to the person who owns those ends. The same end could have different meaning to different people, so that to one it is ultimate and to another the same end is subordinate. For example, a man could marry his fiancé because he delighted in her. For this man, the taking of a wife would be an ultimate end. Another man, with a different set of values, might marry in order to have children, taking no ultimate delight in his wife, so that his new wife, his marriage, would be a subordinate end for him. An ultimate end is, by definition, that which is valued for its own sake.

Also, in Edwards's thinking there are superior and inferior ends which are opposites; a scale upon which ends can be weighted, so that both subordinate and ultimate ends are ranked between these poles. However, at the far end of the scale, beyond the scale, the chief end is that one singular, ultimate end which is superior to all others.[13] Returning to my example, while marrying his fiancé might be an ultimate, rather than subordinate end for a man (another man may not delight in his wife as his wife, but rather loves her, instrumentally, for what she can do for him), his chief end might be to cure polio in the African continent. That is, while both his wife and curing polio

10. Perhaps it is not God's glory to which Beilby and others object, but a fear that other Reformed tenets may be "snuck in" with God's glory. If so, while this concern may be understandable, it should not be a concern. C.S. Lewis could never be accused of being a compatibilist and no one would doubt the central place God's glory found in his writings. He might even be a model in that he resisted fitting into either the libertarian or compatibilist position. An assessment of this observation is left to the reader.

11. Journet, *Meaning of Evil*, 23.

12. J. Edwards, "Dissertation Concerning The End for Which God Created The World," introduction, ¶ 1.

13. Edwards categorizes inferior ends as the opposite of chief ends, and ultimate ends as the opposite of subordinate ends (*End for Which God Created the World*, Introduction, ¶ 1). Synonymously, he uses the terms "last end" and "supreme end" for "chief" within the Introduction.

PART II: The Testing of a Theodicy

are ultimate ends, for they are valued in themselves, he values curing polio above his wife, so that his wife, while an ultimate end, is an inferior end in comparison to curing polio. If so, and in the case that no other ultimate ends exceeds this in his values, curing polio would be his chief end.

On Edwards, that end which God desires above all others, his chief end, is his glory. He writes, "Hence it will follow, that the moral rectitude of the disposition, inclination, or affection of God CHIEFLY consists in a regard to HIMSELF, infinitely above his regard to all other beings; or, in other words, his holiness consists in this."[14] One could imagine that, for God, God's love for his people is his chief end. This clearly is a biblical and an ultimate end for God and so is a candidate for his chief end. Yet, for Edwards, this is not the case, for if this were the case, then Christianity would be anthropocentric. Is Edwards correct? I believe he is and if we walk no further with Edwards than this issue, I would expect strong agreement from all free-will positions. Texts that support this multiply as we read, almost leaping from the page, if we read with an eye looking to God's purpose in creating the world and redeeming a people.

The poetry of David often reflects God's character, his orientation to his people, and his work in those who face evil.[15] In Psalm 23, David reflects on the Lord's shepherding and acknowledges that he is never alone in the valley of death where God "restores my soul; he guides me in the paths of righteousness *for his name's sake*" (verse 3). The great and archetypal shepherd metaphor leads our minds to consider

---

14. J. Edwards, *End for Which God Created the World*, 1.1. There is a point here which must be made. While for many something called an "end" would be seen as a goal to be pursued, God is not pursuing his ends as if they could elude him. This would be a foreign idea to import into Edwards (or into God). If by God's works, his glory is revealed or if his people are brought into his glory, it is human willful-creatures who are changed or brought along and not God. Nothing in Edwards's use of the term "ends" implies a change in God.

15. A word must be said here about the use of the Psalms in a theological argument. Care must be taken in regard to genre and historical setting, at least. But as this thesis sentence has stated, the Psalms are valued timelessly, not because they are simply great poetry or even for their instruction in prayer, but because they theologically address the timeless relationship of God to his people, and of his people to the world. While we cannot apply the Psalms in any way we like, asking of the Psalms any question we desire to have answered, its application in regard to knowing God is not displaced, but crucial to what the Psalms intend to communicate as the hymnody of God's covenant people. As such, the Psalms are theologically dense, prompting John Goldingay to say, "there is a greater concentration of statements about God here than anywhere else" (*Psalms* 1–41, 69). So, Erhard Gerstenberger affirms: "In short, the Psalter does not contain a summa of theological thought or any kind of theological system but a treasury of experiences accumulated by generations of people who lived in the region where the cradle of our own civilization stood.... The contours of this God vary a great deal,... but he always remains the very close, concrete, and personal God of the people" (*Psalms*, 36). That is, the Psalms are a representation of this particular people's understanding of God. This only lays the groundwork, now it must be judged if my theological applications are warranted. Of this specific text of Psalm 23, Goldingay writes, "There are not merely right paths in the sense of paths that lead to the right places,... faithful paths are paths consistent with divine shepherd's faithfulness ... so acting in faithfulness demonstrates that the name is a true reflection of the character [RAS: of God]" (*Psalms*, 350). I take from this that it is more than appropriate to extract God's purposes in shepherding—his character. So this repeated phrase, "for my name," is a theme of the Psalms proclaiming to us God's purpose.

not only the simple safety of the sheep, but God's glory in shepherding his sheep: "for his name's sake." In fact, Psalm after Psalm proclaims this idea in various ways: Psalm 79:9 reads, "Help us, O God of our salvation, *for the glory of Your name*; And deliver us and forgive our sins *for Your name's sake*.";[16] Psalm 106:8 reads, "Nevertheless He saved them *for the sake of his name, that he might make his power known*"; and Psalm 109:21 reads, "But You, O GOD, the Lord, deal kindly with me *for Your name's sake*; Because Your loving-kindness is good, deliver me." Such is the pervasive perspective of the Psalmist. However, there are many counter-examples to this in the Psalms. For example, Psalm 106, cited above, also says in verse 45, "And He remembered His covenant *for their sake*." Does this statement (and many like it which we could also cite), count against this claim that God's chief end, the one end which he values most, is his own glory, since here he saves ("remembers his covenant") for the benefit of his people (and hence not, specifically, his own glory). First, to say God cares deeply (acts for their sake) for his people is to affirm that this is an ultimate end of God. This is not disputed for there is much weighty evidence that God has saved his people because he loves them and desires to give them joy. We can rightly stipulate that God has an ultimate purpose to benefit his people. Beyond this, it is impossible to wholly separate God's love for himself from his love for his people, for God does not work "in parts," loving himself one day and his people another day. Instead, his love is univocal; he loves his people and he loves himself (as indeed he tells us to do, loving others as we love ourselves). But it is still true that he loves everything in a way that is appropriate to each object: he loves a flower as a flower should be loved, human willful-creatures as they should be loved; and himself as an infinitely valuable God should be loved. So, unlike the affirmations of affection and even sacrifice for his people, God holds as his first desire, his own glory. If a disagreement exists between scholars on this issue (though if we are careful with language and the meanings of words, and do not try to import concerns about free-will into this discussion, I suspect it could be avoided), it should not be over whether either of these are ultimate ends of God. However, I do believe that it is the case that God does have a unique chief end, one that is superior to all others and is observable by the way he deals with his people and how he explains his actions.[17] This, according to Edwards, is God's glory. If he is correct, and I believe

---

16. Marvin Tate acknowledges that because God's name and reputation is intertwined with his people, "ultimately it is God's glory which is at stake" because the mockery of Israel by the nations is a mocking of his name and person. All things are ultimately about God and for his glory, including his work in our behalf (*Psalms 51–100*, 301).

17. A clarification might be helpful here. Edwards distinguishes ultimate ends, those which are desired for their own sake, into two classes: original and independent and consequential and dependent. His example is this: "In like manner we must suppose that God, before he created the world, had some good in view, as a consequence of the world's existence, that was originally agreeable to him in itself considered, that inclined him to bring the universe into existence, in such a manner as he created it. But after the world was created, and such and such intelligent creatures actually had existence, in such and such circumstances, then a wise, just regulation of them was agreeable to God, in itself considered. And God's love of justice, and hatred of injustice, would be sufficient in such a case to

he is, it must be shown *not* that "for our sake" is *not* ultimate, but only that it is inferior to God's chief end. I believe this is the case because in all of the text of Scripture, God's glory is never subordinated to creation or confused with creation. This is not a minor point, but it can be confusing, for it is also true that our human flourishing and all of creation is entirely wrapped-up in God's glory and they cannot be fully distinguished. It is not as if we could say that creation is "all about us" or "all about God"; having been created, there is a certain kind of unity for creation itself that necessarily reflects the unity of God. Yet, and this is the crux of the matter, as intertwined as they are, creation has a vector toward God. That is, we are not necessary to God, except that we were created in the past and so have a certain accidental necessity under God's eternal decrees, but God is wholly necessary to us. God's glory includes creation but creation alone (were it possible to draw it out singly) must be "lighter" than the weight of God's glory and creation bound together. If this is a correct perspective, God's glory is his chief end, and that includes his glory in creation.

There is a second biblical reason that could be noted here. The rest of the verse in Psalm 106:45 (which I did not display above) reads, "And He remembered His covenant *for their sake*, and relented *according to the greatness of His lovingkindness.*" Here the phrase "for their sake" modifies God's action in keeping his covenant. So this Psalm is helpful in interpreting itself in this matter. The final phrase tells us that it was out of his character, his own "lovingkindness"—not our intrinsic value—that he saved his people. While I chose this example, and not all examples would be so helpful to my point, this one shows what may be also true of others. That is, even when God says, "I save you for your sake," behind that seems to be that claim that he does so for the sake of his own glorious character and out of his own character of lovingkindness. And while there are other examples that state that human salvation is an ultimate end (with which no one should disagree), and many of these are not bracketed so helpfully with God's chief end of his own glory, there are no counter-examples that would turn this logic around in such a way as to show that "our sake" is a superior end in respect to God's glory. This tends to establish that God's glory is his chief end and does so without importing any of the tenets of compatibilist logic.

I believe this to be a sound case and witnessed by the whole extent of the Bible. Paul writes, "through whom we have received grace and apostleship to bring about the obedience of faith among all the Gentiles *for His name's sake*";[18] and "and he did so *to*

---

induce God to deal justly with his creatures, and to prevent all injustice in him towards them. But yet there is no necessity of supposing that God's love of doing justly to intelligent beings, and hatred of the contrary, was what originally induced God to create the world." So, his original and independent ultimate end is his glory, but his derivative and dependent end is bringing justice (and so love) to his human creatures. So then, only the former can be considered his chief end" ("The End for Which God Created the World," Introduction, §17). Again, we can say that God's glory is his chief end without taking away from other genuine ultimate ends, including both showing his human willful-creation both justice and mercy.

18. Romans 1:5.

make known the riches of His glory upon vessels of mercy, which He prepared beforehand for glory";[19] and "to the end that we who were the first to hope in Christ would be *to the praise of His glory.*"[20] And John tells the church the same thing in his first letter, "I am writing to you, little children, because your sins have been forgiven you *for His name's sake.*"[21] In all things, God's passion toward a thing is appropriate to that thing. So we can truly say God is passionate about his image-bearing creatures and their salvation. But nothing can be understood to exceed his passion for his own name and glory, for such passion is appropriate to that object. His glory is his chief end.[22]

And although I did claim that we should all be able to go this far together, to be fair, I must state that this is not universally appreciated. Stanley Grenz provides at least one example of a free-will theist who is concerned that to accept God's glory into the center will bring with it certain compatibilist (or Reformed) tenets that he finds objectionable:

> God's interest in the creation of the reconciled community arises out of the divine nature itself. Reformed theology has traditionally focused on God's glory as the final rationale and goal for the work of creation and salvation. This is, of course, proper. However, the way theologians frame their understanding of the divine glory is often unhelpful. It so easily leaves us with the impression that God is a cosmic super-egoist demanding all praise and honor. In this way, God appears to be diametrically opposite from what the Bible set forth as the ideal human character. How can God demand that in all our actions we remain humble, if God himself directs all his activities toward his own exaltation?[23]

---

19. Romans 9:23.
20. Ephesians 1:12
21. 1 John 2:12.
22. To this incomplete survey it is helpful to add a sample of the occasions when God glory is referenced as, "his name," "my name," "his glory," or "my glory" to reveal a very God-focused perspective in Scripture. In Exodus 9:16 God made his purposes clear to Pharaoh through Moses, "But, indeed, for this reason I have allowed you to remain, in order to show you my power and in order to proclaim my name through all the earth." When Solomon built the temple, God responded this way: "The LORD said to him, 'I have heard your prayer and your supplication, which you have made before Me; I have consecrated this house which you have built by putting my name there forever, and my eyes and my heart will be there perpetually.' "(1 Kings 9:3). In Isaiah, God trumpets his passion for his name quite loudly: "For the sake of my name I delay my wrath, And for my praise I restrain it for you, in order not to cut you off. For my own sake, for my own sake, I will act; for how can my name be profaned? And my glory I will not give to another" (Isaiah 48:9,11). In Isaiah 42:8 God says, "I am the LORD, that is my name; I will not give my glory to another, nor my praise to graven images." In Isaiah 49:3 God says, "And he said to me, 'You are my Servant, Israel, in whom I will show my glory.' " We see this prophesy fulfilled when Jesus contemplates his own death. His concern is, "Father, glorify your name!" The response of the Father is, "I have glorified it and will glorify it again" (John 12:27–28). God is passionate about his own name and glory. It is his chief end and ultimate purpose.
23. Grenz, *Revisioning Evangelical Theology*, 185.

What is his objection here? Clearly, he is willing to put God's glory at the center; he calls it "proper" to a correct theological understanding: "God's glory as the final rational and goal for the work of creation and salvation." Beyond this point he objects, not comfortable tenting here with the Reformed camp. He objects that they have made God into something terribly self-centered and ungodly. The humility of God is an important subject and one that several of the neo-Puritans have wrestled with in other places.[24] But I suspect this is not the deepest issue for Grenz, but rather what might follow: the superiority of the will of God in all human willing. I suspect that Grenz, if he valued the glory of God so highly, would have been willing to concede the issue of holy humility, if libertarian freedom was not thereby threatened. However, even if I am not correct about his real concern, he himself was willing to go as far as I have gone in this section. It is not the glory of God, but fear of what that entails in other human systems which prevents some free-will theists from making that explicitly central or God's chief end.

The clear testimony of Scripture is that in creation and salvation, and so in all things, the glory of God is his chief end. And this must be the basis of any successful understanding of the problem of evil. Only if we know this first, can we hope to make sense of anything else.

GOD'S CONSEQUENT ULTIMATE END: TO CREATE A PEOPLE FOR HIMSELF

> It is this triune God who has being-in-communion, in love, who has created us as male and female in that image to be "co-lovers" . . . to share in the triune love and to love another in perichoretic unity.[25]
>
> —James Torrance

God has an ultimate and chief purpose: his own glory. But inferior to that chief purpose he has another ultimate purpose in regard to creation, consequent upon his chief end. This is to create a people for himself who can enter into fellowship with him. This is often called theosis, participation in divine union, or human-divine perichoresis.[26]

---

24. God is humble in that he is a servant, but he is not falsely humble about his own glory. John Piper writes, "because God is unique as an all-glorious, totally self-sufficient Being, he must be for himself if he is to be for us" (*Desiring God*, 47).

25. J. B. Torrance, *Worship, Community & the Triune God of Grace*, 104.

26. Paul Fiddes takes an opposing position in his monograph, *Creative Suffering of God*. Strongly influenced by process theology, he sees God, suffering, and creation as inseparable from each other. This is opposed to the view I set forth here in which creation is a result of the character of God and his desire to share himself. He states, "Now God, by his own sovereign will, holds himself in possession through relating himself to creation. That has been the argument of our study" (201). Here creation is essential to "holding himself in possession"—in sustaining his very nature. Even more specifically, he writes (citing Barth), "There is 'no man-less God'" (117). This wholly entangles God with creation so that Fiddes seems to take in not only all of process theology, but also Moltmann's panentheism

David Clotfelter said this well: "God's supreme regard of His own glory is what moves Him to share Himself with His creatures. Their resulting knowledge of God brings them bliss. As Edwards puts it, 'God's esteeming Himself supremely is not contrary to His esteeming human happiness, since He is that happiness.'"[27] Out of his fullness, God gives himself to his people in keeping with his nature. Also, the great psalm preserved or written by the author of Philippians exalts this inclination of God to share himself with his creatures in Philippians 2:5–8. Here we read,

> Have this attitude in yourselves, which was also in Christ Jesus, who, although He existed in the form of God, did not regard equality with God a thing to be grasped, but emptied Himself, taking the form of a bond-servant, and being made in the likeness of men. Being found in appearance as a man, He humbled Himself by becoming obedient to the point of death, even death on a Cross.

The key phrase in this text for this discussion is in verse 6, "ὃς ἐν μορφῇ θεοῦ ὑπάρχων οὐχ ἁρπαγμὸν ἡγήσατο τὸ εἶναι ἴσα θεῷ." In the NASB, RSV, Williams, and many other translations, ὑπάρχων is translated as a concessive participle. Some such as the KJV and NIV translate it neutrally, "who being in nature God." Gerald Hawthorne argues convincingly that in context it must be translated, causally, based on context.[28] It would then read, "who, because he was in the form of God, did not regard equality with God a thing to be grasped." The sense is to link the action explicitly with God's character, revealing that it is the character of God to give himself fully, gratuitously, and without reservation, in order to share himself with us: his nature is in opposition to acquisitiveness. This is reinforced by the context in this psalm of the early church and texts such as 1 Peter 1:20, "He was chosen before the creation of the world," 2 Timothy 1:9, "according to His own purpose and grace which was granted us in Christ Jesus from all eternity," 2 Thessalonians 2:14, "It was for this He called you through our gospel, that you may gain the glory of our Lord Jesus Christ," and many others. In other words, it was God's eternal plan, consistent with his character, to share himself and his glory with us, for the joy of all peoples who turn to him in Christ.

Like the centrality of the glory of God, this ultimate, but consequent purpose of God is broadly accepted.[29] James Torrance in his book, *Community & the Triune*

---

as he hints at throughout the work, even as he debates with Moltmann. Yet, while disagreeing in all these fundamentals, I still find Fiddes to be correct in his bold declaration of the responsibility that God must take for evil in any system, and in noting the very necessity of evil in a world in which God creates as he does create. I will discuss both of these issues in Chapter 5.

27. Clotfelter, *Sinners in the Hands of a Good God*, 241.

28. Hawthorne, *Philippians*, 70. Here also, Hawthorne takes the position that this hymn is written by Paul himself, in response to reflections on the Gospels, particularly, John 13:3–7, which does exhibit a striking parallel (65–66). Arguing that μορφῇ here is best translated as "the essential nature and character of God" (68). This is the context for his argument that ὑπάρχων is not a concessive participle. He prefers the translation of Moule, "Precisely because [RAS: Christ] was in the form of God he reckoned equality with God not as a matter of getting but of giving" (70).

29. James Beilby argues that we should not speculate about God's purposes in creation, and in

PART II: The Testing of a Theodicy

God of Grace, addresses this systematically and echoes some of Moltmann's thinking regarding the importance of the Trinitarian understanding of God and the participation in the life of God, but without Moltmann's attendant panentheism. He begins well, not with creation, but with worship, defining it in this way: "Christian worship is, therefore, our participation through the Spirit in the Son's communion with the Father, in his vicarious life of worship and intercession."[30] Consonant with ancient and orthodox doctrine, he defines the person, the worshiper, not in isolation, but only in communion with God and other people. This is based upon his high view of the Trinity, for God, the creator, can only be understood rightly as three persons in relationship—the Trinity. He is first, a relational God.[31] This is the God who has created us in his image as male and female to find true humanity in perichoretic unity with him and with each other, and who renews fallen humanity by perichoretic union with God in Christ.[32] Here then is how Torrance frames God's goal and intention in creation:

> It is this triune God who has being-in-communion, in love, who has created us as male and female in that image to be "co-lovers" . . . to share in the triune love and to love one another in perichoretic unity. "Then God said, 'Let us make man in our image, in our likeness.' . . . So God created man in his own image, in the image of God he created him: male and female he created them"(Gen 1:26–27). These purposes of God in creation find their fulfillment in redemption.[33]

---

particular he objects to Edwards. He writes, "Edwards lands in the trouble he does because he is willing to speculate about God's purpose in creation" ("Divine Aseity, Divine Freedom," 657). Walter Schultz responds, "Careful deduction from shared assumptions about God and creation (as Edwards proceeds in the first chapter) is not 'speculation' especially when Edwards explicitly indicates his rationale and reservations. Careful and exhaustive induction from Scripture (as Edwards proceeds in the second chapter) is not speculation either. . . . Beilby's views are pervasively misinformed and misguided" ("Jonathan Edwards's End of Creation," 270). While the discussion between Beilby and Schultz is over Edwards, the root issue is the possibility of speaking with integrity to God's purpose in creation. I agree with Schultz in regard to Edwards and assert that it is true for us that careful and non-speculative work has been done in regard to this issue and on this, the church has had broad agreement: God created the world in order to share himself with his people. So I intend to show, and I will also return to dialog with Beilby directly later in this section.

30. J. B. Torrance, *Worship, Community & the Triune God of Grace*, 15. He also writes, "the Christian doctrine of the Trinity, the God who has his being in loving communion, is clearly very different. His primary purpose for humanity is filial, not just judicial—we have been created by God to find our true being-in-communion, in sonship, in the mutual personal relationships of love" (37–38).

31. Ibid., 37. He shows here the various Western images of God and how they are related to our image of ourselves (i.e., "rugged individual" has an image of God as the sovereign monad who is "out there" who is essentially understood by us as in practice as a "Unitarian one"). Also, Thomas G. Weinandy who writes, "The persons of the Trinity are eternally constituted in their own singular identity only in relation to one another" (116) and "They are fully, completely, and absolutely relational. . . . [RAS: They] are verbs . . . they are immutable not because they are static or inert in their relationships, but precisely for the opposite reason" (*Does God Suffer*, 118, 119).

32. J. B. Torrance, *Worship, Community & the Triune God of Grace*, 38.

33. Ibid., 38, 104–5.

Torrance's argument is that God's nature as Trinity leads to creating us in his image with the intent of bringing human willful-creatures into a particular relationship with himself. This is similar to the social Trinity of Jürgen Moltmann[34] and the Cappadocian Fathers' idea of theosis.[35] That relationship is his desire to share himself—so much to be desired by us—so that he makes us in his own image for the joy of his people and his glory. He does this in order that we might be drawn into and delight in perichoretic unity with him—a deeply interpenetrating union of fully differentiated persons.[36] I agree.

Again, I believe there is broad agreement among Christians on this over time and between theological perspectives. Irenaeus wrote, "In the beginning, therefore, did God form Adam, not as if He stood in need of man, but that He might have [some one] upon whom to confer His benefits."[37] So also Anselm wrote, "man, being rational by nature, was created righteous to the end that, through rejoicing in God, he might

---

34. For example, *Trinity and the Kingdom,* 175.

35. We could also consider here the objections of Karen Kilby, who wrote "Perichoresis and Projection." She writes, "This whatever it is, this thing which is beyond our experience which binds the three into a one, however, is given a label—it is called the divine perichoresis. And in order to describe the perichoresis, the social theorist points to those things which do to some degree bind human persons together, into couples or families or communities—interrelatedness, love, empathy, mutual accord, mutual giving and so on. What binds God into one is then said to be like all the best that we know, only of course, unimaginably more so. It has to be more so, since it has to make the three persons into one God and not just into one family of Gods" (9). And "In short, then, I am suggesting we have here something like a three stage process. First, a concept, perichoresis, is used to name what is not understood, to name whatever it is that makes the three Persons one. Secondly, the concept is filled out rather suggestively with notions borrowed from our own experience of relationships and relatedness. And then, finally, it is presented as an exciting resource Christian theology has to offer the wider world in its reflections upon relationships and relatedness" (10).

Kilby's approach follows that of George Lindbeck, which makes the doctrine grammar, rather than truth. She writes, "It can instead be taken as grammatical, as a second order proposition, a rule, or perhaps a set of rules, for how to read the biblical stories, how to speak about some of the characters we come across in these stories, how to think and talk about the experience of prayer, how to deploy the 'vocabulary' of Christianity in an appropriate way" (13). In so doing, she makes ontology secondary to talk about God. Yet, there is appropriate caution in her concern. It is possible for us to project into God our experience (her example is from Anselm). However, as will be discussed in this project, the very work of attempting to understand God is honoring to him. That is not to say that the attempt is complete. There will always be better and worse ways to do this work and there will always be more to say that is true which we have not yet discovered. Just as Theology used to be the Queen of the Sciences, assuming that studies of cosmology will result in apprehension of truth about God (and even worship) from general revelation, so, it is not unlikely that the study of anthropology would be an effective tool to understanding and worshipping God, for we are his image.

36. To James Torrance, we could add Alan Torrance. In *Persons in Communion: An essay on Trinitarian description and human participation,* he (Alan) argues against Barth's view saying "Barth's concept of Trinitarian *seinsweissen* obscures the concept of communion in God" (115). His view, like that of James Torrance, runs parallel to what was displayed above: "The *imago dei* in humanity requires to be interpreted in terms of the participative life of the Body of Christ . . . by grace within the Triune life and God and which 'in Christ' constitutes a *vestigium trinitatis* and thus an *imago Dei*" (368).

37. Irenaeus, *Against Heresies,* in *Ante-Nicene Fathers,* volume 1, 4.14.1.

be blessedly happy."[38] While the perspectives of these theologians are different, at the core, they are both saying that God created people to know joy from communion with God. And even though Leibniz argued that there exists a best possible world which God's character constrains him to create, a position with little support today,[39] still Leibniz's reasoning should be noted as still more subtle than that of his iconic image. He wrote, "I answer that it is goodness which prompts God to create with the purpose of communicating himself."[40]

But here is a sticking point. While there is broad agreement about the centrality of God's glory and God's purpose in sharing himself with us, does this put more emphasis on God's glory than it should properly bear? James Beilby writes, "The essence of the problem is this: the Calvinist's typical assertion that God's fundamental purpose in creation is to demonstrate his glory seems to entail that God have an 'other' to whom his glory must be demonstrated."[41] Moreover, Beilby argues that this improper emphasis implies need in God—a contradiction. He explains, "It is possible to be needy either because of a deficiency—a lack that needs to be filled—or an abundance—a surplus that must be distributed. Either way, there is an unfulfilled need."[42] If correct, this exposes a defect in my argument and those I cited. For Beilby, one way out of this conundrum in God, is to declare a libertarian freedom for God, which permits God to create from a desire to love his image-bearing creatures. But is this an understanding of Calvin and Edwards that truly undermines their position or solves a genuine problem in their argument? For example, of creation, Calvin writes,

> If the cause is sought by which he was led once to create all these things, and is now moved to preserve them, we shall find that it is his goodness alone. But this being the sole cause, is ought still to be more than sufficient to draw us to his love, inasmuch as there is no creature, as the prophet declares, upon whom God's mercy has not been poured out.[43]

Here Calvin's focus on God's goodness and love toward his people, and their loving response, sounds very much like the position which Beilby stakes out for the libertarian.[44] Such statements must at least shape the contours of all that Calvin says in regard to the purpose of creation. What of Edwards?

---

38. Anselm, "Cur Deus Homo," in *Anselm of Canterbury*, 2.1.

39. Swinburne, *Existence of God*, 113–15 where Swinburne concludes this for himself and also John S. Feinberg who concludes this more globally, and others as noted previously.

40. Leibniz, *Theodicy*, 2.228.

41. Beilby, "Divine Aseity," 647.

42. Ibid., 654.

43. Calvin, *ICR*, 1.5.6.

44. "While the Calvinist makes God's glory the chief end in creation, the Arminian calls attention to God's love" (Beilby, "Divine Aseity," 657).

> God may have a real and proper pleasure or happiness in seeing the happy state of the creature; *yet this may not be different from his delight in himself;* being a delight in his own infinite goodness; or the exercise of that glorious propensity of his nature to diffuse and communicate himself, and so gratifying this inclination of his own heart. This delight which God has in his creature's happiness, cannot properly be said to be what God receives from the creature. For it is only the effect of his own work in and communications to the creature; in making it, and admitting it to a participation of his fullness. As the sun receives nothing from the jewel that receives its light, and shines only by a participation of its brightness.[45]

Here Edwards seems to say all that Beilby could desire in regard to God's love for his creatures. Edwards displays God's ultimate end as that of ensuring the happiness of his creatures in himself. Further, the point of God's display of his glory is not out of his own need, as Beilby implies, but rather a confluence of his chief end (his glory) and an ultimate end (to give joy to his creatures). That is, there is not a distinctly Reformed (Calvin-Edwards) position that excludes God's love for humanity as an ultimate purpose. The positions outlined by Beilby, and those of Calvin and Edwards, in regard to the purpose of creation, may intersect—at least at the point I am arguing here.

Before we can move on, it is worth asking: was God compelled to create or was he equally free to create or not to create? It is on this point that I must also make sure I have not overlooked Beilby's challenge. Generally, Christian theologians have insisted that YHWH is wholly free, regardless of the kind of freedom they understand his willful creatures to posses. In describing the coherent God of Christian theism, Richard Swinburne writes:

> The theist also normally holds that all God's actions are free. All that the omnipresent spirit who is God does, he does because he chooses to do. Nothing makes him do what he does. He did not, for example, have to create the world, nor does he have to keep the laws of nature operative.[46]

And of course, God's unencumbered freedom has broad agreement over the spectrum of Christian theology, including Libertarian Free-Will defenders such as Plantinga, Origen, Polkinghorne, or N. T. Wright,[47] and compatibilists such as Feinberg

---

45. J. Edwards, *Dissertation Concerning The End for Which God Created The World*, 1.4 (objection 1, answer 1). Emphasis mine.

46. Swinburne, *Coherence of Theism*, 141.

47. For example, John Polkinghorne (citing Barth) writes, "Creation is the freely willed and executed positing of a reality distinct from God" (*The Faith of a Physicist*, 73). This is well said.

PART II: The Testing of a Theodicy

and Edwards.[48] While we would not find agreement in the rationalist Leibniz,[49] as we noted above, his rationalistic system has few followers today and so he is not a representative.

It is then wholly true to say that all of this is true of God's nature (for nothing he does is other than his nature): to have a passion for his glory, to create the universe, and to give himself to his willful human-creatures. And it is also true to say that God did all of these in his perfect freedom. And in that freedom, it pleased God, because of his character, to choose to show (to communicate, to share) his glory to the human willful-creatures whom he would create in his image for his own glory. God's glory is displayed in the union of his people with him through Christ and this is his desire for his people.

GOD'S CONSEQUENT ULTIMATE END: . . . THAT THEY MAY KNOW HIS JOY

> Delight in the Lord and he will give you the desires of your heart!
>
> —Psalm 37:4

Now we consider more deeply the effect of God's consequent ultimate end. He is not only creating a people to know him, but he does this so that they may know his joy. Again, while this is not his chief end, it is an ultimate end, being valuable to God in and of itself, and a consequent end, dependent upon his chief end. Blaise Pascal wrote,

> All men seek happiness. There are no exceptions. However different the means they may employ, they all strive towards this goal. The reason why some go to war and some do not is the same desire in both, but interpreted in two different

---

48. John S. Feinberg positions God's freedom as compatibilistic, having been circumscribed through all eternity by his own decrees. In *No One Like Him: The Doctrine of God* he writes, "human and divine freedom are not thereby ruled out, if one defines freedom as does a compatibilist" (314); and "Thus, according to compatibilism, God's actions in moral matters are free, even though his moral perfection guarantees that he could only choose the good" (731). For Feinberg, this preserves true freedom (he sees incompatibilist freedom as not free) and responsibility (for otherwise God's foreknowledge of his own acts would render those acts, "in the moment," not free).

49. Leibniz and Swinburne often argue the same case in the same way. For example, in regard to God's freedom, Leibniz writes, "God fails not to choose the best, but he is not constrained so to do: nay, more, there is no necessity in the object of God's choice, for another sequence of things is equally possible . . . and the will is determined only by the preponderating goodness of the object" (*Theodicy*, 1.45). However, per Feinberg, and distinct from Swinburne, Leibniz's system requires that God not only create the best, but that he must create. Of Leibniz, Feinberg writes, "God did not have the option to refrain from choosing a world" (*Many Faces of Evil*, 36, which are alluded to in 2.228 of Leibniz ("this same goodness combined with wisdom prompts him to create the best") and elsewhere, though he rejects that this could be considered to be thought of as "fate." It is clear that his position is highly nuanced). The vast majority of Christian systems disagree with Leibniz and this is not a point of contention. And so, I move on.

ways. The will never takes the least step except to that end. This is the motive of every act of every man, including those who go and hang themselves.[50]

Is it a strange thing for God to share himself with human willful-creatures that his people might know joy? Not so in light of God's character. Historically, Christians have affirmed the mutual love of the Father, Son, and the Spirit for each other.[51] I am struck by the intimacy of the Father and the Son in John 1:1, "In the beginning was the Word and the Word was with God and the Word was God. He was with God in the beginning." John is witness to a deep, eternal, and delightful relationship, one that we would not be amiss to refer to as *the friendship*.[52] So also, we can testify to the association of God's Spirit with love, even as the source or perhaps the means of divine love to his people.[53] So also the Spirit is engaged in the love affair that exists within the Trinity. In Luke 3:22 we read, "and the Holy Spirit descended upon Him in bodily form like a dove, and a voice came out of heaven, 'You are My beloved Son, in You I am well-pleased.' " Here the Spirit seems to be the mediator of the love between the Father and the Son. So also in Galatians 5:22, the first fruit of the Spirit is love. God's Trinitarian love is *a priori* and human love and friendship is derivative. To say that God enjoys a friendship within the Trinity is not anthropomorphism, but rather our understanding of friendship and love is a "theomorphism" derived from the reality of Trinitarian love, which is infinite and perfect and complete, needing nothing.

50. Pascal, *Pensées*, 45. This edition represents this as fragment 148, subordinate to "X. The Sovereign Good."

51. The biblical witness to this is rich: "And a voice came from heaven: 'You are my Son, whom I love; with you I am well pleased.' "Mark 1:11; "Then a cloud appeared and enveloped them, and a voice came from the cloud: 'This is my Son, whom I love. Listen to him!' "Mark 9:7; "Then the owner of the vineyard said, 'What shall I do? I will send my son, whom I love; perhaps they will respect him.' "Luke 20:13; "The Father loves the Son and has placed everything in his hands." John 3:35; "For the Father loves the Son and shows him all he does." John 5:20; "I have made you known to them, and will continue to make you known in order that the love you have for me may be in them and that I myself may be in them." John 17:26; "For he has rescued us from the dominion of darkness and brought us into the kingdom of the Son he loves." Colossians 1:13; "For he received honor and glory from God the Father when the voice came to him from the Majestic Glory, saying, 'This is my Son, whom I love; with him I am well pleased.' "2 Peter 1:17; "For who among men knows the thoughts of a man except the spirit of the man, which is in him? Even so the thoughts of God no one knows except the Spirit of God." 1 Corinthians 2:11; "And because you are sons, God has sent forth the Spirit of His Son into our hearts, crying, 'Abba! Father!' "Galatians 4:6; We also should witness the love of Christ for the Father, shown in his complete obedience and submission (John 14:21) in his life (John 5) and in his death (Philippians 2:5–8).

52. To this text, we could add John 3:35, "the Father loves the Son and has given all things in his hand," and John 5:20, "for the Father loves the Son, and shows Him all things that He Himself is doing."

53. Paul writes, "and hope does not disappoint, because the love of God has been poured out within our hearts through the Holy Spirit who was given to us" (Romans 5:50). To this we could add the association of the Spirit as the source of divine love as seen in the following: "Now I urge you, brethren, by our Lord Jesus Christ and by the love of the Spirit, to strive together with me in your prayers to God for me" (Romans 15:30); and "But the fruit of the Spirit is love, joy, peace, patience, kindness, goodness, faithfulness, gentleness, self-control; against such things there is no law" (Galatians 5:22–23).

PART II: The Testing of a Theodicy

Out of the completeness of his love, while needing nothing for himself, God's nature is to share what is most valuable: himself and the depth of the intimacy between the Three. As was shown above, God wants us to enter into this relationship, and to do so for our joy. The Orthodox church has championed this truth for centuries calling this theosis, deification, or more recently (and perhaps less confusingly for our Western culture), Christification.[54] God's goal is to share himself with human willful-creatures—to bring us into the union that he shares within the Trinity—for our joy. Perhaps no passage demonstrates this more passionately than the prayer of Christ for his people as he prepares to die in John 17:3, 21: "This is eternal life, that they may know You, the only true God, and Jesus Christ whom You have sent. . . . that they may all be one; even as You, Father, are in Me and I in You, that they also may be in Us, so that the world may believe that You sent Me." This text declares that to be a Christian is to be brought into the intimacy of the delightful relationship the Trinity has together and to share in their joy and delight in each other. God's purpose is delighting in his own glory, but he does so by sharing that glory and delight with his special creation—people.

In his after-dinner discussion, which introduces this prayer, Jesus explains the purpose of why he is bringing them into the Trinity. He says in John 15:11, "These things I have spoken to you, that my joy may be in you, and that your joy may be full." He also says in John 16:24, "Until now you have asked for nothing in My name; ask and you will receive, so that your joy may be made full." Jesus, even as he explains that he is leaving the disciples, is pointing toward his purpose for them: joy. He says in his prayer to the Father in John 17:13, "But now I am coming to you, and these things I speak in the world, that they may have my joy fulfilled in themselves."[55]

So if God's purpose in creation is to share himself, and the end of that sharing is human joy, this might explain why the human will is motivated to seek happiness with all our being, even though we are not well tuned to seek it properly. Augustine writes,

> Therefore, since it is true that all men yearn to be happy, and yearn for this one thing with the most ardent love they are capable of, and yearn for other things simply for the sake of this one thing; . . . . All who are happy have what they want, though not all who have what they want are ipso facto happy; but those who do not have what they want or have what they have no right to want, are ipso facto unhappy.[56] But seek we will, and even if we look in the wrong places, we will try to make a show of finding it:

---

54. Ware, *Orthodox Way*, 74. Here citing John 17 he states, "Christ enables us to share in the Father's divine glory." It is interesting that it is here in the revised edition (but not in the 1979 edition) in which he includes the term, "Christified," which is relatively new and possibly coined by Panayiotis Nellas (see *Deification in Christ*, number 5, 34). Also see Boersma, *Violence, Hospitality, and the Cross*, 259–60.

55. To these we could add abundant texts including, Psalm 16:11, Isaiah 51:11, Habakkuk 3:18, 1 Peter 1:8, and Jude 1:24 which connect joy with our salvation and our place with God. Joy is our destiny in God—it is his purpose for his people.

56. Augustine, *The Trinity*, 13.8.

> All people want to be happy; if they want something true, this necessarily means they want to be immortal. They cannot otherwise be happy. . . . But as long as they despair of immortality, without which true happiness is impossible, they will look for, or rather make up, any kind of thing that may be called, rather than really be, happiness in this life.[57]

We see this in the work of Aquinas,[58] Edwards,[59] and Calvin,[60] who write from a tradition that holds to a high view of God's sovereignty, and whose understanding of human freedom is compatibilistic. But we also see this clearly in those who address the issue from an indeterministic or libertarian perspective. This includes Irenaeus,[61] Jacobus Arminius,[62] and others, including many modern writers. For example, Marilyn McCord Adams writes, "The direction of my attempted solution lies in pointing to the incommensurate Good that God is."[63] The word "happiness" does not appear here, but it is clear that the very focus of her theodicy is a vector between God and

---

57. Ibid., 13.11.

58. Thomas Aquinas writes, "Final and perfect happiness can consist in nothing else than the vision of the Divine Essence" (*Summa Theologica*, Ia IIae,q.3,a.8. And also, "Hence it is evident that naught can lull man's will, save the universal good. This is to be found, not in any creature, but in God alone; because every creature has goodness by participation. Wherefore God alone can satisfy the will of man, according to the words of Psalm 102:5: 'Who satisfieth thy desire with good things.' Therefore God alone constitutes man's happiness" (*ST,* Ia IIae,q.2.a.8). It is worth noting here that I take Aquinas's blessedness or happiness ("*beatitudo*") as equivalent terms; the distinction is not significant to this point. So also, is the "beatific vision" of God taken as equivalent to God communicating or sharing himself.

59. Jonathan Edwards writes in *The End for Which God Created the World*, "Thus it is easy to conceive, how God should seek the good of the creature, consisting in the creature's knowledge and holiness, and even his happiness, from a supreme regard to himself; as his happiness arises from that which is an image and participation of God's own beauty: and consists in the creature's exercising a supreme regard to God, and complacence in him; in beholding God's glory, in esteeming and loving it, and rejoicing in it, and in his exercising and testifying love and supreme respect to God: which is the same thing, with the creature's exalting God as his chief good, and making him his supreme end" (2.7).

60. Calvin writes in *ICR*, "If the Lord will share his glory, power, and righteousness with the elect—nay, will give himself to be enjoyed by them and, what is more excellent, will somehow make them to become one with himself, let us remember that every sort of happiness is included under this benefit" (3.25.10).

61. Irenaeus writes, "For as His greatness is past finding out, so also His goodness is beyond expression; by which having been seen, He bestows life upon those who see Him. It is not possible to live apart from life, and the means of life is found in fellowship with God; but fellowship with God is to know God, and to enjoy His goodness" (*Against Heresies*, 4.20.5).

62. "For as he occupied the first place in conferring blessings and doing good, because that high station was his due, since man was about to be called into existence among the number of creatures; so likewise it is his desire that the last place in doing good be reserved for him, according to the infinite perfection of his goodness and blessedness, who is the fountain of good and the extreme boundary of happiness" (*The Works of James Arminius*, volume 1, Oration 1. Here Arminius says that it is the character of God to share himself, that he is the fountain of goodness and that our highest joy is to know God.

63. Marilyn McCord Adams, *Horrendous Evils and the Goodness of God,* 189.

PART II: The Testing of a Theodicy

the human soul seeking joy. And even Clark Pinnock,[64] a proponent of what seems to some to be a radical Libertarian Free-Will, supports this basic concept: everyone seeks happiness. It is also worth quoting Alistair McFadyen, who takes the same position while not supporting Libertarian Free-Will:

> The universality of sin and of accountability for it also achieves an interpretive shift once it is correlated with the dynamics of joy. . . . the primary referent here is not the supposed freedom of human beings, but the dynamics of God. . . . From the perspective of the dynamics of God in creation and salvation, we are born into and for joy in a God whose loves blesses and has joy in us.[65]

So we conclude, still holding-out with some hope of general agreement to this point, that happiness is found in the "fullness of joy" that God desires for his people and it is our purpose because it is God's purpose for his people. God and his glory is then our chief end which is intended to bring his people joy; fullness of joy is to be brought into the life of the Trinity. This is what God has created his people for.

GOD'S CONSEQUENT ULTIMATE END: . . . AND THAT HIS JOY MIGHT BE FULFILLED, ESCHATOLOGICALLY, BY CONFORMING-FREEDOM

> But in the future life it shall not be in his power to will evil; and yet this will constitute no restriction on the freedom of his will. On the contrary, his will shall be much freer when it shall be wholly impossible for him to be the slave of sin.[66]
>
> —Augustine

> One must face the fact that all the talk about His love for men, and His service being perfect freedom, is not (as one would gladly believe) mere propaganda, but an appalling truth. He really does want to fill the universe with a lot of loathsome little replicas of Himself—creatures, whose life, on its miniature scale, will be qualitatively like His own, not because He has absorbed them but because their wills freely conform to His. We want cattle who can finally become food; He wants servants who can finally become sons.[67]
>
> —C.S. Lewis

---

64. "A creation exists because God freely decided to make it. It gives pleasure to God, even though he does not strictly need it. . . . God enjoys the goodness of the world and, by grace, creates (unnecessarily) in order to share his own bliss with others" (Pinnock, *Most Moved Mover*, 125).

65. McFadyen, *Bound to Sin*, 247.

66. Augustine, *Enchiridion on Faith, Hope and Love*, ¶ 105, 123.

67. Lewis, *Screwtape Letters*, 38.

Subordinate to God's chief end, his glory, God has another ultimate and consequential end: to create a people for Himself that they many know his joy, and that this joy might be fulfilled, eschatologically, by Conforming-Freedom. Here we pass beyond the preface to this chapter to the heart of my hypothesis. Since Adam's fall, human willful-creatures live in opposition to holiness. And so on the face of things, God's project appears a failure. If he intended a world with joy, and so without evil and coordinate with his holiness, then that intent collapsed in the rebellion of his willful-creatures. But God's plans did not "fail," nor was "evil" an unfortunate accident or even unlikely, but instead it was a contingency inherent in his plans as he planned them, though not created by him, and his character and goals leads to his intended goal for them, namely, Conforming-Freedom.

One way to understand the possibility of the appearance of evil in God's creation is to perceive that Adam was created good with *perfect* freedom, but not *perfected* freedom. His freedom was corruptible. The kind of freedom which I "give" to Adam here is most like what is called libertarian freedom, as defined earlier in this project, yet I would prefer to call this "unfettered" freedom, emphasizing not Adam's ability of contrary choice, but rather his freedom from necessary conformity to God's character. He was not tied to God's holiness with unbreakable bonds. As such, his goodness (which I take to be the equivalent of perfection) was not unassailable. He had freedom to choose, but by accidental necessity, he did not have freedom to unfailingly pursue the beatific vision of God. Of course, some say he could have remained in perfection (Calvin and others).[68] But it is clear he did not—his perfection was, in fact, *corruptible*.

It is worth defining, "perfect." In this project, perfect means that a thing is "without taint of sin, conforming to the holiness of God." This means that a person, object, or motive is "perfect" because it is untainted by sin, even if that perfection may be tainted in the future.[69] This is not intended to open a discussion in regard to the aseity of God, which is not considered in this context; this definition does not address change: God's perfection is immutable in the sense that he will never act other than from (and in)

---

68. "In this integrity man by free will had the power, if he so willed, to attain eternal life. . . . Adam could have stood if he wished, seeing that he fell solely by his own will. . . . his choice of good and evil was free" (Calvin, *ICR*, 1.15.8). I want to say here that I do not disagree—as far as he goes. It was logically possible that Adam, who was truly free, could indefinitely choose what is good. So it is also logically possible that a die when tossed would always turn up "six." However, unless it was "loaded," this is more than unlikely. God is "loaded." He is fundamentally, characteristically, and by nature, Good. He is Good. He is the Source of Goodness. It flows from within him. That is not the case with Adam who is not so "loaded."

69. James Barr says something like this in his article "Was Everything That God Created Really Good?" On page 64 he notes that the goodness of creation (whatever it meant—he debates this) was corruptible: "the goodness of Adam's world does not prevent the corruption of the world in Noah's time, which suggests that we cannot rely too heavily on that goodness of the original world . . . so there is definitely an uncertainty how far the 'goodness's of the world as first created provides assurance for things long afterward." This is indeed the problem we face. While Barr's solution lies more along the lines, as the title indicates, of questioning the thorough goodness of the original world, my proposal is simpler in that it accords perfection but not sustained perfection.

perfection—freedom from evil. The first humans and God himself shared perfection, but that is distinct from sharing God's unchanging nature, which they did not.[70] We will consider this issue of the "necessity of evil" at length in the next chapter, but here let it be the case that we agree that Adam failed; his perfection was corruptible.

However, the final Era of Freedom will be different: free and conforming. God's people will persevere in goodness, in freedom, possessing what Adam never had. This is the compound idea Conforming-Freedom, two terms which come together in Romans 8. His people will be conformed to the image of Christ—his image—so that, like God, his people will always choose the good, freely. Indeed, as we have seen in so many of the Early Fathers of the church, this is true freedom—the freedom to always choose what is right. D.A. Carson, in his book on the problem of evil, agrees: "Real freedom is freedom to obey God without restraint or reserve. It is not absolute power to contrary; it is wanting to please God at every moment."[71] As noted in the introduction to this section, Augustine talks about this final state of freedom this way: "But in the future life it shall not be in his power to will evil; and yet this will constitute no restriction on freedom of his will. On the contrary, his will shall be much freer when it shall be wholly impossible for him to be the slave of sin."[72] This Conforming-Freedom is a subordinate end for which God has created his people, so that (note: that there is a "so that" is what makes it a subordinate end) they might gain their chief end: knowing God.[73]

This places Romans 8 at the center of the discussion of the problem of evil. N.T. Wright claims, "Romans 8 is the deepest New Testament answer to the 'problem of evil,' to the question of God's justice."[74] And the key to Romans 8 is Conforming-

---

70. Anthony A. Hoekema wrote, "So man at that time had true freedom—but it was not yet perfect freedom. He could still fall into sin and, as a matter of fact, did just that" (*Created in God's Image*, Grand Rapids, MI: W.B. Eerdmans, 1986, 231). It is in this sense that I am using the term perfect. Perfect is the inability to sin. It should also be pointed out that perfection is sometimes considered to be a single point, but there are no biblical reasons to consider this to be the case. Rather perfection is a large set, an infinite set, of all that is untainted by sin, of all that is consistent with God's character.

71. Carson, *How Long, O Lord?*, 191. I will deal with the issue of "power to contrary" and whether our choices in the ultimate (eschatological) Era of Freedom are best represented (as seems implied here) by choosing the good infallibly (even joyfully and without restraint) between good choices and evil choices, or rather, choosing among a infinite number of good choices. I will argue that the latter is the best option. Still on the fundamental point that eschatological freedom is the freedom from failure, I stand with Carson and the Fathers.

72. Augustine, *Enchiridion*, ¶ 105, 123.

73. Here the obvious corollary is that perfection is not a singularity. That is obvious if the first creation and final creation are both perfectly good, yet the second is different in that it will not defect from perfection and it has more people than the first. Perfection is not a precarious balance, then, from which any change will be other than and less than perfect. Paul Fiddes notes this, "This argument in fact [RAS: wrongly] assumes that 'perfection' is a fixed maximal quantity of value, so that change will either get nearer to it or further from it" (*The Creative Suffering of God*, 47). Although he may observe this because of his leanings toward process theology, which I do not support, he is still correct in this observation.

74. N. T. Wright, *Evil and the Justice of God*, 118. A fuller evaluation of Wright's position in this

Freedom. I will print here Romans 8:17–39 in its entirety because of its importance. I have divided it into paragraphs to represent my understanding of how it should be outlined. The thesis is found in verse 17 and 18: Believers must suffer, if they are to share the glory of Christ; verses 18–27 explain this as the author makes it clear that suffering results in freedom; verses 28–39 shows us that freedom is found in conformity to Christ:

> 17 and if children, heirs also, heirs of God and fellow heirs with Christ, if indeed we suffer with Him so that we may also be glorified with Him. 18 For I consider that the sufferings of this present time are not worthy to be compared with the glory that is to be revealed to us. 19 For the anxious longing of the creation waits eagerly for the revealing of the sons of God. 20 For the creation was subjected to futility, not willingly, but because of Him who subjected it, in hope 21 that the creation itself also will be set free from its slavery to corruption into the freedom of the glory of the children of God. 22 For we know that the whole creation groans and suffers the pains of childbirth together until now. 23 And not only this, but also we ourselves, having the first fruits of the Spirit, even we ourselves groan within ourselves, waiting eagerly for our adoption as sons, the redemption of our body. 24 For in hope we have been saved, but hope that is seen is not hope; for who hopes for what he already sees? 25 But if we hope for what we do not see, with perseverance we wait eagerly for it. 26 In the same way the Spirit also helps our weakness; for we do not know how to pray as we should, but the Spirit Himself intercedes for us with groanings too deep for words; 27 and He who searches the hearts knows what the mind of the Spirit is, because He intercedes for the saints according to the will of God. 28 And we know that God causes all things to work together for good to those who love God, to those who are called according to His purpose. 29 For those whom He foreknew, He also predestined to become conformed to the image of His Son, so that He would be the firstborn among many brethren; 30 and these whom He predestined, He also called; and these whom He called, He also justified; and these whom He justified, He also glorified. 31 What then shall we say to these things? If God is for us, who is against us? 32 He who did not spare His own Son, but delivered Him over for us all, how will He not also with Him freely give us all things? 33 Who will bring a charge against God's elect? God is the one who justifies; 34 who is the one who condemns? Christ Jesus is He who died, yes, rather who was raised, who is at the right hand of God, who also intercedes for us. 35 Who will separate us from the love of Christ? Will tribulation, or distress, or persecution, or famine, or nakedness, or peril, or sword? 36 Just as it is written, "for your sake we are being put to death all day long; we were considered as sheep to be slaughtered." 37 But in all these things we overwhelmingly conquer through Him who loved us. 38

---

book is given in my paper, "Evil and the Atonement: A response to N. T. Wright" presented on 16 November 2007 at the annual meeting of the Evangelical Theological Society, San Diego, CA.

PART II: The Testing of a Theodicy

> For I am convinced that neither death, nor life, nor angels, nor principalities, nor things present, nor things to come, nor powers, 39 nor height, nor depth, nor any other created thing, will be able to separate us from the love of God, which is in Christ Jesus our Lord.

The thesis text of the author of Romans (verses 17–18) serves double-duty here, being both the conclusion of the previous section and the theme of what follows. The previous section has been exposing to us the role and effect of God's Spirit at work in his people. His Spirit changes the lives of his people, causing them to desire to obey and actually to obey—but that work is incomplete, for his people do not always obey. And his conclusion makes an interesting claim: if his people are to share in the perfected glory of Christ, they must suffer with him. He wrote that his people are "heirs of God and fellow heirs with Christ, if indeed we suffer with Him so that we may also be glorified with Him." This is a difficult teaching from every perspective. No one likes to suffer. But even worse, could it be the case that suffering is *necessary* in order to share in Christ's glory? Yet, this is what the author is about to reveal.[75] And in doing so, he will show us that Conforming-Freedom is a central part of the glory of Christ, but it must follow suffering with Christ.[76] To get to this explanation, the author moves from our experience of suffering and evil as a necessary part of God's plan, to the effect of that suffering in creation. An illustration of a point he has been making: freedom comes through death—Christ's death, the death of the human sinful nature. Now he shows that freedom comes through death in the context of nature.[77]

---

75. This is such a counter-intuitive idea here that it seems necessary to reinforce it from other texts. Luke 24:26 tells us that it was necessary (δει) for Christ to suffer and this is coordinate with entering his glory. In Ephesians 3:13 Paul links his suffering for them with their glory. In Hebrews 2:9 Jesus is crowned with glory and honor *because of* his suffering. And in 1 Peter, which I will examine in more depth in following chapters, it is his pattern often to associate suffering and glory (1:11; 4:13, 16; 5:1, 10). This is a theme of all of Scripture and more could be added from the Old Testament.

76. It is worth noting texts similar to Romans which also support this idea of Conforming-Freedom, but are less developed in their scope. First Jeremiah 32:40 reads, "I will make an everlasting covenant with them that I will not turn away from them, to do them good; and I will put the fear of Me in their hearts *so that they will not turn away from Me*." The context is God's promise to Israel as he was disciplining them with Babylon and promising restoration as Jeremiah was told to buy a field in anticipation of God's restoration. But this promise goes beyond restoration and looks to a day beyond the exile when "they will not turn away from me." Is this the eschaton? Is this Conforming-Freedom? I suspect so, for this goes beyond the post-exilic experience. We also see something of Conforming-Freedom in 2 Corinthians 3:18, "But we all, with unveiled face, beholding as in a mirror the glory of the Lord, are being transformed into the same image from glory to glory, just as from the Lord, the Spirit." This familiar text says nothing about conforming-freedom, but it does recall that God's purpose is for his people to be fully conformed to the image of Christ, which included freedom from sin. Also, Colossians 3:9–10 gives the same teaching: we are being renewed into the "image of the creator." And Ephesians 4:22–24, which speaks of "the new self, created after the likeness of God" anticipates an experience we have not fully realized. This is ultimately to be experienced as Conforming-Freedom in the fourth Era.

77. Specifically nature here ("creation") does not include his human willful-creatures as they are distinguished in other parts of this text, i.e., in verses 19, 21, 23 (Schreiner, *Romans: Baker Exegetical Commentary on the New Testament*, volume 6, 435).

In the next verses he turns to the inner workings of suffering and death.[78] By way of an illustration from nature, he claims in verses 19–21 that suffering will result in freedom. The "creation" that the author is addressing here does not include God's willful creatures, but only the heavens and earth to which God gave form in Genesis 1 as well as the flora and fauna with which he filled it. People are distinct from "creation" in verse 19 when they appear as "children of God." But neither people, nor fallen angelic beings, nor creation are the primary actors in this drama.[79] Humanity, though a "willing" actor, is not directly responsible for the frustration into which creation was subjected; God is. For that very reason, we might expect to find a word like "punishment." But the author chose ματαιότης which means "futility."[80] If such futility also can include punishment, that is not the aspect the author is highlighting here. C.E.B. Cranfield rightly says that such futility is the frustration of not being able to carry out its God-ordained purpose.[81] The result is that such futility and frustration makes creation "eager for the sons of God to be revealed" and "hoping" in God for its freedom from bondage—just as God's people will receive. And the choice of "futility" is not a surprise—or should not be. A word from the same root is used in only one other place in Romans and that is in a similar context. In Romans 1:21 the result of people's willful sin is God's judgment of futility: "For even though they knew God, they did not honor Him as God or give thanks, but they became *futile* in their speculations, and their foolish heart was darkened."(emphasis mine).[82] People who are not "willing" to carry out their purpose are drawn into frustration because they are further from the will of God.

But the frustration to which creation was subjected also has a God-ordained purpose—to redeem not only a people, but all of creation. Paul writes: "in hope that the creation itself also will be set free from its slavery to corruption into the freedom

---

78. Though I am passing over verse 18 it is worth noting that the author seems to be giving context to the first objection to verse 17, "but I don't want to suffer!". He is helping the reader to keep reading—speaking as one who has suffered more than any of them, an expert. He urges them to understand even this necessary suffering in context—it pales in comparison to what is coming. Even this verse is tied to glory in this way. Cranfield notes that the phrase οὐκ ἄξια which is translated "not worthy" literally means, "not weighing as much" which is a contrast to the Hebrew concept of glory as "weighty" as in 2 Corinthians 4:17 (Cranfield and Sanday, *Critical and Exegetical Commentary on the Epistle to the Romans*, 408).

79. F. F. Bruce notes that the early understanding of this text made Adam the subject, then later Satan was proposed, but clearly God is the only proper subject (*Epistle of Paul to the Romans*, London: 168). So also C. E. B. Cranfield (1975, 414), Leon Morris (1988, 321), Moo (*Epistle to the Romans.*, 516) and many others. John A. T. Robinson (*Wrestling with Romans*, 102), on the contrary, argues unconvincingly for Adam as the subject. The subject, without significant counter-argument, is God.

80. Bruce proposes that the very reason commentators came late to making God the subject, as must be the case, was specifically that what the subject did was to bring "frustration" and not "punishment." This is not an unimportant point and it is something that the author of Romans wants us to understand. He has something more than punishment in mind (*Epistle of Paul to the Romans*, 168).

81. Cranfield, *Romans*, 413–4. So also Thomas Schreiner, "Of course, creation itself was not at fault for the failure to fulfill its purpose" (*Romans*, 436).

82. The word for futile here is not the noun form, but the verb, ματαιόω.

PART II: The Testing of a Theodicy

of the glory of the children of God." In other words, the author is saying that suffering, in order to participate in glory, is in some way critical to God's economy. He uses this illustration from nature as an instance of the more general case that he has made for us above in his theme, "we suffer with Him so that we may also be glorified with Him." He is saying, if this is true for creation, it is true for his people. Of course, he concedes that suffering is negligible compared to what God promises. But he is also saying that such suffering is also instrumental. Humanity's Fall, planned for by God and said here to be necessary for final glory, also led to God's work of frustrating creation that it might be released from decay and brought into freedom—freedom just like that his people are given in Christ. What kind of freedom is this? A quick review of references in previous paragraphs makes it clear that this is a freedom from the possibility of sin:

- Romans 6:6–7: "knowing this, that our old self was crucified with Him, in order that our body of sin might be done away with, so that we would no longer be slaves to sin; for he who has died is freed from sin."

- Romans 6:20–22: "For when you were slaves of sin, you were free in regard to righteousness. Therefore what benefit were you then deriving from the things of which you are now ashamed? For the outcome of those things is death. But now having been freed from sin and enslaved to God, you derive your benefit, resulting in sanctification."

- Romans 7:23: "Wretched man that I am! Who will set me free from the body of this death?"

- Romans 8:2: "For the law of the Spirit of life in Christ Jesus has set you free from the law of sin and of death."

Of course non-willful creation cannot sin, but it longs to live in the world untroubled by the decay ("frustration") resulting when human willful-creatures do not take their rightful place in such freedom. This kind of freedom is a key concept for the author. Not only is this reference to a specific kind of freedom not parenthetical, but these texts show that his point has been building and focusing on this very idea. Such freedom is essential for people and it is something God also intends for creation. That is, though human willful-creatures are subject to "futility" because of their willful sin, even the non-willful part of creation is similarly subject to frustration and futility. But the wonderful and amazing result of this suffering is that even creation will enjoy freedom, though it now suffers the effects of sin that it did not will.[83] The next verses assert that if this is true for creation, which suffers unwillingly and at the hand of God, so his people also will share in this freedom.

Noting that God does not choose to use his power to overthrow evil, Nancey Murphy and George Ellis observe:

---

83. It is worth wondering if the author is here making reference to natural evil: damaging effects of sin which was not willed. That is something worth exploring, but outside the scope of this project.

Holmes Rolston has extended this insight to the world of nature. Rolston's thesis is that suffering in the nature world is, in a sense, redemptive. It is a necessary byproduct of the features of life that allow for the emergence of something higher. And just as God suffers in and with human suffering to bring forth greater good, God suffers, as well, in and with all of life.[84]

Without subscribing to Murphy and Ellis's larger program,[85] they and others are correctly observing a truth about God which calls for our attention: suffering is in some way redemptive.

Returning to Romans, the text is concerned with showing us that this promised freedom, gained by Christ's suffering and which still finishes its work in his people and his creation, is the foundation for hope and the example of the text is that an understanding of this directly affects the prayers of his people (verses 26, 27). My concern here is not this particular application, but the premise, so I will now move on to the next paragraph where we see the next large movement in this text. Paul begins verse 28 with an iconic phrase: "we are more than conquerors." To explain what this means the author begins with God's intimate and prior knowledge of his people, who they are and what they are destined for: "For those whom He foreknew, He also predestined to become conformed to the image of His Son" (verse 29). His people are intended by God to be conformed to Christ, which the author makes identical with glorification (his thesis statement in verse 17) in the explanation of verse 30: "and these whom He predestined, He also called; and these whom He called, He also justified; and these whom He justified, He also glorified." So, the author has tied together the ideas of suffering, conformity with Christ, and freedom in this way: suffering is the means by which God will accomplish human glorification (and that of creation) and glorification is accomplished in Conforming-Freedom.

If we put this together, Paul is saying that suffering is necessary for glorification. His explanation is this: people and creation cry out for freedom from sin and sin's effects. *God brought creation and human willful-creatures on a necessary journey through futility (the inability to live out our created purpose) so that freedom (the ability to perfectly live out our created purpose) might be fully granted to his people.* That freedom is a specific good that God is working out and it will come about in this way: God's people will be conformed to the image of Christ. That is, the freedom that God intends, and is inexorably bringing about, is a Conforming-Freedom.

---

84. Murphy and Ellis, *On the Moral Nature of the Universe: Theology, Cosmology, and Ethics*, 211.

85. In their valuable, but flawed book, Murphy and Ellis argue from a Christian, evolutionary, Darwinian (4), Libertarian Free-Will, based on quantum uncertainty (36), top-down (37) perspective that morality is available to people from within creation without acknowledging the existence of God or his character, just as are the laws of physics. One point (of many) with which I disagree is their belief that it is God's "decision to cooperate with human creatures" that constrains him from using power against evil and necessitates the use of suffering (211). That he does use suffering instead of power is still a valid observation.

PART II: The Testing of a Theodicy

Words like Conforming-Freedom are not naturally conjoined; these words are reasonably considered opposites. Can Conforming-Freedom be a meaningful construct? And if so, what does it mean? Even if my meaning is clear to most readers at this point, let me briefly justify it based on the foundation laid earlier in this chapter and in Part I. Most importantly, God is characteristically good; he is the fountain of all that is good. This was fundamental to Augustine who wrote in *Confessions*, "Is not my God not only good but the supreme good?"[86] God does not participate with what is good, but good flows from him. He is the Source of all Good. Edwards wrote often of this subject, calling God the fountain of Goodness. He wrote, "He is herein infinitely distinguished from all other Gods. He is the great fountain of all good, from whom goodness flows as light from the sun."[87] Also he writes, "He is in the most proper sense, a moral agent. [He is] the source of all moral ability and agency, and the fountain and rule of all virtue and moral good."[88] Also he writes, "He, and his agency, are altogether good and holy, and that he is the fountain of all holiness."[89] There is broad concurrence on this point, but it is worth displaying it here. This must be as clear in our minds as it was in the minds of Calvin and Edwards and no less so in the minds of Pelagius[90] and Arminius.[91] The latter asserted this truth no less directly than the former. This is because the biblical case is so clear. Only a few examples will be needed here. In Luke 18:18–23, Christ claims that no one is good except God, alone. While this verse is exegetically disputed, this works in our favor, here.[92] The text of verse 19 translates simply: "no one is good except only God." The exegetical dispute lies not with the meaning of these words as translated, but with exactly what claim Christ may have been making for himself by citing this truth about God the Father. But the point of the speaker is quite clear in its naked claim—God alone is good; God is good in

---

86. Augustine, *Confessions*, 7.3(5).

87. J. Edwards, "Collections of Sermons: The Most High, A Prayer-Hearing God." Even this exact phrase, "fountain of all good" occurs more than twenty times in Edwards's writings.

88. J. Edwards, "Freedom of the Will," in *Collected Works* (1.5.8).

89. Ibid. (4.9.III).

90. While Pelagius does not make a point of God's supreme goodness, for his focus is on human goodness, he does acknowledge that human goodness is derivative as is observed because he considered God to be full of mercy and eager to give all "help" to his willful-creatures so that they might choose to be good, which implies, "like God."

91. In *The Works of James Arminius* (volume 1, Oration 1), Arminius writes in "The Object of Theology," "He is the best being; he is the first and chief good, and goodness itself; he alone is good, as good as goodness itself; as ready to communicate, as it is possible for him to be communicated: his liberality is only equaled by the boundless treasures which he possesses, both of which are infinite and restricted only by the capacity of the recipient."

92. Here the words from Luke 18:19 are reinforced by an identical text in Mark 10:18. There are no significant textual issues in these verses, but only exegetical ones. This admonition by Christ has been seen by some to identify with God and by others to distinguish himself from God. However, it does not have to be either. Rather in context it is an answer that "is meant to do away with any cheapening of the idea of goodness" (Marshall, *Gospel of Luke*, 684). The dispute over who is good makes the point clear that someone is good characteristically and that someone is God alone.

himself. For our purposes, we need not understand how Christ would apply this in the conversation to himself or to the Jewish ruler who had questioned him. Since no one but God is good, this implies that all goodness observed outside of God is in some way contingent upon God. So also, 1 John 1:5 reads, "God is light and in him there is no darkness at all." This provides a clear reminder of this undisputed theme. God is good, lacking no goodness whatsoever and he is good of metaphysical necessity. God is not just "pretty good," nor does he conform to some good standard, but he is Goodness and all that is good flows from him. Were I to attempt to prove this as the biblical perspective, much more detail (and many unnecessary pages) would be filled, but again, this case is not contested in the church. Far from being contested, it forms the basis of the Trilemma that has driven this conversation. It stands as a stipulation, unless we are willing to "defect" from this position: God is (by nature and in his being) "Omni-Good" (and the source of all that is good). If this were a mutable position, there would be no problem of evil for the Christian.[93]

So, when we say his people will be conformed to himself, we are saying that they will be conformed to the good as God is. And this has been shown not to be the state in which they were created and perhaps it is not a state in which they could have been created. And we have seen that to be conformed to God is the freedom that we have always desired and it is the definition of real freedom throughout the history of the church since the beginning of creation. This is Conforming-Freedom. And it will be shown in later chapters that this is not constrictive. For just as God's freedom is infinite, but always good, so also will be the freedom of his people. Perfection is not a narrow channel, but a wide ocean—if, evil has been destroyed for his people, so that, like God, they do not interact with it. Adam did. They will not. What has God done—what is God doing—to make this the case?

SUMMARY: A PEOPLE WITH CONFORMING-FREEDOM

> Huxley once wrote that if a higher power would undertake to make him always do what is right, on condition of being turned into a sort of clock, he

---

93. It is interesting to note that this idea of God as the source of Goodness may even be preserved in our language in the rather plain and unadorned word we used for the name of YHWH, "God." The English etymology of the word "God" is disputed and most authorities, including the *Oxford English Dictionary*, do not associate it with "good." However, in reverse, it is accepted by the *Oxford English Dictionary* that the Old English word for "good" is "god." So we receive "goodbye" which is commonly understood to be derivative from "God be with ye." And also we receive the word, "gospel," which derives from "god"(good) + "spel" (message). This proves nothing about God, but much about us. We understand, even in our language, that God is synonymous with (the Source of) Goodness. God is the Good. Yet, if we still struggle with this, it is because we too often think that we can define divine goodness as we want it to be: "it seems good to me that God should prevent evil" (or minimize evil, or relieve my evil . . .). But when all is known, that may not be the case. In fact, I will claim that it is not.

PART II: The Testing of a Theodicy

> would close with the offer, since the only freedom he valued was freedom to do the right; freedom to do the wrong he would gladly get rid of.[94]
>
> —J. S. Whale

I have argued that God's *chief end* is to glorify himself and that an *ultimate end* in his creation is to create a world that will allow his human willful-creatures, his people, to share in the relationship between Father, Son, and Spirit. So also, the end for his people in this goal of God is happiness for his people. But evil arose in creation, opposed to God's goodness (which is not distinct from his holiness) and it stands in our way, a barrier to holiness, and our intended joy and hope. We have seen that Adam's unfettered freedom is distinctly different than the freedom that God's people will need to have to know the joy God wants to give them. As we will explore in the next chapter, there is reason to believe that God did not want to control Adam and that he in fact did not. Yet that kind of freedom is not be the same as Conforming-Freedom. God did not make the offer that Huxley would have accepted. Conforming-Freedom, which is the ultimate freedom God intends for his people, is necessary to hope and it is distinctly different than forced conformity. It seems that something deeper, more intricate, more difficult—even more glorious for God—was required. It is the Conforming-Freedom of Romans 8 that will give his people hope. It will do so because they will be conformed freely to God's character and so enjoy the "beatific vision" without hindrance. To understand how, we must investigate what is in the way of that hope: a necessary evil.

---

94. From Huxley's *Collected Essays*, 1.192, as cited in Whale, *Christian Answer to the Problem of Evil*, 49.

5

Hypothesis 2

Evil & Suffering is a subordinate-metaphysical necessity, being both the intrinsic problem and the instrumental solution in God's economy.

HAVING MADE THE CASE in the previous chapter for the kind of freedom that God intends for his people, Conforming-Freedom, I intend to argue here that there is reason to think that the unique means of God to accomplish this great work is Evil & Suffering: he uses Evil & Suffering to destroy Evil & Suffering. Of course, God uses both good works and coercive-power in his battle against Evil. Yet for the teleological destruction of Evil & Suffering, and to create a people for himself who share his freedom from evil, I will argue that he uses Evil & Suffering against itself. The cross is not an example of his work, but normative. To unpack this I will consider in what way God is responsible for the Evil & Suffering that appeared in his world. Then, building on evil as privative, I will make the case that evil may be understood as a subordinate-metaphysical necessity, appearing in creation as a result of God's character and goals for creation. Then, I will argue that Evil & Suffering is the intrinsic problem, arising out of God's creation, but not in God's creation as created. And finally, I will explore the possibility that Evil & Suffering is the unique means that God uses to destroy Evil & Suffering in his creation for his people. Finally, for clarity, I will address some of the concerns that this raises, including: whether God does use or could use good to destroy Evil & Suffering; whether God does use or could use his coercive omnipotence to destroy Evil & Suffering; the problem of consequentialist ethics that "necessary evil" may seem to imply, and what kind of God would permit and use Evil & Suffering in his project.

PART II: The Testing of a Theodicy

EVIL & SUFFERING: GOD'S RESPONSIBILITY IS MEDIATE, ULTIMATE, AND CO-CAUSAL

> The necessary disproportion between human agency and horrendous evils makes it impossible for humans to bear full responsibility for their occurrence.[1]
>
> —Marilyn McCord Adams

In what way is God responsible for evil in his creation? Because responsibility correlates with causation, we could reframe the question: how does the idea of "cause" apply to God in his relationship to Evil & Suffering? God is not a cause among causes in regard to his creation; he is the Cause of all things. What then of the evil which is found in his world? These questions reveal the tension of the non-consequentialist framework which must distance God from direct, causal responsibility for evil. In response, both the compatibilist and the free-will theologian rely (to varying extent) upon the reality of the human will to "offer" God a measure of distance from the evil in his world. Many perceive that this fails for the compatibilist who grants God mediate, causal influence in all things, and so primary causality, restricting his human willful-creatures to secondary and immediate causality. They would observe that mediate and primary causality is thin insulation from evil in his world. But the Libertarian Free-Will theologian, who might hope to relieve God of all responsibility for evil, cannot do so (if that was her intent) by increasing the freedom of the willing agent. The compatibilist observes that in the free-will system God retains responsibility for the world which he instantiated in which evil did occur.[2] So, neither system seems, at first assessment, to have been wholly successful in preserving a non-consequential ethic.

Instead, those on both sides of the free-will discussion might fairly agree that God has "omni-responsibility," a term used by John Hick, for everything in his creation, including evil.[3] Granting this, I propose that the tension in our understanding may find some relief, if we consider that God's role in evil is mediate, as both free-will theist and compatibilists would agree, and we also maintain that God has an asymmetric co-causality in evil with his human willful-creatures, and that God is the ultimate cause of evil in that there is no cause prior to him.[4] If we understand his causality as I have described it here, I hope to show that a non-consequentialist ethic is preserved.

---

1. M. M. Adams, *Horrendous Evils and the Goodness of God*, 38.

2. Even Marilyn McCord Adams would agree. She writes, "I . . . insist on the bankruptcy of free will approaches as a means of shifting responsibility off God on to someone else . . . thus even if disobedient created choice triggered the fall of creation, God would remain fully responsible for the created ruin" ("Evil and the God-Who-Does-Nothing-In-Particular," 112). To this we could add the voice of Kenneth Surin, "The free will defence is an acceptable vindication of God's moral blamelessness. But is it adequate as a defence of his moral perfection . . . or indeed of moral blamelessness?" (Surin, *Theology and the Problem of Evil*, 76). At least in this particular, I agree.

3. Noted by Robert C. Mesle in "Problem of Genuine Evil," 414.

4. The word ultimate has a variety of meanings in English, and specifically in Edwards's scheme of ends, it is one of those ends which is an end in itself. Here, in the case of causes, I am using it to

In Aristotle's system, God's causality could be classified as "efficient," agency, but this would be of little help to distinguish God's specific agency in regard to evil (or Evil & Suffering).[5] Instead, it may be more useful to think in terms of primary and secondary causation which is preserved by Aquinas in his *Commentary on the Book of Causes*. In this scheme, God's responsibility is primary in all things. "Proposition I" states: "Every primary cause infuses its effect more powerfully than does a universal second cause."[6] Aquinas writes in his commentary, "The first cause is more a cause than the second. . . . Therefore, the impression of the first cause arrives first and recedes last."[7] The secondary cause, the human willful-creature, does not in any way mitigate or diminish the causation of the primary agent, God. This is helpful. God, while not the immediate (direct) cause of evil, does retain significant, even primary (indirect and mediated) causal responsibility (though asymmetric in comparison to his causation of the Good). So, I affirm God as the primary cause of evil, mediated by a secondary and immediate cause. Adam triggered the genesis of suffering; he was the immediate and proximate cause, but he was secondary.[8] So while God alone created the world good,

---

indicate a cause which is a cause to itself with nothing causally superior. This does not speak to the value that God places on the instrumental use of evil, nor does it mean that evil is in some way desired by God. That is a different discussion which does not impact the simple statement that God is the ultimate cause of evil.

5. Aristotle, and those who have since developed his system, provides terminology for four kinds of "causation" in the world: the material cause, the substance or composition of a thing; the formal cause, the essence or form of a thing; the efficient cause, the agent who brings something about; and the final cause, the purpose or telos for which a thing comes into being. While it is clear that this use of the word "cause" deviates from our post-enlightenment, Newtonian usage, it is still a helpful place to begin and it is useful to consider how Aristotle's taxonomy of causes might apply to creation. In doing so, I will follow Peter Hicks (*The Journey So Far: Philosophy through the Ages*, 61–62). Per Aristotle-Hicks, the *material cause* of the universe, its primordial substance, is matter and spirit. The *formal cause* is the true form to which a thing conforms, YHWH. The *final cause* of the universe is that end for which it was created. Finally, the *efficient cause*, or agent of creation, is the "cause" which is most like our common usage of the word: the Triune God. Reflecting on this, I would understand that the final cause, the telos of the universe, is to be freely-conforming to God's perfection, the glorious freedom of the children of God. The efficient cause is YHWH. So what of Evil & Suffering which appeared in God's world as he created it? In what way might that implicate God as also the efficient cause of Evil & Suffering? But this only restates the question. The answer lies elsewhere.

6. Aquinas, *Commentary on the Book of Causes*, 7.

7. Ibid., 9.

8. While many Christians subscribe to the Fall as historical, and others do not, the theological meaning intended in the Genesis Fall text (Genesis 3:1–7) infers at least that someone other than God is the immediate author of evil. For those who adopt an evolutionary perspective and have no place for an historical fall (for example, orthodox Christians like John Polkinghorne and other theologians like John Hick), Genesis 3 should still have theological currency in regard to agency—Moses meant something by it: people, not God, are responsible for evil. Yet it is also interesting to note that both systems seem to have a place for a pristine, sinless universe. The evolutionary theologian cannot postulate evil through the first many billions of years of the development of the universe. During this time, nucleo-synthesis, stellar-formation, and the production of heavy elements in super-nova events continued until the galactic densities of heavy elements was sufficient to permit life. And life is arguably necessary for even natural evil to be possible. All the more so in regard to moral evil which must

PART II: The Testing of a Theodicy

even perfect (the independent and efficient cause), he also created it susceptible to diverging from his perfection. God alone decreed that human willful-creatures would be created, good, and with the capacities that they did in fact possess. If this is the case, God must have a mediated causality in regard to evil, for he created the world in which evil arose. Jonathan Edwards makes this point clear when he writes,

> Therefore, I shall take these two things for positions granted and supposed in this controversy, viz., that as to God's own actions and forbearings to act, he decrees and purposes them beforehand; and that whatsoever God designs or purposes, he purposes from all eternity, and thus decrees from all eternity all his own actions and forbearings to act.
>
> Corollary. Hence God decrees from all eternity, to permit all the evil that ever he does permit, because God's permitting is God's forbearing to act or to prevent.[9]

I take this to say nothing less than God is responsible for his world as he created it and nothing occurs that he did not foresee and permit—and in a significant sense, will. This position does not require that God is himself guilty of creating evil or doing evil, but it does assert significant causal responsibility to God. Although God did not create evil, evil appeared in God's creation because God created as he did create. So much Barth rightly allowed when he wrote that evil is "an element in that original plan" and that "the Fall had inevitably to take place, not apart from but in accordance with the will of God."[10] This is a mediate and prior responsibility for evil.

And God's responsibility, his causality, in regard to evil is also ultimate.[11] It is helpful to observe that God and his willful-creatures do not act symmetrically in regard to evil. While humans have a causal immediacy with evil that grants them a certain responsibility and inevitable guilt (which God does not share in any way), God's mediate causality is crucially antecedent and anticipatory. The contribution of God's human willful-creatures is derivative (from God) and consequent (under God); God's contribution enables the contribution of the willful-creature. This asymmetry is well expressed in saying that God is the "ultimate cause" of evil, in the same sense as Edwards speaks of the "ultimate end." So an ultimate cause is a cause for which there

---

have waited billions of years more (unless blue-green algae is considered by some to be a moral agent). So, the universe was initially pristine and without evil, regardless of the system. A moral "fall" from within creation is required to get from the initial pristine state to the problem of evil.

9. J. Edwards, "Miscellanies," #763 (2. second & Corollary).

10. Barth, "The Election of Jesus Christ," *CD*, II.2, §33.1, 128–9. He also writes, "We cannot say that God ordains equally and symmetrically as man's end both good and evil . . . [RAS: yet] it is allowed to be on the basis of the eternal divine decree" §33.2 (171).

11. This can also be seen in Aquinas in *ST*, 1a,q.49,a.2 (article 2), where he writes: "that there should be some things that can, and do sometimes, fail. And thus God, by causing in things the good of the order of the universe, consequently and as it were by accident, causes the corruptions of things." God is the ultimate, or first, cause of evil, but not the secondary and direct cause.

is nothing causally superior. It is important to state clearly that evil is not represented here as an ultimate end of God—not in any respect. Quite the opposite, the *destruction of Evil & Suffering* for his willful-creatures is a subordinate end of God which supports the ultimate ends of his glory and human glorification. It is for these ultimate ends that evil must be faced and defeated. But the battle against evil was not forced on God, nor did it surprise him.[12] God freely chose this battle because it fit his character and perfect plans, his ultimate ends, and his singular chief end, his glory. So I suggest that God is the "ultimate cause" of evil, sovereignly choosing to instantiate the world in which evil would appear and then be defeated by him. That is, there is nothing above or prior to which God's causality "reports" or which conditions it. God is the ultimate cause in that there is no other cause which is not contingent and subordinate to his causation. Like Edwards, I will reserve for God's willful-creatures a limited and immediate causation, considering God's mediate causation as ultimate because he had complete control of instantiating or not, as he did, and with the purposes he sovereignly determined.

Here I must raise an issue for clarity. It might be imagined at this point that I will suggest that God created willful-creatures in order to bring about the appearance of evil, but nothing could be further from the intent of this proposal. God does not desire evil in any ultimate sense and the statement above would invert his ends. Rather, as has been said, God created willful-creatures in order to be glorified by sharing himself with them and in order to give them joy. However, in decreeing such a creation, he also decreed that he would face the problem of evil, which arises necessarily from and subordinate to his character and plans—his plan to create a free people for himself. In so doing he also decreed that he would conquer evil for his human willful-creatures. *This is the problem of evil for God*—not that evil exists, but that his plans meant that he would require himself to destroy it.

So, having argued God's mediate and ultimate responsibility for evil, is it the case that God's causality is necessary and sufficient for the evil act? Briefly, no; God is necessary, but not sufficient. Evil's appearance is conditional upon God's necessary action, creation. But it does not follow that God is the sufficient cause of evil. As has been shown, both Libertarian Free-Will and compatibilist theologians assert, a willful agency apart from God is necessary, given that God is good and what he creates is good as he created it. It is not simply that God "would not" or "should not" create evil; this is true and flows from his character. Nor is it that he "could not," as if he might try but fail—on a "bad day." Rather, God is the fountain and source of all that is good and

---

12. Among Christians who position themselves in the mainstream of traditions and orthodoxy, I am aware only of John Sanders who understands the human turning away from God in the Garden to be a surprise to God: "Now God has to adjust his project in response to this horrible turn of events" (*God Who Risks,* 48). If I expanded the circle, we could name several who see God as reactive, and not able to fully anticipate events which are significantly out of his control and so out of his responsibility. For example, Albert Schweitzer understood Christ's death as a tragedy—a plan gone wrong, and many others. But within circles of orthodoxy, they are still a tiny minority.

PART II: The Testing of a Theodicy

only that which is good. It is better to state it in a positive way: all God does is Good because God does it. If evil arises, an immediate agency, other than God, must be that agent. Both God and his human willful-creatures are necessary, but neither are sufficient. William Frank, proposes such a co-causality. Commenting on Duns Scotus's *Ordinatio* (2.37.2) he writes,

> Each cause's contribution is necessary, but not sufficient, for the effect. Furthermore, the two cohere in such a way as to constitute a total cause.... No increase in accidental features of either cause suffices to overcome the limitation of essence that is overcome only by the holistic integration of the two natures. The concurrence of male and female in begetting offspring is an example.[13]

For Frank, this concept of co-causality extends beyond evil and as I noted earlier, I reject this for the reasons given. Yet as regards evil only, I believe this is correctly stated. Consider: "no increase in accidental features of either cause suffices." It is the case that neither the amplification of the characteristics of God, nor those of his human willful-creatures, would be sufficient for either to produce evil, independently. In fact, it is the very essence of God's human willful-creatures that we are derivative; we are insufficient to anything apart from God's creative work and will. Frank proves quite helpful; co-causality seems to fit reality and the claims of the Text: sufficiency is located in the mediate causation of God and the immediate causation of man.

Co-causality may be parallel to "Proposition I" in Aquinas's *Commentary on Book of Causes*:

> The first cause aids the second cause in its activity, because the first cause also effects every activity that the second cause effects, although it effects it in another way [RAS: which is] higher and more sublime. When the second cause is removed from its effect, the first cause is not removed from it, because the first cause adheres more greatly and more powerfully to the thing than does the proximate cause. The effect of the second cause is only through the power of the first cause.... It is, therefore, now clear and plain that the remote cause is more powerfully the cause of a thing than the proximate cause that follows it, and that the remote cause infuses the thing with its power, conserves it, and is not separated from it by the separation of its proximate cause. Rather, it remains in it and adheres to it powerfully, as we have shown and explained.[14]

I suggest that the primary cause (God) can be understood to share co-causality in regard to evil with the secondary cause, his human willful-creatures. My emphasis here is not intended to minimize God's supreme causality in all things. Quite the opposite, I am trying to call attention to the fact that no understanding of free-will (be it a defense, a theodicy, or even an Augustinian expression of compatibilism) can be understood to diminish God's ultimate responsibility for everything in his creation,

---

13. Frank, "Duns Scotus," 152–3.
14. Aquinas, *Commentary on the Book of Causes*, 6–7.

whether created or arising within creation, including evil. But he neither created evil, nor did he do evil. He did not create suffering. He did not cause it; human (in God's image) willful (exercising a will) creatures (metaphysically dependant) were necessary. So while I propose no parity of causation here between God and his creatures (but rather, asymmetry), and while I insist that God cannot be immediately responsible for evil, an understanding can be put forward that may be more appropriate than that of all free-will arguments.[15] I agree with Frank that neither God nor the human willful-creature could effect evil *on their own*. Such seems to be the intent of Edwards in *Freedom of the Will* where he carefully and clearly explains that all events have causes, natural or moral "antecedents," on which they depend. Further, "what is not necessary in itself, must have a cause,"[16] meaning that all things (and all events), with the exception of God who is the uncaused-cause, have an antecedent cause, including evil. Yet, human willful-creatures alone are morally responsible for evil and so culpable.[17]

---

15. Here I find Paul Fiddes helpful in his critique of free-will arguments that do not include the suffering of God and the (indirect) responsibility of God for all, including evil. He begins by noting, "the most adequate (or the least inadequate) explanation for human suffering lies in human free will, the affirmation that God suffers is still needed to give credibility to such a defense of the world as God's creation. For the Free-Will Defense cannot stand alone" (*The Creative Suffering of God*, 33). This is true for human free-will is incoherent as a theodicy unless the Cross is understood as God's central response, though as I have argued, it is still inadequate. Most importantly, Fiddes adds, "Thus, although God does not create evil and suffering, and though man's own immediate responsibility is not denied, God must bear an ultimate responsibility in choosing to make man as a free creature at all" (33). In doing so Fiddes correctly makes the connection between God's responsibility and evil, even for the free-will theodicy—and I would argue for every theodicy.

16. Jonathan Edwards, *Collected Works*, 2.3.9. Let me also address another concern that is raised by even proposing that evil has a cause: how can that which is privative, and which in that sense does not exist, be said to have a cause? I have already argued that though evil is privative; it is devastatingly privative. And, sin, which is the expression of evil, is embodied in the act of the willful-creature. The use of the verb cause in this context, is not an assertion that evil exists in the sense that rocks or squirrels or human willful-creatures exist, but it is to acknowledge that in keeping with a non-consequentialist ethic, evil was not part of the original creation and evil is part of the creation in which we find ourselves. That which exists, even privatively, is not causeless. It is this cause I am addressing.

17. Co-causality is distinct from moral taint resulting from evil intent and action. In *ICR*, Calvin's title for Book 1, Chapter 18, is "The Instrumentality Of The Wicked Employed By God, While He Continues Free From Every Taint." Indeed this is the case and only the wicked human willful-creatures are tainted. So, in this chapter he writes, "there is no concurrence between God and man, when by His righteous impulse man does what he ought not to do" (*ICR*, 1.18.4, CCEL, Beveridge). That there is "no concurrence" is correctly stated in regard to moral culpability and God's goodness, but such is still "employed by God" for his purposes. Still, no amplification of the abilities of God or his human willful-creatures allow either to corrupt the world independently. In regard to God, his creatures are unalterably derivative and dependant. In regard to evil, God is "impotent" to cause or do sin.

PART II: The Testing of a Theodicy

EVIL & SUFFERING: A SUBORDINATE-METAPHYSICAL NECESSITY

> I could wish, indeed that a better term was available for our discussion than the accepted one, necessity, which cannot accurately be used of either man's will or God's. Its meaning is too harsh and foreign to the subject; for it suggests some sort of compulsion, and something that is against one's will, which is no part of the view under debate.[18]
>
> —Martin Luther

I share Luther's allergic reaction to the word "necessity" as it is used in relationship to the will. In regard to God, freedom is more apt. How much more intensely do we feel this when "necessity" is juxtaposed with the appearance of evil in God's world—as God's good creation? Yet, that is what is proposed here: evil arises by a certain species of necessity in creation as God created it and given the boundary conditions that his character establishes.

Let me restate the definition: *Subordinate-Metaphysical Necessity* is the necessity that arises subordinate to God's singular metaphysical necessity and is therefore conditional upon God. In the context of creation, I apply it to the evil that arose as an intrinsic problem from God's good creation. It arose as a result of God's freedom in creating as he did create; it arose in creation given God's metaphysically necessary character and announced goals. Evil is subordinate-metaphysical necessity; "it had to happen." But it was not there at creation.

Again, this does not make the Creator dependent upon evil in any way. He did not need evil for his project, but rather evil arose out of a kind of necessity and became the enemy God would conquer in order to bring his human willful-creatures into his joy. Evil and its destruction was anticipated by God before all time; when creating, God counted the cost. And, evil arose in God's creation and covered all like a terrible shadow. Of course, Evil & Suffering could be defeated by God's coercive-power. By his power, he could crush evil before it arose or just as it did. While effective, it seems this would not destroy evil *for* his human willful-creatures; instead it would destroy them as well, for they have participated with evil. Rather God desires not only to rid Creation of the shadow of evil, but also to create a people as free from evil as he is himself. And to his glory, and the joy of his people, this will be their *telos*. Evil is not necessary to God, but having created as he did create and having the goals he has, it arose as his necessary enemy.

This is distinct from some theodicy projects which seem to need evil. For example, John Hick "needs" evil to mature humanity. For him, evil is an instrumental necessity. Yet, I can agree with him that we were created, in a certain sense, "immature" in our freedom. That is, we were clearly *not* created free, as God is free—free *from* sin. That is the final state and for this the Bible uses words like eternal, perfect, without sin,

---

18. Luther, "Bondage of the Will," in *Selections from his Writings*, 182.

without tears, freedom, and conforming. That is, in this state, God's people will be not like Adam, but like Christ. In this state they will be "incorruptible."[19] In this narrow sense, corruptible, we were created, immature. But evil was not our God-appointed tutor, nor needed by God in any way, but rather the enemy that God chose to face in order to create us in Christ.

Augustine came close to this when he taught us that Adam fell because he was not the fountain of goodness. While Augustine never quite asserted the Fall as a necessity, John Rist acknowledges that he came right up to the edge of affirming this to be the case when Augustine wrote, "*O certe necessarium Adae peccatum.*"[20] And it was Augustine who told us that Adam became, and we with him, the Fountain of Evil and that this occurred specifically because we are not God. Augustine writes, "From these fountains of evil, which spring out of defect rather than superfluity, flows every form of misery that besets a rational nature."[21] Adam was ontologically "at risk" from birth. At his creation, while not yet a Fountain of Evil, Adam was not and would never be the Fountain of Goodness. That is only God. Adam was neither; he was unfettered and in an ontologically "at risk" position. As such, he must fall.

So, I agree with Paul Fiddes who insists that evil does not arise from a logical necessity in creation. He writes, "the slipping of creation away from the good cannot be logically a necessary consequence of God's creative activity."[22] That is, evil is not logically required as a result of our finitude, nor even because that which is opposite of God must exist, as is the case for Barth's *das Nichtige*. But there is still an inevitability that arises, though not merely from the act of creation. To explain this Fiddes writes, "Reinhold Niebuhr puts the paradox succinctly when he says that sin is 'inevitable, but not in such a way as to fit into the category of natural necessity,' and that 'sin is natural for man in the sense that it is universal, but that in the sense that it is necessary.'"[23] This is a difficult balance for a Process theologian who insists on the need for risk and necessity in the same system. He is even more precise when he cites Macquarrie, "A risk logically excludes necessity.... Macquarrie admits the tragic element in creation, that 'natural evil' and 'human sin' are alike unavoidable possibilities in the

---

19. First Corinthians 15:50–56. ἀφθαρσία, translated in the NASB and other translations as "imperishable" (a better literal translation than the KJV's "incorruptible") is linked in this passage to both the conquest of death, but also of sin, especially in verse 56. So the translation, "incorruptible" stands in context. The future for God's people is without death and without sin; they are incorruptible.

20. Rist, *Augustine: Ancient Thought Baptized*, 282 n. 56. Rist seems to be of two minds, however. Responding to the idea that evil is a "necessary feature of any other soul than His," Rist responds, "We may assume, therefore, that he would not accept that Adam had an option but to sin at some time or other" (107). True. But indeed, assumptions notwithstanding, Augustine comes very, very close to "necessity."

21. Augustine, *Enchiridion on Faith, Hope and Love*, ¶ 24, 31. It could be objected that only Satan is the "fountain of evil" and we are merely conduits. That may be so. In either case, we are stained with evil, suffering is our lot, and we are not merely polluters, but polluted with sin.

22. Fiddes, *Creative Suffering of God*, 213.

23. Ibid., 214.

creation the end of which is good."²⁴ While I have no room for Process thought in my understanding of God, yet here is a term and a concept that is useful: "unavoidable possibilities." I consider this a fair human expression of what is from God's perspective, a subordinate-metaphysical necessity.

In suggesting the *necessity of necessity*, I do so in a way that imposes no antecedent necessity upon God. Gordon Neff, writing for Ockham, and speaking for many, said, "only what is formally in God is necessary,"²⁵ but this is too limited an understanding of necessity. Given that God neither created evil, *nor does he need evil to accomplish his purposes*, it is still the case that evil came to exist in the good world that God created and in the world God chose to create. But no necessity is imposed on God by this, as is the case in some systems, such as Hick's soul-making theodicy. For Hick, epistemic distance and the evil that results seem to be necessary tutors for the maturing of the human soul.²⁶ It also might be the case, if evil was "something," because then God must have created it. But that is not the case for this proposal, which considers that evil has no ontological existence. Along with the broad stream of Christian thought, I hold that evil is privative.²⁷ It is like a shadow, which is nothing in itself. Such a privative understanding of evil is removed from God ontologically. So also, God does not need evil to accomplish his purposes. Instead, given his purposes, evil arises as an obstacle which does not challenge God, but assaults his goals. He could crush evil, and us with it, by a word. Yet, evil is a barrier between God and his elect which God chose eternally to overcome, which arose intrinsically in a good creation, and necessarily, subordinate to the reality of God and his choices.²⁸

24. Ibid., 215. Here he is citing John Macquarrie in *Principles of Christian Theology*.

25. Neff, *William of Ockham: The Metamorphosis of Scholastic Discourse*, 453.

26. While it does not directly touch this thesis, Hick's concept of epistemic distance is troubling. Henri Blocher summarizes his concept of epistemic distance this way, "It would be unthinkable that man, in the divine presence and conscious of that presence, should have sinned, . . . there had to be a distance between the Creator and the Creature. . . . God must be a hidden deity veiled by his creation" (*Evil and the Cross: Christian Thought and the Problem of Evil*, 54). Yet, the lack of epistemic distance did not help Cain when God met with him personally to warn him (Genesis 4), nor did it help Moses when he sinned by trying to refuse God's "offer" at the burning bush (Exodus 3–4). To this list we could add many others, including especially Judas, who lived in the very presence of God for several years—and sinned. We are capable of sinning with no epistemic distance dividing us from God. Blocher notes that this concept was first suggested by Austin Farrer and then rejected and there was no reason for Hick to pick it up again (56)! He writes, "it does not follow that God has hidden himself, to the extent of leaving only ambiguous signs and rendering the fall 'virtually inevitable.'" (56). On this I fully agree with Blocher against Hick. Of course, as Blocher understands, Hick has no event in history in which a Fall occurred. For Hick "The Fall" is the immaturity of an initial state which sins. However, and this is the point of this footnote, my sense of "necessity" in the Fall is unrelated to Hick's epistemic distance or any sense of the hidden-ness of God. The Text presents God as vitally present in his creation and that does not stop sin. Rather the advent of evil in God's creation is related only to the freedom in which God created his human willful-creatures—freedom from being conformed to his Goodness.

27. A further discussion of the rational sense of "privative evil" is discussed in chapter 8, "The Problem of the Existence of Privative Evil."

28. "Consequent Necessity" as defined by John S. Feinberg is quite similar: "once certain choices

EVIL & SUFFERING: AN INTRINSIC PROBLEM

Evil is not intrinsic to creation. This would imply a consequentialist ethic as was discussed earlier. But evil is an intrinsic problem, arising from creation as created, but not in creation when created. Evil is an intruder in God's good world, and it is the problem that arose intrinsically in creation as God created.

Plato's "simile of the sun" is instructive here. It reminds us not simply that we see by the light of the sun, but that the eye's power of sight is dependent upon the sun in that it must also share in the nature of the sun.[29] But so also are shadows, dependent upon the sun. As a shadow "is" but the lack of the sun's light, so evil "is" the lack of God's goodness. So, extending the simile, if the sun existed alone in the universe, there would be no such thing as a shadow. Similarly, because God's image-bearers had in themselves no source of "light" (goodness), the "shadow" (evil) of darkness formed, contingently, but yet of a kind of metaphysical necessity. The real creation is, of course, infinitely more complex than Plato's simile (or my extension). And yet this trope bears its own weight in saying something true about God's creation. Had God created only things which had existence (like rocks), or even only things with existence and life (like squirrels), the shadow of evil would not have darkened his creation. For I am imagining that anything without a will is transparent, casting no shadow. It seems that evil darkened creation only when God made beings that had existence, life, and his image, which included, will. That is, evil arose only in the creation of Adam and his progeny.[30] In some way, we humans can cast the shadow of evil against the holy glare

---

are made (by God or whomever) certain things follow as a consequence. But before these choices are made, no inherent necessity dictates what must be chosen" and "an action is free, even if it is causally determined, so long as it is non-constraining" (Feinberg, "God Ordains All Things," 23–24). This occurs in a good discussion in regard to human freedom in which Feinberg rejects "fatalism" and clarifies the difference between hard and soft determinism, affirming that there is no paradox between deterministic freedom and responsibility. More significantly for this project, he asserts, "it was not absolutely necessary that Adam sin in the sense that there was no other Adam God could have created . . . however, once having made the choice to create Adam as sinning, it was necessary for God to send Christ as redeemer." I fully support Feinberg in this. It is also worth noting that "Consequent Necessity" is a term of Duns Scotus which refers to an action that is necessary in the sense that "once in effect can no longer be changed, but it could have been different" (Luther, *Luther: Lectures on Romans*, 248). Luther notes, "it is meaningless to ask whether this consequent is contingent, as if . . . it could be necessary, inasmuch as only God is necessary in this sense" (249). Here Luther seems to be saying the same thing.

29. Plato, *The Republic*, book 6. The argument here is to instruct us by simile that the "light" of the Good makes all things sensible and rational—knowable, and so also demonstrates the irrationality of evil.

30. It is a strange thing that the "fall" of the angels, which must have occurred prior to the Fall of humanity, did not result in trauma to the universal order according to the biblical narrative. The Adversary was the adversary when he entered the Garden and he was already evil. When he entered, humanity was the target. But as yet, though evil was "in the world," no Fall had occurred. That terrible change in the order of all things (Romans 8:20–21) seems to have required the rebellion of God's image-bearers, not just the angelic beings. I observe this to support the importance of the Fall over the "fall of the angels." Both are important, but only one is specifically narrated in the text, and only

PART II: The Testing of a Theodicy

of the Son; such is the testimony of Scripture concerning Adam and of the Sons of Adam. And like a shadow, evil appears as a parasitic intruder, a problem intrinsic to creation as created, but not within creation as created.

Again, the claim that evil is the intrinsic problem is different than saying it is part of creation. Irenaeus, as noted earlier, suggests that evil was inherent in creation and necessary *for* creation: "Adam was created as a weak creature and so already significantly prone to sin. If (non-suppressed) sinfulness was part of Adam's created nature, it follows that (barring divine intervention) we would have inherited sinfulness whether or not Adam had sinned."[31] But Genesis asserts that Adam was created good, for God pronounced all creation to be "very good." So Adam was not created with an inclination to sin which could arise from sin as composing any part of his nature. Yet, in agreement with Irenaeus, Adam was created weak and sinfulness was free to be exhibited in Adam. While Genesis asserts that Adam's created nature was good, he was not "perfectly good," so that nothing but good came out of him. Christ (Matt 15:10–20, Luke 6:43) and James (Jas 3:11) remind us that our actions reveal what is already in our heart. While this is a post-fall warning, it speaks of the mechanism of temptation and sin in all eras in which evil is possible. So I argue that while Adam was created good, Adam's heart was not tethered to God's perfection. Thomas Boston put it well, "The original righteousness [RAS: of Adam] was universal and natural, yet mutable. . . . It was righteousness that might be lost, as is manifested by the doleful event."[32] But God's righteousness, God himself, is not characteristically mutable. It seems possible that there is a hint here of a kind of necessity arising out of the conditions, though not the creation, and not in God.

This idea may be alluded to by Paul in 1 Corinthians 15:44–49. For sake of the following discussion, I quote the passage here in Greek as well as in English:

> 44 it is sown a natural body, it is raised a spiritual body. If there is a natural body, there is also a spiritual body. 45 So also it is written, "The first MAN, Adam, BECAME A LIVING SOUL." The last Adam became a life-giving spirit. 46 However, the spiritual is not first, but the natural; then the spiritual. 47 The first man is from the earth, earthy; the second man is from heaven. 48 As is the earthy, so also are those who are earthy; and as is the heavenly, so also are those who are heavenly. 49 Just as we have borne the image of the earthy, we will also bear the image of the heavenly.

> 44 σπείρεται σῶμα ψυχικόν, ἐγείρεται σῶμα πνευματικόν. Εἰ ἔστιν σῶμα ψυχικόν, ἔστιν καὶ πνευματικόν. 45 οὕτως καὶ γέγραπται· ἐγένετο ὁ πρῶτος ἄνθρωπος Ἀδὰμ εἰς ψυχὴν ζῶσαν, ὁ ἔσχατος Ἀδὰμ εἰς πνεῦμα ζῳοποιοῦν.

---

one resulted in the futility of all creation. The meaning and significance of the "fall of the angels" can be set aside for this project on that basis, without proposing that it is unimportant. See Chapter 8 on The Problem of the Angels.

31. Summarized by Swinburne, *Providence and the Problem of Evil*, 39 of *Against Heresies* 4.38.1.

32. Boston, *Human Nature in its Fourfold State*, 43, 44.

46 ἀλλ' οὐ πρῶτον τὸ πνευματικὸν ἀλλὰ τὸ ψυχικόν, ἔπειτα τὸ πνευματικόν. 47 ὁ πρῶτος ἄνθρωπος ἐκ γῆς χοϊκός, ὁ δεύτερος ἄνθρωπος ἐξ οὐρανοῦ. 48 οἷος ὁ χοϊκός, τοιοῦτοι καὶ οἱ χοϊκοί, καὶ οἷος ὁ ἐπουράνιος, τοιοῦτοι καὶ οἱ ἐπουράνιοι· 49 καὶ καθὼς ἐφορέσαμεν τὴν εἰκόνα τοῦ χοϊκοῦ, φορέσομεν καὶ τὴν εἰκόνα τοῦ ἐπουρανίου.

Peter Jones rightly reads 1 Corinthians 15 as a refutation of Paganism in the church, writing that the central verse of his argument, 1 Corinthians 15:45, shows that Paul is not making "an extended comparison of sinful humanity with glorified humanity."[33] Instead, in context he reads verse 45 as a clear allusion to prelapsarian humanity, using the word, ψυχή neutrally. Here then, Adam is not the first sinner (as in the sense of verse 22), but rather is the first human. So, the meaning of this key verse in the text becomes, "first the physical, then the spiritual." If his use of ψυχή were not neutral, it would raise the issue that perhaps Paul is "stating programmatically that God condones the Fall as a necessary 'first' event"[34] and this he rejects. But I think Jones may be too quick here. While Jones argues well for the neutrality of ψυχή in verse 45 and also ψυχικός in verse 46, still this soulish existence cannot reach out to God nor can it live for God. It may be neutral ("of the earth") or even perfect in that it has no taint of sin. Yet, the use of "soulish," even in a prelapsarian sense, still demands such a soulish human cannot receive the things of God (1 Corinthians 2:14) and must first die (1 Corinthians 15:44). Is it possible that these verses, while refuting (proto-) Gnostic ideas of an evil creation, might still admit to a certain necessity of evil arising in the context of the world as created by God, though it was created perfect? I think that is exactly what Paul is teaching us here. Evil is the intrinsic problem, an intruder, that arose of a subordinate-metaphysical necessity out of God's good creation.

EVIL & SUFFERING: GOD'S INSTRUMENTAL SOLUTION

>"Be it known unto you, O unhappy and rebellious Mansoul, that the great King Shaddai, my master, has sent me to you with a commission," and he showed them his broad seal, "to reclaim you as his own. And he has commanded me, in case you yield to my summons, to bring this message to you as if you were my friends or brothers. But he also has said that if after summoning you to submit, you still rebel, we should endeavor to *take you by force*."[35](emphasis mine)

---

33. Jones, "Paul Confronts Paganism in the Church," 720. This is distinct from verse 22 which reads, "For as in Adam all die, so also in Christ all shall be made alive" which is a soteriological contrast. Rather in verse 45, "So also it is written, 'The first man, Adam, became a living soul.' The Last Adam became a life-giving spirit." Paul offers a cosmological distinction with "ψυχή" being used in distinct ways.

34. Jones, "Paul Confronts Paganism in the Church," 720.

35. Bunyan, *The Holy War*, 56.

PART II: The Testing of a Theodicy

—John Bunyan

I want to show here that Evil & Suffering is not only the intrinsic problem God chose to face in order to accomplish his ultimate ends, but it is also the instrumental means he uses to destroy Evil & Suffering.

Certainly God can destroy evil powers or evil people, and thwart evil plans. But can God rescue his people *from evil* by coercive force? I propose that it may be the case that he cannot and that this is consonant with the whole of Revelation and biblical history. Romans 5:10 says, "while we were enemies we were reconciled to God by the death of his Son." I suggest that it might be appropriate to amend Bunyan to read, "if after summoning you to submit, you still rebel, we should endeavor to *suffer* that *Mansoul* might be set free." It is in the Cross that we witness God's response to evil and his desire to free his people from evil. This *crucial* act of God in response to our enslavement to sin might be summarized this way: Evil & Suffering is destroyed by Evil & Suffering and that it may be the case that Evil & Suffering cannot be destroyed *for his people* by coercive force. In this section, I hope to offer evidence that this might be an accurate statement of reality.

Stated in this way, this strikes many as unusual. Still the basic idea, evil is corrosive of evil, is often perceived to be generally true even apart from biblical considerations. Aristotle, considering the kind and extent of problems that people face with their temper noted, "for evil destroys even itself, and if it is complete becomes unbearable."[36] That is, all possible characteristics of temper could not appear in one person, for if they did, some of them would be destroyed by the others, so that it is impossible that every kind of bad temper could exist in one person. His principle, whether or not the reader is apt to agree with his logic in regard to temper, is that evil corrodes evil. Some evils destroy other kinds of evils. His principle is correct.

That God did use sin to destroy sin is the perspective of John Piper in his new book, *Spectacular Sins and Their Global Purpose in the Glory of Christ* in which Chapter 8 is entitled: "Judas Iscariot, the Suicide of Satan, and the Salvation of the World: How God Conquered Sin through Sin."[37] It is through his sovereign and instrumental use of sin, that God destroys sin—even the betrayal of Christ by Judas. God conquers sin by using it against itself.

In this section and the next I will examine biblical texts which relate particularly to suffering and to redemption. While no single passage requires that it is the case that Evil & Suffering destroys Evil & Suffering, I believe that the constellation of texts, taken together, strongly endorse this understanding, and show that this proposal is biblically sound. These texts will also show that this perspective sheds light on God's work in

---

36. Aristotle, *Nicomachean Ethics*, 4.5, ¶4.

37. Piper, *Spectacular Sins*, 53. Early in his book he also writes, "First, we see the general pattern that turns up over and over in the Bible, namely, that God's saving victory for his people often comes through sin and suffering" (45). God destroys Evil & Suffering by Evil & Suffering.

and through suffering in order to bring about the Era of Conforming-Freedom for his people, in which evil is no more.

The central point of history is the Cross; the center of Christ's work is his suffering.[38] This is a theme for Jürgen Moltmann throughout his work and one with which I agree. In one place he writes, "Jesus, the crucified, cannot be understood without suffering for the unredeemed condition of the world."[39] This is the core of Christ's mission without which his incarnation makes no sense and the Kingdom does not come.[40] I believe we should listen to him when he speaks in regard to the deep and critical entanglement of God and suffering. And if it is the case that Moltmann is correct in this, we should see an emphasis in Scripture that weights Christ's death heavily in comparison to his incarnation and resurrection. Hints of this can be seen in Paul in 1 Corinthians 2:2 when he writes, "for I determined to know nothing among you except Jesus Christ, and Him crucified" and in the Gospel accounts in which the narrative of Christ's birth and resurrection is given briefer treatment than the events of the night of his death. Of course it would be foolish to call his incarnation, or his death, or his resurrection more important than any of the others, but I suggest that it is the case that his death is central and it may have the greatest weight in this one concern: eradicating evil for his people. In this context, Jonathan Edwards writes that it was the death of Christ that eviscerated Satan:

> And yet it was principally by means of those sufferings that he conquered and overthrew his enemies. . . . The devil had, as it were, swallowed up Christ, as the whale did Jonah; but it was deadly poison to him; he gave him a mortal wound in his own bowels. He was soon sick of his morsel, and was forced to do by him as the whale did by Jonah. To this day he is heart-sick of what he then swallowed as his prey.[41]

So also John Piper wrote, "So it is with Christ. The Lion of Judah, the Root of David, has conquered sin (Hebrews 1:3; 1 Corinthians 15:56) and death (2 Timothy

---

38. Of course, the suffering cannot be divorced from his victory of his resurrection, but that victory was achieved through his substitutionary atonement when he became sin for his people that they might become his righteousness.

39. Moltmann, *Crucified God*, 101. He says elsewhere that a person must grow to perceive "that the history of the world is the history of God's suffering" (*The Trinity and the Kingdom*, 4). Moltmann's emphasis on suffering is not always welcome so he is not quoted here as a representative of what all agree upon, but rather as an insightful theologian whose observations may be of value without ingesting his whole program, including panentheism.

40. Bonhoeffer writes, "God lets himself be pushed out of the world on to the cross. He is weak and powerless in the world, and that is precisely the way, the only way, in which he is with us and helps us" (Bonhoeffer, *Letters and Papers from Prison*, 360). This may be a shocking statement to some. The point is that God's help comes to us in one way: the power of the weakness of suffering. I find myself in fundamental agreement and believe that this position is in agreement with the presentation of Scripture as I hope to demonstrate.

41. In his doctrinal sermon, "The Excellencies of Christ," on the *Collected Works of Jonathan Edwards CD*, in the section, "In His Sacrificial Death," section 7.

1:10; 1 Corinthians 15:25f., 56) and Satan (Hebrews 2:14f.; Colossians 2:15). And he did it when he took on the role of a Lamb and died."[42] This emphasis on the death of Christ does not diminish the whole of his work in the incarnation and resurrection, but rather I propose that the focus of the overthrow of evil is on his work of suffering *in distinction* from God's use of coercive-power.[43] Moreover, unlike Christ's life and resurrection, his suffering is not eternal. It had a purpose and an end. The end is the eschatological destruction of Evil & Suffering for God's people and that seems to be what he accomplished by his suffering.

I want to consider the meaning of the word and concept, "destroy," as it is used in connection with "suffering" or "evil" in New Testament texts in order to understand how Evil & Suffering may be used instrumentally to destroy Evil & Suffering. First, 2 Timothy 1:10 reads, "but now [salvation] has been revealed by the appearing of our Savior Christ Jesus, who *abolished death* and brought life and immortality to light through the gospel." Here Christ's appearing (ἐπιφάνεια) could indicate his incarnation or death, or his Kingdom—or all of his work together. I do not doubt that the author had all of these in mind to some extent, but the specific context of 2 Timothy is the author's suffering for the Gospel.[44] This first movement of the correspondence to Timothy is saturated with suffering as the focus of the work of Christ and his followers, so it is not at all without reason to take "Christ's appearing" as intended to emphasize his suffering and death. Now turning to the verb, καταργέω, it is well translated as "abolish" and it is a frequently used word in the New Testament (though not in the LXX).[45] Here the suffering of Christ is instrumentally used by God to destroy the effects of evil, particularly spiritual death.[46] Such instrumentality can also be seen

---

42. Piper, "Christ: The Lion and the Lamb."

43. In fact, the work of suffering can be considered an exercise of his power, and it works powerfully against evil. However, in the framing of the problem of evil, God's omnipotence is understood as his coercive-power to overthrow those who oppose him, not to cause suffering.

44. He cautions Timothy not to shrink from the painful difficulty of the task (verses 6, 7); he calls Timothy to suffering with himself (verse 8), he reminds him that he has been suffering constantly for the Gospel (verses 11, 12); he notes that all others have turned away because of the difficulty of the task (verses 17, 18); and in the second chapter calls him to suffering with three metaphors: soldier, farmer, and athlete (2:1–7); and finally he ends the section with the psalm in which his people are called to "die with him" (Christ) and "endure with him" (2:11, 12).

45. It is appropriate to read "abolish" or "destroy" though this word has a range of meanings, sometimes far weaker than "destroy." One of the weakest usages of καταργέω is in Romans 7:2, "For the married woman is bound by law to her husband while he is living; but if her husband dies, she is *released* from the law concerning the husband." If "released" was intended, and it makes sense in this context, it seems a somewhat strange use of καταργέω, for other words might seem a better choice, such as λύω which can mean to destroy (but more commonly mean, to loose). It is possible, following Galatians 5:4 "Κατηργήθητε ἀπὸ τοῦ χριστοῦ," that a better translation is "cut off," so NASB has, "severed from Christ." And so Romans 7:2 might read, "she is cut off from (the requirements of) the law concerning the husband." Perhaps. In any case, more than twenty (20) other New Testament usages fall well within the semantic domain, "destroy" and in context of 2 Timothy, such an understanding is wholly justified.

46. Death here is spiritual death, as opposed to mere physical death. See G. Knight III, *Pastoral Epistles*, 376 and also, Marshall, *Pastoral Epistles*, 707. Both emphasize that the work accomplished

in 1 John 3:8 which reads, "the Son of God appeared for this purpose, that He might destroy the works of the devil." Here, we find the verb corresponding to the noun of 2 Timothy, φανερόω, which translates, "appear." Like the 2 Timothy passage, the verb here does not specifically name Christ's suffering, but again the context is helpful to make what is implicit, explicit. The first use of this verb in 1 John is the introduction, "the Word of Life — the Life was made manifest" (verses 1b,2a), which strikes me as very parallel to "the Word was made flesh" of John 1:14. This seems to point to Christ's incarnation above all. But in the context of John 1, the author twice says that the one who appeared is the "Lamb of God"—the sacrifice. This suffering role of his incarnation deeply impressed John as the focus and meaning of his appearing. And also in the immediate context of 1 John 3 we read, "he appeared to take away sin" (verse 5). This again focuses on Christ's work of suffering. So, while this use of φανερόω does not explicitly point to his suffering and death, that does seem to be what the author intends to communicate to us in context. And the effect of the suffering of the Son of God in his appearing is to this purpose, "to destroy the works of the devil." The verb here is λύω and appears in the phrase, ἵνα λύσῃ τὰ ἔργα τοῦ διαβόλου. John, in his Gospel and epistles, uses λύω both to mean, loose, such as in John 1:27 (οὗ οὐκ εἰμὶ [ἐγὼ] ἄξιος ἵνα λύσω),[47] but also, to destroy, as in 2:19 (λύσατε τὸν ναὸν τοῦτον καὶ ἐν τρισὶν ἡμέραις ἐγερῶ αὐτόν). Here the context of 1 John demands the meaning, to destroy, which is without contention in the literature. So, his purpose in appearing is to destroy evil and that is, by contextual inference, his work of suffering. This is also the perspective of Hebrews 2:9-10, 14-15 which reads:

> But we see Jesus, who was made a little lower than the angels, now crowned with glory and honor because he suffered death, so that by the grace of God he might taste death for everyone. In bringing many sons to glory, it was fitting that God, for whom and through whom everything exists, should make the author of their salvation perfect through suffering. . . . Therefore, since the children share in flesh and blood, He Himself likewise also partook of the same, that through death He might render *powerless* him who had the power of death, that is, the devil, and might free those who through fear of death were subject to slavery all their lives.

The core phrase reads, ἵνα διὰ τοῦ θανάτου καταργήσῃ τὸν τὸ κράτος ἔχοντα τοῦ θανάτου. The verb here, καταργέω, now in the subjunctive mood, we have seen and considered in 2 Timothy 1 and its meaning is, to destroy.[48] The phrasing here is very interesting in that it is death which instrumentally destroys (the dominion of and the authority of) death. This is the testimony of Scripture to the singular work of Christ on

---

by suffering is the destruction of spiritual death, and also cite 1 Corinthians 15:26 to reinforce this.

47. The textual issue concerning ἐγω does not affect this discussion.

48. Harold Attridge (*Epistle to the Hebrews*, 92) agrees: "Christ's participation in 'flood and flesh' resulted in his death, whereby he achieved a decisive victory over and (καταργήσῃ) 'destroyed the Power' of the one who holds sway over death."

PART II: The Testing of a Theodicy

the Cross: Evil & Suffering destroys Evil & Suffering. That is, evil is not destroyed by the use of God's coercive-power, but by suffering—note here: his and ours.

I want to also consider Philippians 3:8–11:

> More than that, I count all things to be loss in view of the surpassing value of knowing Christ Jesus my Lord, for whom I have suffered the loss of all things, and count them but rubbish so that I may gain Christ, and may be found in Him, not having a righteousness of my own derived from the Law, but that which is through faith in Christ, the righteousness which comes from God on the basis of faith, that I may know Him and the power of His resurrection and the fellowship of His sufferings, being conformed to His death; in order that I may attain to the resurrection from the dead.

Here the author starts with the idea of loss and suffering which lead to knowing Christ. Then in verses 10, 11 he moves chiastically from resurrection to suffering, to death, to resurrection. This text links the themes of the work of Christ, including his resurrection, but with a specific, chiastic focus on his sufferings, and their effect on our conformity to him. The word destroy is not in this text, but it is clear that the "fellowship of His sufferings" and Christ's death have a destructive impact on the hold that all of Paul's past has on him (that which is "rubbish") and provide for him his future resurrection with Christ. It is by Christ's suffering that death is destroyed.

Jeremiah Burroughs (1599–1646) would take this truth which is shown in the Cross and apply it to our lives as well. In his classic, *The Rare Jewel of Christian Contentment*, he wrote:

> It is the way of God to work by contraries, to turn the greatest evil into the greatest good. . . . This is the way of God, he says, but every one does not understand it. . . . [RAS: He] brings grace out of sin, that is, makes use of sin to work furtherance of grace. . . . It is the way of God to bring all good out of evil, not only to overcome the evil, but to *make the evil work toward the good*. Now when the soul comes to understand this, it will take away our murmuring and bring contentment to our spirits.[49] (emphasis mine)

While "work toward the good" is not arguing that evil is corrosive of evil, Burroughs makes the case that evil carries the burden of bringing about God's ends for his people. His position is one that asserts that it is "the way of God" to work by contraries. It is not simply that God is overcoming evil, but that he is overcoming evil by using evil instrumentally, against itself. But as he acknowledges, this is often not understood by Christians and that lack of understanding results in the evil of discontentment with God. If he does not explicitly assert that Evil & Suffering destroys Evil & Suffering, Burroughs is still expressing something very like what I am proposing and with the strong application that an understanding of this fact would keep us from grumbling

---

49. Burroughs, *Rare Jewel of Christian Contentment*, 48.

when we are suffering. Is not the issue of discontentment and complaining very much related to the problem of evil? Does not the weight of evil tempt us to speak evil against God—something Job was tempted to do in his suffering, but did not do?

While these texts do not prove my case as a linear argument, I find that the possibility that Evil & Suffering destroys Evil & Suffering is not only consistent with the text, but possibly the best understanding of it.[50] Moreover, with Burroughs, it makes good sense of many texts which associate joy and contentment in the context of trials, persecutions, and suffering. If we understand (and trust) that God is using Evil & Suffering to destroy Evil & Suffering, then not only will we refuse to be discontent, but we will know joy. This joy is the not-yet-seen hope of Romans 8 which erupts in the middle of suffering. Consider James 1:2–3 as an example: "Consider it all joy, my brethren, when you encounter various trials, knowing that the testing of your faith produces endurance." This text echoes Romans 5:1–5 which traces the path from suffering to hope because of God's Spirit. In fact, this idea resonates with material found in almost every New Testament work. Evil & Suffering is not only the problem, but they are producing in us, and in God's universe, a creation without Evil & Suffering. Now discontentment is not only precluded by order of God, but joy is produced as we see God's miraculous work of turning evil against itself!

It is also my understanding that this is the perspective of the Garden account. When Genesis tells us about Adam and Eve's rebellion against God, it states that God met them in the Garden along with the Serpent. First, God cursed the Serpent and then in Genesis 3:15, he declared that there would be an ongoing war between God's willful-creatures and the Serpent, "And I will put enmity between you and the woman, and between your seed and her seed; he shall bruise you on the head, and you shall bruise him on the heel." This verse in Genesis, which has been called the proto-evangelion, is interpreted in Romans 16:20 as the victory of Christ over Satan, "I will soon crush Satan under your feet."[51] This was prophetically accomplished by the suffering of

---

50. This is distinct from the position of N. T. Wright who argues for forgiveness as the tool to destroy evil. Of the critical role of forgiveness in "cutting the rope" that binds evil to our souls, he writes, "When we understand forgiveness, flowing from the work of Jesus and the Spirit, as the strange, powerful thing it really is, we begin to realize that God's forgiveness of us, and our forgiveness of others, is the knife that cuts the rope by which sin, anger, fear, recrimination and death are still attached to us. Evil will have nothing to say at the last, because the victory of the cross will be fully implemented" (*Evil and the Justice of God*, 164–5).

51. In Romans 16:20, Paul is reflecting on Genesis 3:15 (Schreiner, *Romans*, and John Murray, *Epistle to the Romans*, 237) in regard to the eschatological fate of Satan (Dunn, *Romans*, 905) or the fate of the contemporary schismatics of verse 17 (Cranfield and Sanday, *A Critical and Exegetical Commentary on the Epistle to the Romans*, 803). I would agree with Schreiner that the fate of both is coterminous (*Romans*, 805). The deepest difficulty with this text is Paul's choice of verb. The Hebrew uses the less aggressive Hebrew word, "bruise," (@wv), to refer to what the Serpent does to the Seed and the Seed to the Serpent. But this verb is strengthened by Paul to "crush" (συντρίβω), and he is perhaps also reflecting on Psalm 91:13 which speaks of "trampling the serpent" (sm;r"). It is interesting to note that Paul is not following a usage of the LXX, which chose the rather odd word, τηρέω (which usually means something like "keep" or "obey" as in 1 Samuel 15:11 and Ezra 8:29). The LXX seems to

PART II: The Testing of a Theodicy

Christ and called a victory. Yet in some way, the author of Romans perceives that it will have its telos, "under our feet." His people are to share Christ's sufferings and victory. This is similar to what Paul indicated earlier in Romans 8:17 when he wrote, "if indeed we suffer with Him so that we may also be glorified with Him." Suffering and victory are closely related. Turning again to Genesis, God declared to the woman that suffering was in store for her as well: "in pain you shall bring forth children." So, 1 Timothy 2:15 reads: "but women will be saved through [the suffering of] childbearing." While this is a most problematic passage, I strongly suspect that this is a soteriological interpretation of Genesis 3:16 and does not refer to the saving of any singular woman by the labor of childbirth and delivery, or even women in general. Rather, I understand it with George W. Knight III and others to be an allusion to the coming of the Messiah through the suffering of childbirth from Eve until Mary.[52] Suffering is not only the effect, but the instrumental means to victory, though even if my understanding does not stand, we are still left with the bare assertion of the writer of 1 Timothy, that suffering is closely allied to salvation and so to the destruction of evil. Returning once more to Genesis, God declared to Adam that the work he previously enjoyed and was created to do, would be filled with suffering, until his own non-redemptive death.[53] In all three cases (including that of Adam), the path for God's people is now suffering. It seems noteworthy that the very narrative that introduces sin into God's creation, introduces the rudiments of the idea that God will use Evil & Suffering instrumentally, at least in the cases of the Seed and the woman, to eventually bring an end to Evil & Suffering.

In the previous chapter, I recognized God's freedom in regard to creation. Now, having created, how free is God in regard to salvation? Of Aquinas's understanding, John Milbank wrote, "the actual means of incarnation and atonement adopted for our salvation were not absolutely necessitated, they were nonetheless 'convenient,' fitting, supremely suitable for this purpose. They possessed the necessity, in Aquinas's

---

have badly misunderstood the intention of the text (Schreiner, *Romans*, 804).

52. Some, including George W. Knight III (*Pastoral Epistles*, 144–48) and Irenaeus (*Against Heresies*, 5.19.1–2), link this text closely with Genesis 3:15 and understand this to indicate the coming of the Messiah, but this position is disputed. Philip Towner understands this to be a teaching that encourages women not to forgo or terminate pregnancy in a radical exercise of their new found freedom in Christ (*Letters to Timothy and Titus*, 233–5). While Marshall notes that σῴζω consistently refers to salvation from sin in the Pauline Epistles he also rejects any allusion to a Messianic understanding of Genesis 3:15. Instead, he understands this as a circumstantial reference to their role (non-instrumental) with a possible link to Galatians 3:16 (468–70). However good reasons exist for taking this position, including the fact that the salvation referred to in this text is rightly taken spiritually and διὰ τῆς τεκνογονίας is well taken as instrumental. One could also note the woman of Revelation 12, who is a representative of God's people, giving birth to the Messiah as a support of the understanding I propose.

53. I want to observe here the curse of Adam as a possible counter example to my argument. Unlike the case of the Seed and the Woman, I see no indication that Adam's suffering has any instrumental purpose: "by the sweat of your face you shall eat bread." This is a change from the blessing of giving humanity all of the seed bearing plants and fruit bearing trees from which people could eat without labor. This curse of the "adamah" (the clay) seems to have no vector pointing to the destruction of evil. This is worth further consideration.

own illustration . . . of traveling, most conveniently, or appropriately, for example, on horseback."[54] This and his extended argument are compelling. No one should desire to bind God's arm or pretend that she can do so. But there are hints in the text that God's freedom was exercised simultaneously[55] in his decrees to create and to save. It is not a limit on God to suggest that something about how he desired to create determined, within his character and goals, what means were fitting for salvation. So from our temporal perspective, viewing creation and salvation as an unfinished project, suffering as the means for salvation is necessary. Christ himself told us that his suffering was necessary in this sense. In Luke 24:25–27 we read:

> And He said to them, "O foolish men and slow of heart to believe in all that the prophets have spoken! Was it not necessary for the Christ to suffer these things and to enter into His glory?" Then beginning with Moses and with all the prophets, He explained to them the things concerning Himself in all the Scriptures.

The point is not that Christ was quoting a single passage as a proof-text, but rather he understood that in this single passage the whole of the Old Testament is fulfilled in his necessary suffering and death. That is, our sin did not make only judgment necessary (it did), but it made Christ's suffering necessary. And by this suffering he enters into his glory which includes the glorification of his people (Romans 8:17, 2 Thessalonians 1:12). In order to be brought into this glory with him, Evil & Suffering must be destroyed for his people and Christ has done this for them. Among the texts he must have opened to them were the suffering-servant passages in Isaiah 42–53. In Isaiah 53:4, it is written, "Surely our griefs He Himself bore, and our sorrows He carried; yet we ourselves esteemed Him stricken, smitten of God, and afflicted." Isaiah is typical of all prophecy in this: suffering characterized Christ's work. And, as a corollary, suffering evil characterizes God's plan to destroy Evil & Suffering for his people. Theologians as diverse as Marilyn McCord Adams,[56] Jürgen Moltmann,[57] and Henri

---

54. Milbank and Pickstock, *Truth in Aquinas*, 60–61. He well adds, using Thomistic terms like *proportia*, *harmonia*, and *ordinato*: "while according to the bare logic of omnipotence, God could have redeemed his people in another way, the aesthetic fittingness of the way actually chosen reflects the way in which the eternal divine Logos itself, in its free compulsion and compelled freedom, is most adequately characterized as the eminent realization of beautiful *proportio*" (63).

55. Simultaneously: let this word of temporal accommodation stand here, in the sense of "decrees." Of course decrees are in fact an accommodation of sorts in and of themselves, for they are only our reach to understand the ways of God. These decrees included creation and salvation, and these were both prior to the act of creation.

56. While the focus of Adams's theodicy is "the incommensurate Good that God is" (Adams, *Horrendous Evil*, 189), the emphasis is God's identification and suffering in Christ (166).

57. Moltmann wrote, "The death of Jesus on the cross is the centre of all Christian theology. It is not the only theme of theology, but it is in effect entry to its problems and answers on earth" (*The Crucified God*, 204).

PART II: The Testing of a Theodicy

Blocher[58] make the Cross and Christ's sufferings the focus of theodicy, so also they make suffering the center of their response to evil.

It is no surprise that the New Testament constantly reflects this truth from the Old Testament. In Acts 3:18 Peter declares to the crowd in Jerusalem, "But the things which God announced beforehand by the mouth of all the prophets, that His Christ would suffer, He has thus fulfilled." Also in Paul, through Luke in Acts 17:2–3 we read, "And according to Paul's custom, he went to them, and for three Sabbaths reasoned with them from the Scriptures, explaining and giving evidence that the Christ had to suffer and rise again from the dead, and saying, 'This Jesus whom I am proclaiming to you is the Christ.'" Not only was Christ's suffering necessary, but this suffering was God's sufficient and perfect victory over evil. So, it would seem, Christ's suffering destroys Evil & Suffering. Also, Colossians 2:15 reads, "When He had disarmed the rulers and authorities, He made a public display of them, having triumphed over them through Him." Here is a positive way to say the same thing: "he triumphed" (θριαμβεύω) over Evil & Suffering (evil powers) by his submission to Evil & Suffering in the Cross.

This is God's plan—to suffer, rather than use coercive-power. And in God's plan, Christ's suffering is normative for his people, calling them to suffer with him. It is exemplary, defining the way God fights this battle. And the battle continues: godly suffering is also part of the battle to finally destroy evil for God's people. Sinclair Ferguson made note of this in his book, *Children of the Living God*. He observed that throughout the Bible, tribulation, suffering and discipline are the road to freedom. And this freedom is like God's own, a freedom from the possibility of evil. He specifically cites Hebrews 12, which begins with Christ's example of suffering to set his people free, and continues with the suffering of his people, and concludes with the shaking of creation so that those things which cannot be shaken may remain.[59] In other words, the end which God intends for his people requires the suffering of Christ, in order to do the work of redemption, and continues with the suffering of God's people to finish the work that Christ began—the ultimate destruction of evil.

Peter Kreeft, a Roman Catholic theologian writes of this in very picturesque language:

> Calvary is judo. The enemy's own power is used to defeat him. Satan's craftily orchestrated plot, rolled along according to plan by his agents Judas, Pilate, Herod, and Caiaphas culminated in the death of God. And this very event, Satan's conclusion, was God's premise. Satan's end was God's means. It saved the world. Christians celebrate the greatest evil and the greatest tragedy of all time as Good Friday.[60]

---

58. In *Evil and the Cross*, Blocher writes, "at the cross evil is conquered as evil" (*Evil and the Cross*, 132).

59. Ferguson, *Children of the Living God*, 114–8.

60. Kreeft, *Making Sense Out of Suffering*, 132.

I like his phrase, "Calvary is judo."[61] The worst evil and the most terrible suffering in all time or space was turned back on itself. And God continues the work through his people—not of redemption, but of "mopping up." Kreeft writes, "All of our suffering can become part of his work, the greatest work ever done, the work of salvation, of helping to win for those we love, eternal joy. How? This can be done on one condition: that we believe. For faith is not just a mental choice within us; it is a transaction with him."[62] That is, when we stand up against evil, and receive its blows, suffering with faith in the one who suffered first and most, we participate in the work. Evil & Suffering—even ours—destroys Evil & Suffering. This is not redemptive; that was accomplished once and for all at the Cross. Rather it is a fellowship with Christ that in some way participates with him as partners in the Gospel and partners in destroying evil.

Paul seems to indicate this same idea when he writes in 2 Corinthians 4:17, "For our light and momentary sufferings are producing for his people an eternal weight of glory far beyond all comparison." It seems that in the suffering of his people, they partner with God in bringing about human glorification in Christ. In Christ's death his people are called to pick up their cross daily with him; God seems to indicate that he is destroying evil and bringing about their glorification. So, F.F. Bruce writes of this text: "It is not merely that the glory is a compensation for the suffering; it actually grows out of the suffering. . . . There is an organic relation between the two for the believer as surely as there was for our Lord."[63] Suffering is linked to future human glorification which is accomplished by the destruction of the enemy on the Cross: the destruction of evil.

Taken together, for no one text can bear the glorious weight I am proposing, these biblical examples seem to argue that it is possible to understand the text in this way: Evil & Suffering destroys Evil & Suffering in order to create a people for God. These texts may also give particular significance to the image of death swallowed up

---

61. Paul Fiddes, reflecting on Barth's *das Nichtige* suggests something similar to "judo" when he writes, Barth "argues that the end-point of sinning is non-being (das Nichtige), and because only Christ is fully identified with human sinfulness only he goes right to the end of the dark pathway of sin and encounters total non-being there. Non-being takes its prey by engulfing the sinner, so that sin is killed. Thus God uses *das Nichtige* to serve him, wiping out the sin which is an obstacle between man and God. In an ingenious move therefore, God employs the punishment for sin as the means to abolish sin" (*The Creative Suffering of God*, 264). To be fair to Fiddes, this is not his whole argument and as a whole, I do not agree, for he continues, "Barth is, nevertheless, surely right to find the center of the atonement in the cancelling of sin, rather than the placating of God's wrath." There is no reason either from analogy or Scripture to suspect that the center of the atonement is not a symphony of intents and effects, one of which must be propitiation. However, atonement theory is beyond the scope of this project, as much as I would like to pursue this.

62. Kreeft, *Making Sense*, 136.

63. Bruce, *Epistle of Paul to the Romans*, 168. Also, and not surprisingly, Moltmann, wrote, "The God of freedom, the true God, is therefore not recognized by his power and glory in the world and in the history of the world, but through his helplessness and his death on the scandal of the cross of Jesus" (*Crucified God*, 195)

PART II: The Testing of a Theodicy

in victory in 1 Corinthians 15:54–55: "But when this perishable will have put on the imperishable, and this mortal will have put on immortality, then will come about the saying that is written, 'DEATH IS SWALLOWED UP in victory.' 'O DEATH, WHERE IS YOUR VICTORY? O DEATH, WHERE IS YOUR STING?' " This is an important use of Isaiah 25:8 by the author of 1 Corinthians. When God's victory is complete, evil ("death") will be gone for God's people. It will not be just out-of-sight or defeated or something we can now deal with by perseverance; evil will be beyond direct interaction with God's people. This may also be what is intended in the image of Revelation 19:3. Here the earth opens up and all sin and sinners and demons are received. It is an image of God's victory in which evil, while not extinguished, for "the smoke from her rises forever and ever," is wholly gone *for his people*. Evil is banished from the experience of his people forever.

The Cross overturns our sense of power and the Cross sheds light on God's revealed work throughout history. God is not just powerful, but omnipotent, exercising his *potentia ordinata* and *potentia absoluta* so that while he can do anything, he can only do what is consistent with his decrees. So it is with the exercise of his power in regard to evil. This can be seen in Acts 10 where Paul and Silas are released from prison. The Philippian jailor was not impressed with the power of the earthquake (nor did Paul and Silas boast of serving a God of great power), but rather by the God who empowered Paul and Silas to joyfully and willingly suffer. It was this power that God's Spirit used to draw the jailor and his whole household to life. In God's decree, it is not coercive-power that destroys evil, but the power of suffering while trusting God, so that it is Evil & Suffering that is powerfully used by God to destroy Evil & Suffering.

If this is the case, it may help us to wrestle with the classic problem of evil, which is usually construed to have three propositions: God is all powerful, God is all-good, and evil exists in God's world. But if Evil & Suffering is used instrumentally by God to destroy Evil & Suffering, then I would suggest that the purposes of an omni-good and omni-powerful God can be discerned with a bit more clarity. No longer can the omni-good God be "convicted" of withholding his coercive-power in the face of evil, but we begin to understand that it is rather Evil & Suffering, and not coercive-power, that is effective against evil. By enduring Evil & Suffering and calling his people to the same, God is doing all that can and must be done to destroy Evil & Suffering, and our belief in the primary effectiveness of coercive-power to destroy Evil & Suffering may be wrong. The result, if this is correct, is that holding to these propositions about God does not lead to pragmatic despair or require that we acquiesce to an unknowable mystery, but rather the result can be hope and even joy. Evil & Suffering is the God ordained instrument used against evil itself.

Does suffering destroy evil or is it simply used by God to accomplish his goals? An overview of 1 Peter in regard to suffering

> Moral evil does not come out of moral goodness, but good does come out of evil and error.[64]
>
> —F.R. Tennant

> For the eyes of the Lord are toward the righteous, and his ears attend to their prayer, but the face of the Lord is against those who do evil.
>
> —1 Peter 3:12

It is difficult to face suffering when suffering seems to testify to the fact that God has forgotten us. But Peter understands this quote from the Psalm 34:15–16 in the context of the experience of the suffering of God's people, not as a promise of avoiding pain.[65] He is calling his people to trust God when pain comes into our lives. But is it the case that Evil & Suffering is used instrumentally by God *to destroy* Evil & Suffering? We have already seen that suffering was, in fact, the chosen method of God to defeat Satan and redeem a people in Christ; Christ's instrumental suffering actually destroyed death *for his people*. But perhaps the Cross was an exception. Or is it also the case that our suffering contributes to the battle to destroy Evil & Suffering? I believe it is and that the biblical witness is consistent in indicating this reading: Evil & Suffering destroys Evil & Suffering. Particularly, I think 1 Peter is helpful in seeing that this is the case.[66]

One of the key threads (perhaps the golden thread) woven into the letter of 1 Peter is suffering. The example is the suffering of Christ and the application is our

---

64 Tennant, *Philosophical Theology*, 194.

65. The context for 3:12 is "but even if you should suffer" (verse 14), and "For Christ also died for sins once for all" (verse 18). Peter is not claiming immunity but rather that his complete confidence is in God in the middle of suffering and a confidence that God sees all and is just.

66. Let me address issues of authorship and date on which scholarship is divided. Repeated citations by Polycarp and Clement make it difficult to place the text of 1 Peter outside of the latter part of the first century (Kelly, *Commentary on the Epistles of Peter and of Jude*, 28). This upper bound is generally accepted, so that, if it was not written by Peter, it was likely to have been written by a apostolic associate, perhaps Sylvanus, Paul's companion (ibid., 33). A lower bound for the date would place it after Sylvanus arrived in Rome with Paul (1 Peter 5:12) in the mid-60's, prior to Peter's death (Davids, *The First Epistle of Peter*, 10). It is a first century document and could have been written by Peter or one associated with him. In regard to authorship, Paul Achtemeier tentatively concludes it is the "anonymous authorship of a pseudonymous letter" (*1 Peter*, 43), but Davids (*The First Epistle of Peter*, 12) sees no reason not to accept Peter as the author. Similarly, Wayne Grudem writes, "there is no compelling evidence to keep us from accepting what the early church universally believed . . . 1 Peter was written by Peter" (*First Epistle of Peter*, 33). And E.G. Selwyn has written one of the most thorough assessments of authorship and he comes to rest on Peter because "the attestation of [RAS: Petrine authorship] is widespread, early, and clear" (ibid., 38). Ultimately, for the purposes of this project, neither authorship nor date is as important as canonical recognition, which is stipulated. I will refer to the author as Peter in deference to the ascription in 1 Peter 1:1.

PART II: The Testing of a Theodicy

suffering. In making this example and application, Peter seems to be drawing an instrumental connection as well: as Christ's suffering destroyed evil, so also does the suffering of his people. Again, for sake of clarity, I am not making any claim about human redemptive suffering—redemption was accomplished by Christ alone. Rather, I am considering the idea that as much as Christ finished redemption, he also left something for his people to complete, "that which is lacking in Christ's afflictions."[67] It seems that God's people have been given a role in completing his work over evil—and evil which, though "finished" on the Cross, continues to haunt our world and our souls today. This is God's grace to us, as it was to Job.

Peter's introductory paragraph (one unbroken sentence in chapter 1 from verse 3 to 12) recognizes this suffering as a key motivation for Peter to write to the exiles. He expresses this in 1:6 when he writes, "In this you greatly rejoice, even though now for a little while, if necessary, you have been distressed by various trials."[68] I want to trace this theme, to which Peter will return in almost every section of his letter, and understand how Peter counsels his "exiles" to understand these trials and the suffering which they are enduring. In this introductory word (verses 8–9), Peter counsels them to understand these trials in the context of the overwhelming joy of their salvation: "you greatly rejoice with joy inexpressible and full of glory obtaining the outcome of your faith, the salvation of your souls."[69] Then in 1:11 Peter ties this counsel into the suffering of Christ, predicted by the Spirit of Christ in the prophets, which accomplished the "glories to follow." In context these glories are Christ's glory but also salvation for his people. Yet Peter does not tell us how this transaction was accomplished. He does not make explicit the instrumental relationship between "suffering" and salvation—except that it exists.

His first argument is that suffering is the calling of his people. In 2:18–20 Peter offers a challenging example of suffering as a slave—a situation not uncommon in the early church.

> Servants, be submissive to your masters with all respect, not only to those who are good and gentle, but also to those who are unreasonable. For this finds favor, if for the sake of conscience toward God a person bears up under sorrows when suffering unjustly. For what credit is there if, when you sin and are harshly treated, you endure it with patience? But if when you do what is right and suffer for it you patiently endure it, this finds favor with God.

---

67. I will consider Colossians 1:24 in greater detail in chapter 6.

68. While NASB has been quoted throughout, it is particularly to be preferred here over the NIV and others in regard to the phrase "εἰ δέον ἐστίν" which is here translated as "if necessary" instead of the NIV's, "you may have had to." However, I do not think the force of this phrase carries any relationship to the necessity of evil as I addressed it earlier in this chapter, a subordinate-metaphysical necessity, but rather the necessity of perseverance in the evil that God sends, necessarily. That is, Peter suggests that is necessary to fellowship with Christ in sufferings in order to rejoice in sufferings.

69. Karen H. Jobes (*1 Peter*, 93) agrees that the reason for joy is an understanding of their salvation.

Here he makes it clear that suffering is to be for righteousness, not unrighteousness, and to be effective (to receive "credit"), it must be done "for sake of conscience toward God." This phrase is somewhat cryptic: "διὰ συνείδησιν θεοῦ." It is translated variously into different English translations in an attempt to capture the sense of Peter's idea, but it is illusive. This same noun for conscience appears again in 1 Peter 3:16 as the ground upon which his people suffer—in good conscience before God. So also, in concept, though not the word, we find conscience in 1 Peter 2:11–12, 3:9, 4:3, 4:15 and others. It seems to be a principle: we should suffer only in the grace of obedience. This will be important for where Peter is going as he drives towards the purpose of suffering. But short of telling us the purpose, he first makes it clear that it is a calling. 1 Peter 2:21 states, "For you have been called for this purpose, since Christ also suffered for you, leaving you an example for you to follow in His steps." Peter declares that suffering, whatever the purpose, is a clear calling for his people. They must follow Christ's example, regardless of the circumstances in which they find themselves.

This idea that his people must endure, suffering patiently within the context in which each person finds herself, includes not only slaves of harsh masters (2:18–25) but also wives of non-Christian husbands (3:1–6, which seems to include not only non-Christians, but also the class of arbitrary, but godly, husbands, for Peter then uses Sarah's obedience to Abraham as an example). In both cases believers suffered unjustly while trusting God. The point is this: this kind of suffering accomplishes something great. One of the things accomplished is that God is glorified in the trust that his people put in him. In the case of slaves such suffering results in "grace" before God for the slave.[70] In the case of wives, the non-Christian husband may be won for the Kingdom, but always the wife will grow in beauty and trust in God. Sandwiched in the middle (2:21–25) is the primary example of Christ who "entrusted himself to him who judges justly." In each case, it is a key that Christ, slaves, and wives, unjustly treated, trusted God and something happened—the destructive intent of this evil was undone; even destroyed. Yes, slaves were killed, Christ died on the Cross, and Sarah was given away to two heathen kings by her husband. But also, Christ glorified God and evil was turned back on itself and destroyed. And so this also is this the case for God's people. Slaves are freed in God (though they may die), Christ is resurrected (death is vanquished), and Sarah (though she suffered humiliation) was the means of the Promise of God in the birth of Isaac. Instead of fighting evil, it is endured patiently with the result that evil is destroyed and freedom is gained from evil's intent upon us.

A second sub-theme in 1 Peter in regard to evil is the blessing that comes through enduring suffering without doing evil. In 3:9 Peter writes: "not returning evil for evil or insult for insult, but giving a blessing instead; for you were called for the very purpose that you might inherit a blessing." As before, the basis for this is the work

---

70. This revealing of God's glory or receiving of God's grace is a theme of this whole section which began in 2:11 and continues through 4:11. All of the admonition here in regard to suffering is within the context of how it can bring glory to God.

PART II: The Testing of a Theodicy

and example of Christ in 3:18. Let's begin with Christ's work, the example, and work forward to Peter's command to us. It is important to see first that Peter understood Christ's sufferings that put him in the position that he "made proclamation to the spirits now in prison" in 3:19. While this is indeed a problematic verse,[71] we need not discern anything more than the fact that Peter connected with the understanding of his audience (and ratified that understanding): Christ's submission to Evil & Suffering resulted in freedom for those who were not free until Christ's work was accomplished. His death destroyed the power that kept "them" in prison and he could then go and announce that freedom. Secondly, we see in 3:22 that as a result of his death, "angels and authorities and powers had been subjected to Him." So also here, we do not need to fully understand who Peter is speaking of as subject to Christ. We need only see Peter's clear claim that a reversal has been accomplished in Christ's suffering—evil lost and was destroyed. What was not subject to Christ before has now been crushed and brought under authority. This is the blessing that his people can hope for in obedience, too. It is the blessing of a world rightly ordered under Christ, with the powers of death, broken and crushed. So, it would seem that Peter is linking endurance of evil (a specific kind of obedience) to partnership in that great work. He expands on this in chapter 4 in the theme of fellowship in Christ's sufferings. In 4:1–2 Peter writes, "Therefore, since Christ suffered in his body, arm yourselves also with the same attitude, because he who has suffered in his body is done with sin. As a result, he does not live the rest of his earthly life for evil human desires, but rather for the will of God." Here Peter makes a connection between suffering and the destruction of sin in human lives and by so doing, evil as well ("he who has suffered in the body has done with sin"). The purifying effect of suffering seems to be related to the idea that suffering destroys evil—in this case that of his own people. Paul says something similar in Romans 6:5–8:

> For if we have become united with Him in the likeness of His death, certainly we shall also be in the likeness of His resurrection, knowing this, that our old self was crucified with Him, in order that our body of sin might be done away with, so that we would no longer be slaves to sin; for he who has died is freed from sin. Now if we have died with Christ, we believe that we shall also live with Him.

Suffering with Christ, the crucifixion of the old nature, results in victory over evil and sin. This principle is applied to all of creation in Romans 8, as we have already

---

71. This may refer to Christ's preaching through Noah's lips (Grudem, *First Epistle of Peter,* 158) or it may refer to Christ's triumph over the wicked men of Noah's generation, parallel to 3:21 over the "authorities" (Achtemeier, *1 Peter,* 245–6) or it could mean that Christ did descend into the holding place of the captives to declare freedom in his conquest of evil. In assessing these options, the "patience" of God (3:20) would weigh against Achtemeier here, but the symmetry with 3:21 (and other textual issues) are a strong argument. Yet, if Achtemeier is correct, it is still true that Christ's suffering of evil resulted in destruction of the power of evil in the realm of people and of the angels. And this is the point. We need not decide the historical reference to which Peter here refers, but only his intent to exalt the effect of Christ's work, which he is affirming.

seen. This is also reflected in the theme of overcoming (νικάω, to conquer) evil which frequently appears in the New Testament (John 16:33; Romans 12:21; 1 John 2:13; 4:4–5; 5:4–5;). While not explicit in such texts, other texts indicate that the theme of overcoming assumes a partnership with Christ in suffering which he taught us was the normal Christian's life. Christ announced in Luke 14:27, "Whoever does not carry his own Cross and come after Me cannot be My disciple" and in John 17:14, "I have given them Your word; and the world has hated them, because they are not of the world, even as I am not of the world." So also we read in 2 Timothy 3:12, "Indeed, all who desire to live godly in Christ Jesus will be persecuted." This is the same idea we read in 1 Peter 4:12–16 in which Peter emphasizes that human suffering is to "share in the sufferings of Christ." And as persecution, temptation, malicious speech, impugned motives, are suffered and his people do not show a lack of courage in obedience, then they shall conquer with him (2 Timothy 2:11–12).

Overcoming is also a key theme in the Revelation of John. In the opening letters to the Seven Churches, each includes a command to overcome (conquer, νικάω) and a promise for those who do. In every case the demand is to overcome through obedience in the context of suffering. In each of the seven letters to the seven churches, νικάω occurs once (except in the seventh letter where it occurs twice). In each case it occurs as a present active participle, the one who overcomes, or better, the one who conquers. The exception to this is the second occurrence in the seventh letter where it occurs in the indicative for which the subject is Christ. While νικάω can be a military or an athletic metaphor, here is more akin to the military metaphor because of the real possibility of death.[72] This is a battle to the death with Evil & Suffering. Further, in the central letter of the seven, the one to Thyatira, νικῶν is coordinated with another participle, τηρῶν (the one who keeps), hence, "the one who conquers and keeps." What we are to "keep" is the call to endure with patience the suffering work of Christ. In the context of John's writings, one might expect to keep either the "words" (John 5:24) or "commands" (John 14:21) of Jesus. It might even be considered a command to "keep" doing his miracles.[73] But this use here is somewhat exceptional in the greater context and I am inclined to understand this as his work of suffering since Christ is depicted in chapters 1–5 of Revelation as the "lamb who was slain" and the one who conquered by suffering. *So, to those in these churches who have conquered Evil & Suffering by patiently enduring, and not by battle or force or coercive-power, God awards eternal gifts.* In each letter, the gifts to the conquerors represent victory over sin (evil) and each recalls times of historic and biblical failure of God's people: the Garden, the desert wanderings, the failure of the Davidic Kingdom, and the failure of Temple worship and more. These failures are now set right (overcome) in Christ and somehow also in human conquering or overcoming. These texts help us to see that the victory over Evil

---

72. Aune, *Revelation*, 151.
73. Ibid., 209.

PART II: The Testing of a Theodicy

& Suffering may indeed come by patiently enduring the Evil & Suffering, and not by coercive-power.

This point is made even more clearly in Revelation 12:11, "and they overcame him [Satan] because of the blood of the Lamb and because of the word of their testimony, and they did not love their life even when faced with death." Here it seems that Satan is conquered by the suffering of those who trusted God. We are partners with God in the work of destroying Satan, through our suffering. This is destruction, not merely victory. Of this text, Peter Hicks writes, "We are called to share in casting him down. We are not just victims of the devil; we are his destroyers."[74] Indeed νικάω is a very strong term, which does not allow for anything less than "overcome" and may indicate, "destroy." G.K. Beale argues that "overcoming" here is not merely the basis, but also the instrumental means by which Satan is destroyed.[75] According to Osborne and also Kistemaker this does not leave room for merely "shaming" or "dishonoring" Satan, but the use of νικάω requires conquering.[76] And the means of destruction is enduring in the face of evil, for the second clause indicates that the means is specifically the suffering resulting from the perseverance in their testimony. So, perseverance in suffering is clearly used by God to destroy the enemy. Osborne agrees, writing, "the real basis of all spiritual victory is always the Cross rather than one's own strength" (also citing D.L. Barr).[77] Also Revelation 15:2a reads, "And I saw something like a sea of glass mixed with fire, and those who had been victorious over the beast and his image." This summary text reinforces John's assertion that evil is conquered, not survived or endured, and that the means of victory is their suffering. The participial use of νικάω references those who conquered in Revelation 13 by martyrdom. Though it appeared that the Beast conquered them (13:7), the Beast was conquered by them in their martyrdom (13:15). G.K. Beale makes an observation which enhances this understanding. He argues that the sea and fire of this verse are "always images respectively of judgment and evil" and that it is just here which is "the place where the Lamb has judged the beast."[78] If that is the case, then it is in and by evil that evil is judged and the saints are freed of their suffering. Our victory is revealed as Evil & Suffering conquers Evil & Suffering.

Returning to 1 Peter, it is this theme of fellowship with Christ that is not only compelling, but is key for Peter's argument; it is what he has been driving toward. And in 4:12–13 he writes: "Beloved, do not be surprised at the fiery ordeal among you, which comes upon you for your testing, as though some strange thing were happening to you; but to the degree that you share the sufferings of Christ, keep on rejoicing, so

---

74. Hicks, *Message of Evil & Suffering*, 121.
75. Beale, *Book of Revelation*, 664–5.
76. Osborne, *Revelation*, 475 and Kistemaker, *Revelation*, 364.
77. Osborne, *Revelation*, 476.
78. Beale, *Book of Revelation*, 789. He further adds, "That the saints are 'standing on the sea of glass's shows that they themselves have been involved in the battle against the sea beast" (791).

that also at the revelation of His glory you may rejoice with exultation." We are bound to Christ in the fellowship of suffering. Here again, as in chapter 1 where this section began, the concepts of "joy" and "glory" (4:13) appear (as they do in Romans 8). These are the anticipated fruits of the destruction of evil in suffering. And to conclude his theme, he tells those who resist Satan, enduring suffering, in 5:10, "After you have suffered for a little while, the God of all grace, who called you to His eternal glory in Christ, will Himself perfect, confirm, strengthen and establish you." Again Peter juxtaposes the idea of suffering with joy, grace, and glory in the closing, just as at the first introduction in chapter 1. These are the fruits of fellowship in Christ, sufferings which result from evil's destruction.

The argument of Peter seems to be that Christ's sufferings gained salvation for his people by conquering and destroying evil, and that his sufferings are normative for them as well. So human sufferings, while not accomplishing salvation, result in a special fellowship with Christ that is used to bring about a state of joy. This is contrasted with those who do not obey the gospel of God (4:17–18). Their judgment follows and they have no joy. Again, the outcome is different for God's people who resist evil (5:9) and suffer evil. God will allow his people to suffer ("for a little while," 1:6 and 5:10), but he will also restore us. It is in this context that Peter says in verse 11, "to him be the dominion." The suffering of Christ, and fellowship with him in suffering for the testimony of Jesus Christ, reveals and brings about God's dominion over evil—and brings to his people hope and joy, because evil is conquered in our suffering with Christ.

ON WHETHER GOD DOES OR COULD USE COERCIVE-POWER TO DESTROY EVIL & SUFFERING

> So a formally contradictory set is one from whose members an explicit contradiction can be deduced by the laws of logic. Is Mackie claiming that set A is formally contradictory? If he is, he's wrong.[79]
>
> —Alvin Plantinga

The very statement of the problem of evil as formulated by Epicurus makes explicit the intuitive sense that God, because he is omnipotent, could use coercive-power to solve our problem of evil. This intuitive sense is strong, yet it is not explicit in the problem. As Plantinga pointed out, the classical statement of the problem of evil is not formally contradictory as generally expressed. It could be altered to be formally contradictory and one way would be to add a fourth proposition that makes the claim that power is an effective means to destroy evil *for his people*. Again, I want to be clear that God has the ability to destroy evil as quickly as it appears within his creation, or even to create in such a way that it does not appear. But there is reason to suspect that were he to do

---

79. Plantinga, *God, Freedom, and Evil*, 14.

PART II: The Testing of a Theodicy

so, in the context of his character and goals, that use of power would not destroy evil *for his people*. Augustine touched on this when he wrote,

> Now would the devil have been overpowered by this most equitable of judgments if Christ had chosen to deal with him by power instead of justice? But *he postponed what he had the power to do, in order to do first what he had to do*; that is why he needed to be both God and man. . . . nor would we have imagined that he was preferring justice to power, but simply that he lacked power. . . . In this way the justice of humility was made more acceptable, seeing that the power of divinity could have avoided the humiliation if he had wanted to; and so by the death of one so powerful we powerless mortals have justice set before us and power promised us.[80]

Here I take Augustine's word "justice" and the "justice of humility" to refer to the justice accomplished by the "powerlessness" of Christ who suffered Evil & Suffering on the Cross. And I understand that Augustine answers the question of why God chose Evil & Suffering over coercive-power to conquer evil: it pleased him to do so for us. Yet, distinct from my proposal, it may seem that Augustine also says God could have used his power if it had pleased him to do so. Yet Augustine argues that God's choice, what he wanted, was limited by his character and goals: his desire to demonstrate his glory to powerless humanity by his restraint of power at the Cross. Ceding this as true, could it be the case that there be other reasons for God's action that are also consistent with his character and goals?

It is important here to say what I intend by words like omnipotence, power, and force. It is not useful, nor possible, to meaningfully separate God's omnipotence from his omni-goodness. When God acts in his goodness, he acts powerfully. When he acts in his power, it is a display of his goodness. I have previously discussed God's goodness as who he is (the Source of the Good) and everything he does.[81] Goodness flows from God in all of his acts. As the Source of all that is good, we know what is good because we observe God by his affect on his universe. So, also he is the source of all power and everything that acts is contingent upon God. But in regard to the problem of evil, and the possibility of God using his power and omnipotence, I am thinking about God's forceful acts, not simply his power. That is, God's power is always displayed, but his force, the sword, is used sparingly and tactically against evil. Yet God always acts powerfully against evil. The Cross and the resurrection could be considered God's most powerful act against evil. So Paul writes in 1 Corinthians 1:17–18: "For Christ did not send me to baptize, but to preach the gospel, not in cleverness of speech, so that the Cross of Christ would not be made void. For the word of the Cross is foolishness to those who are perishing, but to us who are being saved it is the power of God." In

---

80. Augustine, *Trinity,* 13.18. Emphasis mine.

81. This is defined in chapter 2 in the section, "Evil as a Privation of God's Goodness: Augustine," p. 74.

literature and song this phrase often becomes, "the power of the Cross." And it may be that this wonderful phrase, as true as it is, could lead us to forget that the Cross is "powerful" only because it was "suffering." It was not an expression of God's coercive-power in any usual sense. The greatest act of evil and betrayal and suffering was a great revelation of the power of God, but not his naked sword.

But we have an intuitive sense that God could and should snuff out Satan for his people by coercive force. In a certain sense, this *is* the problem of evil for his people. John Piper addresses:

> Have you ever wondered why God does not simply snuff Satan and his demons out of existence now? It is strange that God, with total sovereign rights over Satan, his archenemy, would allow him to do so much harm. God has the right and power to throw him into the lake of fire. . . . Is it because there is a chance the devil and his angels will repent? No. . . . God's aim is to magnify the glory of Christ through the gospel. In other words, God's purpose is to defeat Satan in a way that glorifies not only Christ's raw power, but also his superior beauty and worth and desirability. Christ could simply exert sovereign power and snuff Stan out. That would indeed glorify Christ's power. But it would not display so clearly the superior worth of Jesus over Satan. It would not display the transforming beauty and power of Christ's meekness and humility and lowliness and self-emptying love. The aim of the gospel is to put the glory of the crucified Christ on display.[82]

We do have a desire that God "simply snuff out Satan and his demons" and that this has not occurred is, in some ways, "the problem of evil." But God does not address this as we "desire." This is the message of Romans 3:25–26, "This was to demonstrate His righteousness, because in the forbearance of God He passed over the sins previously committed; for the demonstration, I say, of His righteousness at the present time, so that He would be just and the justifier of the one who has faith in Jesus." While we should be encouraged by this forbearance, it is just that forbearance that disturbs us and causes us to feel, in some measure, the problem of evil. But this text from Romans is telling us that God is glorified in patiently waiting and in the suffering of Christ. This is also the point of what Piper says, including that to wait and act, as God does act, results in his glorification in Christ. This is rightly said, but I do not agree that this is all that can be rightly said, nor does it diminish this truth to wonder if there is more to know. Since God's goal is to display his glory by redeeming his people and conforming them to the image of Christ (without the future possibility of corruption), it may be the case that suffering must be used to destroy evil, which is to accomplish more than the mere destruction of the agents of evil. And if this is the case, even the agents of evil become participants in the drama of redemption.

---

82. Piper, *God is the Gospel*, 113–4.

PART II: The Testing of a Theodicy

Clearly, when Satan became God's enemy, God could have crushed him. Clearly, when Adam rebelled, God could have started over. I say, clearly, not because I can prove it, but because it is an axiom of the problem of evil (omnipotence) and one that I and all Christians who wrestle with the issue stipulate. God created. God could destroy his creation. This includes foremost, rebels, whom he could destroy in perfect justice (a corollary of his goodness). Not only did God not do so, but it was good not to do so—because he did not. Yet, had God destroyed all and started over, evil would have been destroyed, but it would not have been destroyed *for his people*, which is a tautology if we no longer exist. Yet it is a tautology from which we may learn. Once we sin, we become evil and not simply a casualty. Of course, we could imagine that God would destroy evil before it could corrupt us, but that possibility was excluded for reasons which I will explore at more length in Chapter 6. I will say here only that it seems to be the case that God "could not" do so in the sense that it was not "good" for God to create human willful-creatures both free and conforming in one single act of creation. So also, it may be the case that God "could not" destroy evil, *for his people, by the coercive-force* of omnipotent goodness.

Henri Blocher wrote something very close to this idea, seeing it in the sweep of biblical history, but finding it centrally located at the Cross:

> At the Cross we find confirmation that evil does not belong metaphysically to the condition of the human race; to a catastrophe in history, God reacts in human history. At the Cross is revealed how his kingdom comes about: not by might (of weaponry), or by power (of worldly means), but by the Spirit of sacrifice (Zech 4:6); not by the subjection of multitudes to slavery, in the manner of the great rulers of this world, but by the service of the Son of Man (Matt 20:25–28).[83]

Blocher is not saying here that God *cannot* use power against evil (and I agree that God could in fact do so), but he is saying that he does not and he seems to be implying that this arises out of his character as a servant to us, "the service of the Son of Man." The Cross rejects coercive-power as a tool against evil. One might look at the universe with despair, if God refused to use his power to crush evil when he could do so. But if God is already doing all that should be done, must be done, and can be done, by omnipotent goodness, and if he has done so in the Cross, and if he continues to do so actively today through the suffering of his people, then they rejoice in him and in their salvation. His people are engaged in a great battle alongside him, a battle he declares to be a necessary one, if in fact they are to experience all that God intends for them. And it may be there is no other way.

Of course, we can think of many occasions where God uses coercive-power against evil, but it "never works," if by "work" we mean to destroy evil so that it does not appear again. This highlights the important difference between tactical use of

---

83. Blocher, *Evil and the Cross*, 130.

power and strategic use of power. The flood did not destroy evil, but only washed away its accumulation. In Genesis 9, the flood waters had barely receded before Noah got naked-drunk, and worse, the son mocked his father. And worse yet, the whole of the world fell again into rebellion against God, as it was recorded in Genesis 11, at the Tower of Babel. God's use of coercive-power did not destroy sin *for his people*. God used power against Sodom and Gomorrah, but that only rid the world of one cesspool. And the Bible testifies to many other cesspools he did not destroy, as do our newspapers. So also God used power against the enemies of Israel, but not to destroy evil. God's judgment of the Canaanites, delayed for 400 years from the day of Abraham because their sin was not yet ripe,[84] only pushed back the tide of evil just enough to make a womb in The Land for a people who would birth the Messiah. Over and over God used coercive-power to stop evil in its tracks, but it always came back. And this was no surprise to a God who planned the Sacrifice Lamb from the beginning of the world. Could it be that his goal, instead, is to create a people who are free to delight in him forever—and for that he must destroy evil, not just the many instances of evil? And what if to destroy evil strategically, and not only to retard its tactical advance, suffering is required? What if, by his goals and character, he must use Evil & Suffering to destroy Evil & Suffering? What if the Cross is Judo?

I find that although this is the consistent and thorough testimony and example of Scripture and history, yet it is not something that is easily perceived or accepted. Charles Journet gives an example when he asserts that God can use power to destroy evil:

> The evil of nature is permitted in the sense that it is in itself inseparably connected with a good which is intended and directly willed by God. . . . The evil of sin, on the other hand, in itself is inseparably connected to nothing good and acts only to destroy the work of God; . . . . It is permitted, tolerated and suffered in a completely different sense from the evil of nature; it is permitted as a rebellion, an offense, which God cannot will in any way, which he cannot acquiesce in or consent to without denying his own being, which *he could certainly suppress by force and eradicate completely*.[85]

I believe that this position is the common wisdom: God could use coercive-power (force) against evil to destroy it. To this extent the witness of the Scriptures would agree. But if he means "suppress" and "eradicate" evil, *for God's people, I think he is conceding to the general intuition implied by the tension felt in the Trilemma*. But on what is this intuition grounded? What example in the Bible or in human history would provide evidence that such a claim is true? It is merely a postulate or even an *apriori* axiom. I suggest we want it to be true and that it seems to us intuitively that it should be true. But is it? This project proposes that it may be the case that the real destruction of evil and the

---

84. God discusses this with Abram in Genesis 15:16 and the context from 12:1 to the coming of Christ is discipline of his special people that they may accomplish his purposes. One of those great purposes was the Messiah.

85. Journet, *Meaning of Evil*, 147. Emphasis mine.

PART II: The Testing of a Theodicy

suffering it entails, requires facing evil in suffering. Rowan Williams seems to observe this as a fundamental truth of God's world in his Lenten devotional book, *The Truce of God*. Here he is reflecting on the war in Iraq when he writes,

> There is no dispute about the American military capacity, no rival world power any longer, yet this is a might that cannot achieve its ends or deliver a secure environment, peace and prosperity. Irrational evil seems to lurk undetectably and persistently around every corner and has to be fought at all costs. And anyone raising the question of whether terrorism is best combated by the exercise of large-scale force is promptly accused of appeasing terror.[86]

While I am not sanctioning or refuting the wisdom of the "War on Terror" that the United States is waging in Afghanistan or in Iraq, it seems axiomatic to observe as a fact that unrivaled power seems impotent against this evil—and it is just this conclusion that makes the West increasingly uncomfortable. We are all troubled and surprised that main force is so helpless against evil. It is this surprise that I want to notice. And it is just this wrong expectation that leads us to make assumptions about God's work in his world. It inclines us to feel the problem of evil with a relentless acuteness: God could destroy evil for his people with his coercive-power. But what if coercive-power cannot destroy evil?

There is only one clear biblical example of what means can be used to destroy evil. It is the only example we have to show us what the omni-good God of all-power does when he sets out to destroy evil. He used the evil of Good Friday and the suffering of his Son to destroy Evil & Suffering for his people. He used no coercive force. His sword was sheathed. And he conquered evil by the power of the Cross in suffering.

ON WHETHER GOD DOES OR COULD USE GOOD TO DESTROY EVIL & SUFFERING

> The direction of my attempted solution lies in pointing to the incommensurate Good that God is.[87]
>
> —Marilyn McCord Adams

I have argued that God's power (his coercive-power) does not and cannot (in the sense that this is not "good" to do so) destroy evil *for his people*. But what of God's instrumental use of goodness against Evil & Suffering? I must be careful here, for God's goodness cannot be held in any way distinct from everything that God does. All he does is good. All he does is powerful. But just as it is the case that his power is in his weakness, and yet the power of his weakness is distinct from his coercive-power, so also his goodness is in his instrumental use of Evil & Suffering against Evil

---

86. R. Williams, *Truce of God*, 13.
87. M. M. Adams, *Horrendous Evils*, 189.

& Suffering, and this goodness is distinct from the goodness of his instrumental use of the goodness of obedience to destroy Evil & Suffering. And the goodness of obedience is used instrumentally against Evil & Suffering.

Marilyn McCord Adams says that on balance each life must be a good to the person, herself. In that sense, it is goodness that destroys Evil & Suffering in her project by triumphing in degree and at the telos. To the extent that her focus is on the Cross, I could agree. The Cross is the great good—a good work of radical obedience—and it does conquer evil. The Father declares this work of Christ to be good, just as he called the creation, very good. When he was about to die, a voice spoke in the heaving of the disciples, "This is my beloved Son, with whom I am well pleased; listen to him" (Matthew 17:5). The death of the Son, and the Son who died, pleased God; they are Good, and Good does overcome evil.

Romans 12:21 is also a clear statement that good conquers evil, "do not be overcome by evil, but overcome evil with good." Working from the inside out, the immediate context for this verse is its location at the end of a list commonly known as the marks of a Christian: love one another, abhor evil, be patient in tribulation, rejoice with those who rejoice, weep with those who weep, be humble, do not repay evil for evil and many others. Even more directly it is connected by the double use of the word evil (κακός) with verse 17. The author is summing up why love must be genuine—when God's people rightly love one another, they overcome evil. But it is worth noting that this context insists that the good in mind is that of enduring evil that is heaped upon us.[88] Evil need not destroy human willful-creatures, rather God's people destroy evil by enduring Evil & Suffering. But indeed, this is a good as the Cross was a good. Also, this verse is deeply connected to the argument Paul began in 12:1, which commanded us: "to present your bodies a living and holy sacrifice." This is the response of God's people for they have received redemption by grace through the suffering of Christ, which Paul exposed in Romans 1–11. This "living sacrifice" is rightly considered suffering before God and this includes the good of using gifts, loving one another, and all that Paul indicates as the way we are to live in the body. This is done in the context of laying down our lives as a sacrifice, as did Christ. The nature of living out our lives is to be as a "sacrifice." But while I can situate this text in the context of suffering, it is still a text that rightly names doing good before God as instrumental in the battle against Evil & Suffering and I do not desire in this project to minimize that.

While I have shown that a merely coercive understanding of power is excluded as a means of destroying Evil & Suffering, so God's goodness and ours is not excluded as means, though what is good in this text comes under the heading of being a "living sacrifice." For this reason, I suspect that the chief good and obedience that God uses to destroy Evil & Suffering is a form of submissive suffering while trusting him. This is the lesson of Job. In this God turns evil against itself. This is a great good.

---

88. Murray, *Romans*, 144.

PART II: The Testing of a Theodicy

ON WHETHER AN INTRINSIC, NECESSARY EVIL, WHICH OPERATES TO DESTROY EVIL & SUFFERING, REQUIRES A CONSEQUENTIALIST ETHIC

> Woe to those who call evil, good!
>
> —Isaiah 5:20

As I noted earlier in Part I, my proposal is intended to be distinctly non-consequentialist, but I perceive that the very way of stating the hypothesis of this chapter has a ring of consequentialism because Evil & Suffering is both an intrinsic problem and an instrumental solution. It may seem that Evil & Suffering is a "good" because it functions to bring about the ultimate state that God desires. However, I have already argued that my proposal is not consequentialist because good and evil are not defined in light of consequences, but upon God's character. Moreover, the instrumental use of Evil & Suffering to destroy Evil & Suffering for his people, which might sound to some like a consequential good, is a subordinate-metaphysical necessity which cannot be avoided given God's character and purposes. God did not use evil to bring about good, he destroyed the enemy which arose intrinsically in his creation. This, as I have argued above, is not consequentialism.

But there is a wide spectrum of views that seem to be or are that consequentialist. Chris Tiegreen writes in *Why a Suffering World Makes Sense* that evil reveals attributes of God which otherwise would have not been expressed: "There are attributes of our Creator that we never would have experienced if our tragedy had not happened."[89] And he also writes, "The most high God is more clearly glorified, more relevant and visible, in our depths."[90] This is not an exceptional argument and other scholars could be cited including Edwards. But Tiegreen seems to take this position even further when he adds, "There should be no great mystery to the presence of evil, if by context and by contrast, it reveals the manifold character of God."[91] I find the phrase, "no great mystery" to be troubling and I find this argument to be dangerous in that it seems to make evil ontologically instrumental. It is as if God is saying, "I make evil occur in order that my glory may be shown." If that is a correct re-statement of Tiegreen, evil seems necessary to God in his system, because without evil, he would not "be" God because much of his character would be unexpressed. If so, such a position would be difficult to distance from a consequentialist ethic. On the other side of the theological spectrum, John Hick writes that theodicy is "a 'picture' in which evil can be seen as ultimately serving a good and justifying purpose."[92] This goes further in that it defines theodicy that is consequentialist by its very nature.

---

89. Tiegreen, *Why a Suffering World Makes Sense*, 118.
90. Ibid., 103.
91. Ibid., 86.
92. Hick, "Remarks," 124.

This shows something of the range of views which can employ some version of a consequentialist ethic. And, more important to me, this allows me to restate the key difference between "soul-making" and my theodicy (ignoring critical issues of universalism and "many lives"). I see no value in evil, nor do I grant it an ontological reality or ontological necessity in God's project. Rather, evil arose as an enemy because of the choices God made and it was turned back on itself to accomplish his ends. Evil & Suffering is purely contingent and he will extinguish it though Evil & Suffering. This is very different from arguing, as does Hick, that it is necessary in order to mature souls. It is not *important*, to God's project, but *unavoidable* (given God's goals and nature) and in God's wisdom and design it is instrumentally used against itself. There is a great difference between its instrumental use and consequential intent. It is distinct from Moltmann's view which seems to take evil into the very life of God. So Hick's use of evil blurs the distinction between good and evil.

But Bruce Ware reminds us that while God is intrinsically good, he does instrumentally use evil.[93] Evil is an intrinsic problem in the world as it developed, but not as created, and it is not intrinsic to God. Although it is used by God, it never becomes a good, specifically because it is always the enemy. But this might raise the issue of our nomenclature of "Good Friday." Does the Evil & Suffering, which occurred on Good Friday, indicate a consequentialist ethic? In no way. Evil is not transformed into good, thereby becoming a good. Evil does not enter into a partnership with good and they are not in some way both/and. Rather, the Evil & Suffering of Christ have a good effect—the enemy is destroyed. This is a non-consequentialist ethic in that good is good because it is like God and evil is only evil, arising intrinsically and in God's design, used against itself instrumentally.

ON WHETHER A OMNI-GOOD GOD WOULD USE EVIL & SUFFERING IN HIS PROJECT

> Dare one talk in terms of necessity? This intrepid Jesuit does not hesitate, and his position has the merit of being crystal clear: "Evil appears necessarily . . . not by accident (which would not much matter), but through the very structure of system." It is "a rigorously inevitable accompaniment of creation."[94]
>
> —Henri Blocher quoting de Chardin

A further concern that this project may raise is how it could be that a good God makes instrumental use of evil. Could this have the effect of twisting evil into God's character? There are some theologically unsavory fellows who have observed necessity in

---

93. Bruce Ware writes, "So while God controls both well-being and calamity (evil), he does not delight in wickedness, nor does any evil dwell in him, nor can he even look upon evil (i.e., approvingly)" (*God's Greater Glory*, 102).

94. Blocher, *Evil and the Cross*, 23.

evil. In the quote above, Blocher is negatively quoting the ideas of Pierre Tielhard de Chardin. de Chardin espouses a Christianity that is both linked to evolution and man-centered, seeing the universe starting as impersonal and maturing to hyper-personal.[95] This I reject. Further his view of evil is merely developmental, seeing evil arising as we mature and grow, but fading simply because we mature. This I also reject. Yet, like Hick, he seems to be seeing a glimmer of the truth, a certain kind of necessity in evil, given the universe as God created it. In *Doors of the Sea*, David Hart writes, "Hence evil can have no proper role to play in God's determination of himself or purpose for his creatures, even if by economy God can bring good from evil; it can in no way supply an imagined deficiency in God's or creation's goodness; it has no 'contribution' to make."[96] I want to strongly affirm this position. Evil has no role (proper or otherwise) in God or in his purpose for his creatures, and there is no deficiency (imagined or otherwise) in God for which evil must be drummed into service. Evil & Suffering only becomes God's "problem" when he creates a people in his image, for through this, evil came to be. It further becomes God's problem because he purposes to make of these rebels a people for himself and so he wills to accomplish redemption through the incarnation and redemption—He purposed this "problem" for himself before time, as he purposed redemption before time. But evil is not instrumentally brought into existence for God's purpose. Rather is it intrinsically introduced, as shown above, consequent to God's character and goals and it is used instrumentally against itself, distinct from God and adding nothing to God. But could a good God use evil?

Swinburne allows God to "get his hands dirty" in the conquest of evil and writes:

> A theodicist is in a better position to defend a theodicy such as I have outlined if he is prepared also to make the further additional claim that God knowing the worthwhileness of the conquest of evil and the perfecting of the universe by men, shared with them this task by subjecting himself as man to the evil in the world. A creator is more justified in creating or permitting evils to be overcome by his creatures if he is prepared to share with them the burden of the suffering and effort.[97]

D. Z. Phillips responds, "Theodicies, such as Swinburne's, are marked by their order, optimism and progress. . . . if the visit to our world were by a God such as Swinburne describes, those who said that there was no room at the inn would be right. We should not be at home to such callers. And if perchance we were asked to choose between this visitor and another, we should unhesitatingly demand, 'Give us Prometheus!' "[98] In other words, like Hart, he has no room for God to allow evil, but he also objects to God's instrumental use of evil. Yet all of these arguments are argu-

---

95. de Chardin, *Phenomenon of Man*, 260.
96. Hart, *Doors of the Sea*, 74.
97. Swinburne, "Problem of Evil," 103.
98. Phillips, "Response to The Problem of Evil," 119 and 121.

ments of aesthetics, not from the biblical text. We are right to be wary of associating God and evil in our theology. This we cannot do. God is Good. That is absolute. Yet, God is sovereign in all things, including evil. John Piper wrote, "these spectacular sins do not just fail to nullify God's purpose to glorify Christ, they succeed, by God's unfathomable providence, in making his gracious purpose come to pass."[99] This is the consistent testimony of Scripture.

SUMMARY: EVIL &SUFFERING DESTROYS EVIL & SUFFERING FOR GOD'S PEOPLE

> And there was given to each of them a white robe; and they were told that they should rest for a little while longer, until the number of their fellow servants and their brethren who were to be killed even as they had been, would be completed also.
>
> —Revelation 6:11

In this chapter I have attempted to show that God has a co-causality for evil that is mediate and ultimate and that as a result of God's character and goals for creation, evil may have intruded upon creation with a certain subordinate-metaphysical necessity, arising intrinsically in creation, but not intrinsic to God. And that this evil was instrumentally used by God to destroy itself, rejecting the use of coercive-power to destroy evil, but instead using Evil & Suffering to destroy Evil & Suffering that he might create a people for himself who are free to delight in him.

Considering the above text from John's Revelation, could it be that God's people are waiting not only for the Gospel to be preached everywhere and for there to be representatives from every nation, tribe, language, and people, but for the *telos* of the suffering and martyrdom of the people of God, as if suffering was part of their job and something that must be completed before the end? Could it be that this too hints that suffering is at the heart of God's work as he uses Evil & Suffering to destroy Evil & Suffering?

---

99. Piper, *Spectacular Sins*, 8. In other words, God is sovereign even over sin and uses it for his purposes (developed on 10–13).

6

Hypothesis 3
Conforming-Freedom is achieved by God for his people through Evil & Suffering over four Eras of Freedom which are divided by three Creation & Crisis events

I HAVE BEEN ARGUING that evil arises in God's good world as a subordinate-metaphysical necessity, and that it may be possible that Evil & Suffering destroys Evil & Suffering for his people in God's plan for his universe, and that both of these are in accord with God's character and declared purposes. Yet even if Evil & Suffering is the primary tool that God uses against Evil & Suffering, that would not be a complete understanding of God's battle against evil. Although Evil & Suffering may be a weapon that God uses instrumentally to rescue us, I suggest this is not God's strategy, but his tactics. Strategy is perceived at the largest scale, in the great movements spanning the history of the work of God in his human willful-creatures. This large-scale movement is seen in the three Creation & Crisis events in the history and eschatology of his universe: 1/ the creation of the world and the crisis of its subjugation to corruption; 2/ the creation of a new people in Christ which is preceded by the crisis of the incarnation, death, and resurrection of Christ; and 3/ the creation of the new heaven and the new earth, which is preceded by the crisis of the judgment. I suggest that in these three Creation & Crisis events we may discern God's strategy to create a people who are freely-conforming to his character and so able to delight in him forever. Our history then is perceived as a play in four acts, which I propose to be "Eras of Freedom," each of which is bounded by Creation & Crisis events. These acts are "Unfettered Freedom," "Slavery," "Penultimate Freedom" and "Conforming-Freedom."

ON WHETHER FREEDOM COULD BE GRANTED IN A ONE-ACT DRAMA

> Why not forgo this world and create the final perfect one?[1]
>
> —John Feinberg

Before looking at each of the acts within the drama we should consider if this play could have been completed in one act. That is of course up to the play's author, namely YHWH. But many wonder if he could have done so in one act, if he wanted to do so. This includes Descartes who "felt" that God could have arranged things so in our freedom we would never make mistakes.[2] Even John Hick, whose system seems to require a process with evil functioning as a tutor, cannot be pinned down to say clearly if all this could be avoided. Marilyn McCord Adams observed, "Hick equivocates as to whether or not it is metaphysically impossible for God to 'ready make' mature rational humans, or whether such instant virtue is less valuable than that won via a developmental struggle. If the former were true, then not even an omnipotent God could do it."[3] The principle seems to be that God could do anything, but what seems to be missing in this conclusion is well argued reasons history could have been otherwise.

Mackie is another who did not like the world as he found it, especially if a good and omnipotent God was admitted. For Mackie, the "One-Act Drama" question is an argument against God:

> I should have thought, indeed, that the concept of a state of affairs in which men were wholly good, that is of a Kingdom of God on Earth, was an orthodox theistic one, and if that concept is empty or unintelligible, so much the worse for theism. If the theists tell us that God will eventually bring this utopia into being, the critics can hardly be blamed for wondering why he has gone such a long way round about it.[4]

Though Plantinga is well known for silencing the Flew-Mackie challenge in regard to theodicy, this particular challenge by Mackie is different and has not been answered adequately by Plantinga or any of those in dialogue with Mackie: Why has God taken so long? I want to suggest that this truly is how long it takes for God's strategic work to accomplish God's goals. I am posing a partial solution (partial in the sense that I

---

1. Feinberg, *Many Faces of Evil*, 141. I should note that while this is a question that Feinberg raises, it does not assert his position. His position is that God does not have to explain his ultimate reason; it pleased God to make this world as he did (142).

2. "Of course God easily could have arranged things so that, while keeping my freedom and still being limited in what I understand, I never made a mistake. He could do this either by giving me a clear and distinct understanding of everything that I was ever likely to think about; or by forcing me always to remember that I ought not to form opinions on matters I don't clearly and distinctly understand" (Descartes, Meditations, 4, p. 21).

3. Adams, *Horrendous Evils and the Goodness of God*, 51.

4. Mackie, "Theism and Utopia," 154.

am not claiming that this is all there is to say, but rather that it points in a possible direction of fruitful investigation), which I have argued, is wholly consistent with the text of Scripture, with the development of Christian thought in regard to theodicy, with the character of God, and with God's announced goals. I do not argue that my proposal is intuitive or that it is obvious—quite the opposite. Intuition goes with the very question of theodicy which assumes the possibility of a single act play: could not an omni-good and omnipotent God protect his human willful-creatures from evil—even from their own will and self-created evil? But as I understand Feinberg, despite this rhetorical question, he agrees that God cannot accomplish his goals in one act. He writes,

> God can remove evil if that is all he wants to do in our world. However, I will argue that God cannot remove evil without (1) contradicting other valuable things He has decided to do, (2) casting doubts on or directly contradicting the claims that He has all the attributes predicted of Him in Scripture, and/or (3) performing actions that we would neither desire nor require Him to do, because they would produce a greater evil than we already have in our world.[5]

In this I agree—as far as Feinberg goes. Bypassing this human experiment with evil is an impossibility for God, given his goals. So Blocher has noted that "Thomists are closely agreed at this point: 'God cannot . . . create anyone naturally impeccable, any more than he can make a circle square.'"[6] Standing with them, and further offering a discernable purpose in God, I suggest God is taking so long because God has more than the goal of preventing evil for his people (which could be done by his raw power), he wants to destroy evil for his people (which must be done through suffering). To accomplish that, I think the case can be made that he must act within his character. And he is doing this over the sweep of time through multiple Creation & Crisis events.

Before going forward and examining the possibility I offer, it is worth adding Plantinga's objection here. He writes, "Significant freedom, obviously, does not entail wrong doing."[7] This statement is obviously true in regard to God. But why would he or others assert it in regard to God's human willful-creatures who are necessarily exposed to that which God is not exposed? That is, we are exposed to being "not God"—something God cannot experience! As a result, in our "experience" of being "not God," our metaphysical reality, we live out Romans 7:14–25, "For what I am doing, I do not understand; for I am not practicing what I would like to do, but I am doing the very thing I hate." It might be argued that Romans 7 is only the experience of fallen humans, and not humans in the first Era of Freedom (what I have called, Slavery). That is not an argument without merit. Indeed, by definition, first era human willful-creatures had not sinned, for the sin is the crisis that inaugurates the end of the first era and the

---

5. Feinberg, *Many Faces of Evil*, 126.
6. Blocher, *Evil and the Cross*, 28.
7. Plantinga, *Nature of Necessity*, 185.

beginning of the second. Yet, the very fact that we are "not God" means we are able to do what is not like God. Indeed, God prior to the incarnation could in no way interact with evil in this personal way. He did not endure temptation; he could not be tempted. But Adam was tempted after the command was given: "Do not eat!" And not only was Adam tempted, it was his experience to be tempted while still perfect, yet, because he was "not God" and thus subject to defection, Romans 7 is also his experience, while still in the first and perfect era, for he was subject to acting against his good desires. He was taken captive from his perfection; he did not understand what he did, even before he did it. In perfection, Romans 7 was the vector of his existence, if not yet captive to sin and bound over to its penalties. Moreover, John 15:1–11, which calls his people to remain in the vine, reinforces this perspective that it is only those (even those of the era of Penultimate-Freedom) who have the connection to the Source who are able to experience even the beginnings of Conforming-Freedom. Verse 4, which is perhaps the core verse in the famous passage, pictures Christ as the vine and his followers as the branches and this verse calls them to remain connected to this Source: "Abide in Me, and I in you. As the branch cannot bear fruit of itself unless it abides in the vine, so neither can you unless you abide in Me." This is emphasized in all John's corpus that commands them to "remain" (μένω) in Christ: John 6:56; 1 John 2:6; 2:14; 2:27; 3:1–17; 5:15. It is especially worth considering 1 John 3:6, "No one who abides in Him sins; no one who sins has seen Him or knows Him." Here John links the ideas of abiding with Him, the One who is the Source of all Good, and acting in accord with the Source. This internal Source is something that Adam did not have for he was not God and yet he experienced an uncontrolled freedom. He was free from God, but not free from what is not God, because the Source was not within him. To "remain in God" was the voluntary willingness to obey the one negative command, "Do not eat!" And in his freedom from conforming, he did not, nor was there any force acting to maintain that freely given starting point of conformity. He was created good like God, but not being, himself, the Source, there was nothing sustaining this first Era of Freedom in sinlessness.

A similar understanding of the flow of history can be seen in Augustine's famous division of our experience of freedom in *On Rebuke and Grace* and this division is expanded in his *Enchiridion*. In translation, he calls these divisions, stages or epochs: "Of these four different stages, the first is before the law, the second is under the law, the third is under grace, and the fourth is in full and perfect peace. Thus, also, the history of God's people has been ordered according to His pleasure."[8] The first stage is "before the law" in which a person is "able to sin, able not to sin," so that "when, sunk in the darkest depths of ignorance, man lives according to the flesh, undisturbed by any struggle of reason, this is his first state."[9] The second stage is called, "under the

---

8. Augustine, *Enchiridion on Faith, Hope, and Love*, ¶ 118, 137.

9. This quote from Augustine, in his *Enchiridion* and those that follow in this paragraph are all from *Enchiridion*, ¶ 118, 136–7.

PART II: The Testing of a Theodicy

law" in which a person is "able to sin, unable not to sin," so that "when through the law has come the knowledge of sin, and the Spirit of God has not yet interposed His aid, man, striving to live according to the law, is thwarted in his efforts and falls into conscious sin, and so, being overcome of sin, becomes its slave . . . this is man's second state." The third stage is called, "under grace" in which a person is "able to sin, able not to sin," so that "if God has regard to him, and inspires him with faith in God's help, and the Spirit of God begins to work in him, . . . although there is still in the man's own nature a power that fights against him, . . . yet he lives the life of the just by faith . . . this is the third state." The fourth stage is called, "full and perfect peace" in which a person is "able not to sin, unable to sin," so that "he who by steadfast piety advances in this course, shall attain at last to peace, that peace which, after this life is over, shall be perfected in the repose of the spirit, and finally in the resurrection of the body . . . and the fourth [RAS: stage] is in full and perfect peace." While these stages are perhaps only an artificial tool by which the work of God may be understood, still they are helpful. And these states represent for Augustine the progression of a person in his life and also of God's strategic work in his church over time.

Similarly, Thomas Boston, the Puritan theologian, in his work, Human Nature in its Fourfold State suggested four stages of God's work to create the human bliss that was his intent:[10]

I.	Innocence:	Primitive Integrity	(what was)
II.	Nature:	Entire Depravity	(what is)
III.	Grace:	Begun Recovery	(what must be)
IV.	Eternal:	Consummate Happiness / Misery	(what will be)

This is an answer to the question of Feinberg and to the challenge of Mackie. But in his entire book, Boston never asks how it is that God's people will persevere in the eternal state or why this final Era is different than the first. But could it be that there is something strategic that occurs in these stages of history that move us from an initial and perfect state in which Adam was able to sin to a final perfect state in which God's people are not able to sin? Notice that the incarnation, death, and resurrection of Christ are not enough in the third state to grant his people this perfection. I believe that it may be that the daily, tactical operation of God to accomplish this strategy includes a painful period dominated by Evil & Suffering in which Evil & Suffering is destroying itself under God's direction, God's suffering, and the suffering of his people. And ultimately, all of this is leading his creation to a day when there will be no more tears, pain, or suffering.

---

10. Boston, *Human Nature in its Fourfold State*. This outline comes not from one page, but from his work as a whole. In the text above I have preserved (in parenthesis) Boston's expression of the form of the verb "to be" that he associated with each state.

My proposal understands that this drama cannot be resolved in one act—in one single instance of creation.[11] I am not arguing that God "could not" because he lacked the power, but rather that it may be that he "could not" because such a thing is incompatible with his character and declared goals, his desires. In this sense, "one act" is incompatible with his freedom.

It is here that the "necessity of evil" enters into this argument. Not only is it the case that God's ultimate goal is "impossible" in one act of creation, but if the nature of a creation, which is suitable to his character and purposes is such that evil arises necessarily, then evil is a battle that cannot be bypassed by God or us. The necessary appearance of evil is the curtain that divides, creating at least two acts. And given these two acts, the drama could not end there. If that is the case, the necessary appearance of evil might be called, "God's Problem of Evil." Though the evil is a problem only for his people, God has written this drama and he will take it to a conclusion that pleases him—and it is not the appearance of evil! God's problem of evil is that he knows it will arise in his creation as he created it for his purposes and that he, himself, must solve it at infinite cost to himself. Our problem of evil is that it seems to us that, granted his goals and character (act one), and granted evil (act two), God could have completed his work in three acts (and quickly!) by use of the coercive-power of his sword. If my proposal is correct, what foolish children we are to complain in the face of such a great salvation! Our problem of evil is hardly to be compared to God's problem of evil! We are disturbed that it takes four acts, and lasts so long. Like the Jews of Christ's day, who were offended that he did not come in power, we continue to feel the same offense. But God himself pays the infinite price. Ours is finite and relatively brief, though admittedly painful. The heart of this proposal is that all four acts are necessary and the use of Evil & Suffering against itself is as necessary as the appearance of evil.

ON GOD'S USE OF THREE CHIASTIC CREATION & CRISIS EVENTS

The strategic work of God to bring his people into Conforming-Freedom is accomplished in our history through a series of events which can be construed as three Creation & Crisis events. As noted above, these are: the creation of Heaven and Earth and the Fall ; the creation of Christ and a new people in Christ into which falls the central crisis of the death of Christ, and the creation of the New Heavens and New Earth which is preceded by the crisis of the last battle and judgment. An immediate caveat should be made. While these do stand as the three creations and crises within time, their function as a way of thinking about the problem of evil is not indisputable, merely a proposal. I will be stipulating these events, but proposing that the creations, along with their attendant crises, are a model (or perhaps a filter) that may help us to

---

11. It seems to me that an extension of this project would be to interact with Kevin VanHoozer's concept of "Drama of Doctrine" and speech-act theory as he relates to George Lindbeck, Hans Frei, and others (VanHoozer, *Drama of Doctrine*).

PART II: The Testing of a Theodicy

see God's strategy. So, I will be evaluating this model for its utility in helping us discover what God might be doing strategically in regard to Evil & Suffering and to grant us what seems to be his desire, ultimate Conforming-Freedom in which God's people are free from diverging from that which is good. This is a more modest proposal than setting this out as a model that exhaustively encompasses God's strategy to solve his "problem of evil." It will take the whole of eternity to pursue and discover all of God's glory in his work and purposes in allowing evil into his world.

Let me define these terms as I use them. "Creation" is God's constructive work toward his goals, in which some new and critical thing is brought into existence that has never existed before. "Crisis" is God's deconstructive work toward his goals in which an instability is revealed and a great turn is made in the development of history toward his goals. I observe that each of the great creations of God is attended with great crises and so it will be helpful as we begin to consider the components of the three Creation & Crisis events. In doing so, I observe a chiastic structure:

	Display of Chiastic Structure of Creation & Crisis Events	
1	Creation of Heaven & Earth	Old Covenant
1'	The Fall of Humanity	
2	Incarnation of Christ	
2'	**Death of Christ**	
2	Resurrection & Creation of New People	New Covenant
3'	The Judgment	
3	Creation of New Heavens and New Earth	

The numbers on the left side represent the three Creation & Crisis events with historical movement from top to bottom through the chiasm. The prime indicator (') shows the crisis portion of the paired events. Topographically, the first three events occurred under the old covenant order and the last three events under the new covenant order. Parallel items indicate restorations. The central crisis, the crucial event of history, is the crucifixion of Christ. The ultimate movement of history is toward the new creation.[12]

The first "Creation & Crisis" is seen in the account preserved in Genesis 1–3. It is the creation of the universe as the work of God which seems to be described in Genesis one and two.[13] While many have argued that these chapters tell two distinct

12. It must be acknowledged here that there is something about the first Creation & Crisis event which does not readily seem to be parallel with the last event. The first Creation & Crisis event (creation and rebellion) is actually a boundary establishing both sides of the first era, while the events of the third Creation & Crisis inaugurate the final era. One could observe that the first era is finite and must be bounded, while the fourth era is eternal and can only be inaugurated. The lack of symmetry is an indicator that something more can yet be understood here, but this does not necessarily invalidate the observation itself.

13. Other options exist which do not understand this text as a description of the creation of the

stories, making different points,[14] I want to focus on the larger picture of the creation of the universe and its attendant crisis. That is, God created a universe which is fit for human willful-creatures, who, while beginning in perfect relationship to God, became separated from God by their one act of sinful disobedience. This creation was rapidly attended by a crisis (as the story is related in Genesis 3) which shatters the relationship established between God and his human willful-creatures. As was noted in the previous chapter, God takes responsibility for this event in the mediate and ultimate way defined, sharing co-causality with his human willful-creatures. In this crisis, something fundamental is changed. This we observed in Romans 8:20–21: God subjects his perfect creation to frustration. Yet it is this very frustration, this crisis, which is a movement toward God's goal. It is a frustration that is to ultimately bring hope. Already we have a hint that there is strategy. There is movement from what is perfectly created to abject poverty. And while God did not "do it," he is directing. It is his strategy.

The second Creation & Crisis is a composite event: Christ's incarnation (creation), crucifixion (crisis), and resurrection (creation). His coming is creation; it is the Word taking on flesh. But this creation is unwelcome and Christ's crucifixion is the result. This is the crisis of crises in God's strategic movement through history. But it is this crisis that portends the second creation: resurrection and the creation of a new people. 2 Corinthians 5:17 says, "Therefore if anyone is in Christ, he is a new creature; the old things passed away; behold, new things have come." This is the second creation, the καινὴ κτίσις, of a people in Christ, and is tied to the crisis of the Cross which turned Evil & Suffering back on itself, destroying it and giving new birth. We also see this expressed in Galatians 6:14–15, where the suffering of the Cross is tied to the second creation, "But may it never be that I would boast, except in the Cross of our Lord Jesus Christ, through which the world has been crucified to me, and I to the world. For neither is circumcision anything, nor uncircumcision, but a new creation." Here "the Cross" (the enduring of Evil & Suffering) and "new creation" are closely

---

universe. One example that gives the text full and authoritative weight is that of John Sailhamer (*Genesis Unbound*). In this monograph he posits that Genesis 1&2 are not about the creation of the universe, but rather about the preparation of The Land for God's people, wresting it from the Wilderness. This is not the place to critique this proposal, but rather to acknowledge that the subject of creation is disputed among those who understand Genesis "literally." In the case of Sailhamer, if he is correct, my project would still fare well because the point is still that God is making a place which is fit for God's people to have a relationship with him. In regard to the Fall in particular, even if it has theological meaning only at the expense of historical fact, the Fall still stands as descriptive of a change that took place in the relationship between God and his people. The trauma caused a critical break that is shown in God's people being driven into the Wilderness. We cannot rescue ourselves from this Wilderness, but instead our situation must be addressed by God, who promises a Seed who will one day crush the serpent: Evil.

14. For example, Paul Kahn (*Out of Eden: Adam and Eve and the Problem of Evil*) points out that in Genesis, chapter 1, there is a joint creation and a shared image of God and a command to procreate. However, in Genesis, chapter 2, Eve has a very different role, meeting a need in Adam; his loneliness (106–7).

PART II: The Testing of a Theodicy

linked in Paul's thinking. The idea is also seen in Ephesians 4:24, "the new self, which in the likeness of God has been created" and in Colossians 3:10, "and have put on the new self who is being renewed to a true knowledge according to the image of the One who created him." These sister texts in Ephesians and Colossians are not explicitly tied to the crisis of the death of Christ or his resurrection, but it would be most difficult to divorce them from this concept in the Epistles in general or the context in which they lie. In Ephesians the resurrection is linked with the creation of the new self in verse 1:20, "which He brought about in Christ, when He raised Him from the dead" and the likeness which has been created and won by his suffering, the "we have redemption through His blood" in verse 1:7. The context for the Colossians passage is found in 3:1 which begins "if you have been raised with Christ." Perhaps the verse that displays this great and central second creation in its fullness is Philippians 3:10–11: "that I may know Him and the power of His resurrection and the fellowship of His sufferings, being conformed to His death; in order that I may attain to the resurrection from the dead." Here Paul links all of the ideas of suffering, resurrection, and his own recreation ("resurrection from the dead") which inaugurates God's final movement.

This second creation is sometimes overlooked and not represented as a distinct creation account, sandwiched as it is between the old and new creations of the universe. But that is the clear testimony of text, in which each Gospel is committed to revealing the inauguration of a second work of creation. G.K. Beale noted the parallel between the openings of several of the Gospels and the Genesis accounts.[15] Matthew 1:1, which begins "the book of the generations of Jesus Christ, the son of God" is parallel to Genesis 2:4 "These are the generations of the heaven and the earth when they were created, in the day that the Lord God made earth and heaven." And the Gospel of John which begins in 1:1, "In the beginning was the Word, and the Word was with God, and the Word was God" is parallel to the Genesis 1:1 account.[16] There is an identification between the Gospel accounts and creation and so Christ's work is the second creation. And of this second creation, Blocher writes, "He rose on the eighth day, which opens up the new creation after the seven days of the old one."[17] This

---

15. Beale, *Temple and the Church's Mission*, 171–73.

16. While not addressed by Beale, even Mark and Luke have allusions to the Genesis account. Mark begins with the word, ἀρχή which could be of no significance, but it also could be a shadow of Genesis. Yet, the next verse makes a distinction between the "way" prepared by John and the "wilderness." This may reflect the Genesis 2 account in which the Garden is prepared for God's creation in a wilderness in which there was no "shrub of the field was yet in the earth, and no plant of the field had yet sprouted . . . for there was no man to cultivate the ground" (Genesis 2:5). This was a Garden carved out of the wilderness, which still existed and which continues to lie outside the Garden, for it is into this wilderness that Adam would later be condemned. Now in Mark (such could also be noted in John's Gospel), John comes into that wilderness to prepare a place for Christ. Also, Luke alone, when identifying Christ, identifies him as "Son of Adam" in 3:38. Though a weaker allusion than the other three, this is a clear reference to the Garden and the seed which would come through the woman, especially the toledot of Genesis 5:1.

17. Blocher, *Evil and the Cross*, 123.

is a wonderful observation: this second creation is not only new, but it occurs on the first day. So we hear a resonance with John's "light has come into the world" in John 1:9. This is the first day of a new week of the new creation, which moves us on to the third creation.

The third Creation & Crisis begins with a composite crisis: a brief, yet climactic war is followed by the judgment. I am impressed by the simplicity of the description of this final battle. While the victory is total, there is no sign of struggle on the part of the Conqueror. Texts which refer to this final battle between God and evil are scarce, but they sound more like an ending than a great contest. In Revelation 20:9, "fire came down from heaven and devoured them," which may be the end of the battle staged in Revelation 16:16 on the plain of Har-Megiddo, or it may be reference to a second and final battle. Also, in 2 Thessalonians 2:8 we read, "Then that lawless one will be revealed whom the Lord will slay with the breath of His mouth and bring to an end by the appearance of His coming." These texts are ambiguous in regard to their temporal reference. Preterism,[18] defines one end of the spectrum in which the events of Revelation (and others) refer to events now past, which had their complete telos in the first century. Dispensational pre-tribulationalism holds a position on the other end of the spectrum in which these texts are descriptive of the last events of time. But whether these texts refer to events of the past or future, there is no evidence of a sustained or prolonged battle in which God "overcomes" evil by the use of strong exertion of coercive-power, either here or elsewhere. Evil flees before him. In fact, it does so now at his command and has since the beginning of history. The force of His power is overwhelming, no citation of texts or scholars is needed for such an obvious point. Recall that I have stipulated a theodicy arising from this project cannot accept defections: God's power is omnipotent and cannot be diminished by amendment. Our problem of evil is his refusal to use this coercive-power. And it is what Mackie seems to demand: if God is so powerful, why does he wait? Certainly the Christian theist could respond correctly that God is waiting for the fullness of time so that all who are destined to be saved are brought into the Kingdom. As we are told in 2 Peter 3:9–10, "The Lord is not slow about His promise, as some count slowness, but is patient toward you, not wishing for any to perish but for all to come to repentance. But the day of the Lord will come like a thief, in which the heavens will pass away with a roar and the elements will be destroyed with intense heat, and the earth and its works will be burned up." But it may also be the case that something is changing in regard to evil during this time between the first crisis and the last crisis.[19] It may be that there is a

---

18. For a defense of this position, see Russell and Stevens, *Parousia: The New Testament Doctrine of Christ's Second Coming.*

19. It is worth observing here that there is another thread that ties each of these Creation & Crisis events together: the Garden. The first creation focused on the Garden that God made in the middle of the wilderness, to which Adam was later banished. The second creation was born in the lonely wrestling of Christ in the Garden of Gethsemane and he then died in the wilderness, outside of the garden beyond Jerusalem. Finally, the last Creation is the forming of the new Garden, the City of God

PART II: The Testing of a Theodicy

fullness of suffering that must be accomplished as may be indicated by Revelation 6:10–11 which reads:[20]

> and they cried out with a loud voice, saying, "How long, O Lord, holy and true, will You refrain from judging and avenging our blood on those who dwell on the earth?" And there was given to each of them a white robe; and they were told that they should rest for a little while longer, until the number of their fellow servants and their brethren who were to be killed even as they had been, would be completed also.

It is possible to understand Colossians 1:24 in just this light. This text reads:

> Νῦν χαίρω ἐν τοῖς παθήμασιν ὑπὲρ ὑμῶν καὶ ἀνταναπληρῶ τὰ ὑστερήματα τῶν θλίψεων τοῦ Χριστοῦ ἐν τῇ σαρκί μου ὑπὲρ τοῦ σώματος αὐτοῦ, ὅ ἐστιν ἡ ἐκκλησία

> Now I rejoice in my sufferings for your sake, and in my flesh I do my share on behalf of His body, which is the church, in filling up what is lacking in Christ's afflictions.

This text seems to indicate that God's people (or at least Paul) have a critical role in suffering with Christ, and that this role is in some way essential to bringing about what is next. To begin to understand this, there are at least three similar texts to consider. First, Philippians 3:10–11 which reads, "That I may know him and the power of his resurrection, and may share his sufferings, becoming like him in his death, that by any means possible I may attain the resurrection from the dead." Here Paul's identification with Christ in suffering is not "for his body, which is the church," but for his own soul. And like Colossians 1:24, it seems that this suffering is instrumentally tied to the next Era. In Ephesians 3:13 we read, ἐν ταῖς θλίψεσίν μου ὑπὲρ ὑμῶν, which translates, "in my suffering for you," which again identifies Paul's suffering as in some way being of benefit to those he serves, though it is not as clearly tied to bringing about what is next. In 2 Corinthians 1:5–6, Paul writes, "For just as the sufferings of Christ are ours in abundance, so also our comfort is abundant through Christ. But if we are afflicted, it is for your comfort and salvation; or if we are comforted, it is for your comfort, which is effective in the patient enduring of the same sufferings which we also suffer;." Here, too, Paul is engaged in suffering with Christ, for the church. Like Colossians 1:24, there is something critical about the role of suffering for the believer,

---

in which the two trees of life are found and the wilderness is gone, along with evil, which is "banished." This parallel structure is worthy of more investigation.

20. This seems to be the understanding of John Piper in regard to this text. He writes, "Indeed, he says as much about the murder of his saints in Revelation 6:10–11. . . . There is a number of martyrs to 'be filled.' God knows how many murders of his children there must be. And God reigns over every one of them. He does not spare his children death, but he does save them: 'Some of you they will put to death. . . . But not a hair of your head will perish' (Luke 21:16, 18)" (Piper, *Spectacular Sins and their Global Purpose in the Glory of Christ*, 13. This citation is from a manuscript from the author. It has since been published by Crossway Books, 2008.

which goes beyond but is yet tied to the suffering of Christ. And this suffering is of critical value to the souls of his people as well as the souls of those they serve.

Returning to the text of Colossians 1:24, the use of the two words for suffering stand out as unusual: Paul's suffering (παθήμασιν) and Christ's suffering (θλίψεων). That the former is Paul's suffering is clear from context.[21] The surprise is the association of θλίψεων with Christ—something unique to this text and a word never tied to Christ's atonement. It is for this reason that Edward Lohse proposes that these are not the sufferings of Christ as crucified Messiah, but the sufferings of the end times, "the woes of the Messiah."[22] That is, Paul's emphasis is the suffering "in my flesh" so that the emphasis of the word order ("I fill up in my flesh the lack of Christ's afflictions") means that "what is lacking, still to be completed, is then not the atoning sacrifice of Christ but Paul's own share in the sufferings that must be faced in this present age, before the dawn of the new era."[23] There is no substantive lack in Christ's atoning sacrifice—that would contradict the whole of Paul's argument in these epistles (or even the argument of whomever is suggested to have written this in his name). Such a suggestion would result in an internal inconsistency that creates more problems than it solves.[24] Rather, Paul is doing what Christ did not do and did not desire to do. That is, Christ did his job, redemption, but not the job of his people, suffering, which in some way continues to serve the church and contributes to the next Era. The Gospels and Epistles are laden with verses that call his people to suffering with Christ and to what is then lacking in their service on the battle lines of the Kingdom. N.T. Wright suggests that the point of Paul's suffering is that it brings to an end "this present evil age," consistent with current Jewish tradition, to lead us to "the age to come."[25] This path is certainly attended with suffering. But is suffering the sign that the new age is coming, or that work must be done to get us there? Murray Harris suggests that

> Paul viewed the apostolic suffering as his own distinctive contribution toward ending the 'deficiency' in the divinely appointed quota of sufferings to be patiently endured by the messianic community of the last days prior to the end of the Age.... the Christian equivalent of the Jewish apocalyptic notion of the

---

21. In regard to "my sufferings," the textual evidence weighs against the first person possessive, which occurs only in later texts, but the context, including the later use of "in my flesh," supports the implicit reading of "my sufferings" of the NASB and others in this first phrase. Murray Harris adds that the occurrence of τοῖς after χαίρω justifies the use of the possessive in translation (*Colossians & Philemon*, 65).

22. Lohse, *Colossians and Philemon*, 76.

23. Wilson, *Colossians and Philemon*, 171.

24. The use of this term ὑστερήματα in 2 Corinthians 8:14; 9:12, 1 Thessalonians 3:10, and Luke's account of the widow's mite in Luke 21:1–3 ("out of her ὑστερήματα," poverty), makes it clear that the meaning is clearly a "deficiency." But this "deficiency" (lack) cannot be his sufferings that accomplished atonement. Lohse writes, "Paul and all other witnesses in the New Testament unanimously agree that the reconciliation was truly and validly accomplished in the death of Christ, and that no need exists for any supplementation" (*Colossians and Philemon*, 69). The deficiency is our sufferings.

25. N. T. Wright, *Colossians & Philemon*, 90.

PART II: The Testing of a Theodicy

'the birth pangs of the Messiah,' the 'messianic woes' that were to precede the end of the Age.[26]

If Harris and others are correct, this indicates that the suffering of the church is more than a sign of the end, but is the tool of God to bring about the end of this Era and usher in the next. If so, this text fits well into an understanding that God is instrumentally using human patient endurance of Evil & Suffering to somehow bring this age to an end by using Evil & Suffering to destroy Evil & Suffering.

Finally, "this evil age" will end with the coming of Christ. Then, following the judgment, evil will be removed for God's people from recreated "time and space" and there will be no more tears, wars, death, night, seas . . . all that harbored evil has been banished. God's light is everywhere bright and the shadow of evil flees away. This is the miracle that we have been moving toward: the shadow of evil is removed from the back side of creation. Then there will be no shadows and nothing will be hidden from his light. This is the message of Revelation 21:1–5, which was foreshadowed in Isaiah's concluding words in 66:22–24, and which Christ references in Mark 9:41–48. This is the final Creation & Crisis.

Before considering the meaning of this strategic movement of God, it is important to say again what I am not suggesting here. In using phrases like "destruction of evil," I am not saying that evil no longer exists anywhere. I have been careful to use modifiers such as "for his people" and "in the last Era." The final Era of Freedom is only experienced by those who enter the third Era through the work of Christ. Those who never leave the second Era of Slavery, to come into the Penultimate Era, are never welcomed into the fourth Era of Conforming-Freedom. Nor, does this project consider the fate of evil outside of the "New Heavens and New Earth," the "New Jerusalem" or the fate of those who reject Christ. Evil & Suffering is "removed," so that it has no communication with the domain of God's people in the final era of freedom. But the full investigation of this lies beyond the scope of this project, except for this: evil is absent from the experience of those who enter the fourth Era of Freedom.

What is important to see here, and what I am claiming, is that in the strategic movement of God something is clearly missing in the first three acts: the use of God's sword of power to destroy evil for his people. It is drawn and wielded against evil, but it is never drawn and wielded to destroy evil for his people. When it is used, evil is only restrained. Instead, the time between the first and third creations is a time of suffering evil, in which the crucial event of suffering is the Cross. And it appears that

---

26. Harris, *Colossians & Philemon*, 66; citing also Edward Lohse, C.F.D. Moule, and Peter T. O'Brien in support. O'Brien notes that this is true, especially in the context here as Paul writes to a church which he neither started nor served. Whatever Paul means, it must be true in some global way. He writes, "The apostle, through the sufferings which he endures in his own flesh, . . . contributes to the sum total of these eschatological afflictions. By helping to fill up this predetermined measure Paul brings the end, the dawning of the future glory, so much closer. . . . The more of these sufferings he personally absorbed, as he went about preaching the gospel, the less would remain for his fellow Christians to endure" (O'Brien, *Colossians & Philemon*, 80).

the suffering of his people, too, plays a role in bringing about the final act. In the time between, Evil & Suffering is used to destroy Evil & Suffering, so that when we come to the final creation, evil is already defeated. In fact, that seems to be the claim of the texts which we examined. The powerful sword of God was always available to him for the purpose of thwarting evil, but not to make it so that evil does not exist for his people. The three creations show slow and deliberate movement toward what seems to be impossible—to do in three creations what could not be accomplished in one. God is making a people who are as free as God in regard to sin, a people who have Conforming-Freedom, never again to sin.

ON THE FOUR ERAS OF FREEDOM

> On which account we must consider with diligence and attention in what respect those pairs differ from one another—to be able not to sin, and not to be able to sin; to be able not to die, and not to be able to die; to be able not to forsake good, and not to be able to forsake good. For the first man was able not to sin, was able not to die, was able not to forsake good. Are we to say that he who had such a free will could not sin? Or that he to whom it was said, 'If thou shalt sin thou shalt die by death,' could not die? Or that he could not forsake good, when he would forsake this by sinning, and so die? Therefore the first liberty of the will was to be able not to sin, the last will be much greater, not to be able to sin; the first immortality was to be able not to die, the last will be much greater, not to be able to die; the first was the power of perseverance, to be able not to forsake good—the last will be the felicity of perseverance, not to be able to forsake good. But because the last blessings will be preferable and better, were those first ones, therefore, either no blessings at all, or trifling ones?[27]
>
> —Augustine

The three creations and associated crises are the (temporal) boundaries of the Eras of Freedom: Unfettered-Freedom, Slavery, Penultimate-Freedom, and Conforming-Freedom. In each, freedom operates distinctly. The Eras and some of their differences were correctly noted by Augustine and Boston, and here I want to explore these differences.[28]

Before we consider these Eras of Freedom one-by-one, I want to reconsider the application of the standard terms Libertarian Free-Will and Compatibilist Free-Will.

---

27. Augustine, "On Rebuke and Grace," chapter 33. This was written in AD 426 or 427.

28. I should also note the work of Anthony Hoekema in this regard. He also followed Augustine in outlining four eras: True Freedom Not Perfected, True Freedom Lost, True Freedom Restored, and True Freedom Perfected. These are developed in his work, *Created in God's Image*, 231–33. Similar to my development, perfected freedom, as with Conforming-Freedom, is freedom to do only the good and is the intent of God from the beginning.

PART II: The Testing of a Theodicy

While these were carefully defined in Chapter 1, let me briefly suggest here the essential points in the definitions. Both positions agree that there exists freedom of the will: the will functions to choose and the person choosing bears responsibility for that choice. The positions disagree as to how conditioned that choice is by the character of the person and other causal influences, including the corruption of the will. They also differ in regard to the freedom of contrary choice. I will suggest that it may be the case that neither Compatibilistic Free-Will nor Libertarian Free-Will adequately describes the functioning of the human will in every Era. To state my case in an oversimplified way, what the libertarians most want may in fact be granted in the ultimate Era of Freedom, and what the compatibilists describe may have a strict descriptive utility only for the Eras between the first and third creations.

First Era: Unfettered Freedom: Free to Fall (Terminated by the First Creation & Crisis)

> For the first freedom of will which man received when he was created upright consisted in an ability not to sin, but also in an ability to sin.[29]
>
> —Augustine

The freedom that God granted human willful-creatures in this first Era is that freedom which is not tethered (fettered) to God's own goodness. This is reflected in Augustine's words above, "an ability not to sin, . . . an ability to sin" and as noted earlier in the Enchiridion, "before the law." Such freedom is unfettered and unbounded by God's character. It is libertarian in the most natural sense in that it is fully at liberty and unconstrained, having been created good, but not externally sustained in goodness.[30] In certain respects this "unfettered freedom" might be termed a "Defective Free-Will." "Defection" is used here, not as a moral assessment of "unfettered freedom," but as an assessment that such freedom is not free from the pull of sin, as is God's freedom.[31] It is subject to defection; it is able to defect from God's character and this is not the optimum freedom. However, optimized freedom, true freedom, or "freedom" with no

---

29. Augustine, *City of God*, 12.30.

30. By natural, I mean unconditioned by the Fall, and with power of contrary choice. But it is not clear to me what it would mean to be unconditioned by circumstances and by character, or if conditioned, not wholly conditioned. We act within our character and out of our character and our character is perceived by others only by what we actually do—as is God's character. In this sense, such Adamic, first Era freedom could be construed as compatibilist. Whether it is compatibilist or libertarian is not my greatest concern here. We will return to this in the discussion of the fourth Era of Freedom.

31. The words "pull of sin" are deeply troubling in the context of perfection. I am not distinguishing strongly here between the "pull of evil" or even "temptation." All could apply, but the nuance of the phrase "pull of sin," which seems to imply that sin had an attractive force even before the first sin, is not without merit. This is a deep mystery, but it may be bound up in what it means to be "not God" and to be human.

modifier, is to be as free from sin as is God. This was noticed by Augustine,[32] Anselm,[33] Duns Scotus,[34] D.A. Carson,[35] and others. So it would be correct to say, we defected from God's character because of a defect in our freedom. But someone will object to that since I am a non-consequentialist and so must hold that all things were created good, and therefore I cannot permit a defect in Adam's freedom as created by God. To do so would be to include evil in the original creation and to be both a consequentialist in my ethics and a dualist in my ontology. This I reject, again, for I am not suggesting that "defective" is a moral term, but a description of that which permits mutability. That is, while I am using the adjective "defective" in regard to freedom, I am not using it in regard to the first human willful-creatures as created. I am only noting that final persevering freedom has something the original freedom did not possess.[36] Our original freedom was good because it came from a good God and served a godly purpose. It was everything that God intended for this first Era and it was missing nothing he desired in that first Era of Freedom. Nor was it missing anything we needed at that time. And it is the case that the first human willful-creatures were perfectly good. But that freedom was defective in comparison with God's and with the freedom that God ultimately plans for his people. The first human willful-creatures had a freedom that was not perfected. This much Anthony Hoekema wrote, "So man at that time had true freedom—but it was not yet perfect freedom. He could still fall into sin—and, as a matter of fact, did just that."[37] If that is the case, then my argument will show that the Fall was the first step toward that perfection.

Anselm and Pelagius may actually help make this defect visible and bring it into focus. Evans noted, and I agree, that Pelagius's scheme could only work if humanity had a source of goodness within each man and woman.[38] But clearly, this source of

32. Augustine, *City of God*, 14.11, 22.30.

33. Anselm said this well when he wrote, "Teacher. I do not think that free will is the power to sin or not to sin. Indeed if this were its definition, neither God nor the angels, who are unable to sin, would have free will, which it is impious to say" (Anselm, "On Free Will," in *Anselm of Canterbury*, chapter 1 (176)).

34. Duns Scotus writes in *God and Creatures: The Quodlibetal Questions*. In 16.30–31 he agrees with Augustine and Anselm and reason that the will which wills the good is the freer; and "the divine will wills the divine goodness," 16.33.

35. Carson, *How Long, O Lord?*, 191.

36. This seems to be the position of Aquinas when he writes in *ST*, 1a, q49. a2 (article 2), "the evil which consists in the defect of action is always caused by the defect of the agent. But in God there is no defect." God is not the cause of evil, and God is the cause of all that was good, but what was good could defect from the good. The will of God's human willful-creatures was not defective, but it was defectable.

37. Hoekema, *Created in God's Image*, 231.

38. Gillian Rosemary Evans, *Augustine on Evil*, 121. "Pelagius's hypothesis was that if a man can make himself evil by a wrong exercise of his will, he can make himself good by a right exercise of his will. Augustine found two serious faults in this view: it implies that a man can himself be the source of good, and that is a creative act Augustine held to lie with God alone; and it takes no account of the effect Adam's sin had upon all his descendants" (emphasis mine).

PART II: The Testing of a Theodicy

goodness does not exist in humanity now, nor did it exist within Adam or Eve in the Garden. The source is God alone, his nature, and his character. Indeed, we were created good, but we were not created God. The obvious absence of such a source of goodness in any human reveals the nature of the freedom originally given to Adam. The "defect" (clearly visible by accidental necessity) is a freedom which was unfettered, not tied to the Source of goodness, God's character.

By definition, something unfettered and uncontrolled will not be able to conform to a good standard; to be "unfettered" or "uncontrolled" means it is not forced to conform to any external standard. It will "go its own way," which is one way to understand the biblical concept of sin.[39] The root of one Hebrew word for sin is אָטָח. One way of understanding sin can be seen from its morally neutral and metaphorical root in Judges 20:16 as "missing the mark": "Out of all these people 700 choice men were left-handed; each one could sling a stone at a hair and not miss." Similarly the phrase "turn to the right or left" is used descriptively of what it means to sin. In Deuteronomy 5:32 it is used as a warning in introducing the Decalogue: "So you shall observe to do just as the LORD your God has commanded you; you shall not turn aside to the right or to the left." This is also the case in Deuteronomy 17:11, 20; 28:14, Joshua 1:7; 23:6, 2 Kings 22:2, 2 Chronicles 34:2, Proverbs 4:27, and Isaiah 30:21. The New Testament uses a similar idea, and also intensified the same metaphor. Not only are we morally deficient because we cannot "shoot straight," but because we cannot shoot high enough or far enough: "For all have sinned and fallen short of the glory of God" (Romans 3:23). To sin is to be unable to "track" with God and unable to "keep up with" God. The unfettered nature of freedom in this Era seems to provide no force that compels God's willful-creatures to track with him.

Such is the necessity of evil of which I speak here. God in freedom created for his own purposes. But when he created, as he created, sin came with a subordinate-metaphysical necessity from the good creation, specifically because it included his image bearers, the human willful-creatures. For no two objects follow the same path indefinitely, unless both are in some sense guided. In this case, one is guided by his Good nature and one is unguided, having a nature that is unfettered and without The Good. One is the Source, the nature and character of God. One has a created, but not maintained, perfection and is not guided by the Source. So, I will claim, God's creatures, who began with perfection and a certain kind of defective freedom, must defect from God's goodness, necessarily (because of no conforming force), but freely (operating unfettered and with true volitional freedom). This was the first Era of Freedom and its necessary demise.

---

39. There are many biblical definitions of sin including iniquity, pride, wickedness, rejection of God, idolatry, and almost uncountable examples of sin. I do not intend a rigorous definition of sin here, but only to observe that it is possible to consider that all of these represent "missing the mark" of God's holiness. To sin is to fail the command of Leviticus: "be holy as I am holy" (Leviticus 11:44–45, 1 Peter 1:16).

But Calvin seems to object to the idea that we can know why God has taken his people through a progression of "eras." He wrote,

> But the reason he did not sustain man by the virtue of perseverance lies hidden in his plan; sobriety is for us the part of wisdom. Man, indeed, received the ability provided he exercised the will; but he did not have the will to use his ability, for this exercising of the will would have been followed by perseverance. Yet he is not excusable, for he received so much that he voluntarily brought about his own destruction; indeed, no necessity was imposed upon God of giving man other than a mediocre and even transitory will, that form man's Fall he might gather occasion for his own glory.[40]

While asserting that man has "no excuse" for his failure, Calvin acknowledges that the movement from one Era to another was valuable for God's glory, though the reason that God allowed that failure was a mystery "hidden in his counsel." But does Calvin intend to say that this "hidden counsel" should (not just does) remain a mystery, never to be explored by God's human willful-creatures? If so, neither Calvin nor anyone, else offers an argument to that effect. While the infinite glories of God will never be exhausted by human study, I have argued above that all mysteries are subject to human investigation and that what we discover about God is to the glory of God; it glorifies God for his people to know him and delight in him. Could it be that we can understand something more of this specific mystery? Could we understand the holy movement intended by God in permitting human rebellion? Might it be the case that this human failure is a necessary first step toward the glory that God intends for his people? To make a person impeccable seems to require a process in which evil is defeated for his people. In that sense, the first Era of Freedom, unfettered freedom, transitioned into the next by necessity. God was implementing his plan even as we rebelled.

Second Era: Lost Freedom: Slavery to Sin (Terminated by the Second Creation & Crisis)

> "free-will" without God's grace is not free at all, but is the permanent prisoner and bondslave of evil, since it cannot turn itself to good.[41]
>
> —Martin Luther

This second Era of Freedom is that one in which human willful-creatures are (in Augustine like language) "able to sin, unable not to sin." We are in bondage, not freedom, and as Augustine referred to this era in the Enchiridion, we are "under the law." We are in no significant way, free, in regard to sin. We have already discussed the

---

40. Calvin, *ICR*, 1.15.8.
41. Luther, "Bondage of the Will," in *Martin Luther*, 187.

PART II: The Testing of a Theodicy

Irenaean-Origin-Pelagius heritage which views this Era quite differently. I will not examine this here again except to say that the kind of freedom that they desire is not available after the first crisis, which resulted in the whole of the universe being frustrated and brought under bondage to decay. Adam possessed and then lost an unfettered freedom that resembled libertarian freedom (at least in some respects). As a result, people of the second Era of Freedom are found in slavery; having no freedom at all to consistently act in conformity to what is good. The freedom of this Era is most similar to that described as Compatibilistic Free-Will. 2 Timothy 2:24–26 provides a significant picture of this Era into which we are all born:

> The Lord's bond-servant must not be quarrelsome, but be kind to all, able to teach, patient when wronged, with gentleness correcting those who are in opposition, if perhaps God may grant them repentance leading to the knowledge of the truth, and they may come to their senses and escape from the snare of the devil, having been held captive by him to do his will.

In other words, fallen humanity exercises Volitional Free-Will only to discover, that she is not free, but a slave of Satan and deceived into thinking that her choices are freely made in a libertarian sense. But it is a deception because her will is captive to Satan's will. Luther wrestled through this text with Erasmus. When Erasmus says that free-will is "small" without God's grace, Luther retorts that it is non-existent. He writes,

> "free-will" without God's grace is not free at all, but is the permanent prisoner and bondslave of evil, since it cannot turn itself to good. . . . So it befits theologians to refrain from using the term when they want to speak of human ability, and to leave it to be applied to God only. They would do well to take the term out of men's mouths and speech, and to claim it for their God, as if it were His own holy and awful Name. . . . [RAS: Free-will] is the devil's prisoner. Do not use this phrase that deceives the majority of people.[42]

Let me give an example of Alistair McFadyen when he writes of the World War II Jewish ghettos and the internal self-government that the Nazi's required of them. Here let the actions of the Jews be that of "all people" and the actions of the Nazis be that of Satan:

> With the emergence of the Final Solution as the real end of Jewish policy and its primacy over all other objectives, including military ones, all attempts by Jews to operate a rational calculus [RAS: such as making their work indispensable to the war effort] were doomed to failure. . . . The appearance of choice, of plural option which could be exercised, was ultimately illusory.[43]

---

42. Luther, "Bondage of the Will," *Martin Luther*, 187–8.
43. McFadyen, *Bound to Sin*, 101.

This is a grotesque but realistic example of the functioning of our natural will in our universe. While it seems we can act in wisdom in our universe and for our own benefit, or at least to escape a worse situation, we are trapped by Satan; every action that seems wise or beneficial always accounts to the benefit of our enemy and against us. The calculus works inexorably against us. Our will operates "freely," and truly so in every way that Augustine intended when he said that the will operates of itself with nothing higher, yet it is not free in the way we "feel" or "desire." In this Era, our will is overpoweringly influenced. Thomas Schreiner says, "The bondage of the will, then, is slavery to our own desires."[44] And it is also a slavery to the desires of others, especially evil, yet all-the-while we feel free.

It is here I should emphasize that our Volitional Free-Will continues intact throughout all four Eras of Freedom. Jack Cottrell calls Volitional Free-Will, "farcical."[45] That's quite understandable, for many people, perhaps all of us as we are born, like to think of ourselves as self-determining. To say that we choose, but that we act wholly under influences, seems "farcical" to more than a few. But preferences aside, a strong case can be made that our freedom is not as we "choose" or "want" it, but as it is, a kind of slavery. That is not "farcical," but it is frustrating (in the sense of Romans 8:20–21). What remains, Volitional Free-Will, is a shell of what we once had, not a farce. In fact, quite different from a "farce" it is portent of what is to come in the fourth Era of Freedom. We speak truly when we say we exercise our will. Anselm described this well, as the "Teacher" speaks:

> T. But even if the rectitude of the will is absent, the rational nature still has undiminished what is proper to it. I think we have no power sufficient unto itself for action, and yet when those things are lacking without which our powers can scarcely be led to act, we are no less said to have them insofar as they are in us.[46]

Volition exists "without diminution" for it is an essence of what it means to be a human willful-creature. This is also the perspective of Calvin who said, surprisingly to some, that man has free-will and that this is his volition: "Man will then be spoken of as having this sort of free decision, not because he has free choice equally of good and evil, but because he acts wickedly by will, not by compulsion. Well put, indeed, but what purpose is served by labeling with a proud name such a slight thing?"[47] Edwards also said much the same thing.[48] Volition remains and is truly free, though free is a

---

44. Schreiner, "Does Scripture Teach Prevenient Grace in the Wesleyan Sense?," 366.
45. Cottrell, *What the Bible Says about God the Ruler*, 223–44.
46. Anselm, "On Free Will," in *Anselm of Canterbury*, chapter 3 (180).
47. Calvin, *ICR*, 2.2.7.
48. "The plain and obvious meaning of the words freedom and liberty, in common speech, is The (sic) power, opportunity, or advantage that anyone has, to do as he pleases. Or in other words, his being free from hindrance or impediment in the way of doing, or conducting in any respect, as he wills. And the contrary to liberty, whatever name we call that by, is a person's being hindered or unable to

PART II: The Testing of a Theodicy

grand word for such a small seed. But in that seed remains something quite powerful: a responsible choice. It must be acknowledged, even proclaimed, that this is not the same as "true freedom" or as I am calling it in this project, "Conforming Freedom." So Hoekema writes, "By 'choice' or 'the ability to choose' I shall mean the capacity of humans to make choices between alternatives—a capacity that implies responsibility for those choices. . . . By 'true freedom' I shall mean the ability of humans, with the help of the Holy Spirit, to think, say and do what is pleasing to God and in harmony with his revealed will."[49] "True freedom" is what we have always desired—but we have no power to achieve this on our own.

From the perspective of those who will gain the Era of Conforming-Freedom, this second Era is dominated by sovereign rescues of the kind which Christ pictured in the parable of the wedding feast. This is recorded in Matthew 22:1–14:

> Jesus spoke to them again in parables, saying, "The kingdom of heaven may be compared to a king who gave a wedding feast for his son. And he sent out his slaves to call those who had been invited to the wedding feast, and they were unwilling to come. Again he sent out other slaves saying, 'Tell those who have been invited, "Behold, I have prepared my dinner; my oxen and my fattened livestock are all butchered and everything is ready; come to the wedding feast."' But they paid no attention and went their way, one to his own farm, another to his business, and the rest seized his slaves and mistreated them and killed them. But the king was enraged, and he sent his armies and destroyed those murderers and set their city on fire. Then he said to his slaves, 'The wedding is ready, but those who were invited were not worthy. Go therefore to the main highways, and as many as you find there, invite to the wedding feast.' Those slaves went out into the streets and gathered together all they found, both evil and good; and the wedding hall was filled with dinner guests. But when the king came in to look over the dinner guests, he saw a man there who was not dressed in wedding clothes, and he said to him, 'Friend, how did you come in here without wedding clothes?' And the man was speechless. Then the king said to the servants, 'Bind him hand and foot, and throw him into the outer darkness; in that place there will be weeping and gnashing of teeth.' For many are called, but few are chosen."

G. R. Evans showed that this was at the heart of Augustine's understanding of the operation of God in this second Era of Freedom (slavery). All are born into this Era (unlike Adam, we do not "enjoy" the first Era) as slaves to sin and cut off from God. Though God calls all to the wedding feast—all do not come. But some he compels, and they do come.[50] If one seeks to come on his own, and on his own terms, he is not

conduct as he will, or being necessitated to do otherwise" (Jonathan Edwards, "Freedom of the Will," *Collected Works*, 1.5.1).

49. Hoekema, *Created in God's Image*, 228.

50. G. R. Evans, *Augustine on Evil*, 136. These come by Volitional Free-Will, making a choice, yet

welcome. This is the heart of the second Era. I have already suggested that Augustine clearly indicated that he perceived a kind of Libertarian Free-Will for Adam, but a proto-Compatibilistic Free-Will for fallen humanity. So, I also suggest that certain kind of Compatibilistic Free-Will best describes the kind of "non-freedom" experienced by fallen humanity in this second Era. God has handed all over to slavery and it is God who will rescue those who are to be rescued.

Penultimate Freedom: Free to Obey (Terminated by the Third Creation & Crisis)

> And the same reason that has made him create man innocent, but liable to fall, makes Him re-create man when he falls.[51]
>
> —Leibniz

In this Era we are, in Augustinian-like language, "able to sin, able not to sin," or as he labeled it in the Enchiridion, "under grace." And as Leibniz notes, it is an Era of God's re-creation of his human willful-creatures. For the first time since the Fall, we are able not to sin. But the new creation in Christ only has a down-payment on Conforming-Freedom, for in this Era we are still fully able to sin and it is an ability we exercise often! This down-payment is the Holy Spirit who is called our ἀρραβών in Ephesians 1:14, a word meaning "down payment." This is not the final Era. His bi-directional freedom, this sub-freedom, is one that is Compatibilistic Free-Will-like, in that God's people have genuine choices before them, but it is God who controls the causes. Augustine described this Era as he did, rejecting both the dualistic fatalism of the Manicheans and the proto-Libertarian Free-Will of his day, which may have arisen to combat dualism, as discussed earlier. His understanding was Compatibilistic Free-Will-like, in modern terms, in that he looked to God as the one who manipulated the causes.[52]

This is not the place to make a full case for Compatibilistic Free-Will, and I have demonstrated both the historical development and something of the biblical case in Chapter 1.[53] However, I do believe that like the second Era of Freedom, Compatibilistic Free-Will is an adequate model of how God works with his human willful-creatures.

God has so determined the circumstances and causes that they make that choice compatibilistically.

51. Leibniz, *Theodicy: Essays on the Goodness of God, the Freedom of Man and the Origin of Evil*, 1.28.

52. It may be the fact that he was wedged-in between these two rocks that cause some to misunderstand his position as one in which he "progressed" from a Libertarian Free-Will-like position to a radical Compatibilistic Free-Will-like position in later life. In fact, early in life he was fighting with the Manicheans and later in life with the Pelagians; language and emphasis changes depending on to whom you are speaking. Moreover, as was shown earlier, some statements in which he sounded almost libertarian were spoken of the first Era and some in which he sounded more compatibilist were spoken of the second and third Eras.

53. David Clotfelter makes a good and winsome argument of the compatibilist position in his

PART II: The Testing of a Theodicy

It should be also observed that this Era overlaps the previous and is a foretaste of the next. This has been observed by an overwhelming number of scholars, including George Eldon Ladd who wrote:

> God's Kingdom means the divine conquest over His enemies, a conquest which is to be accomplished in three stages; and the first victory has already occurred. The power of the Kingdom of God has invaded the realm of Satan—the present evil Age. . . . [RAS: Satan] was cast down from his position of power; his power was "destroyed." The blessings of the Messianic Age are now available to those who embrace the Kingdom of God. . . . Yes, the Kingdom of God has come near, it is already present.[54]

They are parallel, existing side-by-side, but inhabiting different Kingdoms, or as Ladd understands it, overlapping Ages. Though the Bible presents sin as entering into creation at a point in time and also proclaims the unique work of Christ in time, this Era is experienced asynchronously with people entering into it as they are called by God individually. As a result, they also experience something of the next Era, as well. The Era of Slavery and the Era of Penultimate Freedom exist side-by-side in the same world, but one is not of the other. So also the third Era overlaps with the final Era of Conforming-Freedom. Romans 12:2 references our duty and privilege in the current Era of Penultimate-Freedom, but it is also a glimpse of what is coming: "And do not be conformed to this world, but be transformed by the renewing of your mind, so that you may prove what the will of God is, that which is good and acceptable and perfect." When God's people are fully transformed into the image of Christ, they will desire what is good, acceptable, and perfect, which I take to mean that the will is healed when it desires what God desires. This is a foretaste; this is what can be experienced fully in the Era of ultimate freedom, Conforming-Freedom.

Ultimate Freedom: Conforming-Freedom (Obeying Freely)

> But in the state of glory, every one will see in each thing that he wills, the relation of that thing to what God wills in that particular matter. Consequently he will conform his will to God in all things not only formally, but also materially.[55]
>
> —Aquinas

This Era is parallel to Augustine's final Era in which God's people are "able not to sin, unable to sin." More exactly, he writes in The City of God, "that man should first receive a free will by which he was able not to sin, and at last a free will by which he

---

book, *Sinners in the Hands of a Good God*, Part 2: "At His Mercy" (chapters 4–6), 107–85.

54. Ladd, *Gospel of the Kingdom*, 50.

55. Aquinas, *Summa Theologica*, Ia IIae, q.19, a.10. See also a.9.

was not able to sin,"[56] which means, "the will, therefore, is then truly free, when it is not the slave of vices and sins."[57] True freedom is the freedom from sin. So Augustine describes this era in Enchiridion, "the fourth is in full and perfect peace,"[58] which "will constitute no restriction on the freedom of his will. On the contrary, his will shall be much freer when it shall be wholly impossible for him to be the slave of sin."[59] This is the final or ultimate Era which God has designed for his people over the history of creation—the Era and state for which God's people were not fit before and which seems could not be instantiated for them in a single act of creation.

While some may still object to the necessity of facing and conquering evil, there is significant agreement about what the final state will accomplish for his people. This has been shown to be the understanding of Augustine, Anselm,[60] and Aquinas. Stanley Kane wrote of Anselm's understanding, "Don't you see that someone who possesses what is fitting and advantageous in such a way that he cannot lose it is more free than someone else who possesses the same thing in such a way that he can lose it and be drawn toward what is unfitting and disadvantageous?"[61] Similarly in the contemporary discussion, D.A. Carson has written "Real freedom is freedom to obey God without restraint or reserve. It is not absolute power to contrary; it is wanting to please God at every moment."[62] This is the freedom for which we have always longed.

Of this new creation, Paul Helm wrote, "The freedom of heaven, then, is the freedom from sin; not that the believer just happens to be free from sin, but that he is so constituted or reconstituted that he cannot sin. He does not want to sin, and he does not want to want to sin. And in this respect he is like Christ, who, though tempted, yet could not sin."[63] This final state is something that was lacking in Adam in his initial state. But God in his wisdom decreed the Fall, established the causes so that evil would arise necessarily, yet freely, in the first human willful-creatures, and brought about the strategy that would enact our true freedom. Charles Journet observed this with the words of St. Francis de Sales: "our loss was a gain for us, since human nature has in effect received more graces by the redemption of its Savior than it would have received

---

56. Augustine, *City of God*, 12.30.

57. Augustine, *City of God*, 14.11. This is God's goal, that we might have "fullness of joy."

58. Augustine, *Enchiridion*, ¶ 118, 137.

59. Augustine, *Enchiridion*, ¶ 105, 123.

60. Anselm wrote, through the person of the "teacher": "Do you not see that one who is as he ought to be, and as it is expedient for him to be, such that he is unable to lose this state, is freer than one who is such that he can lose it and be led into what is indecent and inexpedient for him?" (Anselm, "On Free Will," Davies and Evans, chapter 1 (176)).

61. Kane, *Anselm's Doctrine of Freedom and the Will*, 125.

62. Carson, *How Long, O Lord?*, 191.

63. Helm, *Last Things: Death, Judgment, Heaven & Hell*, 92. Though "could not" is correct, because Christ is fully God, yet that is not strictly the meaning of the verse Helm seems to paraphrase here, Hebrews 4:15, which reads simply, χωρὶς ἁμαρτίας or the state of being "without sin." This verse indicates nothing about inability which is explicit in "could not sin."

by the innocence of Adam."[64] This God is accomplishing through the four Eras of Freedom. And God began with the Fall.

There are many texts that deal with this final Era from the perspective of God's goal to finally shape his people into the image of Christ. Some we have already considered, such as Romans 8 which shows the stages of this work in his people (here shortened for clarity): God's call, suffering, and glorification. In context, glorification is equivalent to conforming freedom, for that is the focus of this sentence: "predestined to be conformed to the likeness of his Son." Also, the text in Romans 8:20–21 announces that creation is longing for his people to achieve their freedom so that it may also possess, "the freedom of the glory of the children of God." How does the adjectival phrase, "of the glory" modify freedom when Paul writes, "τὴν ἐλευθερίαν τῆς δόξης"? The answer comes from two phrases in this text. First it is anticipated in Romans 8:17–18, which tells us that in order to be glorified with Christ his people must suffer with him, "if indeed we suffer with Him so that we may also be glorified with Him." Suffering somehow carries his people toward this final Era of freedom. So also, Romans 8:29–30 indicates exactly the means of that glorification through suffering, "προώρισεν συμμόρφους τῆς εἰκόνος τοῦ υἱοῦ αὐτοῦ." The flow shows that conformity is the goal and it is identical with the ultimate consequence of being called, glorification. So the "glorious freedom" of Romans 8:20–21 is "Conforming Freedom." His people will be freely-conforming—something that all creation has been crying out for over all the long ages.

We see this also in 2 Corinthians 3:17–18, "Now the Lord is the Spirit; and where the Spirit of the Lord is, there is liberty. But we all, with unveiled face, beholding as in a mirror the glory of the Lord, are being transformed into the same image from glory to glory, just as from the Lord, the Spirit." The glory of his people, which is here linked in parallel to liberty, is to be conformed to the image of Christ. This is what his people were created for. And as we have seen, 1 Peter 4:1–2 tells us that suffering is the force that drives his people to conformity in Christ, for when they die in Christ, they die also to sin. Also, in Ephesians 4:24 we read, "and put on the new self, which in the likeness of God has been created in righteousness and holiness of the truth." The new self, the final Era which has its beginning now, will be fully experienced in the final Era in full conformity to Christ. It is in this conformity to God that true freedom is found.

It may be helpful here to show the sharp distinction between this proposal and that of John Hick. It might sound to some as if I am suggesting that God's people are moving from immaturity to maturity by the operation of evil. However, while this is Hick's proposal, it is distinctly different from mine. Hick writes, "One who has attained to goodness by meeting and eventually mastering temptations, and thus by rightly making responsible choices in concrete situations, is good in a richer and more valuable sense than one created ab initio in a state of either innocence or virtue."[65] I am propos-

---

64. Journet, *Meaning of Evil*, 258.
65. Hick, *Evil and the God of Love*, 255, as cited in Michael L. Peterson, *God and Evil*, 95.

ing that God takes his people from perfection, through rebellion, to redemption, and finally causes glorification. In opposition to Hick, and problematically for some, my project includes the Fall, which I take to be historical. None-the-less, I hasten to add that a "theological fall," outside of history, would be sufficient for my project, as it is enough to assert that God intends to take his people from one perfection to a greater perfection, through imperfection.[66] In contrast, Hick's "Fall-free" project is from imperfection (immaturity) to perfection (maturity). Secondly, and more important for my project, evil is an enemy that must be conquered. Evil is not a neutral tutor that will make us good, but it is a vicious and privative enemy which appears in the shadow of willful creatures in God's creation. It must be defeated. And it was defeated at the Cross. In our exposure to Evil & Suffering, God's people participate and fellowship with Christ in this work, which in some way contributes to glorification with him in Conforming-Freedom. Finally, evil will not just be left behind in our advance, as if we pass beyond it. Instead, evil is destroyed for us so it has no intersection with us, as it never has with the character of God. Evil is not "trained out" but destroyed through Christ and in his people, by God and not by our efforts. It was destroyed by God when he became susceptible to evil in the incarnation, destroying evil by suffering evil, and triumphing over evil in the resurrection and finally revealing the victory in his return. Until then, his people battle evil along with God in their suffering. Yet, I agree with Hick in this, "God cannot instantly create mature persons," if "mature" means "freely conforming" to Christ (to the Good; to God) in one act of creation. That is, in his freedom, he cannot, for this does not accomplish his goals. Instead I propose that we do not need a soul-making theodicy, but a theodicy in which Evil & Suffering destroys Evil & Suffering. This is a Theodicy by suffering.

Some might object that freedom which is conforming cannot be free. I am sympathetic to that in some ways. The libertarian position wants no freedom that is constrained by internal or external causal forces, which would include an external God or internal character. For some, such constraint would seem to make every choice an a-choice once the causes were exposed. But that is not what I am intending here. When the Bible speaks of conforming to God's character I see nothing that indicates that this must mean human will is "absolutely controlled in every decision" in the final Era. This is like the discussion about the meaning of "apatheia" as it relates to God. Jürgen Moltmann noted that the characteristic of God, which is called "apatheia" by some, has little to do with our modern word "apathy." While apathy means indifference, "apatheia" means freedom from the lower and baser drives.[67] So the freedom that is conforming is freedom from that which is base and from that which is not like God. Then, just as God is free to do anything that is within his character, so in Conforming-Freedom we are in fact freer than Adam and freer even than penultimate-freedom, not under greater restrictions. That which is open to the one who is freed from sin, is

---

66. See the section on Adam and Eve and the Fall in chapter 8.
67. Moltmann, *Crucified God*, 267–69.

greater than that which is open to the one who is constrained by the pull of evil. Of this kind of Conforming-Freedom Moltmann said in echo of Augustine, "Our hearts are captive until they become free in the glory of the triune God."[68] Since theologians, with the exception of rationalists such as Leibniz, affirm that God is free in all his acts, conformity to him, and especially Conforming-Freedom might reasonably include a freedom like God's.

A similar objection would be that this proposal of an ultimate Era of Conforming-Freedom is nothing other than a repackaged compatibilist free-will model: God causes his people to conform to his goodness—and they will like it! Maybe, if that is what the text requires. But if this is what God desired to do, God could have done that in a one-act drama. Rather what I am proposing might be described as an ultimate Compatibilistic Free-Will model, with no higher purpose than the relationship it permits us to have with him. This in no way limits or modifies the reality that God's will is always prior to his contingent universe. But if this proposal is correct, it is also an ultimate Libertarian Free-Will model in which his people will be truly free to do anything that is within the infinite character of God. Dallas Willard makes an interesting observation in this regard. He writes, "It is a curious fact that many today who read that in the period of the judges all did 'what is right in their own eyes' think that something terrible was covered by that phrase. Indeed, the people of this time went wrong in many ways. But to do as one pleases is the ideal condition of humanity, what is often called 'freedom.' "[69] Willard, whose writing is sympathetic with a Libertarian Free-Will perspective, sees something important. This is the freedom that we desire and it is the freedom that his people are destined for in Christ. Such "freedom" is terrible during the period of the Judges, which fell within the Era of Slavery. But, what Willard proposes sounds indistinguishable from what I intend by the phrase Conforming-Freedom in the final Era. I strongly suspect that neither the Libertarian Free-Will or Compatibilistic Free-Will advocate will be content with this proposal, but it may be that Conforming-Freedom contains the best of both Compatibilistic Free-Will and Libertarian Free-Will. This leaves the issue of counter-factuals and the power of contrary choice in the final era. I know of no way to resolve this issue today, in regard to the final Era of Freedom. I am inclined to think that it may be a pointless question at this time, like asking if a person could rightly choose something he desires less than that which he has chosen. That would make no sense when our desires have been healed by him who is the Desire of All. And Ultimate Compatibilistic Free-Will seems to have no need of the same supervisory direction God exercises with human willful-creatures who have broken wills. He could of course, but our desire for this ultimate freedom may turn out to be an echo of the past Garden of Eden, and a memory of the Garden of God, yet to come.

68. Moltmann, *Trinity and the Kingdom*, 222.

69. Dallas Willard writes, "but to do as one pleases is the ideal condition of humanity, what is often called 'freedom,' and does not imply wrongdoing at all" (*Spirit of the Disciplines*, 242).

What will be the nature of freedom in this final Garden? The first Garden had two different trees and that included a choice—one that we would rather not have had, if we had planned the first Garden! And in the new Garden, all is changed, and we have the case that we would have had at first. In the Garden of Eden, God's first human willful-creatures were permitted to eat from "any of the trees"—all was before them. Yet one possibility was a terrible evil. But in the Garden of God that evil choice has been removed; it is gone, perhaps destroyed. This seems to be the "correction" God made between opening chapters of Genesis and the last chapter of Revelation. Most translations read this text, Revelation 22:2, as having only one tree. For example the NIV reads, "on each side of the river stood the tree of life." That is, the tree is planted on one side of the river, but the branches of the single tree overhang both sides. While there is a valid argument for a single tree, the symmetry of two trees in both creations is compelling and perhaps even demanded by this text: "ἐν μέσῳ τῆς πλατείας αὐτῆς καὶ τοῦ ποταμοῦ ἐντεῦθεν καὶ ἐκεῖθεν ξύλον ζωῆς ποιοῦν καρποὺς δώδεκα." The phrase, "τοῦ ποταμοῦ ἐντεῦθεν καὶ ἐκεῖθεν" occurs nowhere else in the text of the NT or LXX, but means something like a tree "on this side and on that side of the river." The first thing to notice is that "tree of life" is anarthrous, contrary to the NIV reading. While the article would seem to limit us to a single tree (with extended branch or some explanation for reaching the other side), the lack of the article grants us freedom to interpret in context whether there is a tree extending over both sides or a tree on each side. Second, a similar Johannine phrase appears in John 19:18 which reads, "καὶ μετ' αὐτοῦ ἄλλους δύο ἐντεῦθεν καὶ ἐντεῦθεν." This is used by John in regard to the trees of the crucifixion. It translates in the NASB as, "and with Him two other men, one on either side" or more literally, "and with him two others on this side and on this side." This indicates at least warrant, if not necessity, that I may take the text of Revelation to read, "a tree of life, on this side and on that side of the river." Greg Beale takes this same position, writing, "First, the original 'tree of life' in Genesis has become multiplied into 'trees for food' and having 'leaves for healing.'" . . . Similarly, Revelation 22:2 pictures the 'the tree of life' as a giant tree or as a grove 'on either side of the river,' bringing healing."[70] The Tree of the Knowledge of Good and Evil is not only gone, but its place has been taken by Life. Heaven is full and rich and nothing is missing. Evil is not just gone, leaving a gap, but fully filled by that which is good (Life), and evil will never be missed. We do not look at the charred stump of evil, and declare, "There it used to be!" We do not notice a tree missing and wonder at its absence. What God began is finished in fullness. In the final creation there are two Trees of Life and they both are for healing. Now, like God, before whom is an infinity of perfect choices,

---

70. Beale, *Temple and the Church's Mission*, 360. John may also be thinking about the text of Ezekiel 47:12 which reads, "By the river on its bank, on one side and on the other, will grow all kinds of trees for food. Their leaves will not wither and their fruit will not fail. They will bear every month because their water flows from the sanctuary, and their fruit will be for food and their leaves for healing." Which using a similar phrase, indicates trees (not the name Tree of Life) on both sides of the river whose leaves are for healing.

PART II: The Testing of a Theodicy

evil is not possible for his people or even missed. It does not exist for his people as a possibility. We, who are redeemed, have returned with God to the state before creation in which no such "thing" as evil existed.[71] In the final Era of Freedom, his people will share with him; they will have Conforming-Freedom. God has made his people safe for his universe by the God glorifying miracle of destroying evil for his people and giving his people the kind of freedom he enjoys, necessarily.

This is Conforming-Freedom. This is the freedom that is greater than that of the first Garden. This is the freedom that God has always had but could not give to his people in one act. It seems he has given it to his people through four Eras by destroying Evil & Suffering through Evil & Suffering.

ON AN ESCHATOLOGICAL THEODICY: REFLECTIONS ON THE BOOK OF JOB

> A theodicy that starts in this way must be eschatological in its ultimate bearings. That is to say, instead of looking to the past for its clue to the mystery of evil, it looks to the future, and indeed to that ultimate future to which only faith can look.[72]
>
> —John Hick

> An ultimate hope will have to rest in an ultimate reality, that is to say, in the eternal God himself, and not in his creation.[73]
>
> —John Polkinghorne

While Polkinghorne and Hick do not eat from the same theological table, they both understand theodicy to be eschatological in nature; it is. Hick's perspective takes a strange route from what he calls an Irenaean perspective of immaturity to a universalism which is achieved by relatively infinite opportunities to mature through "many lives; many worlds." While my divergence from Hick should be obvious by now to the reader, I would affirm his intuition in the quote above. A forward looking theology is necessary to address the present questions of theodicy. So, Polkinghorne, whose conservative approach to special revelation is grounded in natural revelation and logic—an approach he calls bottom-up, affirms that it is only the ultimate reality of God, and the eventual restoration of his people to him in eternity that can grant them hope today. This eschatological approach to theodicy is not exceptional and it crosses systems—as well it should, if it is one of the truths that can be discerned. In this section, I want to investigate whether it is the case that the Book of Job may point us to

---

71. That is, evil truly "is" metaphysically dependent upon the creation of what is good, but not bound to the source of goodness. It is in that sense a privation.

72. Hick, *Evil and the God of Love*, 297.

73. Polkinghorne, *Faith of a Physicist*, 163.

God and restoration to Him in the eschaton as the foundation of our theodicy, and even our theology.

Elihu, the fourth "friend" of Job, may have said something like this to Job in the Book of Job 36:16, "He is wooing you from the jaws of distress to a spacious place free from restriction, to the comfort of your table laden with choice food." Where is this place? We have never yet encountered it. If this translation (NIV) is correct,[74] Elihu may be saying that God is wooing his people from distress to freedom that is beyond present experience. That is, Elihu may be saying that Job can find hope in his suffering only by looking to God and our eschatological end with God. Perhaps his words, "free from restriction" even hints at a kind of freedom God intends for his people, eschatologically. But let it not seem as though I will build a theology (or a theodicy) on a dubious comment tossed at Job by a dubious friend. Yet if this is what Elihu meant, it is not far from the desire for a certain kind of freedom that God seems to have put within all of us. And as noted in this chapter, this kind of freedom may be realized only in the eschaton. And this is what I am suggesting: a right theodicy will be God-centered and eschatological. A successful theodicy does not focus attention on what was or what is, but on God and his eternal plans for his people. And I want to suggest that this is just what the author of Job may have intended in his book.[75]

---

74. Here the NIV is cited against the wooden and almost unreadable NASB translation: "Then indeed, He enticed you from the mouth of distress, instead of it, a broad place with no constraint; And that which was set on your table was full of fatness." All translators struggle with the ambiguities of this text, though the editors of the NASB made no decisions that are helpful to lead the reader to understanding! The difficulty of the text leads some to consider the subject of the verb to be so unclear that it may be God, a missing subject, or the "spacious place" (H. H. Rowley, *Job*, 294–5). If the latter, then the meaning may be that Job has been lured away from righteousness by lack of restriction and choice food, quite the opposite of what I am suggesting. However, there is evidence that God is the subject which includes the conjunctive "also" (וְאַף), which ties this verb to the subject of the previous verse, which is taken to be YHWH. If God is the subject, it then becomes more likely that Elihu is offering Job reason to stop complaining about his situation, namely an eschatological hope beyond any present pain or loss.

75. The majority of scholarship understands Job to be a work that dates from the time of the exile of Israel or afterwards. Gordis places Job between 300–500 BCE: "Virtually all modern scholars date Job somewhere between 700 and 200 BCE . . . I would assign the period between 500 and 300 BCE . . . the early days of the second Temple, which marked the heyday of Wisdom literature, when the concern with the individual became paramount" (Gordis, *Book of God and Man: A Study of Job*, 216). His primary reason is Job's established monotheism. Some cite historical references such as words engraved on stone outlined with lead (19:23–24), references to cultural rankings in the Persian Empire (3:14–15), caravan trade routes (6:19) and others. These points are debatable (Hartley, *Book of Job*, 18). It is Gordis's claim that such monotheism did not exist in Israel until this late date (Gordis, *Book of God and Man*, 216–7). The writers of biblical materials were rarely representatives of their religious culture, but rather prophetic voices. Though some see them as henotheists, I would claim that established monotheists wrote the whole of the biblical text based on repeated statements that other gods (idols) are not true gods. Statements that YHWH or El is more powerful than other gods should be understood as hyperbole for purposes of bragging—contextualization, if you will. But this is a debate for another project. We can say, at least, that a monotheist (if such they were), even monotheists who chased after idols (serial-polytheists, perhaps), are not de facto polytheists, either. Such people may well be idolaters of convenience. While only "believing" in the One, they sought to enjoy

PART II: The Testing of a Theodicy

It is also important to identify the central figure of the Book of Job as YHWH. The spot light is not on Job's friends, nor even Job himself. While not bit players, the friends of Job are under-developed and two-dimensional. They exist in the drama for one purpose: to draw from Job his thoughts about the One who is central to this work, God himself. So also, Job, a more fully developed character, is on the stage to wrestle with God, and with the Adversary. His dominant role is central because of who he interacts with—YHWH. But every speech throughout the work and every activity on earth and in heaven involve God and point us to him. YHWH is central to the thinking of the author and each section of the book drives us to his earth shaking presence in the final chapters. And, while interesting, the central figure is clearly not the Adversary. Indeed, he is the bit player here, carrying out God's plan for Job without passion or creativity; his works are covered in a few sentences. The central figure in this drama is God—yet, with the exception of the introduction, he is off-stage for the first 37 chapters. While not beyond the horizon of the author or audience, God is eclipsed for Job by his Evil & Suffering. And it is just this eclipse of God by evil that

---

the perceived benefits of each god, at least culturally. If it is true that Israel as a whole was changed by the exile into a monotheistic culture, devout and "mature" monotheists existed throughout the history of Israel and only apriori assumptions would date Job later based on the monotheism of its author. In fact, nothing precludes the author of Job from being either a monotheist or a polytheist in any age. Another suggestion is that this is an exilic theodicy in light of the suffering and the loss of the temple and freedom. Hartley observes that it is not likely that this text is an exilic treatise on suffering because the principle, Job, was an innocent man, while the Exile is understood as God's punishment of a less than innocent Israel for gross failure (Hartley, *Book of Job*, 19). Here he rightly cites 2 Kings 22:15–17 and Jeremiah 31:29 as biblical support for their understanding of their situation. Moreover, Eliphaz the Temanite, who is likely from Edom, is on friendly terms with Job. But Edom was a constant harassment to Israel until the exile and a great offense to Israel when they took over Judean cities after the Exile. Eliphaz could hardly have been a friend of Job's, even an accusing one. In light of this and the anger of the exilic Psalm 137 toward Edom, Eliphaz's portrayal seems unlikely after the Exile and questionable even during the Kingdom period. Others have suggested that references to other biblical writings would date Job after those references. But these are ambiguous for it is never clear which text is prior or if both texts cite a common source which is prior to both (these include Psalm 8, 107 and Isaiah 40–55). So Konkel agrees, though he ultimately understands Job to be a work that cites the earlier works of Psalms and Isaiah (August Konkel and Tremper Longmann III, *Job, Ecclesiastes, Song of Songs*, 9–10). But this much is clear, Job is portrayed as ancient and the characters and setting are those of the patriarchal world. Habel writes, "The portraying of Job as a hero of the patriarchal, or better, pre-patriarchal world, is sustained throughout the speeches of Job." While Habel considers that the weight of evidence may favor a late date of writing, more to the point is the era he was describing or the history he was recording (Habel, *Book of Job*, 39). And even Gordis acknowledges this writing, "Because of the patriarchal setting in the prologue he was associated by some with Abraham" (*Book of God and Man*, 225). There is nothing here of a Levitical priesthood, nor a Kingdom of Israel (current or exiled), and a seemingly intentional paucity of historical references to anything that could date Job with certainty, except his culture. What we have in the text are foreign (non-Israelite) names and a patriarchal culture. These show that this is intended to be a portrait of a patriarchal response to evil, and in that sense, the "earliest" biblical response. While the date of writing is important, and on balance most scholars still consider it likely that it is late rather than early, it is more important to understand the intent of the author. It seems he is either recording the oral history of a patriarchal man, Job, or creating a poem in a "timeless" and patriarchal setting to instruct God's people from every age, about how to understand God in the context of undeserved suffering.

troubles Job the most. Job wants God to be center-stage. Job's first lament is primarily focused on the unremitting pain (3:1–26), but even this is understood in context of his relationship to God, who is responsible for his misery (3:23; 6:4, 12:7–10). Job is also concerned that his situation makes it appear to others that God is displeased with him (6:22–30, 12:4). And much of his complaint deals not with the physical pain, but of the emotional or spiritual complaint of being considered guilty or being actually guilty before God (7:20–21; 9:2; 10:7). This is a wrestling with God, not with any man. Most of his complaint is raised toward and against God. It is God that Job ultimately wants to vindicate him—and before whom he will be vindicated.

This terrible eclipse is seen as Job wrestles with the idea of hope. Within Job, there are two key words that have the sense of "wait in hope" (יחל) or "wait patiently" (n. תִּקְוָה or v. קוה). It is not clear if these words are used in distinct ways in the text, though both are used of hope or lost hope. Job 13:15 reads, "Though He slay me, I will hope in Him. Nevertheless I will argue my ways before Him."[76] This is the position he is staking out for himself in the middle of pain. He refuses to let the pain and suffering completely occlude his hope in God (here, יחל). Yet, in Job 14:14 he says, "If a man dies, will he live again? All the days of my struggle I will wait, until my change comes." Now Job falters in his hope; waiting for God is pointless for the dead who will not be raised to continue their earthly life. To wait in hope is pointless—he will crumble like the mountains (verse 18), never to be restored. So, God destroys the hope of a man (verse 19, תִּקְוָה). But this is not the end of the argument Job is having with himself. In his expectation of the grave, he cries out, "If I look for Sheol as my home, I make my bed in the darkness; If I call to the pit, 'You are my father'; To the worm, 'my mother and my sister'; Where now is my hope [תִּקְוָה]? And who regards my hope [תִּקְוָה]? Will it go down with me to Sheol? Shall we together go down into the dust?" (17:13–16). Here Job seems to be making a distinction between hopes he had for his life (that life would be good, verse 11), with his hopes for his ultimate end. In doing so, he seems to be clarifying the difference between the hope of 13:15, which is in God and in seeing him and 14:14–19, which is hope in the plans a man makes for himself in life. One is temporal and fleeting. The other is eschatological. We are now set up for the central argument Job makes in regard to why his pain is so great—it has eclipsed God. And he asserts that this eclipse will not last forever. He returns to his personal hopes in 19:10, "He breaks me down on every side, and I am gone; And He has uprooted my hope like a tree." God is breaking him down and showing him what is most important. Not his "hopes," but his one "hope." He will not return from the grave to pursue his hopes, but his One Hope awaits him. He declares in 19:25–27, "As for me, I know that my Redeemer lives, And at the last He will take His stand on the earth. Even after my skin is destroyed, yet from my flesh I shall see God; Whom I myself shall behold, And whom my eyes will see and not another. My heart faints within me!" I will not take

---

76. Though there is a lack of clarity in the text as to meaning of לא, NIV, ESV, KJV, NASB (above), and a majority of translators take this to mean "to him" as opposed to a negation of hope.

PART II: The Testing of a Theodicy

the time here to validate a claim that this text clearly teaches a belief in resurrection, because that is not central to my claim (though that is my understanding), but I will claim that Job's hope is grounded in once again seeing God, when the eclipse of Evil & Suffering will be completed and past. The face of God will come out from behind evil and he will be satisfied. This is central to understanding Job's pain: the eclipse of God in Evil & Suffering.

Now consider the movements of the text. In this drama, there are three scenes: God's counsel chamber, Job's estate, and Job before God. These could also be understood as what God knows, what human willful-creatures perceive, and what God reveals to his human willful-creatures when he meets us. So also, this could be understood as three movements: heaven, earth, heaven to earth. Or it could also be understood in the context of a time line: Innocence, Evil & Suffering, and Restoration. That Job continued innocent even under Evil & Suffering makes his story distinct from that of the story of Adam and Christ, but still parallel, and perhaps still eschatological.

Choosing the context of time, the first movement is "Innocence." God, and his counsel, is aware of the whole perspective. The view of the drama from God's counsel chamber is not only above and overlooking, but prior and controlling. What happens in the council chamber includes knowledge of the earthly environs and what affects the earthly environs. While on earth, Job continues in innocence of obedience, as well as innocence of knowledge, knowing nothing of the counsels of heaven. In this movement God volunteers Job as his champion. Job knows nothing of this. Job's permission is not solicited.

The next movement is Evil & Suffering. The decisions of the counsel invade the earth and Job's life. Not only does Job endure Evil & Suffering, but his friends must as well, in the sense that they endure Job's suffering and introduce even more evil by the way they represent God. Chesterton wisely wrote, "All they [RAS: Job's friends] really believe is not that God is good but that God is so strong that it is much more judicious to call Him good."[77] Still, they are forced to form an opinion, an understanding, a philosophy—even a theodicy. But they miss their target. The purposes of God are hidden and secret. They occur outside of our perception. What happens in God's counsel chamber affects our lives directly, but we have no access to that which comes by experiencing or even observing Evil & Suffering. Of course, such opacity does not prevent (it even seems to motivate) Job and his friends from trying to make sense of what is occurring. And as they try to make sense of this movement of Evil & Suffering, Evil & Suffering continue unrelentingly. What we learn is that Evil & Suffering has no tag. It is not labeled with product and care instructions; it encodes no return address, nor does it indicate its purpose.

The last movement is "Restoration." One day, after the dreams of the old men have faded (such dreams of understanding as Job's friends had) and after young men have seen their visions (which Elihu had of the gathering storm), God appears on

---

77. Chesterton, *Book of Job*, xviii.

earth and restores all things to Job and even saves Job's friends. It is not exactly as any of them planned, including Job. Job was never permitted to argue his case, but he was marvelously satisfied with the outcome. While neither Job nor Job's friends are mute (Job only claims to be in 40:4–5), who could argue with being proved wrong, forgiven, and seeing Evil & Suffering ended! The author put no argument in their mouth. And in his flesh, Job saw God. The eclipse of Evil & Suffering was over. But this was not Job's due. Carson noted well, "The blessings that Job experiences are not cast as rewards that he has earned by his faithfulness under suffering. The epilogue simply describes the blessings as the Lord's free gift."[78] So they are, and all is restored.

Is this an eschatological text? Perhaps not. It is certainly not in the style of apocalypse which is one eschatological genre. Yet, it is an eschatological in that the focus is on God and it brings about the end of the eclipse of evil in the lives of those who seek him. D.A. Carson wrote, "God will have the last word; we dare to wait for that. Is this one of the reasons that the Book of Job has a 'happy ending'?"[79] I think this understanding of Job contains a hint—a great hint and a clear direction for investigation—that the answer to our problem of evil is in God himself and in his ultimate deliverance of his people from the eclipse of his face. Our hope is eschatological. May he come soon!

SUMMARY

> So then, while Christ is the law, he is also liberty, while he is sin, he is righteousness, and while he is death, he is life. . . . So is Christ the poison of the law, sin and death, and the remedy for obtaining of liberty, righteousness and everlasting life.[80]
>
> —Martin Luther

The blood of Christ has poisoned Evil & Suffering and the slow poison of the Cross has worked itself into every part of evil's privative existence. And though it has worked its worst upon God's human willful-creatures, God has triumphed in the Cross and in the life of the church. His plans to display evil as the nothingness that it is, are revealed in the final Era of Freedom in which liberty and righteousness are experienced together for eternity. In his commentary on Romans, Luther spoke of sin as that which curves a man's nature into itself.[81] So evil is poisoned and its curvedness works not

---

78. Carson, *How Long, O Lord?*, 155.
79. Ibid., 134.
80. Luther, "Commentary on Galatians," in *Martin Luther: Selections from His Writings*, 125.
81. Commenting on Romans 5:4 he wrote, "This is so because, due to original sin, our nature is so curved in upon itself at its deepest levels that it not only bends the best gifts of God toward itself in order to enjoy them" (Luther, *Luther: Lectures on Romans*, 159) and in Romans 8:1–4, "And this is in agreement with Scripture (Isaiah 2:9–22), which describes man as curved in upon himself to such an extent that he bends not only physical but also spiritual goods toward himself, seeking himself in

PART II: The Testing of a Theodicy

only upon the nature of unredeemed people, but now in Christ's suffering, it is forced back upon itself until evil curves itself into its own universe, from which it cannot act upon anything outside of itself—it cannot reach to God's people where they stand in Christ. So we can consider that Christ's suffering, and the suffering of his people while trusting him, has destroyed Evil & Suffering by turning evil in upon itself. In this way, God has destroyed Evil & Suffering for his people.

In this chapter I have attempted to display God's work in history as if it was divided by three events of Creation & Crisis into four Eras of Freedom. These three "Creation & Crisis" events are the creation of the world and the Fall; the Incarnation, Death and Resurrection; and the final judgment and the New Heavens and New Earth. The Eras of Freedom are Unfettered Freedom, Slavery, Penultimate-Freedom, and Conforming-Freedom. This last era is the freedom God has, to this point, reserved for himself. Or perhaps, it is a freedom which is inaccessible to us until Evil & Suffering has run its course and been destroyed. I have suggested there is reason to consider this latter option as quite likely. In considering this, I reflected many biblical texts that, when taken together, seem to commend this possibility, even if they do not require it. Lastly, I considered Job as an example of a text that is both God-centered in its consideration of the problem of evil and sees an ultimate response to the burden of evil in God's restoration. Theodicy is, and must be, eschatological.

In Part III which follows, I will examine how this hypothesis might be applied in pastoral theology, consider objections, and then finally assess concluding matters.

---

all things" (218–9). Also, in Romans 8:5–13 he writes of evil, "this curvedness, depravity, and wickedness" (225).

PART III

A Theodicy in the Face of Reality

> Neither belief in an omnipotent, omniscient and morally benevolent divinity, nor its negation, can "solve" the "problem of evil." This "problem," if it is to be overcome, must be placed in a theological context, void of any apologetic intent.[1]
>
> —Kenneth Surin

> The alternative to disappointment with God seems to be disappointment without God.[2]
>
> —Phillip Yancy

IN PART I, I have laid out the history and development of the thinking of the church in regard to free-will, evil, and theodicy. In Part II, I have attempted to make a case for my proposal: God uniquely uses Evil & Suffering to destroy Evil & Suffering for his people, as well as addressing those ideas which support it or are derived from it. Now I turn to testing the thesis in practical application. And the practical application will be theologically driven and God-centered. As Surin rightly noted, theodicy must not be man-centered and apologetic, defending God, but God-centered and reviving to people who are in pain. In a world of evil, we are going to suffer. And those who suffer will face deep trauma, either trauma and disappointment with God, or trauma and disappointment without him. It is only a forward-looking, eschatological theodicy that can offer real hope in the face of Evil & Suffering.

1. Surin, *Theology and the Problem of Evil*, 104.
2. Yancy, *Disappointment with God*, 253.

7

Practical Theology
Applying the Thesis

IN THIS CHAPTER I intend to offer an apologetic for an eschatological theodicy as an antidote against despair. I will offer a taxonomy of suffering which positions each species of suffering in the context of my proposal. Finally I will evaluate my proposal against the very difficult case of Zosia presented in the Introduction. My goal in this chapter is not to prove my thesis; indeed that was not even my goal in Part II. My intent in Part II was to argue that this thesis is coherent and consistent with the biblical text and that it may prove a helpful direction to pursue for theodicy. Here my goal is to apply this thesis and to attempt to show that it is helpful in the context of real suffering in an evil world. As application, I am operating with a more relaxed standard of argumentation than in Part II, intending only to "test the fit" of a theological solution to human experience.

AN APOLOGETIC AGAINST DESPAIR

> So much of the language... seems to presuppose that the purpose of theodicy is to make the world of human experience capable of being contemplated without despair. Perhaps it is time for philosophers of religion to look away from theodicy.... [RAS: This is] how we remain faithful to human ways of

PART III: A Theodicy in the Face of Reality

> seeing suffering, even and especially when we are thinking from a religious perspective.[3]
>
> —Rowan Williams

MY THEODICY IS AN attack on despair in the face of Evil & Suffering. It is a theodicy intended to free us to delight in God in the face of evil—to see God's face when evil is so very dark, threatening to eclipse the Good. So my theodicy intends to help us "understand God" rather than be a "justification of God to men." And what I propose in our understanding of God is that his coercive-power does not (even cannot) achieve his goals. For God purposes to use Evil & Suffering against Evil & Suffering, destroying it for his people, and to create a people who can delight in him forever, by trusting him as they endure Evil & Suffering. This understanding is an antidote against despair because despair comes not from pain alone, but pointless pain. Despair can arise from thinking that God "could" relieve all pain by his coercive-power and still give himself to us. But if only Evil & Suffering can destroy Evil & Suffering, then a fellowship of suffering evil with him, while not pleasant, could exclude despair and infuse hope.

Yet among some, perhaps many, there seems to be a bias against theodicy (and even theology) which considers all theology to be incompetent in the face of real evil and terrible suffering. There is even a belief that despair is a correct response to Evil & Suffering—or at least a response that we would want neither to intercept nor oppose. So Williams rightly reminds us that the human experience of evil, and its attendant suffering, cannot be separated from intense human pain nor can it be reduced to a "problem" for theodicy. But he goes beyond this point when he insists on sustaining despair. The *Oxford English Dictionary* defines despair as "the action or condition of despairing or losing hope; a state of mind in which there is entire want of hope."[4] By this definition (which I will abbreviate as "to lose hope"), despair is neither sorrow nor disappointment nor an intensification of either. Despair is a turning away from hope and in so doing, is a turning from God to an anthropocentric life.[5] So, for purposes of this discussion, I will consider "hope in God" and "human despair" to be antonyms.

---

3. Rowan Williams, "Reply: Redeeming Sorrows," 146–47. In this response to Marilyn McCord Adams he is concerned about her "calculus" of evil which seems to allow us to replace compassion with theology. To that extent I would agree. But later he writes, "In plain English, I suspect that it is more religiously imperative to be worried by evil than to put it into a satisfactory theoretical context, if only because such a worry keeps obstinately open the perspective of the sufferer, the subject, from whom this is never a question of aesthetics" (147). I believe that he is over the top here, making an argument for the superiority of "love" over "truth." But grace requires both in equal measure: love and truth incarnate. And this is experienced when we share the suffering of the sufferer and speak truth from within. In this way, it is good for theodicy to attempt to allow both the observer and the sufferer to contemplate suffering without despair. The world of the happy and the world of the unhappy are not incommensurables. They are bridged by God's grace.

4. Murray, *Oxford English Dictionary*, sb. definition 1.

5. This is the argument of Francis Schaeffer in *Escape from Reason*. For example he wrote, humanity "did not accept the Line of Despair and the [RAS: Hegelian] dichotomy because he wanted to. He accepted it because, on the basis of the natural development of his rationalistic presuppositions, he had to. He may talk bravely at times, but the end it is despair" (82).

Despair then could be rightly considered a goal of God's Enemy and antithetical to God's goals for his people. Calvin writes in reference to the Book of Job, "Satan's aim is to drive the saint to madness by despair."[6] Here Calvin reminds us implicitly that there is a fundamental distinction between God's effective will and his permissive will. While God is responsible for all, Satan, even in acting for God, acts with a different goal and agenda. Satan summons despair. Despair is the domain of the Enemy, not the locus of intimacy with God in the middle of suffering. Instead, if we meet God in suffering he will draw us from despair to a place of hope. This should be and is a legitimate goal for any theodicy.

Let me be quick to acknowledge that I do not suppose that Williams is advocating a turn away from God. But words are important. To "look away from theodicy" and the acceptance of "despair" comes too close to advocating despair. It seems to argue against the great good of right thinking about God for the suffering person. Still there are competent and incompetent ways to amend despair. And there are selfish and unselfish motives for doing so. The most banal is the hortative, "don't cry," which expresses too much about the needs of the speaker and too little about the person in despair. Certainly applying bad theology is unacceptable, as in the case of Job's friends. But neither the application of bad motives nor of poor theology is the standard by which we could assess whether "despair" is a correct response to Evil & Suffering. Of course, good theodicy is insufficient, for the common graces must accompany the grace of truth. Love and truth must come as inseparable twins, mirror images of each other. I propose that a God-ward (built upon trusting God in all things), Cross-centered (rooted in the singular act that destroyed evil), incarnational (in which God's common graces are offered through human agents who are willing to suffer as agents), eschatological (grounded in God's future grace) theodicy offers the sufferer hope over and against despair.

It seems that Gabriel Marcel would disagree when he writes that hope and despair are inseparable:

> But it is the essence of hope to exclude the consideration of cases; moreover, it can be shown that there exists an ascending dialectic of hope, whereby hope rises to a plane which transcends the level of all possible empirical disproof— the plane of salvation as opposed to that of success in whatever form. . . . the correlation of hope and despair subsists until the end; they seem to me inseparable.[7]

Marcel speaks of hope here as if it is something deceptive and contrary to reality. Further he seems to understand an eternally dualistic world of hope and despair. Again, in a sense he is correct, descriptively, but the world does not have to be that way. Paul speaks prescriptively of banishing despair and running toward hope on the basis of

---

6. Calvin, *ICR*, 1.18.1.
7. Marcel, *Philosophy of Existentialism*, 28.

PART III: A Theodicy in the Face of Reality

the work of Christ on the Cross (as in Romans 8, previously considered). Here he represents hope as the partner of suffering, even in the present, and knows nothing of despair.[8] Despair is banished in the work of Christ and in its application to us. Yes, suffering continues, and sorrow also, but hope is a substantive token of the coming reality. It is the hope to which we were saved according to Romans 8:24. It is the hope that comes when Evil & Suffering is conquered by Evil & Suffering leading us to the glory of the presence of Christ and our own Conforming-Freedom. True, we do not see this yet, but we will. And "if we hope for what we do not see, we wait for it with patience" (Romans 8:31).

I am not ignoring the descriptive reality of despair which the Bible clearly acknowledges. Let me briefly survey a biblical approach to despair. If we seek for biblical terms for despair, we should consider, שׁיח,[9] which is used in Psalms 42 and 43, two Psalms which continue one idea to completion.[10] Here the Psalmist counsels his own soul not to despair or to be down-cast, but instead to hope in God: "Why are you in despair, O my soul? And why have you become disturbed within me? Hope in God" (Psalm 42:12). This chorus is repeated three times in this psalm, each time a prescriptive antidote to his overwhelmingly painful circumstances. The circumstances do not change, the pain and sorrow still exist, yet a greater reality enters that banishes his despair. The greater reality is that the deepest desire of his soul is to be refreshed in God (42:1) and he finds that he can do that when he contemplates his salvation and praises his God (42:5, 42:11, 43:5). This meditation on his salvation calls his soul from despair to hope. Despair is acknowledged as the human condition in suffering, but a God-ward theology (not here a theodicy) is needed to turn him from despair to hope.

In the New Testament, Paul's word, ἐξαπορηθῆναι, is very like what we might mean by despair. He uses it twice:

> For we do not want you to be unaware, brethren, of our affliction which came to us in Asia, that we were burdened excessively, beyond our strength, so that we *despaired* even of life; (2 Corinthians 1:8).

And

> We are afflicted in every way, but not crushed; perplexed, but not *despairing*; persecuted, but not forsaken; struck down, but not destroyed; always carrying about in the body the dying of Jesus, so that the life of Jesus also may be manifested in our body. For we who live are constantly being delivered over

---

8. Let me acknowledge that Paul speaks of "despairing of life" (1 Corinthians 1:8) but this is rather a statement that he "feared for his life" than that he despaired so that he contemplated taking his own life or that he lived in and with despair as a partner in ministry. Nor is despair to be taken as a synonym for sorrow, which does accompany Paul in ministry, as will be shown below.

9. Another Hebrew root is vay, which means something like, "give up," as in 1 Samuel 27:1 when Saul was said to give up looking for David. However, while it can be translated as "despair" it is not used in laments or to express hopelessness.

10. This term also occurs in Psalm 44 and Lamentations 3:20.

to death for Jesus' sake, so that the life of Jesus also may be manifested in our mortal flesh. So death works in us, but life in you (2 Corinthians 4:8–12).

In chapter 4, it is clear from context that Paul thinks that despair is not a fitting response to suffering evil. Though his severe afflictions (in chapter 1) drove him to fear that he had no hope of life, they did not cause him to give up hope. Paul calls us to hope and away from despair.

Another term, μεριμνάω, could be translated as anxiety, and it represents another species of lost hope. But this too, we are told to abjure—as if it was in our control to do so. In Philippians 4:6 we read, "Be *anxious* for nothing, but in everything by prayer and supplication with thanksgiving let your requests be made known to God." In 1 Peter 5:7 we are charged: "casting all your *anxiety* [n. μέριμνα] on Him, because He cares for you." This same root is used many times in Christ's instruction to us in the Sermon on the Mount (Matthew 6:25–34): "Therefore I tell you, do not *worry* about your life, what you will eat or drink; or about your body, what you will wear. Is not life more important than food, and the body more important than clothes?" If anxiety is a mild species of despair, it is nonetheless a form of despair, a move away from hope in God.

This brief survey does not prove my case, but it does indicate a direction. First, these examples indicate a scriptural bias against despair. It is not something to accept as necessarily parasitic with grief. Second, it indicates a direction for repairing despair: a God-ward theology (perhaps even a God-ward theodicy) is important to turn us away from despair toward hope.

One could object that Christ, our model, despaired in the garden, but is this the case? Matthew 26:38 reads, "Then He said to them, 'My soul is deeply grieved [περίλυπος], to the point of death; remain here and keep watch with Me.'" There is nothing here of surrendering to despair nor is he falling into the yawning maw of hopelessness. Was Christ tempted to despair? I suspect so, for this word is a synonym for despair.[11] Yet it is clear that he was not despairing, so that he sank into hopelessness. Like Paul and the Psalmist, he struggled toward hope. We can see this because despair could never have spoken the words of his high-priestly prayer, which he prayed at just this same moment in time, recorded in John 17. Despair could never have trusted the Father so that he still accepted the cup of suffering with peace. Despair could never have risen from the ground and boldly greeted his betrayer as a friend and his captors with compassion. This was indeed sorrow and grief, but it was not despair; he was not overwhelmed by hopelessness.

In Hebrews 11 we can hear a whole chorus singing a song in opposition to despair and hopelessness. This text is a tribute to those who acted in faith, against the debilitating reality of the pain which drives people toward hopelessness and away

---

11. In the LXX, this is the word used by David in Psalm 42:5, 11, and 43:5, "Why are you [περίλυπος], o my soul?," so it is here a synonym for "despair." It is also the word used to describe the feelings of the rich young ruler who could not follow Jesus at the expense of his possessions (Luke 18:23–24).

from God. This chapter reads like a genealogy of the "suffering but hopeful." It begins with these words: "and without faith it is impossible to please Him, for he who comes to God must believe that He is and that He is a rewarder of those who seek Him" (Hebrews 11:6). Here, despair is not just the opposite of hope, but the opposite of faith.

My argument in this chapter is intended as a hopeful response to the challenge of despair: not only can despair be banished by proper theological application, but it must be. I argue that a Cross-centered, eschatological, and God-ward theology and theodicy must be applied, specifically to turn us away from hopelessness and despair in the middle of our pain. This is a turn toward hope. This hope is in the Cross and in the God-man who knows our griefs and sorrows because he is a man of sorrows. For that reason, I do not propose that suffering produces no sorrow, but that good theology, rightly applied, can move the sufferer toward hope. For this reason, I prefer the direction Chris Tiegreen argues:

> The theological answers to the problem of evil do not deny that the pain and suffering are real. In fact, they depend on the pain and suffering being intensely real. God's mercy means nothing if the need for it is quick, painless, or superficial . . . . No, the theological answers don't make it all better. But they are still answers. . . . Is that a pat answer? So be it. Just because the pain is real doesn't mean the answers aren't.[12]

Tiegreen offers us an incarnational response to pain and suffering, which makes room for sound theology (and even theodicy). This sound theology does not promise to remove evil from our current experience (for that would indeed be a "defection" as noted in Part II), nor does it promise to remove the pain of evil (for that would be false), but it does intend to deliver a God-ward response to evil and suffering. This God-ward response to evil and suffering has its focus on Christ and its hope in his return, demonstrated by living it out today in the midst of painful circumstances. Tiegreen makes his direction very clear: "You are the response of God."[13] This God-ward response produces hope that is to be delivered in human form, incarnationally. Following the example of Christ, who gave up his rights and took on human form in order to suffer for us and with us, "you are the response of God."

---

12. Tiegreen, *Why a Suffering World Makes Sense,* 167–68. I could even, with some trepidation in light of fundamental disagreements with her theodicy, cite Marilyn McCord Adams for support here. She writes, "They demand of us, their friends and counselors, not only that we sit shiva with them, but also that we help them try to make sense of their experience. They look to us for hints, beg for coaching as they embrace, and struggle to sustain the spiritually difficult assignment of integrating their experiences of the Goodness of God and horrendous evil into the whole of a meaningful life. . . . Philosophical reflection on horrors takes up the challenge. . . . Survivors have to deal with their experiences afterward. And here philosophy can be of help" (*Horrendous Evils and the Goodness of God,* 188).

13. Tiegreen, *Why a Suffering World Makes Sense,* 176.

A theological theodicy is not "morally repugnant," as Bart Ehrman seems to propose.[14] It is not the fact that a theodicy is theological or biblical that would exclude it, but only if it is *only* theological or biblical. Even as I write this, thousands of Chinese of Sichuan Province are dead and dying.[15] The images of this tragic earthquake appear on our computer and television screens and the world weeps. Where is God's grace in the suffering of those buried and of those who experience the deaths of those they love? Grace will come in at least two ways. It will come through the church, and in particular the Chinese Christian church, who will give what only the church of Christ can give—the God-ward truth of the Cross in the context of their demonstrations of love.[16] It will also come with God's common graces of mobilized aid and rescue workers from throughout the world, the comfort of families, and the tears of friends. These are God's graces to dispel despair and point us in the direction of hope. But what of the persons now trapped and dying? Surely many who do not know Christ are despairing, dying alone with no common grace and no saving grace? And what of Christians trapped under the rubble? I will not say they are not despairing, but I do affirm that Romans 8 announces that despair is not in any way normal or basic to the people of God. Quite the opposite, what is basic is hope in suffering. What is the difference between the one who hopes and the one who despairs? The difference is not suffering or pain, which is common to all who face death, in the overwhelming sorrow at the thought of never again seeing loved ones, not being able to marry, not living to help aging parents, or not being permitted to see yet-unborn grandchildren. Nevertheless, the person who knows the Man of Sorrows and is known by him, who has the Godward theology of David, Paul, and Christ, and who may even lack the common grace of water to wash out the dust of the rubble from his mouth, can have hope in death. We cannot say this without tears, but we still must say this clearly. I could rehearse the death of Stephen (c. 35) or the death of Polycarp (c. 155) as examples of just this response. Despair may be normal in our world, but that does not make it a response that we must protect and expect. Jesus came to destroy despair through his incarnation and death on the Cross. May God do so today in Sichuan through his church and through many common graces.

14. Bart D. Ehrman cites Ken Surin and Terrence Tilley and his own experience in order to reject most works of theodicy and ultimately even all forms of biblical theodicy as he exegetes them—except the book of Ecclesiastes (*God's Problem*, 121–22, 276).

15. On 12 May 2008, a 7.9 magnitude quake struck the Sichuan Province in China. The death toll is already in excess of 10,000 with another 20,000 known to be buried under the rubble. As I am revising this chapter, Japan is still recovering from the 9.0 magnitude earthquake of 11 March 2011 that produced a tsunami and compromised multiple nuclear power generators. More than 20,000 people were killed or missing and more than 300,000 were displaced.

16. Moll, "Great Leap Forward." This article notes that the Christian Church in China may constitute up to 130 million (54–130 million), according to government figures. Moreover, some congregations are finding that they can emerge from the illegal house church to the open by showing care and concern toward their community, beyond the members of their church. I expect they will be on the front lines of giving care to survivors of the recent earthquake.

PART III: A Theodicy in the Face of Reality

A TAXONOMY OF GODLY SUFFERING

Still, it does seem like the obvious "shortcoming" of any theodicy applied is that it does not change the circumstances: a train wreck is still a train wreck, the dead are still and cold, the exploited continue to suffer, losses are not restored. Evil is evil. What good is a word of truth in such an ocean of despair? But it is appropriate, as well as just and merciful, that despair is the target of theodicy. Theodicy has never meant to change circumstances but is instead intended to help the sufferer wrestle with circumstances which are not mitigated by common graces. It certainly is not intended to make evil, and its attendant suffering, acceptable. But a God-centered theodicy can rightly strive to inject hope into the darkness of pain. Again, it must be said that theodicy alone is insufficient. As noted above, it must be attended with grace. And to grace, I would add an attendant engagement against evil, for evil is the enemy and must always be confronted by us, for it will be destroyed by God. Indeed, in our realized eschatological way of thinking, it *has* been destroyed, as I discussed in the previous chapter. But in the case of this theodicy, if it points in the direction of truth, a well employed theodicy is also right action against evil. Still, a theodicy applied without grace can increase the weight of despair if it is used to protect the speaker from pain instead of giving hope to the hearer. A God-ward theodicy, applied in and with grace, is effective in combating evil and despair in the real world, far from the theologian's writing table.

So I want to apply my thesis, which was offered in Part II, in the context of a taxonomy of suffering: suffering of persecution, involuntary-suffering, suffering of correction, suffering of obedience, and the suffering of the ungodly (and incarnational suffering).[17]

Let me say that in some ways there is only one kind of suffering for the People of God; all suffering (persecution, discipline, folly, accidental or any other "species") is actually a participation with Christ's sufferings, regardless of what it may look like to the person suffering or to the person watching. Peter Hicks makes a similar point: "I am still convinced that, biblically speaking, because I am a child of God, the suffering I go through, even as the result of my own folly or sin, is still part of the suffering of Christ."[18] He is correct. To make that point clear, I want to consider in detail how God might use each species of suffering as part of the suffering of Christ.

---

17. It might be fairly objected that these are not necessarily biblical species of suffering. Indeed there is no verse that makes such a list and no collection of verses, taken together, that intends such a taxonomy. Others have suggested biblical taxonomies, including Bart Ehrman: redemptive, test of faith, evil forces, mystery, and meaningless (*God's Problem: How the Bible Fails*, 275–76), Walter Kaiser: retributive, educational or disciplinary, vicarious, empathetic, evidential or testimonial, revelation, doxological, eschatological or apocalyptic (cited in Morgan, *Suffering and the Goodness of God*, 68). I am not offering a "standard set" or an exegeted norm. Instead, these are offered as a tool for discussion, which when taken together, cover the range of suffering that is experienced in life and exposed in Scripture (by definition). Another person could suggest twelve different species and they would also serve. These allow us to consider experience and biblical texts and offer significant internal coherence for purposes of discussion.

18. Hicks, *Message of Evil & Suffering*, 170.

Let me make three caveats. First, I remind the reader that any taxonomy is imputed from outside as a tool for understanding and it is not intrinsic. While a taxonomy should describe internal realities, it is still an imperfect construct, intended to allow for useful progress in a discussion. In this case, it is to test the "fitness" of this theodicy. And even if the species of suffering reflects reality with a measure of accuracy, any specific act of suffering will likely be a hybrid, containing characteristics of other species. Yet, such taxonomy makes it possible to consider ways that suffering, as much as it participates in a species of suffering, could be used by God in the battle against evil. Second, let me acknowledge that all types of suffering are instrumentally used by God to refine us and this project has no interest in minimizing this parallel truth about this effect of suffering in God's economy.[19] I do not intend to say here that God has a singular instrumental use for evil, but rather, as I have argued in Part II, God has an intent to instrumentally use Evil & Suffering to destroy Evil & Suffering, and that an understanding of its instrumentality could give hope to those who suffer. Finally, I want to remind the reader that I am applying the thesis of a God-ward theodicy in which Evil & Suffering destroys Evil & Suffering in the lives of Christians. While the reader may or may not consider herself to be a Christian, this theodicy, as I noted in the introduction, is of no value to a person who rejects the God of the Bible, and rejects salvation in Christ alone. I do not say that there is nothing to say in regard to theodicy for such a person, but that their problem with evil is an inherently different one than the one which I am addressing here.[20] With that long caveat, I will test my thesis against each species.

---

19. Examples of texts making this claim include 1 Peter 1:6–7; 2 Timothy 2:3,15; 1 Thessalonians 2:1–4; James 1:12; and Romans 5:1–5.

20. Again, my theodicy is primarily directed toward "how to understand God" and is not a "justification of God to men." It is a theodicy intended to free us to delight in God in the face of evil—to see God's face when evil is so very dark. In that sense, it is biblical, not philosophical and not apologetic. As Bart Ehrman noted, this is the concern of the Bible: "What they wanted to know was how to understand God and how to relate to him, given the state of the world. The question of whether suffering impedes belief in the existence of God is completely modern, a product of the Enlightenment" (*God's Problem: How the Bible Fails*, 121). In this, at least, I agree. Yet, it is possible to note that if this theodicy is correct, it might have an externally apologetic value. If it is problematic for a person to believe in a God who is all-Good and all-powerful, but does not act against evil (per the Flew-Mackie thesis), such a non-Christian (or even non-theist) could come to understand that God does not use his coercive-power to stop evil because coercive-power is ineffective to destroy evil for his people. Believing this, such a person might come to an appreciation of the non-coercive-power of the Cross and its norm-establishing authority to define proper use of power: Evil & Suffering alone destroys Evil & Suffering. She might find in herself a growing willingness to surrender to Christ and take up her own Cross in the battle against Evil & Suffering. As fruitful as this may be, this is not a direction that I am exploring here.

PART III: A Theodicy in the Face of Reality

Suffering of Persecution or Voluntary Suffering

The most obvious and clear example of instrumental suffering is that of the suffering of the church for Christ's name, the suffering of persecution. This suffering is most obviously parallel to Christ's own voluntary suffering for the redemption of his people. Jesus' suffering for the redemption of his human willful-creatures was voluntary. Jesus said in John 18:10, "No one has taken [my life] away from Me, but I lay it down on My own initiative." And with Christ, those who follow him are called to be volunteers: "If anyone wishes to come after Me, let him deny himself, and take up his Cross daily, and follow Me" (Luke 9:23). This is also the command of 1 Peter 2:21, "For you have been called for this purpose, since Christ also suffered for you, leaving you an example for you to follow in His steps." While a command, this verse has a clear sense of volunteerism, which is reflected even in Paul's words to Timothy in 2 Timothy 1:8, "join with me in suffering for the gospel." Of course, we are not carrying the Cross of Christ. Christ did that and it was sufficient for our salvation. These are texts previously considered in greater detail and they remind us that we carry our own cross for Christ, suffering in the battle against evil, voluntarily.

How can the idea that Evil & Suffering destroys Evil & Suffering be of pastoral help to those who voluntarily suffer for the testimony of Christ? If Evil & Suffering destroys Evil & Suffering then the person who suffers for the Gospel, is truly a partner in a fellowship with Christ in the battle. Suffering is not only something to be endured, but a battle to be fought and won with Christ. It is not that in battle the circumstances are changed, but rather that the battle matters and has great significance. This difference is clear. Hope comes from our significant work as co-laborers with God; despair comes from meaninglessness and when evil occludes the face of God. If it is the case that our suffering is joining in the battle with God to destroy Evil & Suffering, a work that Christ truly left for us to do, then our suffering is not pointless, but glorious as Paul says in Romans 8:17, "we will be glorified, if we suffer with him." While we might grieve the cost, we are justified to counsel the sufferer that they should take heart—as Paul did for Timothy. Their suffering is not meaningless. It is no strange thing that they suffer. They are joining Christ as partners in the Gospel, completing what was lacking in Christ's afflictions. God disemboweled evil on the Cross by turning Evil & Suffering against itself. Now those who suffer voluntarily with him, fight in the battle against a defeated but still dangerous enemy.

Involuntary-Suffering

This is the kind of "unfair" suffering that comes for "no reason" to every person who is following God. Job considered his suffering to be unfair. But while such suffering may be "unfair" in the sense that it does not come because we failed in any way that was worse than our neighbor, "unfair" is not the best choice of words to describe such suffering. The word "unfair" could predispose us, and perhaps even Job, to grumbling, which is a terrible sin. In such "unfair" circumstances, and by God's grace, no grumbling shall be allowed to come from our mouths. Let me instead propose the term, involuntary-suffering, for that suffering which seems to have no cause that we can discern.

Involuntary-suffering is also a kind of biblical and godly suffering which God uses to overcome Evil & Suffering. While 1 Peter speaks often of suffering because of our testimony, Peter also speaks about involuntary-suffering. In 1 Peter 2:19 he writes, "for this finds favor, if a man bears up under sorrows when suffering unjustly, because he is conscious of God." In context, it is the suffering of a slave who experiences suffering as a result of an inconsiderate master. It is not the suffering experienced due to standing for Jesus, but for being alive and in the "wrong place at the wrong time." Here the slave is being beaten for no purpose and not even for his testimony. Involuntary-suffering is to be on the receiving end of either a "random act of violence" or an act of directed personal venom when the sufferer did not provoke the attack.

Peter tells us that we can find favor with God when we bear up without complaining because we are "conscious of God." But what does it mean to be "conscious of God"? That's what Job's story demonstrates quite well. First, it is important to understand that Job was not a volunteer in any normal sense of the term. He was appointed by God (not even by The Adversary) for suffering. He had not torn down his neighbors' idols like Gideon. He was not a "preacher of righteousness" like Noah. He simply lived his life righteously. And though *we know* that there was a contest between God and The Adversary (specifically because Job honored and treasured God), God sent no angel to reveal to Job the heavenly discussion of Job 1–2. He volunteered to serve God, but he was neither prophet nor evangelist. There was no visible (to him) connection between his suffering and his loyalty to God. And Job's response shows that he was "conscious of God." As I discussed in Part II, he was conscious of God throughout all of his lament. While he did not always honor and worship God in his suffering, his entire lament was God-ward. His every response was to worship and honor God, even if he did demand an audience before God so that he might have an answer. This is God-ward suffering because of (or due to) a consciousness of God.

How does my thesis apply to this species of suffering? In this context we are warriors. If we find ourselves experiencing involuntary-suffering, it is indeed a battle and we are not casualties (as Job was tempted to think), but warriors. Christians are called to live in God's "ready-room" from which he can dispatch us into battle without our permission. And, if it is true that such involuntary-suffering is part of the battle against Evil & Suffering, knowing this will help us not to lose heart. It is not meaningless, but one more step toward the final victory. When we suffer, we do not lose heart. We can know this even when we cannot see the connection between our suffering and our testimony or between our pain and our passion for God. We patiently endure our involuntary-suffering because we are conscious of God's plan to use our suffering, not redemptively (for this was done singularly in Christ), but to complete the destruction of Evil & Suffering. God's army has no civilians and no observers.

Suffering of Obedience

This kind of suffering includes the suffering of Christ when he was tempted, as Luke recorded in Luke 4:1–13 and elsewhere. Here we are told that Christ resisted Satan's temptations in the desert and his very temptations were sufferings—the suffering of obedience. Hebrews 2:14 (previously exegeted in Part II) tells us that his own resistance against temptation was deep suffering. And when he had resisted, Satan was defeated and fled to wait for a better opportunity to engage him again. The Enemy lost this battle. Evil was defeated through the suffering of obedience.

The suffering of obedience is our suffering when we resist temptation and set our face toward obedience. Like Christ, we are told to suffer temptation also, anticipating a victory over the enemy. We read in 1 Peter 5:8–10:

> Be of sober spirit, be on the alert. Your adversary, the devil, prowls around like a roaring lion, seeking someone to devour. But resist him, firm in your faith, knowing that the same experiences of suffering are being accomplished by your brethren who are in the world. After you have suffered for a little while, the God of all grace, who called you to His eternal glory in Christ, will Himself perfect, confirm, strengthen and establish you.

If we suffer temptation and resist, no matter how painful, Satan is defeated in his attempt to destroy us and God will himself restore us in his time. Also, in James 4:7 we read, "Submit therefore to God. Resist the devil and he will flee from you." Here again, we suffer temptation while resisting the enemy with our perseverance and obedience. As a result the enemy loses and flees. All of our godly suffering as we resist temptation, as was that of Jesus, is a battle against the enemy.

How does the thesis apply? If this battle, this suffering of obedience, is used by God to destroy Evil & Suffering, then we are not simply, "being good" (instead of "being bad"), but joining God in a critical battle. Obedience in itself is something God has called us to, for we are to be perfect as our heavenly father is perfect. But if temptation leads to suffering when we obey, and if in that suffering we entrust ourselves to a faithful creator and continue to do good, and if (as I argue) suffering is part of God's work to destroy Evil & Suffering, then we are not just avoiding sin, we are winning a battle with God against evil.

How then to counsel one who is suffering under temptation? Our counsel must be to endure. And it would be justification enough if we were counseling each other to avoid evil, for that is sufficient reason under grace, but I am suggesting much more: we call each other to a battle to defeat Evil & Suffering. It is amazing how innocuous temptations may seem to us at the time: "turn these stones into bread." What is wrong with that? Who would it hurt? But we are warriors who obey the call of our Master and we suffer when we obey despite being tempted, for that too is a battle with a victory to be won. And in suffering with perseverance, if my argument is correct, Evil & Suffering is destroyed. This is hope to those who face the suffering of obedience.

Suffering of Correction

One of the mistakes of Job's friends was to mis-type Job's suffering as God's correction for Job's sins. They were flatly wrong. Anyone would be wrong to suggest that all suffering is correction or disciplinary action for specific evil acts, as I have displayed above. If it is difficult to identify this species of suffering in another, it is still a challenge to discern in oneself. Yet it is true that God does bring corrective suffering into the life of his children as discipline.[21] We can see this in one of the most famous passages of The Revelation of John in which Jesus speaks to the church of Laodicea (3:19–20), "Those whom I love, I reprove and discipline; therefore be zealous and repent. Behold, I stand at the door and knock; if anyone hears My voice and opens the door, I will come in to him and will dine with him, and he with Me." God also gives this message in Hebrews 12:7–10:

> It is for discipline that you endure; God deals with you as with sons; for what son is there whom his father does not discipline? But if you are without discipline, of which all have become partakers, then you are illegitimate children and not sons. Furthermore, we had earthly fathers to discipline us, and we respected them; shall we not much rather be subject to the Father of spirits, and live? For they disciplined us for a short time as seemed best to them, but He disciplines us for our good, so that we may share His holiness.

Could the application of this thesis be of use to those suffering under the correction of God? David disobeyed God and committed adultery and murder (2 Samuel 11–12). Later, when the prophet Nathan confronted David, he repented. Still, God disciplined David; his son, who was born to Bathsheba, would die. He pleaded with God for the life of the child while the baby still lived. But when the child died, this is how David responded (2 Samuel 12:20): "So David arose from the ground, washed, anointed himself, and changed his clothes; and he came into the house of the LORD and worshiped." Evil (the willingness to rebel or grumble against God) and suffering (the effect of rebellion) were destroyed when David responded like Job. But this

---

21. To suggest that suffering can be an act of God's discipline is an offensive statement to many. Citing Bart Ehrman, "The problem with this view is not only that it is scandalous and outrageous, but also that it creates both false security and false guilt. If punishment comes because of sin, and I am not suffering one bit, thank you very much, does that make me righteous?" (*God's Problem: How the Bible Fails*, 55). It is not only a self-identified non-Christian such as Ehrman who would have a problem with this view. The Bible both identifies suffering in correction (or discipline) and cautions against foolish identification of the same (the Book of Job, Matthew 7:3–5). Nor does the Bible give justification for assuming that because we do not suffer, we are righteous (Luke 13:4, Tower of Siloam).

was different. David responded with worship specifically when he understood that his suffering was actually discipline for his own personal rebellion against God. And in that response, Satan was defeated, for he could only have desired David to curse God and to despair. Consider also, Jonah. His disobedience led to his discipline: a great storm and being thrown overboard on one day, and a scorching sun and near death by heat-stroke on another. Jonah's repentance, though partial and temporary, led to the salvation of Nineveh through Jonah's preaching, the Spirit's conviction, and God's mercy. Jonah's discipline was godly suffering that was used to destroy evil (Nineveh's and Jonah's) and suffering (they did not suffer God's wrath in that generation and the consequences of their evil were mitigated) in his own life and spread hope in the lives of others—even against his will. Consider Achan. In Joshua chapters 6 and 7 he participated in the battle for Jericho, but he plundered what belonged to the Lord and brought a curse upon himself, his family, and Israel. When the people of Israel attacked Ai, thirty-six men of Israel died and the army of Israel were routed. All of Israel came under the lot to determine who had stolen the consecrated things from Jericho, and Achan was taken. Guilty, exposed, and already condemned, Achan stood before a grieving Israel and an offended God. Then Joshua said the most amazing thing, "My son, I implore you, give glory to the Lord, the God of Israel." How can God give or receive glory in this? When we accept even the suffering of discipline, God is glorified and evil is in some sense, defeated.

At ground level, we need not necessarily determine whether suffering is the involuntary-suffering of the righteous, like Job, or the disciplinary suffering of the disobedient, like Jonah or David or Achan. Every day we should ask God to lay bare our hearts and purify us. When suffering comes, we are to let it have its effect while we honor and obey him, conscious of him. And if it is the case that Evil & Suffering destroys Evil & Suffering even in the middle of the suffering of correction, which in this case may be due to evil of our own making, this is medicine for hope.

Suffering of the Ungodly and Incarnational Suffering with the Ungodly

What about people who suffer, who do not know God? What of the suffering of those who are ungodly? Much of the suffering of the world is by people who know nothing of God in Christ or who reject him. This is perhaps the most difficult kind of suffering to comprehend. What value can it have for redeeming creation or the sufferer herself? It seems to be the kind of suffering considered in the introduction, gratuitous evil, which I said I would not consider here. Yet, it could be pointed out that this is what Christ did for us. He gave up his place and his right to heaven and entered into the ugliness of our world in the form of a servant, not a detached visitor. He entered into our delirium, not succumbing to it, knowing that the way back to glory was complete identification and a substitutionary death. And as he suffered with us, he stayed wonderfully sane, focused on the Father and led by the Spirit, seeing evil as evil and good

Practical Theology

as good—and he obeyed. He was obedient even to death. The God-man suffered for the godless—the enemies of God. So we are to be like-minded and voluntarily give up what we have to enter into the suffering of others, incarnationally. And if it is the case that we suffer with those who are not seeking God, like Christ, we are defeating evil.

If my argument is correct, this is a call to join in the suffering of others, not redemptively, for only Christ can or did accomplish that, but incarnationally, to complete the work of defeating Evil & Suffering. The Sermon on the Mount seems to call us in this direction when it calls God's people to voluntarily suffer with others who do not know Christ. He tells us to enter into the pain of those who are actually fighting *with God* by causing pain in *our lives* (Matthew 5:39–40):

- But I say to you, do not resist an evil person; but whoever slaps you on your right cheek, turn the other to him also.
- If anyone wants to sue you and take your shirt, let him have your coat also.
- Whoever forces you to go one mile, go with him two.[22]

If my argument is correct, this kind of suffering is also part of the destruction of Evil & Suffering. It is not that such incarnational suffering with those who oppose God changes their circumstances; it often does not. Yet in the greater battle against Evil & Suffering, Evil & Suffering lose, even in these wretched circumstances. There is an interesting phrase in Paul's discussion of marriage, children, and divorce in 1 Corinthians 7:14–16:

> For the unbelieving husband is sanctified through his wife, and the unbelieving wife is sanctified through her believing husband; for otherwise your children are unclean, but now they are holy. Yet if the unbelieving one leaves, let him leave; the brother or the sister is not under bondage in such cases, but God has called us to peace. For how do you know, O wife, whether you will save your husband? Or how do you know, O husband, whether you will save your wife?

Here he writes in the first phrase, "Ἡγίασται γὰρ ὁ ἀνὴρ ὁ ἄπιστος ἐν τῇ γυναικί." The verb, ἀγιάζω (I make holy), which is in first position of emphasis here, is indicative, perfect, passive: "the unbelieving husband has been made holy in (or perhaps instrumentally, by) the (believing) wife." This is the type of suffering of a wife who

---

22. We might conclude from what we see here that any kindness in the face of pain or evil amounts to godly suffering, but it does not. Godly suffering is different. In 1 Corinthians 13:3 Paul extols the greatest and most excellent way of love, "If I give all I possess to the poor and surrender my body to the flames, but have not love, I gain nothing." The context here is the dispute that Paul was having with the Corinthians, who were acting like his enemies. To them Paul insists that a person could race into a burning building to save a child and not do it from love (that is, from godliness). He says, a person could give all her money to Habitat for Humanity but not be a loving person (that is, a godly person). Love is more than doing the godly *type* of thing; it is doing the godly thing for the right reason. The right reason is to "have the same mind as Christ." So it is when we enter into the suffering of another voluntarily, because we are conscious of God.

PART III: A Theodicy in the Face of Reality

suffers at least the isolation of seeking God alone (and perhaps worse) and her suffering (or the parallel suffering of the husband, if the situation is reversed) is used incarnationally to draw her husband to God. Similarly, in 1 Timothy 6:1, Paul also calls slaves to stay in the condition they are in for the sake of the Gospel. Here also, incarnational suffering has sanctifying effect—evil is destroyed.

So, while I see nothing in the text that indicates that Evil & Suffering destroys Evil & Suffering when one is not conscious of God, yet it is the case that when the godless suffer, we are called to join them, suffering with them. One could counsel such a person that in their godly, incarnational suffering with and for the ungodly, Evil & Suffering is destroyed. Their suffering hope may become the faith of another—a defeat of the enemy.

What have I shown? I have not proven my thesis, but I hope I have shown that my thesis, if correct, has significant application to sufferers. In the words of Timothy Keller, "Though Christianity does not provide the reason for each experience of pain, it provides deep resources for actually facing suffering with hope and courage rather than bitterness and despair."[23] I have attempted to show that with each species of suffering that I have identified, a battle can be won by the sufferer against Evil & Suffering. A war is being fought and if the battle is waged so that the sufferer is "conscious of God," a victory is offered regardless of the pain or the outcome on this earth. Evil & Suffering is not merely to be endured, but a battle to be fought beside God to the destruction of Evil & Suffering. Not only is each species of suffering not meaningless, but if such a battle cannot be won by coercive force, such knowledge changes not the pain, but the meaning of the pain; suffering evil is the instrumental means of God to win the battle and bring the Era of Penultimate-Freedom to a close, inaugurating the Era of Conforming-Freedom and Hope. This is a battle whose story is being written down in heaven wherein the sufferer is the God-appointed champion. In her obedience, God is glorified, and when Evil & Suffering is endured in hope, Evil & Suffering is destroyed for God's people.

APPLICATION TO THE EXAMPLE OF ZOSIA

In my introduction I reported the account of the true story of Zosia, a young girl whose eyes were callously put out by Nazi soldiers for their own entertainment before they took her away to be killed. It is an ugly story we would like to forget, but we dare not. Weinandy writes, "all of humankind, through his body the church, is adjoined to the risen Christ. Thus all human suffering must be interpreted from within the context that all who suffer are united, to a greater or lesser extent, to the risen Christ."[24]

---

23. Keller, *Reason for God*, 27–78. The chapter called, "How Could God Allow Suffering" is an excellent incarnational response that makes the tie between suffering and glory: "not a future that is just a consolation for the life we never had but a restoration of the life you always wanted" (32).

24. Weinandy, *Does God Suffer?*, 246.

While I cannot subscribe to all of Weinandy's project,[25] I find myself in significant agreement here: all human suffering is only understood at the Cross and all suffering is a call to God's people to join in that suffering. We cannot stand back in safety, even if we weep. As I noted above, the suffering of humanity calls God's people to an incarnational response, just as our Lord did and still does through us. But how does it help that Zosia is united to the risen Christ in the middle of her torture?

We know so little of her case. We do not even know if Zosia knew God, but let us assume here that she did not, in order to make the case as difficult as it can be. Consider several other unknowables:

- We do not know what work God did in Zosia herself, or in her pain. James 1:2–4 tells us that God uses suffering to draw us to himself. Who is to say that Zosia was not drawn to God in this?

- We do not know that Zosia is innocent. We can say that she is young and "should" have had more time to repent, but she, like all, is born under God's wrath. She is born a rebel and condemned until she surrenders to Jesus (John 3:16–18). I deserve far worse then she received.

- We do not know who God moved through Zosia's sacrifice to resist evil.

These (and many more) are examples of what we do not know and perhaps cannot know. But I know this: God is in control of his universe. Zosia is not one of those times that "God lost." As I argued above, my project accepts that nothing happens without his permission, even without his will. All that happens is by his sovereign will.[26] Someone must have wondered why I did not list gratuitous suffering (meaningless, dysteleological) as a species of suffering in the taxonomy above. I did not address it for reasons I gave in the Introduction and because she who accepts my premise must maintain that meaninglessness is not a species of suffering, but a dangerous accusation against God's holiness. It is a result of our limited horizon—such suffering is meaningless only "as far as we can see." In this case, meaninglessness is more honestly a complaint that we cannot see far enough into the design of God, and not a kind of suffering. It is truly a charge

---

25. In chapter 8, "The Incarnation—The Impassible Suffers," Weinandy takes a position against Moltmann saying that it is wrong to assert that God suffered. For example he writes, "within the Incarnation the Son of God never does anything as God. If he did he would be acting as God in a man" (205); and he writes, "confining the suffering to his human state, far from limiting the significance of the Son's suffering, actually enhances it" (214). Perhaps he is rightly eager to avoid the sense that God suffered "as a human." But the Council of Chalcedon asserted that the two natures of Christ were unmixed and indivisible. Weinandy seems to emphasize the sense of being unmixed at the expense of the indivisible and it seems to me that it is improper emphasis to suggest "confining suffering to his human state." In so doing, he divides the indivisible. We must say, at the Cross, the Trinity suffered in the God-man, Jesus Christ.

26. In a private correspondence, John Piper wrote, "It seems straightforward and clear to me that when God does this [RAS: i.e., choose to create the world where he knows a bad thing will happen], the bad thing is a part of his plan, NO MATTER WHAT his way of causing or not causing it is" [emphasis original] (email, August 2008).

against God; it is grumbling. That Zosia's pain is worse than we want to imagine, and worse than we want to experience, is true. That we dare not speak of her pain without tears is certain. Yet the full meaning of her pain is beyond our ability to assess. That it is meaningless (in any absolute sense with reference to God's sovereignty) is something we cannot assert; in fact, this theodicy explicitly rejects that possibility.

Does that seem callous? Quite the opposite is true. A person who has no confidence in God and his work in the world has nothing to say to Zosia as she dies, or to her parents who must live with the vision of her death, or to the German guards who wrestle with their barbarous actions forty years later. If Zosia is not a Christian, as is supposed here, it is the case that her suffering, while rejecting God or cursing him, or dying in passive grief, has no destructive effect on evil. Worse, if Zosia is not a Christian, then her suffering at the hands of the Nazis is small compared to the suffering of eternal separation from God. Yet even then her suffering is meaningful in this—and it is hard to say, but true—it is meaningful when it calls God's people to step in and suffer with her. That is something we do know from the story. No one stepped in and suffered with her. There was no incarnation of grace in her last moments. Where was the author of the account when he witnessed this? Where was the church? Where was I? And still today her suffering is a call to incarnational suffering in a world which knows only despair, and a call to declare, from that place of suffering, the only truth that brings hope. And hope results when we turn to God. This is a God-ward theodicy of the incarnation and the Cross, in which enduring both evil and suffering are the only weapons against Evil & Suffering.

SUMMARY

By saying that despair is a turn from hope and a turn from God, I have argued that despair is a sin, and that if correct, this thesis, this theodicy, applied rightly with grace, is properly a tool against despair and a tool to lead us toward hope. I have tested the thesis against a taxonomy of suffering to see how this thesis might be practically applied, in order to lead the sufferer to hope. I have argued that, if the sufferer endures while trusting God, as did Christ, her Evil & Suffering destroys Evil & Suffering and that this realization dissolves the despair of meaninglessness, allowing hope in the middle of the pain. I have argued that we must not only endure suffering ourselves, but enter incarnationally into the suffering of others in order to bring the grace and hope of God. Evil and its attendant suffering must be destroyed—and God is not doing this alone.

8

Remaining Issues and Disconfirmatory Evidence

THERE ARE MANY ISSUES raised by this thesis; I consider only a few here. Some offer interesting side-trails that should be explored. Others raise significant objections to this proposal. I will now explore some of these issues that have been raised in conversation over the last several years. I do not propose to resolve any of them here, but will merely raise the issues and begin to explore them. Whether or not they are fruitful directions for more work or serious objections, I leave for the reader to decide.

THE PROBLEM OF ADAM AND EVE

> The Fall is a view of life. It is not only the only enlightening, but the only encouraging view of life. It holds . . . that we have misused a good world, and not merely been entrapped into a bad one. It refers evil back to the wrong use of the will, and thus declares that it can eventually be righted by the right use of the will. [RAS: The Fall is] a hope, but also in some strange manner a memory; and that we are all kings in exile.[1]
>
> —G. K. Chesterton

As G. K. Chesterton observed, the Fall is a doctrine of hope. So it is for this project, which makes the claim that human freedom exists in four distinct Eras and that the first Era spanned the time between creation and creation's radical corruption by the first human sin. Specifically, I accept that Adam and Eve were the first humans, the first beings created in the image of God, and that their sin ended the first Era of Freedom which is often referred to as the Fall by authors of various theological works.[2]

---

1. Chesterton, *The Thing*, chapter 31.
2. At greater length (*The Thing*, chapter 31), Chesterton makes an argument for "theological space" for the Fall when he compares it to the "Myth of Magna Carta." He asks if we would think it astonishing

PART III: A Theodicy in the Face of Reality

Yet, as I noted above, this raises *a priori* objections among many. The Adamic fall, and even the existence of Adam himself, is not universally accepted by all who consider themselves Christian theologians. John Hick is a clear example of one who rejects the Fall, but we do not have to wander so far from orthodoxy to encounter a challenge.[3] John Polkinghorne observes, "From St. Paul onwards, the story of Adam and Eve's disobedience and expulsion from Eden (Gen. 3) has played a significant role in Christian thinking, in rather striking contrast to its apparent lack of importance in Jewish tradition. . . . [RAS: Yet] original sin . . . was the only empirically verifiable Christian doctrine!"[4] In this he rejects the historical Fall and proposes a new kind of Fall, which is constituted in a self-awareness and guilt before God:

> Clearly an Irenaean account is much more compatible with an evolutionary understanding of terrestrial life than is Augustine's theory of primal catastrophe. One may picture the developing line of hominid evolution as coming to contain within itself both a dawning of self-consciousness and also a dawning of God-consciousness. At some stage, the lure of the self and the lure of the divine came into competition and there was a turning away from the pole of the divine Other and a turning into the pole of the human ego. Our ancestors became, in Luther's phrase, "curved in upon themselves." . . . Self-consciousness, with its power to envisage the future, made our ancestors able to anticipate that, one day, they would die. At the same time, their increasing alienation from God cut them off from the only true source of hope for a destiny beyond death, thereby making the realization of human transience a bitter one. In such a way it is possible to reconceptualize the Christian doctrine of the Fall.[5]

While I do not subscribe to Polkinghorne's position, he offers a possible "lowest common denominator" approach that permits me to take a position that still relies heavily upon the Fall. His position is still historical, but accounts for evolution and the "mythical" quality of the story of Adam. His position, while not mine, provides one

to abandon all expressions of democracy if it could be proven that King John did not actually sign the document on the island in the Thames.

3. John Hick writes, "The accompanying notions of an original but lost righteousness of man and perfection of his world, and of inherited sinfulness as universal consequence of the fall, which jointly render that event so catastrophic and therefore so crucial for the Augustinian theodicy are both rejected." In this, he speaks of Irenaean-type theodicy as well as his own (*Evil and the God of Love*, 263). Later he adds that Adam is not only "myth" but a-historical (281–5). Although I radically disagree with Hick, let me say that this limited set of assumptions, if granted, would not adversely affect my main point. My focus is on God's goal: eschatological and Conforming-Freedom for God's willful creatures. If my description of the kind of freedom possessed and lost by Adam and Eve is disputed because neither a real Adam and Eve, nor a fall, can be shown to be historical, it is still the case that the "myth" of the Bible speaks of this "event" and these people. I argue that such fits the larger picture, which I believe the Bible paints. If, moreover, it could be demonstrated that Adam and the Fall are not historical, still my hypothesis of God's goal of Conforming-Freedom is not, by that, damaged. It would only lack one aspect of supporting, historical credence.

4. Polkinghorne, *Science & Theology*, 63–64.

5. *Science & Theology*, 64–65.

example of what I would call "theological space," a theological and narrative change from perfection and obedience to rebellion.[6]

Robert Williams considers the value of the "Adamic myth" to Schleiermacher (as well as Hick and Ricoeur) and the Irenaean scheme of theodicy:

> In these myths evil is either antecedent to creation (cosmogony) or coincident with finite existence (tragedy, Gnosticism). Evil is thus structural, necessary, belonging to the very nature of existence. Against such views the Adamic myth asserts (1) that evil is not coincident with finite existence because existence is good, and (2) the origin of evil is separate from the origin of existence. Evil is thus understood as occurring within a good creation already completed. The origin of evil is traced not to God, or to creation as such, but to man, to the ancestors of the human race. The Adamic myth is an anthropological account of the origin of evil.[7]

While I believe the "Adamic myth" to be presented as historical assertion by the author of Genesis (and the whole of the Bible), the one who chooses to reject the historical content of this text and yet still reject both the preexistence of evil and the necessity of evil in a finite existence (from the moment of creation), must explain how to do so without the Fall. It seems that their problem is much more challenging than mine.

Most importantly, I propose that I do not have to prove that the Fall of Genesis 3 is historical, but only that it is theologically meaningful in a way that does not weigh against my proposal. I note that my argument does assume that the Bible, properly interpreted, is true in every claim it makes. Still, let us suppose that all of Genesis 1–11 is written within the genre of myth. As myth, let us agree that it intends to convey truth through story, even if that truth does not include the historicity of the stories themselves.[8] What then is the point of the Garden myth in particular? I propose that this includes at least: (1) that God created (neither means nor timing are assumed here) and his creation was good; (2) that God created (by direct or indirect means) image-bearers with whom he desired a relationship; and (3) that creation has been

---

6. Tom Schreiner also notes of Romans 5:12–21, "There is little doubt that Paul believed he [RAS: Adam] was historical. He did not confront the theory of evolution, which has caused people to reconsider the historicity of Adam. The question of Adam's historicity, therefore, relates more to the area of apologetics than it does to exegesis" (Schreiner, *Romans,* 292). In this he is correct: there is no exegetical issue here. What I ask for, then, is the theological space created by Paul's understanding: there was a change from obedience to rebellion.

7. Robert Williams, "Theodicy, Tragedy and Soteriology," 397.

8. John S. Feinberg has outlined four basic types of literary myth, which include: irrational, symbolic, religious ideals, and religious history. The last type of myth is theologically rich and based on history. Feinberg writes, "myth can be so defined as to harmonize with history, even if some details of the myth don't match exactly with what happened in history" (*No One Like Him,* 574–5). Many theologians use "myth" more simply as "not-true." Such is the case, for example, for John Hick who writes, "a myth is a story which is told but which is not literally true, or an idea or image which is applied to someone or something but which does not literally apply, but which invites a particular attitude on its hearers" (Hick, "Jesus and the World Religions," 179).

PART III: A Theodicy in the Face of Reality

altered negatively, and that alteration has its origin in that which is anti-God, namely, evil.[9] That I refer to this as "the Fall" might be problematic for some, but I offer that this term may be taken in its broad meaning of "the Change."[10] In the case of Hick, where even the idea of "the Change" would not settle well, I would argue that a change of some kind is unavoidably required by the text and that Hick is in error. In this context, such a Change need not be historically situated in the person named Adam (as I understand it), but could be of only theological significance, represented in the Adamic myth (as the text requires, minimally). If it is taken in this way, I suggest that the thesis presented here is not in any way hindered, at least on that account. I will leave it to others to prove or disprove the historicity of the Fall.

Second, in the New Testament, Romans 5:14, 1 Timothy 2:13–14, and 1 Corinthians 15:22, 45 make references to Adam in the context of theological argument. For example, in Romans 5:14 we read, "Nevertheless death reigned from Adam until Moses, even over those who had not sinned in the likeness of the offense of Adam, who is a type of Him who was to come." Whether the author is validating Adam's historicity or simply using the common understanding or "Parable of Adam" to make his point, Adam stands as representative of fallen humanity and that is taken to be an event that took place in our history. This is supported by a great number of scholars,[11] and few Christian theologians would disagree that the creation was fundamentally changed after God created it, and that in Christ, creation was radically renewed, even recreated, in his death and resurrection. Similarly, I am proposing no more, and likely

---

9. The term "anti-God" used here is not to be taken as dualistic, but in its more mathematical sense of that which is not God-like or that which is the opposite of God.

10. Not all would even allow that any such change occurred. Hick, for one, who understands that we were all created in God's image and must grow to be in his likeness, sees a continuous line from our creation to the day of completeness in which our souls have been fully matured. For Hick there is no discontinuity such as a Fall or Change (*Evil and the God of Love*, 196–7). So be it. I do not believe that this specific assumption of Hick is correct and I will choose to stand within the tradition that is as wide as Pelagius and Augustine and their progeny. If I am incorrect, the responsibility to prove otherwise rests with the novel position. This thesis of a human fall from God's goodness, or corruption of the "very good" creation, has a broad and continuing historical-theological validity, which until proven otherwise, is not in fundamental jeopardy.

11. It is common for scholars to take Adam and Christ as theological representatives. So, James Dunn writes, "Adam is the exemplar or pattern of Christ in that they are both epochal figures" (*Romans,* 292). Also Ernst Käsemann writes, "Even Adam as the primal man is not an interchangeable example" (*Commentary on Romans,* 147). Doug Moo (*Epistle to the Romans*) and Robert Jewett (*Romans*) assume Adam's historicity and use him as a type, just as the text asks us to do. William Sanday and Arthur Headlam speak to this passage with the words, "the contrast between the two great Representatives of Humanity—Adam and Christ" (*Critical and Exegetical Commentary on the Epistle to the Romans*, 131). Also, C. E. B. Cranfield in his famous commentary on Romans, understands Adam to be a significant person in the theological discussion of the author of Romans (*A Critical and Exegetical Commentary on the Epistle to the Romans*). Also, the *Interpreter's Bible* says, "Adam was the founder of one race, Christ another" (467). These few examples do not prove that Adam was an historic person or that we must consider him so, only that there is legitimate and historical and exegetical grounds for practicing theology based on the biblical use of Adam and the Fall. In fact, it would seem even necessary to do so unless texts like Romans 5 were to be terribly distorted.

much less, than did the author of Romans and in that light, I would beg the reader to offer me just this "theological space." So, the reader need not agree with me that "Adam" and "the Fall" were historical in order to evaluate my thesis, but she need only to accept the more fundamental change from good to corrupt. This is not unlike the position taken by Swinburne, who writes, "I shall wish to accept a historical Fall and give it some role in my theodicy, but not the kind of prominence which Augustine gave it."[12] I ask the reader to allow me to use the terms with at least the minimum theological weight required by the biblical story: they are pointers to a fundamental change in God's good creation.

THE PROBLEM OF THE ANGELS

> The good angels themselves were not created incapable of sin. Nevertheless I would not dare to assert that there are no blessed creatures born, or such as are sinless and holy by their nature.[13]
>
> —Leibniz

> "I repeat that [the angels'] freedom consists in their obedience. This is a further reason to extol, not themselves, but God who made them thus, with this nature."[14]
>
> —Karl Barth

If the Fall, the defection of human willful-creatures from the Good, is contingently necessary, as I have argued it is, then the angels seem to present a problem to that argument. That is, if both humans and angels are created beings with a will which is free to choose for good or to create evil, and if some of the angels did not defect from God, then our human defection from God's goodness is not a subordinate-metaphysical necessity, but rather only an accidental necessity. Yet, as all acknowledge, the Bible gives a paucity of information about the angels and even less about their "fall." Chris Tiegreen observed correctly that "speculating about angels is a risky endeavor."[15] Yet, we were created to seek understanding of all that God has done, so it is worth plunging into this endeavor.[16]

---

12. Swinburne, *Providence and the Problem of Evil*, 41. For Swinburne, Adam is a creation of God, but he is possibly an evolutionary creation—the first to think morally and to understand the nature of temptation. And while his Fall unleashed human suffering and death, it did not result in Augustinian original sin and our sinful penchant. My position is different in some significant respects, but not in regard to what is most important in this context: the historicity of the Fall and the resultant damage to all of creation (35–41, 108–10).

13. Leibniz, *Theodicy*, 2.120.

14. Barth, *CD*, III.3, §51, 498.

15. Tiegreen, *Why a Suffering World Makes Sense*, 113.

16. For the sake of this discussion, I accept without argument, the historic assumption that demons are angels who rebelled. I can do this because if an "angelic fall" is not granted, the objection evaporates.

PART III: A Theodicy in the Face of Reality

Augustine asserted that the "those [RAS: angels] who are now evil did of their own will fall away."[17] But in Book 12 of *The City of God*, which takes up the question, "What is the reason of sinlessness of Good Angels?" he writes, "These [RAS: bad] angels, therefore, . . . received less of the grace of divine love than those who persevered in the same . . . or one fell by their evil will."[18] That is, Augustine maintains a kind of pre-fall freedom for both groups of angels such that they acted by volitional freedom of their will, though one sustained of God and the other not sustained; they were created with differing connections to God's sovereign goodness. Anselm takes a slightly different approach to understanding this problem, but the effect is the same. That is, he suggests that all angels had potential for good or evil, but they received or did not receive perseverance from God. And in the failure of some, the perseverance of the others was confirmed by the punishment of those who failed.[19] The perseverance or defection, while free in compatibilistic terms, is determined by God's sovereignty, not the free actions of the angels. In this perspective, the angels did not "enjoy" Adam's original freedom. Similarly, the reformers denied a free-will in the angels, if by free-will it is meant that their will was the determining factor in their perseverance. When Calvin writes, "although [RAS: the will of the elect angels] cannot turn away from good, yet it does not cease to be will," he preserves their volitional will and God's sovereignty over their perseverance.[20] Similarly Martin Luther denies sufficient free-will to the angels in *Bondage of the Will*:

> For if we believe it to be true that God foreknows and foreordains all things; that He cannot be deceived or obstructed in His foreknowledge and predestination; and that nothing happens but at His will (which reason herself is compelled to grant); then, on reason's own testimony, there can be no "free-will" in man, or angel, or in any creature[21]

So, Augustine, Anselm, Luther, and Calvin were agreed in this: there was something that distinguished angel from demon even prior to the so called "fall of the angels."[22] It is interesting to note that angels are spoken of as a vast and mighty host,

---

17. Augustine, *City of God*, 11.13.

18. Augustine, *City of God*, 12:7 with similar statements in, 11.11, 11:13, and discussed also in *Enchiridion* ¶ 28–30.

19. Anselm, "De Casu Diaboli," chapters 5–6 (203–4).

20. Calvin, *ICR*, 2.5.1.

21. Luther, "Bondage of the Will," *Martin Luther: Selections from his Writings*, 203.

22. Michael Lloyd in his dissertation on *The Cosmic Fall and the Free Will Defence* notes that Karl Barth also denies the free-will of the angels (*CD,* III.3.480, 493, 498), but neither does he see demons as "fallen angels." He quotes Barth, "Although the demons derive from God, they are utterly inimical to Him. They are neither divine nor creaturely, and they exist only in their opposition to God and creation: They can only hate God and His creation. They can only exist in the attempt to rage against God and to spoil His creation." Lloyd then goes on to say, "how personal terms such as 'hate' may be used of nothingness, or how nothingness came to be differentiated, individualized and personalized, Barth does not try to explain. . . . On the question of origin however, Barth rejects the traditional view.

though people were described as only two—and even as one in their bond of marriage. Minimally, there is something quite different about the angels: number, image of God, duty and role, and perhaps even their relationship to freedom. Angels could conceivably have a freedom that was compatibilistic from the day of their creation so that they fell or were sustained by God's will, while the situation for human willful-creatures was different in that they were created in libertarian freedom.

But in the end, we do not know. We do know that for his own glory, God could have created some angels with a freedom that permitted them to defect and created others who could not defect. But this we can assert: the Bible does not describe angelic freedom; there is nothing in the text that requires that all angelic beings were created equally or equally sustained in perseverance; and it is not explicit that all angels have a will which is free to rebel. This we know: God created us lower than the angels so that one day (through a process of three "Creations & Crisis") we will be re-created above them and will share in God's freedom—Conforming-Freedom. By accidental necessity, we can safely say he did not do this for the angels. They are a distinctly different creation and so may be their will.[23]

THE PROBLEM OF THE EXISTENCE OF PRIVATIVE EVIL

> Several factors helped to keep zero aloof from numbers. Each number pertains to specific collections of things but zero to no thing at all.[24]
>
> —Robert Kaplan

In his book, entitled, *The Nothing That Is*, Robert Kaplan traces the deep philosophical problem that zero is fundamentally "different" from the other integers. Each integer can be mapped to a unique number of "things"; but zero cannot and is not. Zero does not exist. When proposed as part of the set of the integers it was widely rejected as non-existent. Yet zero eventually gained a necessary reality that defied its nothingness. Over hundreds of years, acceptance came from another direction: "The

---

Having denied that angels have free will, he cannot have recourse to the story of the fall of the angels, and, indeed he explicitly attacks it as 'one of the bad dreams of the older dogmatics' (*CD*, III.3.531)" (264). This is an interesting position, as we can always expect from Barth, however, it is helpful in that it shows there are many positions that anticipate a great difference between the angels and humans as "created," though Lloyd notes, not surprisingly, that Balthasar disagreed (269).

23. It is also interesting to notice in this respect that the defection of the angelic world is never treated by the text of Scripture as a Fall that radically changed creation. No one claims with certainty that an account of the Fall of Lucifer is even preserved in Scripture. This Fall is at best, off-stage, background information. Instead, it was the Fall of God's human willful-creatures that takes center stage (regardless of one's perspective of its historicity). In Genesis 3, the storyline takes a shocking, radical, and theologically crucial shift. The whole of the rest of the Old Testament and the Gospel is concerned with the remedy to this event for all of God's people. But there is no remedy for fallen angels. The focus of God's attention in the story is on his people. The angels are a side-bar.

24. Kaplan, *Nothing That Is*, 68.

uncomfortable gap between numbers, which stood for things, and zero, which didn't, would narrow as the focus shifted from what they were, to how they behaved. Such behavior took place in equations—and the solution of an equation, the number which made it balance, was as likely to be zero as anything else."[25] In experience, zero, though it was nothing, acted like that which is.

It appears to me that when the existence of a privative evil is rejected by some, it is rejected on the same metaphysical grounds that zero was rejected for many years. I suggest that in making the universe good (including numbers) God provided us with "integer" zero out of a kind of necessity (given his decree of the existence of "things"). Yet it was difficult for us to assent that zero has a metaphysical reality and that it should be included in the set of integers. Here is a strong creation-analogy in regard to the privative nature of evil. It is privative, but it "is." It may not "exist" nor was it "created," but it has undeniable force and reality in our world. The very fact of its negative existence calls for recognition. And it is proper, in a certain sense, to say that this privation *exists* in God's creation. Evil is the "nothing that is." It is intrinsic, but uncreated.[26]

Our language seems to lack the precision necessary to adequately describe the *privatio boni*. That the absence of good is a trauma in our world is without dispute. That evil exists must be stated, however imprecise. But here is the deeper mystery—a wonderful mystery that makes God's redemptive work even more awesome and shocking to us: one day "the nothing that is" will be destroyed for God's people. It will be "impossibly removed" and never missed—for it never was.

---

25. Ibid., 75.

26. I began this project with the intent to answer the basic question of theodicy: "If God is all-Good and all-powerful, why does he not use his coercive-power to save each of us from Evil & Suffering?" My answer was to suggest that coercive-power is not effective in the battle against Evil; instead God uses the power of the Cross. He turns Evil & Suffering against itself, in the Cross and through our lives. But along the way, I encountered another question which I cannot entertain in this project, but is worth stating here: Of what need does God have of Satan? Some would claim he has no need of Satan and that Satan does not exist. While I would grant Satan actual existence, God's Story minimally requires Satan theologically; Satan has a purpose in God's Story theologically, or he would not appear. I do not know the answer, and an investigation of this is beyond the scope of this project. However, I suggest that it might be worth considering whether in God's design, evil could be released in his creation only in a personal form. I hesitate here. I am not sure what it means for Satan to be "personal." Certainly, he is not in the image of God; he is not a person in the sense that God has created his human willful-creatures, personal. Yet, in comparison to the "nothing that is" in evil, he is very personal. Could it be that God's plan required that evil not begin with humanity and that it not ever be impersonal? Chris Tiegreen suggested something like this when he wrote, "the temptation in the garden of Eden came from a serpent, not a principle" (*Why a Suffering World Makes Sense*, 154). Is personified evil a kind of mercy to God's human willful-creatures? Is it a mercy that the "nothing that is" came in the form of the Adversary and not simply a negation? This is worth further study.

THE PROBLEM OF BINDING THE STRONG MAN

> Then a demon-oppressed man who was blind and mute was brought to him, and he healed him, so that the man spoke and saw. And all the people were amazed, and said, "Can this be the Son of David?" But when the Pharisees heard it, they said, "It is only by Beelzebul, the prince of demons, that this man casts out demons." Knowing their thoughts, he said to them, "Every kingdom divided against itself is laid to waste, and no city or house divided against itself will stand. And if Satan casts out Satan, he is divided against himself. How then will his kingdom stand? And if I cast out demons by Beelzebul, by whom do your sons cast them out? Therefore they will be your judges. But if it is by the Spirit of God that I cast out demons, then the kingdom of God has come upon you. Or how can someone enter a strong man's house and plunder his goods, unless he first binds the strong man? Then indeed he may plunder his house. Whoever is not with me is against me, and whoever does not gather with me scatters. Therefore I tell you, every sin and blasphemy will be forgiven people, but the blasphemy against the Spirit will not be forgiven. And whoever speaks a word against the Son of Man will be forgiven, but whoever speaks against the Holy Spirit will not be forgiven, either in this age or in the age to come."
>
> —Matthew 12:22–32

Does Christ's teaching on the "binding of the strong man" argue against my proposal? Could this be an argument that God does use coercive force against evil? As I discussed in Chapter 6, God does use coercive force against evil, tactically. He did so with Noah, by the Canaanites, against demons, and on many other occasions. But in no case of coercive action against evil are we told, nor is it the effect, that evil is destroyed. In every case, evil came back strong or stronger afterwards. Chapter 20 of Revelation (however "the thousand years" is interpreted) speaks of Satan being restrained, but after his release, he attacks again. Restraint is not destruction. Battles against the demonic do not free the possessed person forever. My proposal claims that it is possible that God's humble weakness in Christ's work, and ours as we endure Evil & Suffering while trusting God, is used uniquely (as opposed to God's coercive-power) to destroy Evil & Suffering. So also in the text from Matthew, there is no hint of destruction, but only tactical binding.

THE PROBLEM OF PRAYING TO BE DELIVERED FROM EVIL

If it is the case that Evil & Suffering destroy Evil & Suffering how could God call us to pray for deliverance from Evil & Suffering? In Matthew 6:13, Christ teaches us to pray, "deliver us from evil," which asks that we be excused from the battle altogether. If this verse teaches that we are to be delivered from evil now by supernatural intervention,

PART III: A Theodicy in the Face of Reality

how can it be maintained that godly suffering will be used by God to destroy Evil & Suffering? Instead, one might argue that if my thesis is correct, we should pray that God should bring *more* Evil & Suffering into our lives. Do our prayers and the prayers of the Bible argue against this thesis?

I suspect not. The context of the Lord's Prayer is not that we be delivered from suffering, but from temptation: "lead us not into temptation, but deliver us from evil." We know that God does not tempt anyone: "Let no one say when he is tempted, 'I am being tempted by God'; for God cannot be tempted by evil, and He Himself does not tempt anyone" (James 1:13). Given that Christ and James must agree, "lead us not into temptation" could instead be understood as a request to God to make us strong *against* temptation. This would be very like the injunction of 1 Corinthians 10:13 which says, "No temptation has overtaken you but such as is common to man; and God is faithful, who will not allow you to be tempted beyond what you are able, but with the temptation will provide the way of escape also, that you may be able to endure it." Here God promises to give each of us a way out of every temptation. The next phrase in the Lord's Prayer, "but deliver us from evil" could then be understood as an epexegetic expression of the same idea. We are petitioning God not for deliverance from suffering, but deliverance from the temptations of evil.[27]

In the larger context of many other examples where God's people pray for relief, God sometimes grants relief and at other times, he does not. He is the Lord, as Shadrach, Meshach, and Abednego understood when they declared to Nebuchadnezzar, "[our God] will deliver us out of your hand, O King, but if not . . . ." So, we affirm that God gives us good things and delights in doing so when it pleases him to do so, brings him glory, and is good for his children—and he leads us to suffer for the same reasons. And he leads and directs in our suffering. My thesis is not a call to suffer always, but to understand and trust that God-appointed suffering as right and good and effective in his economy and plans for his glory and our joy. It is appropriate to pray for relief for others and for ourselves—and especially for delivery from temptation. Even Christ prayed for release from suffering in the Garden, but that was not granted to him. Instead, when the Father led him in suffering, the Evil & Suffering which he

---

27. David gives us an example of this from his own experience. In 1 Samuel 25, David is not yet king, but is still running from Saul. He and his men had received an offense from a local man named Nabal. Taking the repayment of the offense upon himself, he set out with his men to kill Nabal. Abigail was Nabal's wife. When she learned of Nabal's foolish offense and David's intent, she sent David and his men a gift of food and wine and came herself to beg David's forgiveness of her husband's foolishness. David's responded, "Praise be to the LORD, the God of Israel, who has sent you today to meet me. May you be blessed for your good judgment and for keeping me from bloodshed this day and from avenging myself with my own hands. Otherwise, as surely as the LORD, the God of Israel, lives, who has kept me from harming you, if you had not come quickly to meet me, not one male belonging to Nabal would have been left alive by daybreak" (1 Samuel 25:32–34, NIV). In this case, this was God's deliverance for David. We could wonder where his deliverance was in the case of his sin with Bathsheba! Could it be that it is not recorded because David never took advantage of the offered deliverance? We should pray intensely for God's promised mercy to accept the offered way out of sin. We should ask him, "Lead us not into temptation, but deliver us from evil."

endured did destroy Evil & Suffering. The call to pray for relief does not contradict this project, for God sovereignly appoints suffering and relief and he directs the battle against evil.

WHAT IF I AM WRONG?

The fate of most books is to gather dust in a library. They are like a party that never gets going: people nibble at the food, engage in stilted conversation, and then slip away. So, because its fate is likely "dust-to-dust," it is hardly likely to cause any damage. But what if it is both wrong and actually read? Even that would be very good. God often uses wrong ideas to force us to frame the right one—that is the history of theology. One would like to be right, but the instrumental use of the incorrect can bring about more clarity of truth.

However, that is no excuse for sloppy theology or bad theology and some errors are more dangerous than others. They can terribly mislead individuals and even whole groups of people down paths that wander further from the truth and from God. Though truth stands, people are injured by what is false when they depend upon it. I do not think this thesis is of that type. If I am wrong, and some trust in my words beyond their merit, they would cause no injury. In fact, I think an astute reader might say, "So what is Shenk saying that is different from that which we have always known?" I think she would have a point. There is a sense that what I am saying is quite obvious, but not often asserted or articulated in a way that is so encompassing. That is, God disemboweled Evil & Suffering by his display of power in the weakness of the Cross; 2 Timothy 1:8 says he destroyed evil. Yet, mortally wounded, we are called to endure patiently with him in our own sufferings as a fellowship with him and to participate with him in order to complete his work. I am merely tying these together with: 1/ the contingent necessity of evil; and 2/ the ongoing work of God to destroy Evil & Suffering as we suffer evil and trust him. My project is not of the species of ideas that diminish God and threaten those who trust it. If I am wrong, I am still asserting rightly that the universe is about God and his glory, and not us. I am still calling God's people to patient endurance while trusting him when we suffer. One cannot go far wrong in that, I think.

But if I am right in some significant part of my thesis, and if the direction I offer is a fruitful direction to explore, it could provide a dimension of meaning to our suffering that has been little explored. It has a meaning like that of the Cross. It could free people from assuming that it is right and good and possible for God to eradicate evil with coercive-power. This hermeneutic could help us find joy in our partnership with Christ in a way we might never have imagined otherwise. May God reveal his truth and accomplish his will in and through us in our fellowship of suffering with him.

Conclusion

> The theist's not knowing why God permits evil does not by itself show that he is irrational in thinking that God does indeed have a reason.[1]
>
> —Alvin Plantinga

THIS QUOTE BY PLANTINGA is at the center of my argument. Much of the debate about the problem of evil surrounds assumptions that we understand enough of God to rule on what he could and could not do. For example, that he is able because he is infinite, and willing because he is good, to destroy evil by coercive force.[2] But I respond, that we do not know enough of God to pronounce against him. My thesis, should at least demonstrate that it is very possible to assert a biblically sound reason for dispelling disaffection with God for those who want to trust him. That is, it may be the case that destroying evil by coercive force would destroy us—and God does not desire to destroy us but save us! So great is his desire and so much does it add to his joy to bring us into fellowship with him that he paid the ultimate price for us as is indicated by Hebrews 12:2: "who for the joy that was set before him endured the Cross." What if the only possibility open to God, given his character and goals, was to destroy us along with evil, or to destroy evil for us by suffering—and to require us to suffer with him? If right, this changes everything. If wrong, it is at least a sufficient demonstration that our framing of the Trilemma is short-sighted.

AN ASSESSMENT AGAINST THE BASINGERS'S CHALLENGES

> It is the way of God to work by contraries, to turn the greatest evil into the greatest good. . . . This is the way of God, he says, but every one does not understand it. . . . [RAS: He] brings grace out of sin, that is, makes use of sin to work furtherance of grace. . . . It is the way of God to bring all good out of evil, not only to overcome the evil, but to *make the evil work toward the good.* Now

---

1. Plantinga, *God, Freedom, and Evil*, 11.

2. It might be considered that this is similar to the argument that suggests God could "just forgive us" without the Cross. I cannot examine this here, but it is worth pursuing as a follow-up argument in favor of this thesis.

Conclusion

> when the soul comes to understand this, it will *take away our murmuring* and bring contentment to our spirits.[3] (emphasis mine)
>
> —Jeremiah Burroughs

If I have a desire in this project, it is just what Burroughs has expressed in this paragraph. I desire, by a proper understanding of God's work in suffering, to train my heart toward contentment, which is, I think, an apt definition of hope. If this thesis is correct, and more work must be done to establish this, its truth would urge us in this direction. It takes us away from grumbling, the sin of the Israelites at Sinai for which many died, and moves us toward hope in God.

In bringing this work to a close, I want to consider the challenge of David and Randall Basinger that I referred to in the introduction to Part II:

> *Challenge #1*: It is quite likely that God could have done more to eliminate evil without negatively affecting the relevant divine goals. In fact, it is so unlikely that all of the evil we experience is necessarily connected to divine goals that the theodicy (and thus theism) in question must be considered implausible.
>
> *Challenge #2*: Even if all of the evil we experience is necessarily connected to divine goals, it is unlikely that all of the relevant divine goals are, or could be, morally acceptable. In fact, in relation to some evils, it is so unlikely that any morally acceptable goal necessitating such evil could exist that the theodicy (and thus theism) in question must be rejected as implausible.
>
> *Challenge #3*: Even if all the evil we experience is necessarily connected to morally acceptable goals and the inherently negative value of evil is appropriately acknowledged, it is doubtful that the God postulated by the theodicy in question remains worthy of worship. In fact, since the relevant being so clearly fails to possess the minimum attributes required of a deity, any theodicy (and thus theism) that postulates a being with such attributes must be viewed as an implausible response to the evil we experience.[4]

In regard to Challenge #1, I believe I have established that if my thesis is correct, there is not an over abundance of evil, as if God created or permitted a particular amount of evil as necessary for his project. Instead, evil exists in abundance and parasitically upon God's creation, unavoidably, because it is a subordinate-metaphysical necessity, and contingent upon God's character and announced goals. And, in God's character and announced goals, it will be destroyed for God's people, eternally. But this cannot be accomplished without first "subjecting creation to frustration," and if I am correct, God could not eliminate evil by coercive force without also eliminating us. Instead he is doing the "impossible." He is eliminating evil for his people by suffering himself and calling us to suffer with him in order to fully destroy Evil & Suffering by

---

3. Burroughs, *Rare Jewel of Christian Contentment*, 48.
4. Basinger and Basinger, "Logic of Theodicy," paragraphs 37, 42, and 49.

using Evil & Suffering against itself—for us. If this thesis is correct, Challenge #1 is surmounted.

In regard to Challenge #2, if my thesis is correct, evil is necessary and unavoidable, if the goal of theosis (Christification or being brought into full fellowship with the Trinity) is to be achieved. The way of getting beyond Evil & Suffering requires Evil & Suffering. As intense and painful as it is, over the short period called time, eternity is inaugurated with all Evil & Suffering eternally destroyed for God's people. Evil is the battle that cannot be avoided given God's character and announced goals. Challenge #2 is surmounted.

In regard to Challenge #3, if my thesis is correct, God needs no defense. He has offered us fullness of joy and he himself paid a necessary (given his goals for his people and his glory) and infinite price to gain theosis for his people. Our loss, no matter how painful now, is very limited and does not begin to compare to the loss he suffered at the Cross. God needs no defense. He has done it all. If this is correct, Challenge #3 is surmounted.

If this is the case for this project, hope will be the result.

WHAT I DID NOT SAY

As I have had conversations with many in regard to my thesis, I have noticed that sometimes confusion arises not (only) because of what I said, but because of what I did not say, but which some think I did say or imply. Let me attempt to clarify what I did and did not say. As a point of style, the following bullet-points may seem awkward to some, yet in the interest of clarity, I think they will prove helpful.

- I did not say that evil (or Evil & Suffering) is useful to God, but that God uses evil. Evil is not used in the proposal as in a consequentialist ethic, but it is the enemy that is unavoidably faced by God's people and by God because of his character and announced goals.

- I did not say that in being ultimately and co-causally responsible for evil, God in any way is taking evil into himself. He does not. God is uniquely Good and the Source of the Good and eternally free of evil.

- I did not confuse evil with suffering by combining them into the singular term, Evil & Suffering. While they are distinct, they have a common beginning and a common end, and they cannot exist in isolation. It is my claim that they are each corrosive of the other: suffering, while trusting God, and evil, if left to flower, bear fruit, and then decay, destroy Evil & Suffering in God's economy.

- I did not say that we will have Libertarian Free-Will in the new creation. Our freedom will be like God's, conforming to his character, bringing him glory.

- I did not say that we will have Compatibilistic Free-Will in the new creation. Our

Conclusion

freedom will be like God's, free to choose unpredictably (to a created observer) from an infinity of perfect choices, all of which glorify God.

- I did not say that because evil is privative, it is in any way trivial. It is as far from trivial as the east is from the west, for evil cost the life of Jesus Christ.

- I did not say that privative evil exists in the sense that God exists. Yet it does exist in the sense that zero is an integer, functionally, but not objectively.

- I did not say that evil should not be battled because it is the problem intrinsic to creation. It is *the* enemy and it must be battled by God's willful-human creatures by suffering and trusting God while enduring evil.

- I did not say that Evil & Suffering is the only means by which God combats evil. My focus has been on the limited effectiveness of coercive force and the necessary use of Evil & Suffering against itself to accomplish God's goal of destroying evil for us. But Goodness (discussed in a limited way in Part II) and the Revelation of Christ (the second coming) are critically important in this battle against evil and its attendant suffering.[5]

- I did not say that my proposal is correct. I said that it fits well in the biblical, historic, and theological tradition of the church and may lead us to truth, which will help us to find hope in suffering.

WHAT I DID SAY

> The problem of evil remains without any rational solution . . . at the cross evil is conquered as evil.[6]
>
> —Henri Blocher

In Part I, I have considered the historical development of the concepts of free-will, evil, and theodicy and attempted to show the need for more work to be done. In Part II, I have put forward a thesis which I divided into three hypothesis:

- Hypothesis 1: Conforming-Freedom is the ultimate and singular human freedom required by God's character and goals for his people (Chapter 4).

- Hypothesis 2: Evil & Suffering is a subordinate-metaphysical necessity, being both

---

5. The Revelation of Christ is only an implicit concern of this project, but it has been implicitly argued, for this has been a theological and biblical project and the revealed Word of God is basis for all my claims—even if I am wrongly interpreting the Word itself and wrong in my conclusions based on that interpretation. To that extent, the eschatological Revelation is a tool against despair. There are hints throughout the Bible of an explicit use of Revelation against evil (and so against its attendant suffering). One is in Thessalonians: "And then the lawless one will be revealed, whom the Lord Jesus will kill with the *breath of his mouth* and bring to nothing by the appearance of his coming" (2 Thessalonians 2:8). This is worth further study.

6. Blocher, *Evil and the Cross*, 128, 132.

the intrinsic problem and the instrumental solution in God's economy (Chapter 5).

- Hypothesis 3: Conforming-Freedom is achieved by God for his people through Evil & Suffering over four Eras of Freedom which are divided by three Creation & Crisis events (Chapter 6).

In Part III, I have attempted to assess the practical application of this thesis and to consider some of the challenges which might overturn it.

What are the means by which God deals with the Evil & Suffering of our world? I have suggested the tactical use of coercive-force and the strategic use of Evil & Suffering in which Evil & Suffering is turned back upon itself. Does God use one of these or some combination of all to destroy Evil & Suffering? Christians believe and declare that the Cross stands at the center of history. It defines love and justice simultaneously and indivisibly. It is also the standard of hope in suffering. It is our unique redemption. It occurred once for all and will never be repeated. Now, the high priest has taken his seat. It is finished. In the Cross and in the resurrection, God destroyed death and displayed life and immortality for all to see. In the Cross, he created a holy people from an evil chaos. But is the suffering of the Cross an exception or the definition of the nature of the battle against evil?

Of course God has used great force against evil. He has used punishment, including death, force of arms, plagues, and even demons to attack evil in the world. But that has hardly slowed evil down in the world. The flood served God's purposes, but that purpose was not to destroy evil or the suffering that attends it. And if it temporarily diminished the amount of Evil & Suffering in the world, it hardly destroyed it. It only destroyed many who were instrumentally evil. So also, God has used revelation. But the Revelation of the Law did nothing other than increase the trespass and "stop our mouths" (Romans 3:19) in our guilt before God. Sin actually blossomed and bore fruit under the Law. Both punishment and revelation have their place in God's sovereign work, but they do not destroy or overcome evil. At best, they mitigate suffering for a time, but they often seem to increase suffering, as if fertilizer!

But there is one other means—the means of the Cross: Evil & Suffering turned against Evil & Suffering. In Christ, we see that evil was destroyed in the evil of suffering Christ endured while he was patiently trusting the Father. Evil & Suffering was turned back on itself—and routed. The destruction of evil and of suffering was the result. And it has affected all of history. In fact, the shadow of the Cross reaches back over the life of the prophets, who died with angry shouts in their ears, spit on their face, and their own blood on their robes. The shadow of the Cross falls upon David's sufferings; its outline is seen in the Psalms. The shadow of the Cross fell over the desert when Moses lifted up the bronze snake. The shadow of the Cross is painted upon the rock altar of Abraham and Isaac. The shadow of the Cross reached into the garden and loomed over the head of the snake. And the shadow of the Cross is over the church today. In fact, not only does the church exist beneath that shadow, but each saint carries his own cross—a real life sized relic. This is our inheritance.

It is also our command. The Cross is not only central because its redemptive work uniquely stretches over all of history, it is central because it is the vocation for every man and woman of God. We are called to be people of the Cross, who also carry our own cross on our back. But how is it that we are to be people of the Cross, ourselves? On the Cross, was not all accomplished for our salvation? Indeed it was. But all was not accomplished. We continue to fill up in our bodies that which was lacking in Christ's afflictions. Death was conquered; the war against evil was won, but there is left for his people to finish the mopping up. We still await the redemption of our bodies. Creation still cries out for release from the bondage to decay. There is something yet to be completed. We are to participate in the sufferings of Christ. Our sufferings are still overcoming evil as we do the good of entrusting ourselves to a faithful creator, while continuing to suffer and patiently endure.

But what of the obedience of faith? Could this not be a fourth means—even the primary means, beyond force, revelation, or suffering? Perhaps it was the obedience of Christ, more than the sufferings of Christ, which destroyed death and brought life and immortality to light? Indeed obedience is a means of destroying Evil & Suffering. And perhaps the focus of that obedience is a particular kind of obedience: suffering obedience. And perhaps that suffering obedience is a particular kind of suffering: the suffering of patient endurance. And perhaps that patient endurance has a singular focus: trust in God. When we suffer while trusting God, maintaining our integrity before him as Job did, Evil & Suffering is turned back upon Evil & Suffering. Evil & Suffering is overcome in that kind of obedience. Thus, Evil & Suffering is necessary for the destruction of Evil & Suffering in God's economy.

What I am saying is that, as a "problem," evil does remain without a rational solution. Evil is inherently irrational and resists reason. We cannot defeat it by knowledge. In fact, it is a chimera in that it has no proper being—as terrible as it is. But proper or not, it must be destroyed. Perhaps it is for that reason that it cannot be destroyed by main force. It is instead conquered in the humility and submission of the Cross. This is the wonder of the Cross: Evil & Suffering is conquered by enduring evil and suffering while conscious of God. And we are called to continue that work. In God, Evil & Suffering is destroying Evil & Suffering. At the Cross, evil is conquered *by* evil. And in God's destruction of evil at the Cross, we rest our hope in the person of Christ.

Bibliography

Achtemeier, Paul. *1 Peter: A Commentary on First Peter*. Hermeneia. Minneapolis: Fortress, 1996.
Adams, Marilyn McCord. "Evil and the God-Who-Does-Nothing-In-Particular." In *Religion and Morality*, edited by D. Z. Phillips, 107–31. New York: St. Martin's, 1996.
———. *Horrendous Evils and the Goodness of God*. Ithaca, NY: Cornell University Press, 1999.
———. "The Problem of Hell: A Problem of Evil for Christians." In *God and the Problem of Evil*, edited by William L. Rowe, 282–309. Oxford: Blackwell, 2001.
———. "Redemptive Suffering: A Christian Solution to the Problem of Evil." In *The Problem of Evil: Selected Readings*, Library of Religious Philosophy, number 8, edited by Michael L. Peterson, 169–87. Notre Dame, IN: University of Notre Dame Press, 1992.
———. *William Ockham*. Notre Dame, IN: University of Notre Dame Press, 1987.
Adams, Robert Merrihew. "Must God Create the Best?" In *God and the Problem of Evil*, edited by William L. Rowe, 24–36. Oxford: Blackwell, 2001.
Ahern, M.B. "An Approach to the Problems of Evil." *Sophia* 2/1 (1963) 18–26.
———. "Good and Evil—a Note." *Sophia* 6/3 (1967) 23–26.
———. "The Nature of Evil." *Sophia* 5/3 (1966) 35–44.
———. "A Note on the Nature of Evil." *Sophia* 4/2 (1965) 17–25.
Allen, G. W. *The Mission of Evil: A Problem Reconsidered, Being a Suggestion Towards a Philosophy of Absolute Optimism*. London: Skeffington & Son, 1900.
Anglin, W. S. *Free Will and the Christian Faith*. Oxford: Clarendon, 1990.
Anselm. *Anselm of Canterbury: The Major Works*. Edited and translated by Brian Davies and G. R. Evans. Oxford: Oxford University Press, 1998.
Aquinas, Thomas. *Commentary on the Book of Causes*. Translated by Vincent A. Guggliardo. Thomas Aquinas in Translation 1. Washington, DC: Catholic University of America Press, 1996.
———. *Summa Contra Gentiles of St. Thomas Aquinas*. Volume 1. Translated by Fathers of the English Dominican Province. London: Burns, Oates and Washbourne, 1923.
———. *The Summa Theologica of St. Thomas Aquinas (ST)*. 2nd ed. Translated by Fathers of the English Dominican Province. New York: Benziger, 1920. Online: http://www.newadvent.org/summa/.
Aristotle. *Nicomachean Ethics*. Translated by W. D. Ross. Online: http://classics.mit.edu/Aristotle/nicomachaen.html.
Arminius, Jacobus. *The Works of James Arminius*. Grand Rapids: Christian Classics Ethereal Library, 2002. Online: http://www.ccel.org/ccel/arminius/works1.html.

Bibliography

Attridge, Harold. *Epistle to the Hebrews*. Hermeneia. Philadelphia: Fortress, 1989.

Augustine, St. Bishop of Hippo. "Against the Two Letters of the Pelagians." In *A Select Library of Nicene and Post-Nicene Fathers of the Christian Church*, series 1, volume 5, edited and translated by Philip Schaff and Henry Wace. New York: The Christian Literature Company, 1890.

———. *The City of God*. Translated by Marcus Dods. New York: Modern Library, 1993.

———. *Confessions*. Translated by Henry Chadwick. New York: Oxford University Press, 1991.

———. *Confessions*. Translated by Edward B. Pusey. Kindle Edition (no date), Springfield, OH: Collier, 1961.

———. *Enchiridion on Faith, Hope, and Love*. Translated by J. B. Shaw. Washington, D.C.: Regnery Publishing, 1996 (1961).

———. *Free Choice of the Will*. Philadelphia: Peter Reilly, 1937.

———. "On Nature and Grace." In *A Select Library of Nicene and Post-Nicene Fathers of the Christian Church*, series 1, volume 5, edited and translated by Philip Schaff and Henry Wace. New York: Christian Literature, 1890.

———. "On Rebuke and Grace." In *A Select Library of Nicene and Post-Nicene Fathers of the Christian Church*, series 1, volume 5, edited and translated by Philip Schaff and Henry Wace. New York: Christian Literature, 1890.

———. "A Select Bibliography of the Pelagian Controversy." In *A Select Library of Nicene and Post-Nicene Fathers of the Christian Church*, series 1, volume 5, edited and translated by Philip Schaff and Henry Wace. New York: Christian Literature, 1890.

———. *The Trinity*. Works of Saint Augustine: A Translation for the 21st Century. Translated by Edmund Hill. Edited by John Rotelle. Brooklyn, NY: New City, 1990.

Aune, David. *Revelation*. Word Biblical Commentary. Volume 52a. Dallas: Word, 1997.

Barr, James. "Was Everything That God Created Really Good? A Question in the First Verse of the Bible." In *God in the Fray: A Tribute to Walter Brueggemann*, edited by Tod Linafelt and Timothy K. Beal, 55–65. Minneapolis: Fortress, 1998.

Barth, Karl. *Church Dogmatics*. Edited and translated by G. W. Bromiley. Edinburgh: T. & T. Clark, 1960.

———. *The Theology of the Reformed Confessions: 1923*. Translated and annotated by Darrell L. Guder and Judith J. Guder. Columbia Series in Reformed Theology. London: Westminster John Knox, 2002.

Basinger, David. "Divine Control and Human Freedom: Is Middle Knowledge the Answer?" *Journal of the Evangelical Theological Society* 36/1 (1993) 55–64.

Basinger, David, and Randall Basinger. "The Logic of Theodicy: A Comparative Analysis." *Journal for Christian Theological Research* 3/3 (1998) 1–12. Online: http://www.luthersem.edu/ctrf/JCTR/Vol03/basinger.htm.

Beale, Greg. *The Book of Revelation*. The New International Greek Testament Commentary. Grand Rapids: Eerdmans, 1999.

———. "Eden, the Temple, and the Church's Mission in the New Creation." *Journal of the Evangelical Theological Society* 48/1 (2005) 5–32.

———. *The Temple and the Church's Mission: A Biblical Theology of the Dwelling Place of God*. New Studies in Biblical Theology, volume 17, edited by D.A. Carson. Downers Grove, IL: InterVarsity, 2004.

Beilby, James. "Divine Aseity, Divine Freedom: A Conceptual Problem for Edwardsian-Calvinism." *Journal of the Evangelical Theological Society* 47/4 (2004) 647–58.

Blocher, Henri. *Evil and the Cross: Christian Thought and the Problem of Evil*. Translated by David G. Preston. Downers Grove, IL: InterVarsity, 1994.

Boersma, Hans. *Violence, Hospitality, and the Cross: Reappropriating the Atonement Tradition*. Grand Rapids: Baker Academic, 2004.

Boethius, Anicius. "The Consolation of Philosophy." *The Consolation of Philosophy*. Edited by Irwin Edman. New York: The Modern Library (Random House), 1943.

———. *The Consolation of Philosophy*. Translated by Victor E. Watts. London: Penguin, 1999.

Bonhoeffer, Dietrich. *Letters and Papers from Prison*. New York: Touchstone, 1997.

Boston, Thomas. *Human Nature in its Fourfold State*. London: Banner of Truth Trust, 1964 (1720).

Boyd, Gregory. *God at War*. Downers Grove, IL: InterVarsity, 1997.

———. *God of the Possible*. Grand Rapids: Baker, 2000.

———. *Satan and the Problem of Evil*. Downers Grove, IL: InterVarsity, 2001.

Boyd, Gregory, and Edward K. Boyd. *Letters from a Skeptic*. Wheaton, IL: Victor, 1994.

Bruce, F. F. *Epistle of Paul to the Romans*. London: Tyndale, 1963.

Bryden, James Davenport. *Letters to Mark on God's Relation to Human Suffering*. New York: Harper, 1953.

Buber, Martin. *Good and Evil: Two Interpretations*. Upper Saddle River, NJ: Prentice Hall, 1953.

Bunyan, John. *The Holy War*. New Kensington, PA: Whitaker House, 1985.

Burroughs, Jeremiah. *The Rare Jewel of Christian Contentment*. Grand Rapids: Sovereign Grace, 1971 (1648).

Buttrick, George, editor. *Interpreter's Bible*. Volume 9. New York: Abingdon-Cokesbury, 1954.

Calvin, John. *Institutes of the Christian Religion*. Translated by Ford Lewis Battles. Edited by John T. McNeill. Library of Christian Classics 20. Philadelphia: Westminster, 1960.

———. *Institutes of the Christian Religion*. Translated by Henry Beveridge. Grand Rapids: Christian Classics Ethereal Library. 2002. Online: http://www.ccel.org/ccel/calvin/institutes.html.

Carson, D. A. *How Long, O Lord?* 2nd ed. Grand Rapids: Baker Academic, 2006.

Chardin, Pierre Tielhard de. *The Phenomenon of Man*. Translated by Bernard Wall. New York: Harper & Row, 1965.

Cheetham, David. "Transforming John's Hick's Eschatology." PhD diss., University of Wales, 1994 (also published as *John Hick: A Critical Introduction and Reflection*. Aldershot: Ashgate Publishing, 2003).

Chesterton, Gilbert Keith. *Introduction to The Book of Job*. 1st ed. London: Cecil Palmer & Haywood, 1916.

———. *The Man Who Was Thursday*. London: Penguin, 1937.

———. *The Thing*. Martin Ward, Software Technology Research Lab, De Montfort University, Leicester, 2005. Online: http://www.cse.dmu.ac.uk/~mward/gkc/books/The_Thing.txt.

———. *Thomas Aquinas: The Dumb Ox*. New York: Image/Doubleday, 1956.

Ciocchi, David M., and J. P. Moreland. *Christian Perspectives on Being Human: A Multi-disciplinary Approach to Integration*. Grand Rapids: Baker, 1993.

Clendenin, Daniel. *Eastern Orthodox Theology: A Contemporary Reader*. Grand Rapids: Baker, 1995.

Clines, David. *Job 1–20*. Word Biblical Commentary 17. Dallas: Word, 1989.

———. *Job 21–37*. Word Biblical Commentary 18a. Nashville: Thomas Nelson, 2006.

Bibliography

———. *Job 38–42*. Word Biblical Commentary 18b. Nashville: Thomas Nelson, 2006.
Clotfelter, David. *Sinners in the Hands of a Good God: Reconciling Divine Judgment and Mercy*. Chicago: Moody, 2004.
Cook, Robert R. "*A Representative Survey and Critical Analysis of Theological and Philosophical Discussions of Divine Foreknowledge in the English Speaking World from 1970–1989.*" DPhil diss., London Bible College, 1990.
Cottrell, Jack. *What the Bible Says About God the Ruler*. Joplin, MO: College, 1984.
Cranfield, C. E. B., and W. Sanday. *A Critical and Exegetical Commentary on the Epistle to the Romans*. Edinburgh: T. & T. Clark, 1980–1983.
Crisp, Oliver. "Creating Evil? An Inquiry into the Logical Problem for Theodicy." MTh thesis, University of Aberdeen, 1998.
Cyril of Jerusalem. "The Catechetical Lectures." In *A Select Library of Nicene and Post-Nicene Fathers of the Christian Church*, series 2, volume 7, edited and translated by Philip Schaff and Henry Wace. New York: Christian Literature, 1890.
Davids, Peter. *The First Epistle of Peter*. New International Commentary on the New Testament. Grand Rapids: Eerdmans, 1990.
Dawkins, Richard. *River out of Eden: A Darwinian View of Life*. New York: Basic, 1996.
Descartes, Rene. *Meditations on First Philosophy in Which are Demonstrated the Existence of God and the Distinction Between the Human Soul and the Body*. E-text was constructed upon the translation by John Cottingham (Cambridge University Press). Edited by Jonathan Bennett. Online: http://www.earlymoderntexts.com/pdfbits/de.html.
Dionysius (Pseudo-Dionysius the Areopagite). "On Divine Names." In *The Works of Dionysius the Areopagite*, translated by Reverend John Parker. Online: http://www.ccel.org/ccel/dionysius/works.i.html.
Dostoyevsky, Fyodor. *The Brothers Karamazov*. Translated by Constance Garnett. New York: The Modern Library, 1950.
Dunn, James. *Romans*. Word Biblical Commentary 38 (a/b). Dallas: Word, 1988.
Duns Scotus, John. *Duns Scotus on the Will and Morality*. Selected and translated by Allan B. Wolter. Washington, DC: The Catholic University of America Press, 1997.
———. *God and Creatures: The Quodlibetal Questions*. Translated and introduction by Felix Alluntis and Allan B. Wolter. Princeton, NJ: Princeton University Press, 1975.
Edwards, Jonathan. *The Collected Works of Jonathan Edwards CD*. Edited by Michael Bowman. Austin, TX: NavPress Software, 1998.
Edwards, Paul, editor. *Encyclopedia of Philosophy*. New York: McMillan Company, 1967.
Ehrman, Bart. *God's Problem: How the Bible Fails to Answer Our Most Important Question—Why We Suffer*. New York: HarperCollins, 2008.
Elfred, Michael Williams. "The Role of the Passion of Christ in a Christian Answer to the Problem of Suffering." MPhil thesis, University of Nottingham, 1981.
Erickson, Millard. *What Does God Know and When Does He Know It?* Grand Rapids: Zondervan, 2003.
Evans, Gillian Rosemary. *Augustine on Evil*. Cambridge; New York: Cambridge University Press, 1982.
Evans, Robert F. *Pelagius: Inquiries and Reappraisals*. New York: Seabury, 1968.
———. *Four Letters of Pelagius*. New York: Seabury, 1968.
Farley, Edward. *Ecclesial Reflections: An Anatomy of Theological Method*. Philadelphia: Fortress, 1982.
Farley, Edward. *Good & Evil: Interpreting a Human Condition*. Philadelphia: Fortress, 1990.

Feinberg, John S. *Deceived by God*. Wheaton, IL: Crossway, 1997.

———. "God Ordains All Things." In *Predestination and Free-Will*, edited by David Basinger and Randall Basinger, 19–43. Downers Grove, IL: Intervarsity, 1986.

———. *The Many Faces of Evil: Theological Systems and the Problem of Evil*, first edition. Grand Rapids: Zondervan, 1994.

———. *The Many Faces of Evil: Theological Systems and the Problem of Evil*, revised and expanded edition. Wheaton, IL: Crossway, 2004.

———. *No One Like Him: The Doctrine of God*. Wheaton, IL: Crossway Books, 2001.

Ferguson, Niall. *The War of the World: Twentieth-Century Conflict and the Descent of the West*. New York: Penguin, 2006.

Ferguson, Sinclair. *Children of the Living God*. Carlisle, PA: Banner of Truth Trust, 1989.

Fiddes, Paul. *The Creative Suffering of God*. Oxford: Clarendon, 1988.

Flew, Antony. "Divine Omnipotence & Human Freedom." In *New Essays in Philosophical Theology*, edited by Antony Flew and Alasdair Macintyre, 144–69. The Library of Philosophy and Theology. New York: MacMillan, 1955.

Flew, Antony, and Gary Habermas. "My Pilgrimage from Atheism to Theism: A Discussion Between Antony Flew and Gary Habermas." *Philosophia Christi: Journal of The Evangelical Philosophical Society*. Winter 2004. Orlando, FL. Online: http://jmm.aaa.net.au/articles/14169.htm.

Flint, Thomas P. *Divine Providence: The Molinist Account*. Corness Studies in the Philosophy of Religion. Ithaca, NY: Cornell University Press, 1998.

Floyd, William Edward Gregory. *Clement of Alexandria's Treatment of the Problem of Evil*. London: Oxford University Press, 1971.

Forsyth, P.T. *The Justification of God: Lectures for War-time on a Christian Theodicy*. New York: Scribner's, 1917.

Frank, William. "Duns Scotus on Autonomous Freedom and Divine Co-Causality." In *Medieval Philosophy and Theology*, volume 2, edited by Mark D. Jordan and Norman Kretzmann, 142–64. Notre Dame, IN: University of Notre Dame Press, 1992.

Freddoso, Alfred J. *Introduction to On Divine Foreknowledge: Part IV of The Concordia* by Luis de Molina. Ithaca, NY: Cornell University Press, 1988.

Fretheim, Terence. *The Suffering of God: An Old Testament Perspective*. Philadelphia: Fortress, 1984.

Geivett, R. Douglass. *Evil and the Evidence for God: The Challenge of John Hick's Theodicy*. Philadelphia: Temple University Press, 1993.

Gerstenberger, Erhard. *Psalms, Part I with an Introduction to Cultic Poetry*. Volume XIV. Forms of Old Testament Literature. Grand Rapids: Eerdmans, 1988.

Goldingay, John. *Psalms*. Volume 1: Psalms 1–41. Baker Commentary on the Old Testament. Edited by Tremper Longman III. Grand Rapids: BakerAcademic, 2006.

Gordis, Robert. *The Book of God and Man: A Study of Job*. Chicago: University of Chicago Press, 1995.

Gregory of Nyssa. *Gregory of Nyssa: The Life of Moses*. Translated by A.J. Malherbe and E. Ferguson. Malwah, NJ: Paulist, 1978.

Grenz, Stanley. *Revisioning Evangelical Theology*. Downers Grove, IL: Intervarsity, 1993.

Griffin, David Ray. "Augustinian Theodicy." In *The Problem of Evil: Selected Readings*, edited by Michael L. Peterson, 197–214. Library of Religious Philosophy 8. Notre Dame, IN: University of Notre Dame Press, 1992.

Bibliography

Grudem, Wayne. *The First Epistle of Peter: An Introduction and Commentary.* Tyndale New Testament Commentary. Grand Rapids: Eerdmans, 1988.

Habel, Norman C. *The Book of Job: A Commentary.* The Old Testament Library. Philadelphia: Westminster, 1985.

Harris, Murray. *Colossians & Philemon.* The Exegetical Guide to the Greek New Testament. Grand Rapids: Eerdmans, 1991.

Hart, David Bentley. *The Doors of the Sea: Where was God in the Tsunami?* Grand Rapids: Eerdmans, 2005.

Hartley, John E. *The Book of Job.* The New International Commentary on the Old Testament. Grand Rapids: Eerdmans, 1988.

Hasker, William. *God, Time, and Knowledge.* Ithaca, NY: Cornell University Press, 1989.

Hawthorne, Gerald. *Philippians.* Word Biblical Themes. Waco, TX: Word, 1987.

Helm, Paul. *The Last Things: Death, Judgment, Heaven and Hell.* Carlisle, PA: Banner of Truth Trust, 1989.

Henry, Carl F. *God, Revelation and Authority: The God Who Stands and Stays.* Part II. Volume 6. Wheaton, IL: Crossway, 1999.

Herbermann, Charles G., et al., editors. *The Catholic Encyclopedia: An International Work of Reference on the Constitution, Doctrine, Discipline and History of the Catholic Church.* New York: Robert Appleton Company, 1907–1912.

Hick, John. *Evil and the God of Love.* New York: Harper & Row, 1966.

———. "Jesus and the World Religions." In *The Myth of God Incarnate*, edited by John Hick, 167–85. Philadelphia: Westminster, 1977.

———. *John Hick: An Autobiography.* Oxford: Oneworld, 2002.

———. "Remarks." In *Reason and Religion,* edited by Stuart C. Brown, 122–8. Ithaca, NY: Cornell University Press, 1977.

Hicks, Peter. *The Journey So Far: Philosophy Through the Ages.* Grand Rapids: Zondervan, 2003.

———. *The Message of Evil & Suffering.* The Bible Speaks Today, edited by Derek Tidball. Downers Grove, IL: InterVarsity, 2006.

Hoekema, Anthony A. *Created in God's Image.* Grand Rapids: Eerdmans, 1986.

Honderich, Ted, editor. *Oxford Companion of Philosophy.* Oxford; New York: Oxford University Press, 1995.

Hopko, Thomas. "On God and Evil." In *Abba: The Tradition of Orthodoxy in the West*, edited by John Behr, 179–92. Crestwood, NY: St. Vladimir's Seminary Press, 2003.

Horne, Milton P. "Theodicy and the Problem of Human Surrender in Job." DPhil diss., Regent's Park College, 1989.

Howard-Snyder, Daniel T. "Surplus Evil." *The Philosophical Quarterly* 40/158 (1990) 78–86.

Hughes, C. T. "Philosophers, Theologians and Evil: Toward a Union of Philosophical and Theological Concerns in Theodicy." DPhil diss., Oriel College, 1988.

Hume, David. *Dialogues Concerning Natural Religion.* Edited by J. C. A. Gaskin. Oxford: Oxford University Press, 1993.

Ingham, Mary Beth. *Scotus for Dunces: An Introduction to the Subtle Doctor.* Saint Bonaventure, NY: Franciscan Institute, 2003.

Ingham, Mary Beth, and Mechthild Dreyer. *The Philosophical Vision of John Duns Scotus: An Introduction.* Washington, DC: Catholic University of America Press, 2004.

Irenaeus. *Against Heresies*. In *The Ante-Nicene Fathers: Translations of the Writings of the Fathers Down to AD 325*, volume 1, edited by Alexander Roberts and James Donaldson. Buffalo, NY: The Christian Literature Publishing Company, 1885.

Jacobs, Alan. *Shaming the Devil: Essays in Truthtelling*. Grand Rapids: Eerdmans, 2004.

Jewett, Robert. *Romans*. Hermeneia. Minneapolis: Fortress, 2007.

Jobes, Karen H. *1 Peter*. Exegetical Commentary on the New Testament. Grand Rapids: Eerdmans, 2005.

Jones, Peter. "Paul Confronts Paganism in the Church: A Case Study of First Corinthians 15:45." *Journal of the Evangelical Theological Society*. Volume 49/4. December 2006: 720.

Jordan, Mark D. *Rewritten Theology: Aquinas After his Readers*. Challenges in Contemporary Theology. Edited by Garreth Jones and Lewis Ayres. Malden, MA: Blackwell Publishing, 2006.

Journet, Charles. *The Meaning of Evil*. Translated by Michael Barry. New York: P.J. Kenedy & Sons, 1963.

Julian of Norwich. *Revelations of Divine Love*. Translated by Elizabeth Spearing. Edited by A.C. Spearing. New York: Penguin Books, 1998.

Kahn, Paul. *Out of Eden: Adam and Eve and the Problem of Evil*. Princeton, NJ: Princeton University Press, 2007.

Kane, G. Stanley. *Anselm's Doctrine of Freedom and the Will*. Texts and Studies in Religion. Volume 10. New York, NY; Toronto: Edwin Mellen, 1981.

———. "Theism and Evil." *Sophia* 9/1 (1970) 14–21.

Kaplan, Robert. *The Nothing that Is: A Natural History of Zero*. Oxford; New York: Oxford University Press, 2000.

Käsemann, Ernst. *Commentary on Romans*. Translated and edited by Geoffrey W. Bromiley. Grand Rapids: Eerdmans, 1980.

Keats, John. *The Letters of John Keats*. Edited by H. E. Rollins. 2 vols. Cambridge, MA: 1958.

Keller, Timothy. *The Reason for God: Belief in an Age of Skepticism*. New York: Dutton, 2008.

Kelly, J. N. D. *A Commentary on the Epistles of Peter and of Jude*. London: Adams & Charles Black, 1969.

Kelsey, David. *Proving Doctrine: The Uses of Scripture in Modern Theology*. Harrisburg, PA: Trinity International, 1999.

Kilby, Karen. "Perichoresis and Projection: Problems with Social Doctrines of the Trinity." First published in *New Blackfriars*, October 2000. Online: http://www.theologyphilosophycentre.co.uk/papers/Kilby_TrinNBnew.doc.

Kistemaker, Simon. *Revelation: Exposition of the Book of Revelation*. New Testament Commentary. Grand Rapids: Baker Academic, 2001.

Knight, George W., III. *The Pastoral Epistles: A Commentary on the Greek Text*. Grand Rapids: Eerdmans, 1992.

Knight, Mark James. "The Concept of Evil in the Fiction of G.K. Chesterton: With Special Reference to his Use of the Grotesque." PhD diss., King's College, 1999.

Konkel, August, and Tremper Longman III. *Job, Ecclesiastes and Song of Songs*. Cornerstone Biblical Commentary. Carol Stream, IL: Tyndale House, 2006.

Kreeft, Peter. *Making Sense Out of Suffering*. Ann Arbor, MI: Servant, 1986.

Kushner, Harold S. *When Bad Things Happen to Good People*. New York: Avon, 1981.

Lactantius. *A Treatise on the Anger of God*. In *The Ante-Nicene Fathers: Translations of the Writings of the Fathers Down to AD 325*, volume 7, edited by Alexander Roberts and James Donaldson. Grand Rapids: Eerdmans, 1983.

Bibliography

Ladd, George Eldon. *The Gospel of the Kingdom*. Grand Rapids: Eerdmans, 2000 (Paternoster, 1959).
L'Engle, Madeleine. *Two-Part Invention*. San Francisco: HarperSanFrancisco, 1988.
Leff, Gordon. *William of Ockham: The Metamorphosis of Scholastic Discourse*. Manchester: Manchester University Press, 1975.
Leibniz, Gottfried Wilhelm. *Theodicy: Essays on the Goodness of God, the Freedom of Man and the Origin of Evil*. Translated by E. M. Huggard. Peru, IL: Open Court Company. The Project Gutenberg, 1985. Online: http://www.gutenberg.org.
Lewis, C. S. *A Grief Observed*. New York: Bantam, 1961.
———. *The Problem of Pain*. San Francisco: HarperSanFrancisco, 1940.
———. *Screwtape Letters*. New York: HarperCollins, 2001 (1959).
Lindbeck, George. *The Nature of Doctrine: Religion and Theology in a Postliberal Age*. Louisville: Westminster John Knox, 1984.
Lloyd, Michael. "The Cosmic Fall and the Free Will Defence." DPhil diss., Worcester College, University of Oxford, 1997.
Lohse, Edward. *Colossians and Philemon: A Commentary on the Epistles to the Colossians and to Philemon*. Hermeneia. Philadelphia: Fortress, 1971.
Luther, Martin. *Luther: Lectures on Romans*. Library of Christian Classics. Volume 15. Philadelphia: Westminster, 1961.
———. *Martin Luther: Selections from his Writings*. Edited by John Dillenberger. Garden City, NY: Anchor Doubleday, 1961.
McFadyen, Alistair. *Bound to Sin*. Cambridge: Cambridge University Press, 2000.
Mackie, John Langshaw. "Evil and Omnipotence." *Mind* 64 (1955) 200–212.
———. "Theism and Utopia." *Philosophy* 37/140 (1962) 153–8.
McKim, Robert. "Worlds Without Evil." *International Journal of Philosophy of Religion*. Volume 15 (1984) 161–70.
Maitland-Cullen, Patrick S. "The Theodicy Problem in the Theology of Jürgen Moltmann." DPhil diss., University of Edinburgh, 1990.
Marcel, Gabriel. *The Philosophy of Existentialism*. Translated by Manya Harari. Secaucus, NJ: The Citadel, 1956.
March, Jenny. *Cassell Dictionary of Classical Mythology*. London: Cassell, 1998.
Marenbon, John. *Boethius*. New York: Oxford University Press, 2003.
Marshall, I. Howard. *The Gospel of Luke: A Commentary on the Greek Text*. New International Greek Testament Commentary. Exeter: Paternoster, 1978.
———. *The Pastoral Epistles*. The International Critical Commentary. Edinburgh: T. & T. Clark, 1999.
Mathewes, Charles T. *Evil and the Augustinian Tradition*. Cambridge; New York: Cambridge University Press, 2001.
Mautner, Thomas. *A Dictionary of Philosophy*. Cambridge, MA: Blackwell Reference, 1996.
Merillat, Herbert Christian. " The Gnostic Apostle Thomas." Bardic, 1997–2005. Online: http://www.bardic-press.com/thomas/gnosticapostle.htm.
Mesle, C. Robert. "The Problem of Genuine Evil: A Critique of John Hick's Theodicy." *The Journal of Religion* 4/66 (1986) 412–30.
Meyendorff, John. *The Orthodox Church: Its Past and Its Role in the World Today*. Translated by John Chapin. New York: Pantheon, 1962.
Milbank, John, and Catherine Pickstock. *Truth in Aquinas*. Radical Orthodoxy Series. London: Routledge, 2001.

Milton, John. *Paradise Lost*. London: Penguin Books, 2000 (1667).

Molina, Luis de. "Disputation 25." Translated by Alfred J. Freddoso. Online: www.nd.edu/~afreddos/translat/molina25.htm.

———. *On Divine Foreknowledge: Part IV of The Concordia*. Edited and translated by Alfred J. Freddoso. Ithaca, NY: Cornell University Press, 1988.

Moll, Rob. "Great Leap Forward." *Christianity Today*. May 2008. Online: http://www.christianitytoday.com/ct/2008/may/19.22.html.

Moltmann, Jürgen. *The Crucified God: The Cross of Christ as the Foundation and Criticism of Christian Theology*. Translated by R. A. Wilson and John Bowden. New York: Harper and Row, 1974.

———. *The Trinity and the Kingdom: The Doctrine of God*. Translated by Margaret Kohl. San Francisco: Harper & Row, 1981.

Moo, Douglas. *The Epistle to the Romans*. Grand Rapids: Eerdmans, 1996.

Morgan, Christopher, and Robert A. Peterson, editors. *Suffering and the Goodness of God*. Theology in Community. Wheaton, IL: Crossway, 2008.

Mosser, Carl. "Evil, Mormonism and the Impossibility of Perfection *Ab Initio*: An Irenaean Defense." Paper read at The Evangelical Theological Society, Washington, D.C., November 2005.

Murphy, Nancy, and George F. R. Ellis. *On the Moral Nature of the Universe: Theology, Cosmology, and Ethics*. Theology and the Sciences. Edited by Kevin Sharpe. Minneapolis: Fortress, 1996.

Murray, James Augustus Henry. *Oxford English Dictionary*, Oxford: Clarendon, 1961 c.1933.

Murray, John. *The Epistle to the Romans*. The New International Commentary on the New Testament. Grand Rapids: Eerdmans, 1959.

———. *Redemption Accomplished and Applied*. Grand Rapids: Eerdmans, 1955.

Neff, Gordon. *William of Ockham: The Metamorphosis of Scholastic Discourse*. Manchester: Manchester University Press, 1975.

Nellas, Panayiotis. *Deification in Christ: Orthodox Perspectives on the Nature of the Human Person*. Contemporary Greek Theologians. Number 5. Crestwood, NY: St. Vladimir's Seminary Press, 1987.

O'Brien, Peter T. *Colossians and Philemon*. Word Biblical Commentary. Volume 44. Waco, TX: Word, 1982.

Origen. *Against Celsus*. In *The Ante-Nicene Fathers: Translations of the Writings of the Fathers Down to AD 325*, volume 4, edited by Alexander Roberts and James Donaldson. Buffalo. NY: The Christian Literature Publishing Company, 1885.

———. *On First Principles: Being Koetschau's Text of De Principiis*. Translated by G.W. Butterworth. New York: Harper Torchbacks, 1966.

———. "Putting to Death the Works of the Flesh." In *Romans: New Testament VI*, edited by Gerald Bray, 214–5. *Ancient Christian Commentary on Scripture*, edited by Thomas Oden. Downers Grove, IL: InterVarsity, 1998.

Osborne, Grant. *Revelation*. Baker Exegetical Commentary on the New Testament. Grand Rapids: Baker Academic, 2002.

Pagels, Elaine. *Adam, Eve and the Serpent*. New York: Random House, 1988.

Palau, Luis. *Where Is God When Bad Things Happen?* New York: Galilee Doubleday, 1999.

Pascal, Blaise. *Pensées*. Translated by A. J. Krailsheimer. London: Penguin Classics, 1995.

Bibliography

Pelagius. *Pelagius's Commentary on St. Paul's Epistle to the Romans.* Oxford Early Christian Studies. Translated and introduced by Theodore de Bruyn. Oxford: Clarendon; New York: Oxford University Press, 1993.

Peterson, Michael L. *Evil and the Christian God.* Grand Rapids: Baker, 1982.

———. *God and Evil: An Introduction to the Issues.* Boulder, CO: Westview, 1998.

Phillips, D. Z. *The Problem of Evil and the Problem of God.* London: SCM, 2004.

———. "Response to The Problem of Evil." In *Reason and Religion.* Edited by Stuart C. Brown, 103–21. Ithaca, NY: Cornell University Press, 1977.

Pike, Nelson. "Hume on Evil." *Philosophical Review* 72/2. April 1963: 180–97.

Pinnock, Clark. *The Most Moved Mover.* Grand Rapids: Baker Academic, 2001.

Piper, John. "Christ: The Lion and the Lamb." Minneapolis: Desiring God, 1986. Online: http://www.desiringgod.org/ResourceLibrary/Sermons/ByDate/1986/535_Christ_The_Lion_and_the_Lamb/.

———. *Desiring God: Meditations of a Christian Hedonist.* Sisters, OR: Multnomah, 1996 (1986).

———. *God is the Gospel.* Wheaton, IL: Crossway, 2005.

———. *God's Passion for his Glory: Living the Vision of Jonathan Edwards.* Wheaton, IL: Crossway Books, 1998.

———. *The Justification of God: An Exegetical and Theological Study of Romans 9:1–23*, second edition. Grand Rapids: Baker, 1993.

———. *Spectacular Sins and Their Global Purpose in the Glory of Christ* (preprint manuscript from the author). Wheaton, IL: Crossway, 2008.

Plantinga, Alvin. *God and Other Minds: A Study of the Rational Justification of Belief in God.* Ithaca, NY: Cornell University Press, 1990 (1976).

———. *God, Freedom, and Evil.* New York: Harper & Row, 1974.

———. *The Nature of Necessity.* Oxford: Clarendon, 1974.

———. "The Probabilistic Argument from Evil." *Philosophical Studies* 35 (1979) 1–53.

Plato, *The Republic.* Translated and introduced by Desmond Lee. London: Penguin Classics, 2003 (1974).

Polkinghorne, John. *Belief in God in an Age of Science: The Terry Lectures, 1998.* New Haven, CT: Yale Note Bene, 2003.

———. *The Faith of a Physicist: Reflections of a Bottom-Up Thinker: The Gifford Lectures for 1993–1994.* Princeton, NJ: Princeton University Press, 1994.

———. *Science & Theology: An Introduction.* Minneapolis: Fortress, 1998.

Pomazansky, Michael. *Orthodox Dogmatic Theology: A Concise Exposition*, second edition. Translated by Hieromonk Serphim Rose. Platina, CA: Saint Herman of Alaska Brotherhood, 1994.

Ramberan, Osmond. "Evil and Theism." *Sophia* 17/1 (1978) 28–36.

Ratzinger, Joseph (Pope Benedict XVI). *Communion and Stewardship: Human Persons Created in the Image of God.* The July 2004 Vatican Statement on Creation and Evolution. Online: http://www.vatican.va/roman_curia/congregations/cfaith/cti_documents/rc_con_cfaith_doc_20040723_communion-stewardship_en.html.

Rees, Brinley Roderick (B.R.). *Pelagius: A Reluctant Heretic.* Woodbridge, Suffolk; Wolfeboro, NH: Boydell, 1988.

Ricoeur, Paul. *The Conflict of Interpretations: Essays in Hermeneutics.* Edited by Don Ihde. Evanston, IL: Northwestern University Press, 1974.

Rist, John M. *Augustine: Ancient Thought Baptized.* Cambridge; New York: Cambridge University Press, 1994.

Roberts, Alexander, and James Donaldson, editors. *The Ante-Nicene Fathers: Translations of the Writings of the Fathers Down to AD 325.* Grand Rapids: Eerdmans, 1983.

Robinson, John A.T. *Wrestling with Romans.* Philadelphia: Westminster, 1979.

Rodin, Robert Scott. "A Study of the Doctrine of Evil and Theodicy in the Theology of Karl Barth." PhD diss., Aberdeen University, 1993.

Rowe, William. "The Problem of Evil and Some Varieties of Atheism." *American Philosophical Quarterly* 16/4 (1979) 335–41.

Rowley, H. H. *Job.* The New Century Bible. London: Thomas Nelson, 1970.

Russell, J. Stuart, and Edward E. Stevens. *The Parousia: The New Testament Doctrine of Christ's Second Coming.* Bradford, PA: International Preterist Association, 2003 (1887).

Sailhamer, John. *Genesis Unbound: A Proactive New Look at the Creation Account.* Sisters, OR: Multnomah, 1996.

Sanday, William, and Arthur Headlam. *A Critical and Exegetical Commentary on the Epistle to the Romans.* The International Critical Commentary. Volume 32. 5th edition. Edinburgh: T. & T. Clark, 1980.

Sanders, John. *The God Who Risks: A Theology of Providence.* Downers Grove, IL: InterVarsity, 1998.

Schaeffer, Francis. *Escape from Reason.* Downers Grove, IL: InterVarsity, 1968.

———. *He is There and He is not Silent.* Wheaton, IL: Tyndale, 1972.

Schaff, Philip. *History of the Christian Church.* Grand Rapids: Christian Classics Ethereal Library. First published in 1882. Online: http://www.ccel.org/s/schaff/history/7_ch02.htm#_ednref68.

Schreiner, Thomas. "Does Scripture Teach Prevenient Grace in the Wesleyan Sense?" In *The Grace of God—the Bondage of the Will: Historical and Theological Perspectives on Calvinism*, edited by Thomas Schreiner and Bruce Ware, 2:365–82. Grand Rapids: Baker, 1995.

———. *Romans.* Baker Exegetical Commentary on the New Testament 6. Grand Rapids: Baker, 1998.

Schultz, Walter. "Jonathan Edwards's End of Creation: An Exposition and Defense." *Journal of the Evangelical Theological Society* 49/2 (2006) 247–71.

Scott, Alan. *Origen and the Life of the Stars: A History of an Idea.* Oxford: Clarendon, 1991.

Selwyn, E. G. *The First Epistle of St. Peter.* London: MacMillan, 1961.

Smith, J. C. *Ancient Wisdom of Origen.* Cranbury, NJ: Associated University, 1992.

Spinoza, Benedict. *On the Improvement of the Understanding.* Translated by R. H. M. Elwes. Champaign, IL: Project Gutenberg, 1997. Online: http://www.gutenberg.org/dirs/etext97/spint10.txt.

Stackhouse, John G. Jr. *Can God be Trusted? Faith and the Challenge of Evil.* New York: Oxford University Press, 1998.

Stump, Eleonore. "The Problem of Evil." *Faith and Philosophy: Journal of the Society of Christian Philosophers* 2/4 (1985) 392–423.

Surin, Kenneth. *Theology and the Problem of Evil.* Signposts in Theology. New York: Basil Blackwell, 1986.

Swinburne, Richard. *The Coherence of Theism.* Clarendon Library of Logic and Philosophy. Oxford: Clarendon, 1977.

———. *The Existence of God.* Oxford: Clarendon, 1979.

———. "The Problem of Evil." In *Reason and Religion*, edited by Stuart C. Brown, 103. Ithaca, NY: Cornell University Press, 1977.

———. *Providence and the Problem of Evil*. Oxford: Clarendon, 1998.

Tabb, Mark. *Out of the Whirlwind*. Nashville: Broadman & Holman, 2003.

Tate, Marvin. *Psalms 51–100*. Volume 20. Word Biblical Commentary. Dallas: Word, 1990.

Tennant, F. R. *Philosophical Theology*. Volume 2. Cambridge: Cambridge University Press, 1930.

Tertullian. *Against Marcion*. In *The Ante-Nicene Fathers: Translations of the Writings of the Fathers Down to AD 325*, volume 3, edited by Alexander Roberts and James Donaldson. Buffalo, NY: Christian Literature, 1885.

———. *Against Praxis*. In *The Ante-Nicene Fathers: Translations of the Writings of the Fathers Down to AD 325*, volume 3, edited by Alexander Roberts and James Donaldson. Buffalo, NY: Christian Literature, 1885.

Tiegreen, Chris. *Why a Suffering World Makes Sense*. Grand Rapids: Baker, 2006.

Tiessen, Terrance. *Providence & Prayer: How Does God Work in the World?* Downers Grove, IL: InterVarsity, 2000.

Tilley, Terrence. "The Use and Abuse of Theodicy." *Horizons* 11/2 (1984) 304–19.

Ton, Joseph. *Suffering, Martyrdom, and Rewards in Heaven*. Oxford; New York: Lanham, 2000.

Torrance, Alan. *Persons in Communion: An Essay on Trinitarian Description and Human Participation*. Edinburgh: T. & T. Clark, 1996.

Torrance, James B. *Worship, Community & the Triune God of Grace*. Downers Grove, IL: InterVarsity, 1996.

Towner, Philip. *Letters to Timothy and Titus*. The New International Commentary on the New Testament. Grand Rapids: Eerdmans, 2006.

Trigg, Joseph Wilson. *Origen: The Bible and Philosophy in the Third-century Church*. Atlanta, GA: John Knox, 1983.

VanHoozer, Kevin J. *First Theology: God, Scripture, and Hermeneutics*. Downers Grove, IL: InterVarsity, 2002.

———. *Is There a Meaning in This Text?: The Bible, The Reader, and the Morality of Literary Knowledge*. Grand Rapids: Zondervan, 1998.

———. *The Drama of Doctrine: A Canonical-Linguistic Approach to Christian Theology*. Louisville, KY: Westminster John Knox, 2005.

Velde, Rudi te. *Aquinas on God: The "Divine Science" of the Summa Theologicae*. Ashgate Studies in the History of Philosophical Theology, edited by Stone, Byrne, Antognazza, and Steel. Aldershot: Ashgate, 2006.

Voltaire (François-Marie Arouet). *Candide, or Optimism*. Translated by Henry Morley. New York: Barnes & Noble, 2003 (1759).

Wall, Robert. *Revelation*. New International Biblical Commentary. Peabody, MA: Hendrickson, 1992.

Walls, Jerry. "Why Plantinga Must Move from Defense to Theodicy." In *The Problem of Evil: Selected Readings*, edited by Michael L. Peterson, 328–32. Library of Religious Philosophy, 8. Notre Dame, IN: University of Notre Dame Press, 1992.

Ware, Bruce A. *God's Greater Glory: The Exalted God of Scripture and the Christian Faith*. Wheaton, IL: Crossway, 2004.

Ware, Timothy (Bishop Kallistos Ware). *The Orthodox Way*, revised edition. Crestwood, NY: St. Vladimir's Seminary Press, 1995 (first edition, 1979).

———. *God's Lesser Glory: The Diminished God of Open Theism*. Wheaton, IL: Crossway, 2000.
Weinandy, Thomas. *Does God Suffer?* Notre Dame, IN: University of Notre Dame Press, 2000.
Whale, J. S. *The Christian Answer to the Problem of Evil*. London: Student Christian Movement, 1936.
Whitehead, Alfred North. *Process and Reality: An Essay in Cosmology*. Gifford Lectures Delivered in the University of Edinburgh During the Session 1927–28. Corrected edition by David Ray Griffin and Donald W. Sherburne. New York: The Free Press, 1978.
Wiggers, Gustave Friedrich. *An Historical Presentation of Augustinism and Pelagianism from the Original Sources*. Translated by Ralph Emerson. Ann Arbor, MI: University Microfilms, 1979.
Willard, Dallas. *The Spirit of the Disciplines*. San Francisco: Harper Collins, 1990.
Williams, C. J. F. "Where the Semipelagians Went Wrong." *Sophia* 2/3 (1963) 19–24.
Williams, Norman Paul. *The Ideas of the Fall and of Original Sin: A Historical and Critical Study*. London: Longmans, Green, 1927.
Williams, Robert. "Theodicy, Tragedy and Soteriology: The Legacy of Schleiermacher." *Harvard Theological Review* 77/3–4 (1984) 395–412.
Williams, Rowan. *On Christian Theology*. Challenges in Contemporary Theology, edited by Gareth Jones and Lewis Ayres. Oxford; Malden, MA: Blackwell, 2000.
———. "Reply: Redeeming Sorrows." *Religion and Morality*, edited by D.Z. Phillips, 132–48. New York: St. Martin's, 1996.
———. *The Truce of God*, second edition. Grand Rapids: Eerdmans, 2005.
Williams, Thomas. "A Most Methodical Lover: On Scotus's Arbitrary Creator." *Journal of the History of Philosophy*. Volume 38. Berkeley, CA: University of California Press, 2000: 169–202.
———. "Reason, Morality, and Voluntarism in Duns Scotus: A Pseudo-Problem Dissolved." *The Modern Schoolman* 74:73–94. St. Louis: St. Louis University Press, 1997.
———. "The Unmitigated Duns Scotus." Originally accessed on his academic page on the University of Notre Dame website. Now available on his University of South Florida site. Online: http://shell.cas.usf.edu/~thomasw/archiv.pdf.
Wilson, R. *A Critical and Exegetical Commentary on Colossians and Philemon*. The International Critical Commentary. New York: T. & T. Clark, 2005.
Wojtyła, Karol Józef (Pope John Paul II). "Salvifici Doloris." *Apostolic Letters*. 11 February 1984. Online: http://www.vatican.va/holy_father/john_paul_ii/apost_letters/documents/hf_jp-ii_apl_11021984_salvifici-doloris_en.html.
Wolter, Allan B. "The Unshredded Scotus: A Response to Thomas Williams." *American Catholic Philosophical Quarterly: Journal of the American Catholic Philosophical Association* 77/3. Washington, DC: The Association, 2003: 315–56.
Wright, Nicholas Thomas. *Colossians and Philemon*. The Tyndale New Testament Commentaries. Grand Rapids: Eerdmans, 1986.
———. *Evil and the Justice of God*. Downers Grove, IL: InterVarsity, 2006.
———. *The New Testament and the People of God*. Christian Origins and the Question of God, volume 1. Minneapolis: Fortress, 1992.
Wright, R.K. McGregor. *No Place for Sovereignty: What's Wrong with Freewill Theism?* Downers Grove, IL: InterVarsity, 1996.
Yancy, Phillip. *Disappointment with God: Three Questions No One Asks Aloud*. Grand Rapids: Zondervan, 1988.

Bibliography

Yandell, Keith E. "The Greater Good Defense." *Sophia* 13/3 (1974) 1–16.

Yannatos, Michael. "Good and Evil in the Teaching of Saint Basil of Caesarea." MA thesis, Durham University, 1985.

Zupko, Jack. "Review: Marilyn McCord Adams, Horrendous Evils and the Goodness of God." *Sophia* 41/1 (2002) 135–38.

Scripture Index

GENESIS

1	60, 181
1–3	234–35
1:1	236
1:26–27	138, 125, 168
2	236
2:4–5	236
3	189, 235
3:1–7	189
3:15–16	205–6
4	196
5:1	236
6	111
8:21	111
9	221
11	221
12:1	221
15:16	221

EXODUS

3–4	196
9:16	165
32	92

LEVITICUS

11:44–45	244

DEUTERONOMY

5:32	244
17:11	244
17:20	244
28:14	244

JOSHUA

1:7	244
6–7	278
23:6	244

JUDGES

20:16	244

1 SAMUEL

15:11	205
27:1	268

2 SAMUEL

11–12	277
12:20	277

1 KINGS

9:3	165
14:22–24	108

2 KINGS

22:2	244
22:15–17	258

Scripture Index

2 CHRONICLES

16:9	103
34:2	244

PSALMS

1–41	162
8	258
16:11	174
23	79, 162
23:3	162
34:15–16	211
37:4	172
42–43	268
42:5	268–69
42:11–12	268
43:5	268–69
44	268
51–100	163
79:9	163
91:13	205
102:5	175
106:8	163
106:45	163–64
109:21	163
111:10	27
112:7	79
137	258

PROVERBS

4:27	244
25:2	2, 150

JOB

1 & 2	117, 275
3:23	259
6:4	259
7:20–21	259
9:2	259
10:7	259
12:7–10	259
13:15	259
14:11	259
14:14–19	259
19:10	259
19:25–27	259
36:16	257
37–41	117
40:4–5	261
42	117

ISAIAH

2:9–22	261
5:20	111, 224
7:9	9, 27
25:8	210
30:21	244
40–55	258
42:8	165
42–53	207
45:7	60
48:9	165
49:3	165
51:11	174
53:4	207
66:22–24	240

JEREMIAH

2:19	122–23
19:5	108
31:29	258
32:40	180

LAMENTATIONS

3:20	268

EZEKIEL

47:12	255

EZRA

8:29	205

HABAKKUK

3:18	174

ZECHARIAH

4:6	220

Scripture Index

MATTHEW

1:1	236
5:39–40	279
6:25–34	269
7:3–5	277
15:10–20	198
16:17	44
17:5	223
20:25–28	220
22:1–14	248
26:38	269

MARK

1:11	173
4:28	86
9:7	173
9:41–48	240
10:18	184

LUKE

3:22	173
3:38	236
4:1–13	276
6:43	198
9:22–25	142
9:23	274
13:4	277
14:27	215
18:18–23	184
18:23–24	269
20:13	173
21:1–3	239
21:16 18	238
21:29–30	86
24:25–27	207
24:26	180

JOHN

1	203
1:1	173, 236
1:1–3	75
1:4–5	44
1:9	237
1:14	203
1:27	203
2:19	203
3:16–18	281
3:35	173
5	173
5:20	173
5:24	215
6:44	44
6:56	231
8:32	121
8:56–57	121
12:27–28	165
13:3–7	167
14:21	173, 215
15:1–11	231
15:11	174
16:24	174
16:33	215
17	174, 269
17:3	157, 174
17:13	174
17:14	215
17:17	121
17:21	174
17:26	173
18:10	274
19:18	255

ACTS

3:18	208
10	210
13:9	25
17:2–3	208

ROMANS

1–11	223
1:1–5	25
1:5	164
1:18–25	59
1:21	181
3:21–26	25
3:23	244
3:25–26	219
3:28	25
4:5	126
5&6	43
5:1–5	205, 273
5:1	126
5:4	261
5:10	200
5:50	173
6:5–8	214
6:6–7	182
6:20–22	182

ROMANS (continued)

7	230–231
7:2	202
7:14–25	230
7:23	182
8	xvii, 17, 178, 186, 205, 214, 217, 252, 268, 271
8:1–4	261
8:2	182
8:3	26
8:5–13	262
8:13	124
8:17	179, 181, 206–7, 274
8:17–18	252
8:17–39	179
8:18	108, 144
8:19	181
8:20–21	197, 235, 247, 252
8:21	60
8:24	268
8:28, 29	183
8:29–30	252
8:30	183
8:31	268
9	22
9:1–23	70
9:13–14	70
9:20	117
9:20–23	22
9:23	165
10:9–10	25
12:1	25, 223
12:2	250
12:17	223
12:21	215, 223
15:30	173
16:17	205
16:20	205

1 CORINTHIANS

1:8	268
1:17–18	218
2:11	173
2:14	199
2:2	201
4:7	74
7:14–16	279
12:3	44
13:3	279
15	199–203
15:22	199
15:26	203
15:44–49	198–99
15:45	286
15:50–56	195
15:54–55	210
15:56	201–2

2 CORINTHIANS

1:5–6	238
1:8	268
3:17–18	252
3:18	180
4:8–12	269
4:17	109, 181, 209
5:17	235
8:14	239
9:12	239

GALATIANS

3:16	206
4:6	173
5:4	202
5:22	173
6:14–15	235

EPHESIANS

1:7	236
1:12	165
1:14	249
1:20	236
3:13	180, 238
4:22–24	180
4:24	236, 252

PHILIPPIANS

2:5–8	167, 173
2:6	167
3:8–11	204, 236, 238
4:6	269

COLOSSIANS

1:13	173
1:24	212, 238–39
2:15	202, 208
3:1	236

Scripture Index

3:10	236
3:9–10	180

1 THESSALONIANS

2:1–4	273
3:10	239

2 THESSALONIANS

1:12	207
2:8	237
2:10–13	27
2:14	167

1 TIMOTHY

2:15	206
6:1	280

2 TIMOTHY

1	203
1:8	202, 274
1:9	167
1:10	111, 201–2
1:11	202
1:17	202
2	22
2:3	273
2:11–12	215
2:20–21	22
2:24–26	246
3:12	215

HEBREWS

1:3	201
2:14	202, 276
2:14–15	203
2:9	180
2:9–10	203
4:15	251
5:14	110
11	269
11:6	270
12	154, 208
12:7–10	277

JAMES

1:12	273
1:2–3	205
1:2–4	281
1:13–14	96
1:13–15	93
3:11	198
4:7	276

1 PETER

1:1	211
1:3–12	212
1:6	212, 217
1:6–7	273
1:8	174
1:8–9	212
1:11	180, 212
1:16	244
1:20	167
2:11–12	213
2:11—14:11	213
2:18–20	212
2:19	275
2:21	213, 274
3:9–22	211–14
4:1–2	214, 252
4:11–16	215–16
4:13	180
4:16	180
5:1	180
5:7	269
5:8–10	276
5:10	180, 217
5:12	211

2 PETER

1:17	173
3:9–10	237

1 JOHN

1:5	185
1:9	81
2:6	231
2:12	165
2:13	215
2:14	231
2:27	231

Scripture Index

1 JOHN (continued)

3	203
3:1–17	231
3:5	203
3:6	231
3:8	203
4:4–5	215
5:4–5	215
5:15	231

2 JOHN

2 1:4	121

JUDE

1:24	174

REVELATION

1–5	215
6:10–11	238
6:11	227
12	206
12:11	216
13	216
15	216
16:16	237
19:3	210
20	291
20:9	237
21:1	60
21:1–5	240
22:2	255

Name and Subject Index

Abraham, 55, 116, 126, 213, 221, 258
Achtemeier, Paul, 211, 214
acrasia, 30
Adamic, 25, 242
Adams, Marilyn McCord, 5, 37-38, 82-83, 104, 142-45, 149, 151, 175, 188, 207, 222-23, 229, 266, 270
Adams, Robert Merrihew, 47, 134
Ahern, M. B., 61, 78, 94-95, 98, 140-141
Alaric, 25, 75, 127
Allen, G. W., 38, 110
Ambrose, Aurelius, 27
Anglin, W. S., 20
Anselm of Canterbury, 31-33, 40-41, 80-82, 130, 169-70, 243, 247, 251
apocalypse, 145, 239, 261, 272
apostle, 25, 120, 126, 138, 164, 211, 239-40
Aquinas, Thomas, xi, 2, 18, 28, 33-37, 40-42, 44, 49, 53, 55-56, 60, 78-79, 82, 89, 130-31, 134, 137, 149-50, 175, 189-90, 192, 206-7, 232, 243, 247, 250-51
Aristotle, 28, 30, 33-34, 78, 107-8, 189, 200
Arminian, 16, 51, 54-55, 170
Arminius, Jacob, 18, 45-46, 56, 175, 184
aseity, 168, 170, 177
atheism, ix, 60, 94, 102, 113-14, 134, 140, 142, 150
atonement, 26, 147, 179, 201, 206, 209, 239
Augustine, ix, xi, 4, 6, 8-10, 18, 20-21, 23-31, 33-34, 37, 40-44, 49, 51, 53, 55-57, 60-61, 72-87, 89-91, 93, 95, 103, 105, 115, 117, 121, 123, 125-31, 134-35, 137-38, 144, 149-50, 174, 176, 178, 184, 195, 218, 231-32, 241-43, 245, 247-51, 254
Augustinian, 21, 24-25, 30, 34, 55-56, 78-79, 83-84, 90-93, 95, 105, 135, 137-38, 192, 249

Bañez, Domingo, 19, 48-49, 86
Barr, James, 177, 216

Barth, Karl, 46, 67, 90-91, 132, 166, 169, 171, 190, 195, 209
Basinger, David and Randall, 48, 154-55
Beale, Greg, 60, 216, 236, 255
Beilby, James, 161, 167-68, 170-71
Benedict, 110, 124
Best of All Possible Worlds. *See* Theodicy types
Blocher, Henri, 1, 11, 60, 95, 98-99, 115-16, 146-48, 151, 196, 208, 220, 225-26, 230, 236
Boersma, Hans, 174
Boethius, Anicius, 16, 31, 41, 49, 51, 53, 55, 80, 129
Bonhoeffer, Dietrich, 62, 201
Boston, Thomas, 198, 232, 241
Boyd, Gregory, 7-8, 54, 59, 91, 105, 109-10, 158-59
Bruce, F. F., 181, 209
Buber, Martin, 111
Buddha, Buddhism, 101, 110, 145
Bunyan, John, 199-200
Burroughs, Jeremiah, 204-5

Calvin, John, 9, 18, 26, 42-45, 52, 56, 84-85, 98, 105, 131, 150, 170-71, 175, 177, 184, 193, 245, 247, 267
Calvinism, 45-46, 48, 54, 93, 105, 170
Canaan, 107, 221
Carson, D. A., 1, 178, 243, 251, 261
Chardin, Pierre Tielhard de, 225-26
Chesterton, G. K., 1, 28, 33-34, 260
Ciocchi, David, 3, 19
Clement of Alexandria, 21, 23, 25-26, 49, 55, 69-70, 120, 126, 211
Clendenin, Daniel, 56
Clotfelter, David, 167, 249
compatibilism, xvii, 15-16, 18-21, 23, 27, 29-31, 36-37, 41, 46, 48-49, 51, 55-57, 67, 77, 93, 96-97, 130, 133, 141, 143, 158-61, 164-65, 171-72, 175, 188, 191-92, 241-42, 246, 249, 254

321

PART III: A Theodicy in the Face of Reality

Compatibilistic Free-Will. *See* Free-Will

conforming, 11, 21, 150, 153, 160, 177–78, 185, 189, 195, 219–20, 228, 231, 244, 248, 252–53

Conforming-Freedom. *See* Era(s) of Freedom

consequentialist, 64, 104–6, 122, 124, 129, 148–49, 151, 187–88, 197, 224–25, 243

correction (suffering of). *See* suffering

Cottrell, Jack, 247

counterfactual, 47–49, 52

Cranfield, C. E. B, 59, 181, 205

Creation and Crisis, xvii, 11, 55, 228, 230, 233–35, 237, 240, 242, 245, 249, 262

Cross (of Christ), ix, xi, xiii, xvii, 1, 11, 60, 95, 98–100, 107, 111–12, 116, 142, 144, 146–48, 151, 153–54, 167, 174, 187, 193, 196, 200–201, 204–5, 207–13, 215–16, 218–23, 225, 230, 235–36, 240, 253, 261, 267–68, 270–71, 273–74, 281, 282, 290, 293, 295, 297–300.

Cyril of Jerusalem, 126

Davies, Brian, 32–33, 81, 251

Dawkins, Richard, 102

Descartes, Rene, 86–87, 91, 132, 229

Decrees, of God, xviii, 16, 37, 42–49, 65–66, 87–88, 105–6, 133, 164, 172, 190–91, 207, 210, 251, 290

defect, xvii–xviii, 16, 26, 31–32, 35, 73, 76, 83, 88, 91–92, 178, 195, 231, 242–44, 287–89

Defection. *See* Theodicy types

Defense. *See* Theodicy types

Deism, Deist, 114, 134

depravity, 43, 52, 84, 89, 95, 98, 141, 232, 262

despair, 44, 109, 116–17, 175, 210, 220, 265–80

Devil, 71, 81, 84, 119, 147, 201, 203, 216, 218–19, 246, 276

discipline (suffering of). *See* suffering

Dostoyevsky, Fyodor, 8, 145, 149

Duns Scotus, 19, 27–28, 37–40, 86, 192, 197, 243

dysteleological (suffering). *See* suffering

Edwards, Jonathan, 9, 16, 18, 49–51, 64, 66–67, 83, 86–89, 105–6, 144, 150, 159–63, 167–68, 170–72, 175, 184, 188, 190–91, 193, 201, 224, 247–48

Ehrman, Bart, 158, 271–73, 277

Epicurean, 3, 5, 7, 11, 13, 103–4, 107, 112–13, 155, 217

Era(s) of Freedom, xvii–xviii, 11, 16–17, 21, 30–31, 42, 55, 61, 97. 153, 178, 228, 230–31, 240–49, 252, 256, 261–63

Conforming-Freedom, xvii, 11, 16–17, 21, 31–33, 57, 97, 157, 176–78, 180, 183–87, 201, 228, 231, 233–34, 240–241, 248–50, 253–54, 256, 262, 268, 280

Penultimate Freedom, xviii, 17, 228, 249–50

Unfettered Freedom, xviii, 16, 177, 186, 195, 228, 241–42, 244–46, 262

Forfeit Freedom (Slavery), xvii, 16, 32, 42, 131, 179, 181, 203, 228, 230, 240–241, 245–50, 254, 262,

Erasmus, Desiderius, 40, 42, 246

Erickson, Millard, 7

Evil & Suffering, xvii, 6, 11, 16, 61–63, 99–100, 106, 116–17, 129, 136, 139, 144, 146, 151, 159–60, 187–89, 191, 194, 197, 199–200, 202, 204–11, 214–18, 221–28, 232–35, 240–241, 253, 256, 258, 260–263, 266–68, 272–80

Feinberg, John, 4, 17–18, 20, 38, 48, 56, 59, 66, 93–94, 96, 98, 104–6, 115, 131, 134, 137, 140–141, 149, 159, 170–172, 196–97, 229–30, 232

Ferguson, Niall, 111

Ferguson, Sinclair, 208

Fiddes, Paul, 65, 142, 166–67, 178, 193, 195, 209

Flew, Antony, 4–5, 16, 19, 31, 56, 103, 113–14, 140–143, 149, 159, 229, 273

Flew-Mackie, 4–5, 140, 143, 149, 229, 273

Floyd, William E.G., 21, 69–70, 120

foreknowledge, 7, 15–16, 19, 22–23, 28–29, 32, 40–41, 43–44, 46–51, 53–55, 63–65, 86, 109, 133–34, 172, 179, 183

Forfeit Freedom, (see Eras of Freedom)

Freddoso, Alfred J., 19, 44, 46–47, 63–66, 86

freedom, xvii–xviii, 3–4, 7, 10–11, 15–19, 21–33, 35–38, 40, 42–44, 46–57, 59, 61, 64–67, 70, 72, 77–78, 83, 86–88, 91–93, 97, 102–3, 109–10, 113–14, 119, 125–26, 130, 133–34, 136, 140–141, 147–48, 150–151, 153, 157–60, 166, 168, 170–172, 175–89, 193–97, 206–9, 213–14, 217, 228–31, 233, 240–258, 261–62, 280

Free-Will, xvii–xviii, 4, 11, 13, 15–23, 25–37, 39–57, 59–60, 64–65, 67, 72–74, 76–77, 82, 91, 93–98, 101–3, 105, 107, 109, 111–13, 115, 117, 119, 121–27, 129–31, 133–35, 137, 139–41, 143, 145, 147–49, 151, 155, 158–63, 165–66, 171, 176, 183, 188, 191–93, 241–42, 245–49, 254, 263

Compatibilistic Free-Will, xvii, 15, 18–21, 30, 55–57, 67, 77, 96–97, 133, 141, 143, 159–60, 242, 246, 249, 254

Libertarian Free-Will, xviii, 15, 18–23, 29–30, 35–37, 40, 46, 49–50, 52–57, 60, 67, 73, 77, 94–97, 126, 141, 143, 149, 158,

160, 171, 176, 183, 188, 191, 241–42, 249, 254
  Volitional Free-Will, xviii, 17–20, 22, 32, 36–37, 41–42, 44, 47, 49–51, 55–57, 88, 97–98, 105, 244, 246–48, 288
Free-Will Defense. *See* Theodicy types
Fretheim, Terrence, 53–55, 158
futile, 59, 109–10, 179, 181–83, 198

Geivett, R. Douglass, 27, 63, 76, 78–79, 113, 134, 138, 140
Gerstenberger, Erhard, 162
glorify, 2, 5, 43, 99, 105–6, 109, 150, 165, 179–80, 182–83, 186, 191, 199, 206–7, 209, 213, 219, 224, 227, 245, 252–53, 256, 274, 278, 280
glory, 2–3, 19–20, 22–23, 27, 42–43, 45, 47, 49, 59, 83–84, 99, 109, 117, 150, 159–67, 169–77, 179–82, 186, 189, 191, 194, 200, 203, 207, 209, 212–13, 217–19, 224–25, 234, 238, 240, 244–45, 250, 252, 254, 268, 274276, 278, 280
Gnostic, ix, 21, 64, 68–69, 71, 119–21, 123, 125–26, 131, 199
Goldingay, John, 162
Gordis, Robert, 114, 257–58
gratuitous suffering, (see Suffering)
Greater Good defense, (see Theodicy)
Gregory of Nyssa, 90, 124
Grenz, Stanley, 165–66
Griffin, David Ray, 78
Grudem, Wayne, 211, 214

Habel, Norman C., 258
Habermas, Gary, 114, 142
happiness, 50, 60, 75, 130, 167, 171–72, 174–76, 186, 232
Harris, Murray, 239–40
Hart, David Bentley, 113, 134, 226
Hawthorne, Gerald, 167
Hegelian, 147, 266
Helm, Paul, 80, 251
Henry, Carl F., 61
Henry, Matthew, 118
Hick, John, 4–6, 18, 62, 65, 70, 72, 78, 90–93, 102, 105, 117, 129, 132, 134–39, 149–51, 158, 188–89, 194, 196, 224–26, 229, 252–53, 256
Hicks, Peter, 34, 61, 63, 68, 101, 189, 216, 272
Hinduism, 58, 64, 110
Hoekema, Anthony, 17, 178, 241, 243, 248
holocaust, 5
hope, x, xviii, 2–3, 6, 21, 60, 76–77, 102, 111, 116–17, 119, 128, 137–38, 146–47, 150–151, 153–55, 158, 161, 165–66, 173, 176,
179, 181, 183, 186, 188, 195, 200–201, 205, 210, 214, 217, 231, 235, 256–57, 259–61, 263, 266–74, 277–78, 280
horrific, 5, 7–8, 54, 75, 98, 102, 128, 134, 143–46, 154, 175, 188, 207, 222, 229, 270
human willful-creatures, 17, 21, 26, 28, 31, 77, 157–58, 162–63, 169, 172–74, 177, 180, 182–83, 186, 188–94, 196, 220, 223, 228, 230, 235, 242–45, 247, 249, 251, 254–55, 260–261, 274
Hume, David, 3, 103

incarnational suffering, (see Suffering)
incompatibilist, 143, 148, 172
instrumental, 11, 65, 81, 106, 123, 136, 148, 151, 182, 187, 189, 194, 199–200, 206, 211–12, 216, 222–26, 273–74, 280
intrinsic, 11, 64–66, 106, 144, 153, 160, 164, 187, 194, 197–200, 224–25, 227, 273
involuntary suffering, (see Suffering)
Irenaean, 65, 91, 93, 120, 122, 129, 135, 137–38, 158, 246, 256
Irenaeus, 18, 70, 91, 105, 117, 119–26, 129, 134–39, 169, 175, 198, 206
Islamic, 34, 108

Jacobs, Alan, 118–19, 123, 129, 131
Jerome, 23–26, 125
Jesuit, 46, 49, 56, 225
Journet, Charles, 6, 98, 107, 148–49, 160–61, 221, 251–52
Judas, 126, 196, 200, 208
Julian of Eclanium, 72
justification, x, 25, 55, 70, 111, 121, 266, 273, 276–77

Kaiser, Walter, 272
Kaplan, Robert, 289
Keats, John, 136
Keller, Timothy, 280
Kelly, J. N. D., 211
Kelsey, David, 9
Kierkegaard, Søren, 111
Kilby, Karen, 169
Kistemaker, Simon, 216
Kreeft, Peter, 208–9
Kushner, Harold S., 108–9

Lactantius, 103
Laplace, Pierre-Simon, marquis de, 102
Leibniz, Gottfried Wilhelm, 4, 52, 65, 78–79, 86–87, 90, 110, 114, 130–34, 141, 170, 172, 249, 254
Leibniz Lapse, 52, 141
Lewis, C. S., 104, 161, 176

Libertarian Free-Will. *See* Free-Will
libertarian, xviii, 15–16, 18–24, 26–27, 29–31, 34–37, 40, 46–50, 52–57, 60, 67, 70, 73, 77, 91, 94–97, 125–26, 130, 141, 143, 148–49, 158–61, 166, 170–71, 175–77, 183, 188, 191, 241–42, 246, 249, 253–54
Lloyd, Michael, 72, 288–89
Locke, John, 17
Lombard, Peter, 82
Luther, Martin, 18, 40–42, 83–84, 131, 137, 194, 197, 245–46, 261

Mackie, John, 4–5, 31, 94–95, 113–15, 139–43, 149, 159, 217, 229, 232, 237, 273
Macquarrie, John, 195–96
Manichean, 21, 24, 27, 30, 68, 73–74, 91, 119, 126, 249
Marcel, Gabriel, 2, 267
Marcion, 68–69
Marshall, I. Howard, 184, 202, 206
Mathewes, Charles T., 78–79, 95
Mcfadyen, Alistair, 58, 176, 246
meaningless suffering. *See* suffering
Mesle, Robert C., 158, 188
Messiah, 206, 221, 239–40, 250
Meyendorff, John, 56
Milbank, John, 206–7
Milton, John, 114, 116
Molina, Louis de, 19, 26, 44, 46–49, 53, 56, 63, 85–86
Molinism, 47–49, 56, 86, 133
Moltmann, Jürgen, 15, 54, 68, 102, 146–47, 151, 153–54, 166–68, 201, 207, 209, 225, 253–54, 281
Monarchianism, 69
monism, 68, 97, 110
Moo, Douglas, 181
Moreland, James P., 3, 19
Mormonism, 120
Moses, 92, 124, 165, 189, 196, 207
Moule, C. F. D, 167, 240
Murphy, Nancy, 182–83
Murray, John, 66, 205, 223, 239, 266
mystery, x, 1–3, 6, 101, 114, 116, 145, 150, 210, 224, 242, 245, 256, 272

necessity, xi, xviii, 16, 26, 28–29, 35–38, 40–41, 51–53, 56, 58, 61, 63–67, 92, 94–95, 97–99, 106, 112, 114, 120, 122, 132–33, 141, 164, 167, 172, 177–78, 185, 187, 194–99, 206, 212, 225–26, 230, 233, 244–45, 251, 255
Neff, Gordon, 196
Newton, Isaac, 1–2, 189

Nicene, 22–23, 68–69, 72–73, 103, 120, 123, 169
Nichtige, nothingness, 85, 90, 149, 195, 209, 261
nonconsequentialism, 105, 149, 193

obedience (suffering of). *See* suffering
Ockham, William of, 20, 37–38, 51, 53, 65, 82–83, 196
omnipotence, xviii, 3–4, 9, 19, 47, 53–54, 56, 80, 84, 94, 103, 107, 113, 119, 136, 139–42, 159, 187, 202, 207, 210, 217–18, 220, 229–30, 237, 263
omnipresence, 9, 145, 171
omniscience, 3, 9, 47, 54, 63, 98, 263
Origen, 21–26, 42, 55–56, 70–71, 79, 96, 120, 123–26, 129, 138, 171
Osborne, Grant, 216

paganism, 107, 199
Pagels, Elaine, 126
panentheism, 147, 166, 168, 201
paradox, 3, 98, 195, 197
Pascal, Blaise, 172–73
Pelagian, 21, 24–26, 30, 32, 45, 49, 56–57, 73–74, 77, 80, 83, 124–25, 249
Pelagius, 4, 18, 21, 23–27, 30, 40, 42, 55–56, 72–73, 76–77, 79, 83, 119, 124–26, 129–31, 138, 184, 243, 246
Penultimate Freedom. *See* Era(s) of Freedom
perichoresis, 166, 168–69
persecution (suffering of). *See* suffering
Peterson, Michael L., 61, 102, 115, 252
Pickstock, Catherine, 207
Pinnock, Clark, 54, 110, 176
Piper, John, 70, 166, 200–2, 219, 227, 238, 281
Plantinga, Alvin, 3–5, 16, 19, 31, 51–54, 59–61, 66, 95, 98, 112–14, 139, 141, 143, 149, 158–59, 171, 217, 229–30
Plato, xi, 21, 27–28, 33–34, 107, 197
Platonic, ix, 27–28, 34
Plotinus, 72
Polkinghorne, John, 2, 27, 142, 171, 189, 256
Polycarp, 120, 211, 271
Porphyry, 72
prayer, 34, 56, 154, 162, 165, 169, 173–74, 183–84, 211, 269
Praxeas (Praxis), 68–69
privative, ix, xi, 21, 69–90, 93–99, 103, 126, 130, 132, 137, 148–49, 187, 193, 196, 218, 253, 256, 261
Probabilistic (Evidential, Logical) defense. *See* Theodicy types
problem of evil, x, xiii, xviii–8, 10–11, 21, 26–27, 49, 54, 59–61, 69–70, 78, 91, 93, 102,

104–9, 111–21, 123, 128–32, 134–39, 141–43, 147, 149, 151, 153, 158–59, 166, 178, 185–86, 188, 190–191, 196, 198, 202, 205, 210, 217–20, 222, 226, 233–35, 237, 261–63, 270
propitiation, 25, 209

Ratzinger, Joseph (Pope Benedict XVI), 124
redemption, 24, 26–27, 46, 62, 66, 69, 78, 120, 123, 125, 129, 142–46, 149, 159–60, 162, 168, 179, 181, 183, 197, 200, 206–9, 211–12, 219, 223, 226, 236, 239, 251, 253, 256, 259, 266, 272, 274, 276, 278–79
Rees, William, 24
Reformation, 16, 26, 44–46, 52, 54, 56, 74, 83, 86, 95, 105–6, 127, 129, 131, 138, 159, 161, 165–66, 171
riches, 22, 165
Ricoeur, Paul, 115
Rist, John M., 29–31, 74, 77, 195
Robinson, John A. T., 181
Rousseau, Jean-Jacques, 57
Rowe, William, 60

Sagan, Carl, 102
Sailhamer, John, 235
sanctification, 22, 25, 34, 55, 121, 126, 182, 279–80
Sanders, John, 48, 54, 65, 110, 158, 191
Satan, 7, 41, 54, 59, 67, 77, 84–85, 91, 97, 105, 159, 181, 195, 200–202, 205, 208, 211, 216–17, 219–20, 246–47, 250, 267, 276, 278
Schaeffer, Francis, 58, 112, 266
Schleiermacher, Friedrich, 9, 129, 135, 138
Schreiner, Thomas, 59, 180–181, 205–6, 247
Schultz, Walter, 168
Schweitzer, Albert, 191
Scotus, Duns. *See* Duns Scotus
sin, 25–26, 29, 45, 60, 71, 83, 93, 98–99, 124, 135, 180, 189, 198–99, 209, 231, 235
sinner, 167, 199, 209–10, 250
Slavery. *See* Era(s) of Freedom
Socinius, Faustus, 26
soteriology, x, 25, 115, 124–25, 139, 142, 145, 147, 199, 206
soul, 3, 70, 72, 79, 104, 131, 136, 158, 199, 205, 212, 225, 239
Soul-Making theodicy. *See* Theodicy types
sovereignty, xvii, 9, 13, 16, 19, 22, 25, 36–37, 41, 43, 45–46, 48, 53–55, 60–61, 64, 66–67, 73–74, 76, 84, 92, 96, 102, 108, 110, 114, 117, 120–121, 126, 130, 134, 166, 168, 173, 175, 191, 200, 219, 227, 248, 281
Spinoza, Baruch, 110

Stoic, 68, 71
Stump, Elanore, 3
subordinate-metaphysical necessity, xviii, 11, 65–67, 98–99, 187, 194, 196, 199, 212, 224, 227–28
suffering, 107, 109, 128, 147, 153, 179, 201, 204, 206, 208–9, 212, 214–17, 236, 238–40, 266–67, 270, 272, 274–76, 278, 280
 correction (suffering of), 272, 277–78
 discipline (suffering of), 92, 208, 221, 272, 277–78
 dysteleological suffering, 5–6, 62, 136, 281
 gratuitous suffering, 5, 7, 60–63, 278, 281
 incarnational suffering, 272, 278–80
 involuntary suffering, 272, 274–75, 278
 meaningless suffering, 5, 61, 63, 101, 136, 272, 274–75, 280–281
 obedience (suffering of), 272, 276–77
 persecution (suffering of), 21, 179, 205, 215, 272, 274
 voluntary suffering, 231, 245, 274, 279
suicide, 107, 128, 200
Surin, Kenneth, 118–19, 121, 123, 129, 138, 158, 188, 263, 271
Swinburne, Richard, 27, 106, 142, 159, 170–172, 198, 226

Tertullian, 68–69, 124, 126, 137
theonomy, 37–39, 63, 82–83, 131
Thomist, 1, 33, 39, 46, 49, 207, 230
Tiegreen, Chris, 224, 270
Tiessen, Terrance, 34, 56
Tilley, Terrence, 113, 271
Theodicy types
 Best of All Possible Worlds, 4, 52, 87, 65, 114, 130–134, 141, 170, 172, 249, 254
 Defection (type), xvii, 106–7, 110–112, 119, 237, 270
 Defense (type), xvii–xviii. 4–5, 52–53, 64, 72, 91, 93, 106, 112–15, 118, 120, 133–34, 140–141, 143, 148–50, 158, 188, 192–93, 237
 Free-Will defense, 91, 112–13, 133, 140–149, 158. 193
 Greater Good defense, 60, 106, 148–49, 183
 Probabilistic (Evidential, Logical) defense, 6, 95, 112–15, 141, 159
 Soul-Making theodicy, x, 4–5, 92, 134–36, 138, 196, 225, 253
 Theodicy (type), xvii–xviii, 4–8, 10–11, 13, 15–18, 20, 22, 24, 26, 28, 30, 32, 34, 36, 38, 40, 42, 44, 46, 48, 50–56, 60, 62, 64–66, 68, 70, 72, 74, 76, 78, 80, 82, 84, 86–88, 90, 92–96, 98–151, 153–55, 158, 160–162, 164, 166, 168, 170, 172, 174–76,

325

PART III: A Theodicy in the Face of Reality

178, 180, 182, 184, 186, 188, 190, 192–94, 196, 198, 200, 202, 204, 206–8, 210, 212, 214, 216, 218, 220, 222, 224–26, 229–30, 232, 234, 236–38, 240, 242, 244, 246, 248–50, 252–54, 256–58, 260, 262–63, 265–74, 276, 278, 280
Ton, Joseph, 199, 203
Torrance, Alan, 166–69
torture, 79, 127, 154, 281
trials, 205, 212
Trigg, Joseph Wilson, 21
Trilemma, xvii–xviii, 3–4, 7, 11, 13, 112–13, 139, 142, 155, 160, 185, 221
Trinity, 6, 8–9, 15, 27, 68–69, 102, 137, 145–47, 153, 166–69, 173–74, 176, 189, 201, 218, 254, 281

Unfettered Freedom. *See* Era(s) of Freedom

Valentinian, 121, 126
Vanhoozer, Kevin, 10, 233
violence, 41, 174, 275
Volitional Free-Will. *See* Free-Will.
Voltaire (François-Marie Arouet), 102, 134
voluntary suffering, (see Suffering)
voluntarism, 19, 28, 37–40

Ware Bishop Kallistos (Timothy), 56, 90, 157, 160, 174

Ware, Bruce, xvii–xviii, 19–20, 47–48, 56, 90, 99, 157, 160, 174, 225
Warfield, B. B., 72–73
Weinandy, Thomas, 168, 280–281
Whitehead, Alfred North, 108
Wiesel, Elie, 102
Wiggers, Gustave Friedrich, 24–25, 30
wilderness, 235–38
Willard, Dallas, 254
Williams, Rowan, 145, 167, 222, 266–67
Williams, Thomas, 38–39
Wojtyla, Karol Jozef (Pope John Paul II), 89–90
Wonder (of the Cross), xiii, 1, 11, 100, 219, 255, 290, 300
worship, 59, 108, 118, 154, 166, 168–69, 215, 275, 277–78
wrath, 22, 59, 165, 209, 278, 281
Wright, N. T., 111, 171, 178–79, 205, 239
Wright, R. K. McGregor, 25, 55, 73

Yancy, Phillip, 263
Yandell, Keith, 148–49

Zoroastrianism, 68
Zosia, 7–8, 265, 280–81
Zupko, Jack, 104